D0463645

11/16

GULLIVER ABE, IN THE WHITE HOUSE, ATTACKED BY THE LILLIPUTIAN OFFICE-SEEKERS.

Frank Leslie's Budget of Fun, March 15, 1861. Courtesy of the Abraham Lincoln Presidential Library and Museum.

LINCOLN'S
WHITE HOUSE

LINCOLN'S WHITE HOUSE

The People's House in Wartime

James B. Conroy

ROWMAN & LITTLEFIELD
Lanham • Boulder • New York • London

Published by Rowman & Littlefield
A wholly owned subsidiary of The Rowman & Littlefield Publishing Group, Inc.
4501 Forbes Boulevard, Suite 200, Lanham, Maryland 20706
www.rowman.com

Unit A, Whitacre Mews, 26–34 Stannary Street, London SE11 4AB

Distributed by NATIONAL BOOK NETWORK

British Library Cataloguing in Publication Information Available

Library of Congress Cataloging-in-Publication Data Available

978-1-4422-5134-2 (cloth)
978-1-4422-5135-9 (electronic)

♾ ™ The paper used in this publication meets the minimum requirements of American National Standard for Information Sciences—Permanence of Paper for Printed Library Materials, ANSI/NISO Z39.48–1992.

Printed in the United States of America

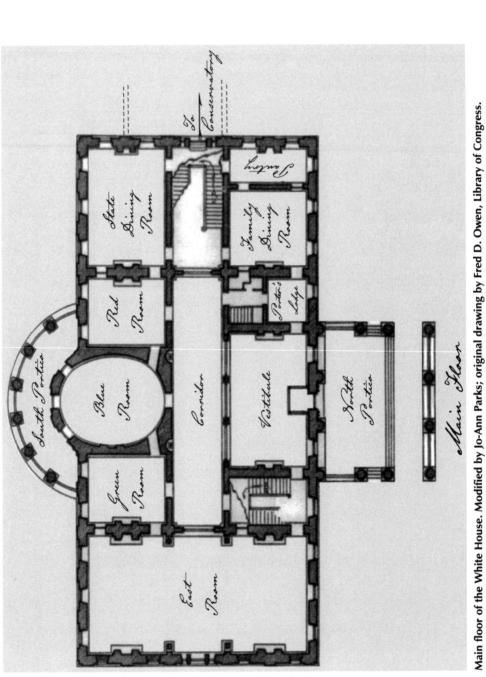

Main floor of the White House. Modified by Jo-Ann Parks; original drawing by Fred D. Owen, Library of Congress.

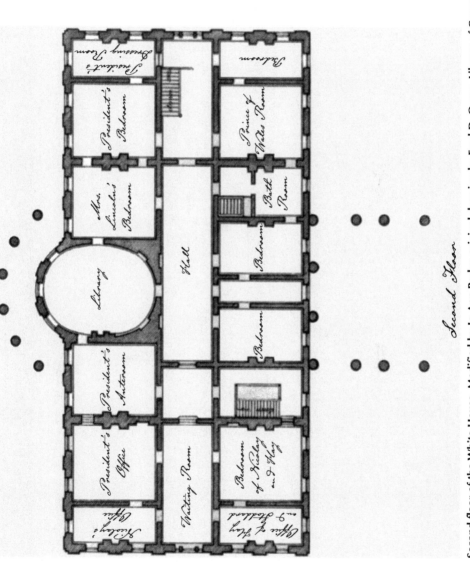

Second floor of the White House. Modified by Jo-Ann Parks; original drawing by Fred D. Owen, Library of Congress.

CONTENTS

CONTENTS

INTRODUCTION

L ate on a winter night in 1864, the massive White House gates on Pennsyl-vania Avenue stood open to the world. Just inside both entrances, a pair of stoic cavalrymen sat mounted face to face across the gravel carriageway on the matched black horses of the Union Light Guard. It was not an easy watch. "Sitting quietly on horseback for two hours on a cold night is, to say the least, disagreeable," a guardsman later said, but the view was agreeably calm. Barren trees spread their limbs in the dark, a few of the house's windows shone with yellow-tinged gaslight, and flickering jets of flame lit the curved stone path to the white-pillared portico, washed in a pale gold glow. Two sentries paced their beat a few feet in front of the mansion, starting at opposite ends and crossing in the middle with muskets on their shoulders and deer tails on their hats. Said to be "more ornamental than useful," neither the Pennsylvania Bucktails nor the Union Light Guard challenged any sober citizen who approached the President's House.

Leaning on a pillar under the portico, a bright young corporal named Rob-ert McBride, fresh from Ohio with the rest of the Union Light Guard, heard the front door open, and a tall, thin, awkwardly moving man came out alone, looking weary in a long black coat and a poorly kept stovepipe hat. McBride had seen his face in *Harper's Weekly* and *Frank Leslie's Illustrated Newspaper*, but the gaslight caught the furrows that the portraits left out.

As Lincoln closed the door, clasped his hands behind him, and slowly crossed the portico with his head bent forward and his eyes cast down, McBride drew his saber to his chin, and the nearest Bucktail sentry presented arms, but the commander in chief noticed neither man's salute. Alone with his burdens, directly under the gaslight as if he were on stage, he paused at the top of the steps for what seemed like minutes, long enough for McBride's arm to quiver. Then he absently lifted his hat to his guards and walked to his left toward the War Department down a wooded, brick-paved path barely lit by a single flame. McBride sheathed his sword, the sentry resumed his beat, and they both watched the president anxiously as he passed "into the shadows of the trees."

Back on duty the next morning, McBride saw Lincoln leave the White House again and start toward the War Department. The Bucktail sentry swung his musket to his chest in a rigid salute, but the president passed him by as if he were invisible. Lincoln had walked a dozen paces down the path before he stopped short, turned around, raised his hat, and bowed like "one gentleman apologizing to another for an unintentional slight." Only then did the soldier resume his beat.

After Lincoln was out of earshot, McBride asked the Bucktail why he had held his position after the president passed. Lincoln ignored his salute all the time, the sentry said, but he always stopped and returned it before he had gone very far, alone on his walk through the trees at the height of a civil war.

Later that year, a British writer and a fellow Englishman approached the White House with an editor of the *New York Times* and found not a "dog on the watch." Lincoln had not yet arrived for their meeting, but his wartime home and headquarters were as open as a barn. Passing freely through the portico, the editor took the Londoners into the lobby, led them up the stairs past a servant who was cleaning them, and walked them into the office of the president of the United States as if it were a shop. His British companions followed "in mute amazement, half ashamed of treading unasked on this sacred ground," but the American had no such qualms. "The people paid for this house," he said, "and they had a right to see the inside of it; they paid the President to live there, and they had a right to see him in it."

The President's House is not his castle, the Englishman told his readers; "it is not even his house."

*　　*　　*

Many years ago, a distinguished professor of medieval history wrote a note on a paper I had worked hard to write, a rare event in my misspent youth. He called it a "very good" job. Faint praise, it seemed to me. "You have done your research carefully," he wrote, "and written it quite well, though so many short paragraphs indicate a little weakness in organization." I could have lived with a little weakness, and I still like digestible paragraphs. It was the last line that stung: "History is inquiry, engaging with the past, which we engage in because it has a purpose. You have not indicated your purpose. B +."

The professor was a kindly man, and he made me a generous offer. If I gave him a revision that stated and served a purpose, the paper might earn an

A. I cannot recall the purpose, but I do recall the A, and the lesson that went with it. Thousands of books on Lincoln, including one of my own, have blessed and burdened the world. No one should write another unless it has a purpose.

When I started researching this one, curiosity about the Civil War White House was purpose enough. No book had ever captured in one place how it looked, felt, and smelled; its plumbing, heat, and light; its servants, guards, and aides; their alliances of power and convenience; their collisions over matters of jealousy, integrity, and race; what Lincoln was like to work for and how he used his staff; his literally open door in a city full of angry men; his wife's lavish refurbishments and entertainments; the shady company she kept and the scandals they provoked; the mobs of persistent job seekers ranging up the scale from madmen to Herman Melville; a host of guests and callers as diverse as Nathaniel Hawthorne, Sojourner Truth, P. T. Barnum, a dozen Plains Indian chiefs, a magician called Hermann the Prestidigitator, assorted generals, thieves, and spiritualists, Walt Whitman, Julia Ward Howe, Ralph Waldo Emerson, and a nine-year-old Venezuelan piano prodigy. Many of their observations of the President's House and its residents, upstairs and down, had not seen print since the nineteenth century, some had never been published at all, and no one had woven them together to bring Lincoln's White House to life.

As my work on the book progressed, a deeper purpose worked its way through the material, revealing Lincoln's character and tracking his growth as he made "this big white house" a rallying point for the war, a sounding board for the people, a platform for social change, and an engine for racial progress. In the short and long paragraphs that follow, the men, women, and children who knew his White House will speak plainly for themselves, shedding light on him and his times and perhaps a glint on our own.

1

THE PAINFUL SENSE OF BECOMING EDUCATED

On a pleasant March 4, 1861, a bright Inauguration Day in Washington City, Abraham Lincoln and James Buchanan left the Capitol side by side and were seated in an open coach for a risky ride to the White House. A squad of nervous cavalry surrounded them, sharpshooters scanned the crowd, and infantry with loaded muskets prepared for a military movement in the shape of a parade. For a young theology student from upstate New York, there was no festivity in the air. "On the contrary, there was an air of foreboding—a half expressed fear of danger or tragedy." Looking back in better times as a veteran of Lincoln's cabinet, an old Connecticut Yankee named Gideon Welles recalled his own unease: "A strange state of things existed in Washington at that time," he said. "The atmosphere was thick with treason."

Seven angry states had already left the Union, provoked by the mere election of an antislavery president. Several others were on the edge, and Washington was a thoroughly Southern town, surrounded by the slave states of Maryland and Virginia. Bands of armed secessionists drilled openly in the city, and all but a tiny slice of the miniature U.S. Army was in Indian country, hundreds of miles from a railroad. As an Illinois congressman said, few of the Northern and Western visitors in the capital for the celebration were aware that its public buildings "were full of plotting traitors." Despising the happy interlopers who had come to cheer for Lincoln, the city rang with threats that he would never reach the White House.

As the presidential coach rattled down the cobblestones past the oddly mixed crowd lining Pennsylvania Avenue, Lincoln raised his hat to scattered applause, Buchanan looked at his shoes, and the wind blew in grit from the dirt cross streets. The presidential carriage passed smart hotels and shops on the right, gambling halls and brothels on the left. Horse soldiers blocked the intersecting streets, riflemen lined the roofs, sappers led the carriage, and its clattering cavalry escort surrounded and almost hid it, keeping their horses dancing to spoil any marksman's aim. Top-hatted marshals rode beside them, sashed from shoulder to hip.

Adding more pathos than charm, an elaborate flatbed cart with "Constitution" on its side and "Union" on the backs of its six white horses carried thirty-four little girls in white, one for each state, whether in the Union or out. They were waving tiny flags. A gallows humorist claimed that the Southern girls were quarreling with their Northern friends. A column of nervous infantry marched behind them with fixed bayonets.

To imperial British eyes, there was shockingly little to march through. The London *Spectator*'s correspondent called Pennsylvania Avenue "a secondhand Broadway out at elbows," with side streets that ran "short distances, ending abruptly in brickfields or in open country; and that is all. . . . The whole place looks run up in a night." For the English novelist Anthony Trollope, Washington City was "a straggling congregation of buildings in a wilderness . . . a ragged, unfinished collection of unbuilt broad streets, as to the completion of which there can now, I imagine, be but little hope." Sportsmen shot snipe near the White House, which anchored the most finished part of town, for there one could find "a house, and then a blank; then two houses, and then a double blank. After that a hut or two, and then probably an excellent, roomy, handsome family mansion." Bullfrogs croaked in the side lanes in spring.

As the inaugural parade neared the White House and the city's finest streets, the Republican crowd grew deep and began to roar. Just past Willard's Hotel on the right—"Willard's menagerie," as a British guest called it, full of anxious, bearded men hungry for appointed offices—the parade turned north along the granite colonnade of the half-built Treasury Department on the left, then west at the corner where the drab brick State Department stood. The War Department was several hundred yards further down Pennsylvania Avenue, "a dingy-looking old brick building of the dry goods box style of architecture," a cavalryman said, with the matching Navy Department beneath it. Together, the four most important Executive departments lined the rectangle known as the President's Park, with the White House in the middle of its manicured grounds.

As the parade came in sight of the President's House, cheering Republicans jammed the broad stone sidewalk that fronted its lawn. Across Pennsylvania Avenue, the crowd had spilled over into Lafayette Square, a public park enclosed by a railed fence, with a network of brick-paved, gas-lit paths and an equestrian statue of Andrew Jackson in the middle, rearing his horse in a circus pose. Trollope thought the horsemanship "most absurd, but the man sitting on the horse is manifestly drunk. I should think the time must come when this figure at any rate will be removed."

Approached on a sunny day, there was something down at heels about the President's House, too much decay under too many coats of paint. "The White House is beautiful on a moonlight night," an Englishman said, "but not otherwise." A kinder European writer admired "the unpretending White House, which has obtained its name from the color of innocence."

Lincoln's White House. The driveway is out of sight to the left and right. Library of Congress. Restoration by Derek Jensen.

Atop a low stone wall running parallel to the sidewalk, a black-painted fence of iron spears gave the house a stately air but little protection. On an ordinary day, low-wage White House laborers wielding brooms and long-handled rakes kept the granite sidewalk swept and the gravel driveway combed, but no one guarded the open carriage gates or the pedestrian gates beside them. On every day but Sunday, the public roamed the President's Park at will.

Wooded ground framed the groomed front lawn, in the center of which stood a neglected bronze statue of Jefferson, looking less like a founding father to a young Lincoln aide named William Stoddard than "a moldy old Indian, just dug up." A broad stone walk ran along the semicircular driveway from Pennsylvania Avenue to the portico, lined by a decorative wrought iron fence.

As the parade curled into the driveway, Charles Francis Adams Jr., twenty-five years old and a descendant of two presidents, looked on: "I drew a long breath when I saw Mr. Lincoln leave his carriage, and turned away confident that the last danger was passed."

The infantry formed in line as Lincoln and Buchanan stepped down from their coach and were greeted by the general in chief of the army, Winfield Scott, the military architect of the Mexican War, in a blue dress uniform with hairbrush epaulettes and a fore and aft bicorn hat. Born in Virginia in 1786, Scott was too fat to mount a horse and had been driven ahead of the parade. Mrs. Lincoln arrived in a separate carriage.

Despite its timeworn dinge, or perhaps in part because of it, no thoughtful citizen could approach the Executive Mansion without a sense of presence that never went away, even for its residents and staff. For William Stoddard, "the shadows, the ghosts, if you will, of all sorts of events, past, present, and to come, trooped in and flitted around the halls and lurked in the corners of the rooms." The White House had scarcely changed since Washington approved its design, and every president had lived there since 1800, a living link to Adams, Jefferson, Madison, and Monroe, John Quincy Adams, and Andrew Jackson. The very paving stones under the portico, "foot-worn into furrows," evoked the past, Stoddard thought, every one a "historical wrinkle."

At a little past noon, Buchanan walked Lincoln to the door. A courtly old man with wispy, bone-white hair, he took his successor's hand, bid him welcome, and wished him well. A few days earlier, during a cabinet meeting in his second-floor office, a card had been brought in that Buchanan had read with pleasure. "Uncle Abe is downstairs!" Rather than have him shown in for his courtesy call, the Pennsylvania Democrat had gone down and brought him back.

Buchanan had served for forty years as a congressman, senator, minister to the Court of Saint James's, and president of the United States. Lincoln had spent a single term in Congress, in which he had been ignored, and had not set foot in Washington since 1849. He had never run anything more elaborate than a two-man law firm. As he freely confessed, he took command of the White House "entirely ignorant not only of the duties, but of the manner of doing the business." Most sophisticates thought him a fluke, the leader of "a frontier community" desperately over his head in an existential crisis. He was not entirely sure that they were wrong.

As one cruel critic said, Buchanan was afflicted with "a peculiar nervous twitching always to the left, as if some unseen spirits were plucking him by the sleeve" and "whispering distasteful counsel." Having passively watched the dissolution of the Union he had sworn to preserve and protect, he had little to share with his successor, distasteful or otherwise. To Lincoln's private secretary, John George Nicolay, Buchanan seemed released from a waking nightmare.

Before he left the Lincolns, he gave the new First Lady a note commending the servants. He had already given her husband all the wisdom he had. At the Capitol, handing him his burdens on the cusp of a civil war, Buchanan had taken him aside in the presence of John Hay, Lincoln's assistant private secretary, all of twenty-two years old, who had "waited with boyish wonder," as he later recalled, for whatever "momentous counsels were to come from that gray and weather-beaten head. Every word must have its value at such an instant."

The outgoing president said, "I think you will find the water in the right-hand well at the White House better than that at the left," and described the kitchen and the pantry in detail. Lincoln listened "with that weary, introverted look of his" and soon told Hay he had not heard a word.

Buchanan had declined Lincoln's invitation to stay as a guest while he made his transitions. As his coach rolled past an honor guard and out of sight for good, Lincoln walked into the White House for the first time as president. The high-ceilinged storm entrance, built of simple window sash in Van Buren's time to keep out drafts and rain, had been redone in glass and iron under Franklin Pierce and still made a poor first impression. Stoddard called it "a mere coop of a lobby." A tourist guidebook suggested more gently that it was "far from imposing, and might be greatly improved."

To the right of the coop was the porter's lodge, a tiny room staffed by two Irish-born doorkeepers in common business suits, the white-haired conniver Edward McManus and his gawky assistant Thomas Burns. The Washington elite knew Old Edward by name. A little slip of a man appointed by Zachary Taylor, he habitually wrung his hands as if he were washing them, a "half smile of suppressed humor flickering across his face." Armed with nothing more than the porter's lodge window that let them see who was coming, Old Edward and Burns made the whole of the White House guard.

As Lincoln and his party left the coop, they entered a double-height lobby, crowned by layered moldings, a frescoed ceiling, and a tall chandelier, with Gothic revival furniture of unforgiving oak positioned around the perimeter. The vestibule it was called, smartly carpeted, with matching marble mantels on the left and right under striking ten-foot mirrors. The White House firemen kept the coal fires stoked on a cold March day. At the far end of the vestibule, a floor-to-ceiling screen of ground-glass panes in a decorative cast iron frame ran from wall to wall with a door in the middle, protecting the formal rooms from drafts.

William Howard Russell, the American correspondent for the stately *Times of London*, was not impressed. The vestibule had the air of a bank or a public registry, he said, as if forms could be found on a counter.

The servants may have been gathered to greet the Lincolns. Many of them were British or continental born. The government paid the doorkeepers, messengers, gardeners, laborers, and watchmen. The president paid the steward, the usher, the cook, the coachman, and several waiters, maids, and scullions himself, enabled by his princely $25,000 salary. He had brought his own valet, a young black man from Springfield named William H. Johnson.

The presidential party moved on from the vestibule through the door in the ground glass screen, crossed a wide hall, and entered the oval-shaped Blue Room. Often called the finest room in America, the Blue Room had been blue since 1837, "deeply, darkly, beautifully blue." Under a sky blue frescoed ceiling, Buchanan's rococo revival sofas and chairs, upholstered in blue and silver satin, were gilded to match the Blue Room's elaborate cornices. Blue and gold hangings draped the walls, reflected in oversized mirrors. Monroe's contrasting white marble table still stood where he had left it, and Hannibal still leaned on Monroe's bronze mantel clock. Japanese fans and lacquered boxes brought home by Admiral Perry lent the room an exotic touch. Its floor-to-ceiling windows and tall French doors opened onto the pillared south portico, where the president and his family and guests could sit in painted rockers in season, take the air, and enjoy the view of the gardens on the south lawn, the unfinished stub of the Washington Monument, a swath of the Potomac, and the green hills of Virginia. The *New York Herald* told its subscribers that "when not overcrowded with men, but conveniently full of beautiful women and tasteful costumes," the Blue Room made "a charming picture with its mingled fascinations of nature and art."

Here Lincoln greeted his inaugural guests, the well-fed investor Benjamin French among them, a Washington City official, marshal of the inaugural parade, relieved to have brought it off safely. A lifelong friend of his fellow New Hampshire Democrat Franklin Pierce, French had jumped ship to the Republicans in time for Lincoln's election and would play a key role in his White House. When the thirty-four little girls personifying the states were handed down from their float, it was French who led them inside. According to French's diary, the president asked to kiss them all, and did, a scene that drew much interest and warm applause.

Once Lincoln and his retinue had prepared themselves for the charge, the front door was thrown open and thousands of ordinary citizens poured through in line. Pundits often called them the sovereigns when they took to the White House en masse as if it were their own, which they surely felt it was and regularly did. Lincoln met them head on, in an excellent mood, said the *New York Times*, and the marshals of the parade "kept all rudeness at a distance." Determined to honor protocol in a White House receiving line, the first of many to come, the president wore white kid gloves with "a rather ghastly effect on his large, bony hands," a plainspoken woman would say. Ill at ease in formal dress, he told a friend at one event, "I suppose it is polite to wear these things," but they made him "positively uncomfortable."

Formality came with the house. With thirty-one rooms, it was the biggest in America. Its pompous first occupant, John Adams, had called it the Executive Mansion, which the *Boston Journal*'s correspondent said "the royalty-apers hereabouts" still favored, but Lincoln preferred "what is called the White House," a term used with growing frequency. He sometimes called it the people's house, and tried to make it so, but his duty to greet the sovereigns was a painful ordeal. After gripping literally thousands of hardened hands, many of them unwashed, his once white glove would be filthy enough to tempt his wife to pick it up with tongs and drop it in the fire.

No one screened the crowd in the inaugural reception line, and no one stood armed and ready to protect the president but the beefy Ward Hill Lamon, his former junior law partner, eighteen years his junior. Soon to be appointed marshall of the District of Columbia, Lamon would obsess over Lincoln's safety throughout his presidency, often guarding him personally as he did today, standing beside him in the receiving line with two big pistols, two Derringers, and two vicious knives under his coat. A friend was convinced that "you could put no more elements of attack or defense in a human skin."

A few weeks later, a colleague in the law named William Orme stayed with Lamon in his rooms near Willard's Hotel and found them full of "all the modern inventions in the shape of arms" and "spiritual comforts" in the shape of bottles and jugs. On his first night with Lamon, Orme told a mutual friend, he stirred a bit in bed and was jolted awake by the jarring sight of weapons of every kind and combination. "You have no idea of the armory in which he sleeps. He calls it his bedroom."

*   *   *

John George Nicolay, who called himself George, was the President's private secretary, twenty-nine years old and unremarkable by the look of him. His

John George Nicolay, ca. 1861. Courtesy of the Gilder Lehrman Institute of American History, Image No. GL05111.02.0113.

$2,500 salary was ample, but Congress provided for only one presidential assistant, and Nicolay, utterly innocent of Washington, was it.

Born poor to illiterate parents in 1832 in a village in Rhenish Bavaria, George was brought to Ohio when he was six, young enough to absorb English without an accent, and orphaned at fourteen. Taken in by relatives in western Illinois, he reckoned at the time that the woman of the house beat him because she liked it, but he did not.

With two years of schooling at age sixteen, Nicolay happened into an apprenticeship at the *Pittsfield Free Press*, a haunt for local Whigs whose owner all but adopted him in fortuitous Dickensian style. Housed in a furniture shop touting COFFINS and FURNTURE CHEAP, the *Free Press* published local gossip and news wired in from New York. Moving up the ladder from printer's devil to writer to editor in eight years, George called the paper a poor man's college. His penmanship was elegant and his prose was strong, his sentimental poetry not particularly.

Tall at five feet ten, thin to the point of frailty, and often in tenuous health, Nicolay was a likeable fellow despite a "Teutonic" temperament and "a slow smile," but even for a quiet young man, Pittsfield was short of amusements. He played the little organ at the Congregational Church, whose pastor deplored worldliness in all its insidious forms. Dancing, for one, might not be a sin, "but the ten-den-cy" was bad. George danced nonetheless with the dark-haired, dark-eyed, well-read Therena Bates, "the only girl in town who smiled at him when he was poor and ragged."

In 1852, Nicolay traveled to Washington to patent a printing press. He marveled at the Capitol grounds, with their "walks as smooth as a ballroom floor," and shook the hand of Millard Fillmore at a White House reception.

He bought the *Free Press* from his benefactors in his early twenties. In 1856, so the story goes, Lincoln visited Pittsfield, asked for an honest printer, and was led to George Nicolay, who was captured for life. Nicolay sold the *Free Press* in 1857, took a clerkship in Springfield with Lincoln's friend and ally Ozias M. Hatch, Illinois's prickly Secretary of State, and studied the law by reading it. At Hatch's Statehouse office, Lincoln was drawn to Nicolay's command of the election tables and befriended him playing chess, literally and figuratively.

When the Republicans nominated him for the presidency in 1860, Lincoln made Nicolay his secretary at $75 a month, supplemented by the State of Illinois. Working round the clock as a presidential campaign staff of one, Nicolay stayed on the public payroll while Hatch's other clerks did his work, which seems to have troubled no one, least of all Honest Abe.

Election Day ended for Nicolay at 4 a.m. There was never any question that he would follow Lincoln to Washington. His fiancée, Therena Bates, stayed in Pittsfield.

*   *   *

Lincoln called his private secretary "Nicolay," a familiar form of address for casual friends and associates. Nicolay's twenty-two-year-old assistant he called "John."

As his younger sister recalled, John Hay grew up "stringing his words

John Hay leaning against the shutters of a White House window. From the Lincoln Financial Foundation Collection, courtesy of the Indiana State Museum and Allen County Library.

together into rhymes" in the quaint little village of Warsaw, Illinois, in a house on a bluff overlooking the Mississippi. The slight, delicately handsome son of a physician and a physician's daughter, Hay was not yet seventeen when he went east to Brown and acquired an Eastern polish from its 225 students and its faculty of eleven. His roommate quickly saw what would serve him all his life. Despite a certain reticence, Hay had "so winning a manner that no one could be in his presence, even for a few moments," without being hopelessly charmed. A casually brilliant wit, he graduated with honors as the elected class poet in 1858, attracted to girls and theology, "indifferently fond of mathematics," with "the best vocabulary in our tongue."

Like many a campus luminary, Hay went home reluctantly and agreed to study law at his uncle's Springfield firm, both partners of which were friends of Lincoln's, whose office adjoined theirs, a stroke of good luck of the sort that blessed John Hay. Taking to him immediately, as almost everyone did, Lincoln spotted talents "not needed in the practice of provincial courts."

The 1860 campaign rescued him from the law when Lincoln's correspondence overwhelmed Nicolay, a boyhood friend of Hay's, though Nicolay was six years older. When Lincoln asked his supporters to find him a second assistant, they settled on Hay, whose uncle's place on the selection committee did not hurt his chances.

Lincoln hesitated when Nicolay suggested taking Hay to the White House, wary of bringing "all of Illinois," but he quickly came around. To overcome the budgeted limit of one private secretary, he was prepared to pay Hay out of his own pocket until Nicolay found that Hay could be made an Interior Department clerk assigned to White House duty at a comfortable $1,600 a year.

William Howard Russell, *The Times of London*'s resident cynic in Washington, was a hard man to beguile, and even he liked Hay, "the nice smart odd witted young Secretary of the President." The distinguished American writer John Russell Young admired Hay's old-school style and thought he brought to Lincoln what Hamilton had brought to Washington, an instinctive sense of tact and "the soft answer which turneth away wrath."

Hay's diplomatic skills were assets in the rough and tumble of Washington politics, but his rosy cheeks were not. He was "honest as sunshine," Young said, with a natural sort of grace and "a peach blossom face," none of which impressed a leathery politician who called him "a handsome and unusually bright boy hardly out of his teens" trying hard to produce a moustache. For the *Philadelphia Evening Star*'s reporter, Hay was "a proper ladies' man" who "might with due change of garb have passed creditably as a lady's maid."

Lincoln was among the keener judges of talent who saw Hay's brilliance as a friend later did: "It was simply impossible for him to talk for any length of time without saying something that delighted you inexpressibly," something you couldn't wait to take to others to delight them too. In casual conversation he nearly always made some remark that lingered in the mind, and he dropped his little gems "as if he owed their inspiration to the listener." Everyone who spent half an hour with him "was sure to go away not only charmed with Hay but uncommonly well pleased with himself."

Hay was also well pleased with Hay, and to some perceptive minds it showed. Beneath the charming surface was "just a shade of pride that did not make acquaintanceship spontaneous," the *Star*'s correspondent said. One was "not quite sure whether it was the reserve of diffidence or aristocracy."

It was both. Thoughtful enough to write an old flame in Providence to help his sister find an Eastern school, he was affected enough to add, "She is, I think, about 17 years old." He often indulged an urge to look down his handsome nose. Newly arrived at the seat of power, he answered a letter from a boyhood friend who called Warsaw as dull as ever. Warsaw was "a social paradise" compared to Washington, Hay said, "which imagines itself a city because it is wicked, as a boy thinks he is a man when he smokes and swears." He sent a friend an English novel because it was new, which he thought was "its only recommendation. It sketches with miraculous fidelity characters that are not worth sketching." Its title was *Silas Marner*. As he leaned against a cigar stand at Willard's Hotel, someone congratulated him on winning a White House job at the age of twenty-two. "Yes," he replied, "I'm the keeper of the President's conscience."

The ironic self-deprecation must have helped him carry it off. In the fashion of the day, he had a calling card made with his photograph on it, which reminded him "of the desperate attempts of a tipsy man to look sober. But coat, trousers, and gloves are irreproachable."

*　　*　　*

On his first afternoon in the White House, probably with Nicolay and Hay, Lincoln climbed the stairs to the eastern end of the second floor, where every president since Jackson had done business. Lincoln would call it the shop.

If he skipped the grand ceremonial staircase at the western end of the house and took the informal business stairs between the East Room and the vestibule, he passed through a small reception room at the second-floor landing then walked up several steps to the office wing. To accommodate the towering East Room beneath it, the office wing's floors were a few feet higher than the ones in the family quarters down the hall, making the ceilings seem a bit lower.

A new Ohio congressman was surprised by the look and feel of the business end of the White House that Buchanan had left for Lincoln, "bare, worn and soiled," like "the breaking up of a hard winter." The big rectangular waiting room in the middle of the office wing had paneled walls, tasteful moldings, and a glorious lunette window, but its varnished oilcloth floor was stained near the spittoons. The president's good-sized anteroom, adjoining the western side of his south-facing office, was furnished with old-fashioned horsehair sofas and chairs, dusty busts of former presidents, dusty prints of founding fathers, a faded copy of the Declaration of Independence in a badly stained sandalwood frame, and a "worn and not particularly clean carpet."

The Chief Executive's spacious office matched the anteroom, starting with the carpet. John Quincy Adams may have been the first president to work there, and much of its hand-me-down furniture was old when he did. Not that anyone considered it precious. A San Francisco newspaper called it "too rickety to venerate." Every cabinet since Jefferson's had sat at the walnut table in the middle of the room, every president since John Adams had worked at the simple desk between the windows, and the boots of many statesmen had soiled the threadbare rug. The wicker scrap basket and leather-bottomed armchairs might have come from a secondhand shop.

Buchanan had left a second-rate engraving of Jackson over the carved marble mantel, a bell rope to call the staff, and "a bust of poor Pierce staring down from a bad eminence on his still more unfortunate successor." The stagnant scent of Buchanan's cigars hung over the room, and his plain, varnished maps hung hit or miss on the walls. A wood fire burned in the hearth, and the mantel's old brick arch bore the marks of Jackson's feet, deployed in what Charles Dickens called the American position. The gas chandelier with a thin rubber hose running down to a lamp on the table cast a faintly yellow light on the dinge.

The office's best feature was its view. Two floor-to-ceiling windows overlooked the south lawn; the long, blunt tooth of the Washington Monument; the adjoining herd of cattle; a swath of the Potomac; the "bastard Gothic" red brick castle of the Smithsonian Institute, as Trollope called it; the steeples of Alexandria; and Robert E. Lee's pillared mansion on Arlington Heights.

Rarely interested in his surroundings, Lincoln may scarcely have noticed. "The first thing that was handed to me as I entered this room," he soon told a friend, was a message from Major Robert Anderson, in command of Fort Sumter in Charleston Harbor. Overwhelming rebel forces were demanding its surrender. The fort must be given up ignominiously or it must be reinforced, almost certainly starting a war.

*   *   *

The bachelor President Buchanan's niece and hostess, Harriet Lane, had thoughtfully made arrangements for the servants to give the Lincolns and their guests an elegant dinner on the evening of the inauguration. Seventeen sat down to supper, all of whom had come with the Lincolns from Illinois. An editor among them passed gossip to reporters about the ladies' inaugural ball gowns, gleaned from talkative maids.

Part way through dinner, the voices of hundreds of New York Republicans drifted into the room, the first of many White House serenades that Lincoln would enjoy or endure. It was an honor that called for a speech, and he came out and gave his thanks. When told in times to come that a serenade was planned, Hay would warn him and ask if he planned to speak, which every crowd cajoled him to do. Like many master speechwriters, he was a weak extemporaneous speaker, and he knew it. Sitting one night with a friend, he heard approaching music with a show of exasperation and hauled himself to the center window over the north portico, a traditional presidential rostrum. Serenade speeches made him feel like a steam doctor, he said (a sort of quack physician who claimed to drain toxins with steam) who was asked to mend a broken leg.

After dinner, the Lincolns and their guests went upstairs to rest before the inaugural ball, to be held in a barnlike hall newly built for the purpose. Henry Adams, a grandson of John Quincy Adams and a great-grandson of John Adams, like his older brother Charles, was there when the Lincoln's arrived. Henry was new to Washington himself as his congressman father's secretary. Looking for signs in Lincoln's face, he thought he saw a mind "absent in part and in part evidently worried by white kid gloves," with "the same painful sense of becoming educated and of needing education" that troubled Henry too.

*   *   *

The president needed educating in many things, not the least of which were his wife's expensive tastes, cheap companions, and disloyal relatives, all of which infected the White House from the start.

The Kentucky-born Mary Todd Lincoln quartered many Todds in the house for the inaugural festivities, including her older sister, Elizabeth Todd Edwards, an influential figure in Springfield; her cousin Elizabeth Todd Grimsley; her half-sister Margaret Todd Kellogg of Cincinnati, who brought two daughters; and Martha Todd White, a "brilliant young woman, more than usually attractive," who had come with her husband from Selma, Alabama, which had already gone over to the Confederacy. It was awkward to explain that the Whites had too. Mrs. Lincoln's rebel brothers stayed away.

Mrs. Edwards said, "Mary was quick, lively, gay—frivolous it may be, social, and loved glitter, show, pomp, and power," all of which would ruin her in the White House with the help of unscrupulous men. Just before the inauguration, some influence-seeking New Yorkers improved the White House stable, and William S. Wood, a shifty former organizer of pleasure excursions, helped her fill it. While managing the Lincolns' trip from Springfield, Wood had oiled his way into Mrs. Lincoln's favor. Now he made her a gift of two exquisite black horses after inquiring about her choice of colors. To give them something to pull, another set of New Yorkers sent the Lincolns a custom-made coach with a crimson brocade interior and "all the conveniences of a modern carriage," according to the *New York Tribune*, which admired the donation and its donors.

The stunning new coach arrived two days before the inauguration. Far from sending it back, Lincoln canceled his appointments and went for a ride. It was all above board, and no laws were broken, but poisonous seeds were sown.

2

A STRANGE MIXTURE
OF ENTHUSIASM
AND GREED

Hordes of eager job seekers had invaded the President's House in the opening days of every administration since Jefferson succeeded Adams in 1801. It was said that they had killed poor William Henry Harrison in his first month in office, and young William Stoddard thought it "no fault of Abraham Lincoln that they did not kill him." Even before he left Illinois, aspiring public servants had descended on him from every part of the country, including the South, drawn by the lure of 1,500 public offices. "Were it believed that vacant places could be had at the North Pole," Lincoln said, the road to the Arctic Circle "would be lined with dead Virginians."

"A host of ravenous partisans from Maine to California" had put him in the White House, said his Secretary of the Navy Gideon Welles (who was said not to know which end of a ship went out first), and they followed him there in force. With the country coming apart, Lincoln spent most of his first weeks in office choosing a postmaster for Brick Meeting House, Maryland; a commissioner to the Sandwich Islands; the land office registrar at Clarksville, Arkansas; and some less consequential officials. He wished he could attend to the Southern question, he said, and avoid a civil war, but the office seekers took all his time. Aware of the ludicrous irony, he likened himself to a man too busy letting rooms at one end of his house to put out a fire in the other.

He could hardly do otherwise. Many Southern-born officials had resigned, leaving scores of vacancies, all but a few other Democrats would soon be dismissed, and Lincoln's choice of replacements could make or break his presidency. With far more applicants than jobs, the chore of rejecting half a dozen supporters for every one he could satisfy was grim.

On the morning after the inauguration, they pushed their way into the White House like a mob at a failing bank. For weeks to come, tobacco-chewing men commandeered the halls and corridors, most of them nattily dressed and many irregularly bathed. They hit the place hard when it opened at nine and stayed until the doormen pushed them out in the afternoon. There were days when they filled the East Room, the Red Room, the Green Room, the Blue Room, and whatever color rooms they liked. On the staircase "you could hardly squeeze your way up or down." They took the office wing like an occupying army and fouled the vicinity of the spittoons. Some slipped into the family quarters and importuned Mrs. Lincoln's relatives. They paraded up and down the walks and caucused under the porticos. Coining an apt oxymoron, a newspaper said the house was overrun by a "mob of gentlemen." Many were Southerners in a city full of spies, but security drew little thought and less action.

Office seekers in the waiting room. Nicolay's door is on the left, Lincoln's on the right. *Frank Leslie's Illustrated Newspaper*, **April 6, 1861. Courtesy of the Boston Athenaeum.**

Not everyone wanted a job. Some wanted an autograph, a federal contract, or a pardon for a wayward son, and the White House was open to them all. The onslaught stopped at noon on Tuesdays and Fridays when the cabinet met, and Nicolay made some progress on the night of March 30, convincing the president to receive the public only between ten and three. Nicolay wrote his fiancé, Therena Bates, that the shorter office hours relieved the president and "all the rest of us from a burden of labor which it would be impossible to sustain." Three days later, Lincoln cut them back again from ten to one, giving his secretaries time to eat and sleep, Nicolay wrote, but the crowd "hangs on with a wonderful perseverance, and although it is five weeks since the inauguration, I cannot yet begin to estimate when we shall be free from them."

They would never be free from them. The Private Secretary on duty, usually Nicolay but often Hay, tried to manage the president's appointments with less than scant success. Lincoln lapsed and saw the public indiscriminately throughout his presidency. His secretaries wasted their time setting limits, Hay said. "He would break through every regulation as fast as it was made."

*　　*　　*

Fresh from Illinois at the age of twenty-five, prepared to bring the presidential staff to a bloated total of three, William Stoddard had not yet been appointed, but "I did go to admire the dense pack of office seekers which had taken possession of the White House," he later recalled. Working a path through the vestibule, he pushed his way to a servant halfway up the stairs and asked him to take his card to Nicolay, who appeared at the bannister and shouted Stoddard's name while three or four applicants "tugged at his coat tails." Stoddard hollered back, and Nicolay yelled over the din.

"Do you wish to see the President?"

"No! I don't. Tell him I'm here, 'cording to orders. That's all. He'll know what to do. I won't bother him." Inconceivable as it was, the very idea brought laughter from the mob and a quiet smile from Nicolay.

A few days later, Stoddard stepped into a bureaucratic cover for an extra presidential aide that had served since the 1830s, when Jackson had sworn not to spend the rest of his presidency signing grants of federal land to private parties and appointed a land patent secretary. The $1,500 salary had not been raised since. For a week or two, Stoddard did his signing at the Interior Department. Returning to the White House several times, he found the staircase "still corked," but "I did get up once or twice and got acquainted with Nicolay and Hay."

Born in 1835 in rural New York to a mother who loved books and a father who sold and published them, Stoddard inherited from his parents his fervent

William O. Stoddard. From the Lincoln Financial Foundation Collection, courtesy of the Indiana State Museum and Allen County Library.

Baptist faith, his abolitionist politics, his "natural obstinacy" as he called it, and "not a drop of humility." His ability to hit two calling cards with a pistol in each hand at thirty feet said as much about his nerve as it did about his eye. "He carried himself like a West Pointer" and had left the University of Rochester to go west. He was editing the *Central Illinois Gazette* when Lincoln came by in 1859. The *Gazette* backed Lincoln for the presidency in its next issue, one of the first papers to do so, and Stoddard dove into the campaign. After the election, Lincoln recruited him to his staff.

Never short of confidence, Stoddard wanted the private secretary's job but admitted years later that Nicolay deserved it. "On the whole, I think he was much better qualified than I was. He was older, more experienced, harder, had a worse temper, and was decidedly German in his manner of telling men what he thought of them."

*　　*　　*

Old Edward McManus, the crafty Irish doorkeeper, had an endless stock of tales about the figures who had passed through the White House in his time. Lincoln often repeated his favorite Edward story. After rising from the vice presidency when Zachary Taylor died, Millard Fillmore had asked Edward if he thought it would do for the president to buy a secondhand coach. "Sure, your Excellency," Edward said, "you're only a secondhand President, you know." Lincoln said Fillmore told the story himself.

Edward's real task was not to keep the door but to open it. It was usually unlocked, and any visitor could open it himself, but the most conventional callers rang for the doorman. When General Scott and Lincoln's Secretary of War Simon Cameron came to formally present their officers, Cameron, "the least conventional of men," simply opened the door and walked in, but Scott stayed on the threshold until Cameron came back to find him. Without a word, the general pulled the doorbell "in a stately way" and entered gravely "on the appearance of the proper attendant."

Edward greeted callers according to their station and his mood and brought their cards to the president when their rank or mission called for it. A touring Englishman and his friends recognized Edward's type when he sized them up as small potatoes and failed to take their coats: "There is a porter who stands in the vestibule of the White House and cracks nuts in a familiar manner," the British tourist said. "He is an old Irishman, and has seen many generations of Presidents. . . . He asked us no questions as we passed on, and it was quite a matter of choice as to whether I should leave my hat and overcoat on a table in the hall or not. It was suggested, indeed, that I should take these articles of apparel with me, 'all kinds of people' being about."

When Stoddard first reported for duty, Edward handed him three brass keys to the front door, for "the young gentlemen," he said, "one for Mr. Nicolay, one for Mr. Hay, and one for yourself." Two of the keys were new. The third was old and tarnished. Edward said it "belonged to the lock when it was put on," but ancient as it was it could still open the door, just like Edward himself. Stoddard took the relic. "That's the key I want, Edward. Give Nicolay and Hay the new ones." When Stoddard used his key, he liked to think it had turned the lock in the hand of Jefferson or Jackson.

*   *   *

In their first days in the White House, Lincoln's secretaries tried to hold the job seekers at bay, with poor results. On his way from his meals to his desk, the president inched his way through waves of shouting men thrusting papers in his hands. There were times when cabinet members had to push through the crowd and pull him into a corner to discuss the dissolution of the Union. On Thursday, April 4, to grapple with ways and means to keep Virginia in it, Lincoln led an important Virginian to a bedroom and locked the door behind them, the office wing being full of uninvited eyes and ears. "It was a sort of epidemic" a respected House member said, "and Mr. Lincoln, at times, was perfectly appalled by it."

So was John Hay, who had come to the White House expecting to be awed and was horrified instead by the "bull-dozing Congressmen" and less distinguished boors who charged the public trough. Hay found the "swinish selfishness" of it all "unspeakably repulsive" but eventually came to the more forgiving view that the crowd was "inspired by a strange mixture of enthusiasm and greed." There were good men among them, he said, eager to serve their country at their own financial cost, though few were indifferent to prestige. One polished gentleman sold his business to accept an unpaid consulate in Norway "where he shivered through an Arctic night of six months" to show his friends and neighbors that the president had confidence in him. "But the numbers were so great and the competition was so keen that they ceased for the moment to be regarded as individuals, drowned as they were in a sea of solicitation."

The *Times of London*'s William Howard Russell lived at Willard's Hotel, the home of the Excelsior Stationer, who pledged to prepare calling cards for office seekers "in superior penmanship." Willard's almost shook with their tread, Russell said, every man "heavy with documents." After one was told he would not be made a judge, he "condescended to seek a place in the Post-Office" and finally applied to keep a lighthouse, "he was not particular where."

Several of Mrs. Lincoln's relatives nosed their way to the feedbag, some successfully, some not. Her friend and cousin Elizabeth Todd Grimsley stayed at the White House for six months. "The papers announce the presence of 100 Todds and all wanting office," she wrote in a letter home, but she made no apology for coveting Springfield's prize. "I have heard nothing about my appointment as post-mistress except Mary often suggests it is to be." It wasn't.

"The thieves hunt in gangs," said Horace Greeley, the editor of the *New York Tribune*, "and each helps all the rest." Attorney General Edward Bates said the cabinet was squabbling over "the distribution of loaves and fishes," and Lincoln did not always flatter their choices even when he blessed them. The insufferable Charles Francis Adams Sr. had let it be known in public that Lincoln was out of his depth. When Adams called at the White House with his fellow aristocrat William Seward, Lincoln's charming Secretary of State, to tell the president he was grateful to be appointed minister to London, Lincoln snubbed him on the spot. "Very kind of you to say so, Mr. Adams, but you are not my choice, you are Seward's man." Then he turned to his Secretary of State: "Well Seward, I have settled the Chicago Post Office."

Governors, senators, and congressmen fought for spoils. Only half facetiously, Lincoln told Stoddard that the more they succeeded the more it cost them. Of every six men they helped, they disappointed five, and the one who got a job thought he should have gotten better. Naming the congressman to whom he had given the most positions, Lincoln said he liked him and did not want to see him hurt. "I guess I won't give him any more."

There was ample proof of his point. A Springfield Republican told a fellow Lincoln man that Nicolay got him a Census Bureau job "at a salary of $1,200—the very lowest—I had been promised a $1,400 place, but promises in this latitude are hardly considered obligatory." The Illinois Secretary of State Ozias Hatch wrote his former employee Nicolay on a friend's behalf:

> George, I want this man to have a place *on my account, darn it*. Some other gentlemen obtain favors. *I ask this of you*. Mr. Browne was *my friend in my youth*. He will not ask for a place that he cannot discharge the duties of . . . George I mean all I have written here. Your friend O. M. Hatch.

The wife of another former neighbor wrote directly to the president: "I hope you may never feel as deep and bitter a disappointment as Mr. Moody and I felt last night when we heard you had given the Post Office to Mr.

Armstrong." She had ruined her health taking care of her injured son, she said, and Mr. Moody had no business and no prospect of any. "Please give my sincere regards to your wife."

Many of Lincoln's supporters were baffled by the time he gave to job seekers on the edge of a civil war. Senator William Fessenden of Maine said he "would turn the federal bayonets" on them if he were in Lincoln's place; but Lincoln was in that place, and he felt duty bound to see them. Most of them had waited days or weeks, many had worked to elect him, and it was painful to disappoint them. He said more than once that his one true vice was an inability to say no. "Thank God for not making me a woman."

He often filled his office with half a dozen applicants at once, processing them in bulk. According to Hay, he received everyone with "a gentle patience," an "astonishing" patience Stoddard thought, though they rarely got what they wanted. After a parting presidential handshake and a noncommittal word, Hay sent their papers to the relevant bureaus "and that was all; the fatal pigeon-holes devoured them."

When he turned them down on the spot, the president tried to soften the blow. After a simple man asked to be made a White House doorkeeper, Lincoln disappointed him gently.

"Have you ever had any experience in doorkeeping?"
"Well no, no actual experience sir."
"Any theoretical experience? Any instruction in the duties and ethics of doorkeeping?"

The man had no such credentials.
Had he ever attended lectures on doorkeeping or read a doorkeeper's textbook?
He admitted that he had not.

"Well then my friend, don't you see that you haven't a single qualification for this important post?"
"Yes, I do," he said, and went away "humbly, almost gratefully."

Like a cloud of Egyptian locusts, Hays said, the first swarm of job seekers moved on after the crop was consumed, but a lesser infestation never left. On one of the calmer days, a gentleman named F. J. Whipple was waiting when the president came through from the family quarters. "What can I do for you?" Lincoln asked.

"Nothing sir. You have not an office I would accept." He had only come to shake the president's hand.

Lincoln grasped his shoulder. "Is it possible! Come into my office. I want to look at you. It is a curiosity to see a man who does not want an office." Whipple was pleased to oblige, and Lincoln doodled as they chatted. A senator called on him a few days later, saw a sketch on his desk, and asked him what it was. "It is the portrait of the one man who does not want an office."

*   *   *

Three days after the inauguration, the White House contained a thousand eager white men seeking jobs and one dejected black man who had just lost his. On Lincoln's recent trip from Illinois, the *New York Herald* had reported from the train that William H. Johnson, his bodyguard, messenger, handyman, barber, and valet, "although not exactly the most prominent, is yet the most useful member of the presidential party." But Lincoln was less than a week in office when Johnson was dismissed for the color of his skin.

Some people thought the White House servants were exclusively white, but a number were descended from household slaves and their unchaste masters, a number that the Lincolns would increase. Years later, a black historian named John Washington, who grew up under their wings, said White House servants were the cream of "colored society" and often led its religious and social organizations. Accustomed to the simple girls she had hired in Springfield, Mrs. Lincoln was as surprised by the White House domestic staff's confidence as she was by their skills. Many had served presidents for years and "knew better than she what was to be done, how it should be done, and why it should be done."

But the veteran White House servants made life hard for interlopers, and they made William Johnson's intolerable. "Johnson's color was very dark," John Washington wrote, "and White House servants were always light." Descended from Virginia's "finest families," they shunned and abused him mercilessly.

When Johnson could stand no more, the commander in chief surrendered to his servants. Not yet prepared to upset racial norms even in his own house, or perhaps especially there, he had Johnson tend the White House furnace at $50 a month and gave him a letter to help him find a better job: "William Johnson, a colored boy, and bearer of this, has been with me about twelve months; and has been, so far as I believe, honest, faithful, sober, industrious, and handy as a servant."

There were no takers. Then Lincoln wrote a note to his avuncular Secretary of the Navy Gideon Welles, "Uncle Gideon" he sometimes called him, and handed it to Johnson.

> The bearer (William) is a servant who has been with me for some time and in whom I have confidence as to his integrity and faithfulness. He wishes to enter your service. The difference of color between him and the other servants is the cause of our separation. If you can give him employment you will confer a favour on yours truly, A. Lincoln.

When Welles did not or could not comply, Lincoln tried his Secretary of the Treasury Salmon Chase, perhaps the most racially enlightened member of his cabinet. Chase made Johnson a laborer on the Treasury Department grounds the next day. Impressing his supervisors, Johnson soon became a messenger, a position of trust. Lacking quicker communications, the White House and other federal offices employed messengers to run notes by foot, horseback, and carriage, some as important as diplomatic exchanges, others as simple as a message carried from Lincoln to Seward a few hundred feet across the President's Park: "Please call over, and bring the 'Marque and Reprisal' bill with you."

Johnson still came to the White House in the mornings to tend the president's wardrobe and shave him. It was said that Lincoln arranged it "as his family are poor."

*   *   *

On March 7, the foreign diplomatic corps came to the White House to pay their respects, and Secretary of State Seward, Lincoln's guide to diplomacy, introduced them. On behalf of all the diplomats, the Portuguese minister addressed the president in French, the lingua franca. For Lincoln it might have been Martian. A translation had been sent in advance, which a messenger took to Seward with Lincoln's draft reply: "To whom the reply should be addressed, that is, by what title, or style, I do not quite understand; and therefore I have left it blank."

Nicolay wrote home to his friend Ozias Hatch that night: "Don't get impatient that I have written no letters back." Things had started as well as they could have hoped, but the labor had been "terrible," and God knew how they would get through it. "We have scarcely had time to eat, sleep, or even breathe." There were more friends in Washington than jobs. "Illinois is here in perfect hordes. You may look out for a tremendous crop of soreheads."

*   *   *

The White House had never been heavily guarded, but several presidents had wanted protection and found it. Suspicious of the common man, Monroe hired plainclothes guards and kept firearms in the porter's lobby. The White House sentry box was built after a housepainter misfired two pistols at Jackson in 1835, provoking Old Hickory to beat him with his cane. In the 1840s, Tyler asked Congress for a security contingent and got one, over no small objection to a Praetorian Guard. To cover the scent of fear, his hulking "doormen" wore common dress and announced his guests. As sectional tensions grew, Fillmore requisitioned muskets from the armory and limited public access to the grounds. Pierce engaged a guard who scrutinized all comers in the vestibule.

In a city full of Southerners steeped in a culture of violence, Lincoln resisted any protection at all. A New Yorker named Charles Tuckerman glimpsed his vulnerability soon after his inauguration. Pausing on an early morning stroll through the White House grounds, Tuckerman was leaning on a fence when a tall, poorly tailored, "ungainly-looking man" came toward him "with an expression of curiosity, if not of suspicion." It was not until the awkward man stopped within speaking distance that Tuckerman recognized the president and raised his hat. Lincoln did the same and asked where he was from. Apparently satisfied from his answer and his accent that he posed no threat, Lincoln said he had been walking the grounds for the first time. He gestured toward the house, noted changes since Madison's day, and was walking the New Yorker toward his favorite view of the river when a passerby started toward them. "Upon this, Lincoln bade me an abrupt 'good morning,'" Tuckerman said, "and turned with a shambling gate into the mansion."

Everyone was on edge, but the thought of civil war seemed absurd to Nicolay. To be sure, he told Therena, "a little brush at Charleston or Pensacola is quite possible," but "that any general hostilities will result from it I have not the least fear." Hay did his best to impress a young lady with a jaunty report of his own: "We are very jolly here now, on a war footing. We are hoping for a little brush with the traitors, but are very much afraid they will deprive us of that pleasure."

3

PLAIN AND SIMPLE IN
ITS APPOINTMENTS

On January 8, 1861, two months before the inauguration, Mrs. Lincoln had left Springfield to shop in New York for the first goods available to ornament herself as well as the White House, a sight she had not seen since 1849. Properly escorted by three distinguished men and the credit of the President Elect, she walked "The Ladies' Mile" below Madison Square on Broadway for days, delighted with the likes of Macy's, B. Altman, Brooks Brothers, Lord & Taylor, and A. T. Stewart's Marble Palace, the biggest, most luxurious store on earth. The merchants were at least as delighted with her redecorating plans as she was. A. T. Stewart's clerk sent a note to an influential senator, hoping "to refurnish and put in order the White House for the reception of a Republican President" with "a disposition to do it for a fair equivalent without robbing the government."

Two months later, Mrs. Lincoln arrived at the White House expecting grandeur and was shocked to be shown a "dilapidated mansion" instead. An Illinois congressman agreed that the house was unattractive. Even the elegant parlors were frayed around the edges, and the family quarters were a melange of dingy carpets, greasy wallpaper, and ancient grime.

Buchanan's niece Harriet Lane gave Mrs. Lincoln a tour on the Friday before the inauguration, a gesture more gracious than the house. Early on the morning of their first full day in residence, Mrs. Lincoln and her cousin Mrs. Grimsley took a closer look. If they started on the ground floor, misleadingly called the basement, they did not save the best for last. Built on sloping terrain, the White House was two stories high on Pennsylvania Avenue and three in the back, where the basement became the ground floor, with big windows facing the sunny south. Even so, William Stoddard said, the basement had the air of "an old and unsuccessful hotel."

Predictably enough, the basement was the servants' domain, "perennially overrun with rats, mildew, and foul smells," with a dozen or more rooms on both sides of a vaulted central hall and wings on both sides. To venture into the basement was to be "reminded of old country taverns," Stoddard said, "if not of something you have smelled in the edge of some swamp."

The big, high-ceilinged, whitewashed kitchen, adjoining a scullery and a larder, had iron-barred, north-facing windows from which you could peer onto Pennsylvania Avenue if you stood on a chair. The sand on the brick-paved floor absorbed grease and whatever spilled, and the cooking fire had never gone out since John Adams's servants lit it in 1800.

Acknowledged as one of the city's best, the White House cook, Cornelia Mitchell, was later recalled by her peers as "well educated for a colored girl of her day," with "a splendid old Southern family background." Her range ran from corn pone and cabbage and chicken fricassee, two of Lincoln's favorites, to lobster and terrapin. She lived in the basement servants' quarters with her children, "and her oldest daughter was allowed to receive her company there." The Lincoln boys were known to borrow her old umbrella.

Elsewhere in the basement were the steward's big office with its desk and locked cupboards, the wine cellar, storage rooms, laundry, and ironing rooms. The wash was dried in the vaulted corridor, avoiding a public display of the presidential linen.

The mansion's heating, plumbing, and lighting systems led the state of the art. Progressive in little else, Lincoln's predecessors of the past two decades had equipped the President's House with every modern marvel of domestic tranquility, ahead of almost every wealthy house in the city.

The huge, coal-fired furnace was a modern wonder when Van Buren had it installed in 1840 in the oval space beneath the Blue Room. Hot air ducts terminating in brass or iron grates and the heat of the furnace room itself ran up to the first floor. Ducts warmed the second floor less effectively. When the dining rooms and parlors were used on cold nights, the White House firemen lit their coal-fueled fireplaces, supplementing the furnace and drawing its heat, but the office wing could be uncomfortable. Nicolay composed a letter to Therena, "so cold that my hand is almost too numb to write, sitting here in my own office, as you will see from this."

An obscure breed of basement pump kept the water moving through the pipes until it failed in May of 1861. Lincoln tracked down an army captain who knew its ways, personally helped him fix it with a monkey wrench, and invited him to lunch.

As they did in all but a few American homes, whale oil lamps and candles lit the Lincolns' house in Springfield, but the White House had been lit by gas since 1848, lowering the risk of fire in exchange for the risk of asphyxiation. After Lincoln nearly succumbed, nodding off to a leak in his office, it took the gasfitters hours to find it.

The system took some getting used to. To operate a lamp, you attached its rubber hose to an outlet on a wall or a gas-fed chandelier, turned a valve, and touched a match to the gas for a bright, clear, faintly yellow light. Some called it harsh. Others called it brilliant. To extinguish it, you disconnected the hose or turned the valve back. Servants came around at dusk with poles tipped with wicked oil lamps to light the chandeliers.

The gas was made from coal at the Washington Gas Light Company plant on Capitol Hill and sent through a buried pipe down Pennsylvania Avenue that fed the adjoining streetlamps, the White House, and the Capitol. On an ordinary night, the gas flickered out at nine when the plant shut down, leaving nothing but ancient sources of light. A servant recalled years later that after a long day at work the president "would lie on his couch, and I would bring him his candle and the *Star*. I would cut the candle in three pieces and place one of the short pieces in the candlestick. Then Lincoln would place the candlestick on his chest and read the *Star*."

*　　*　　*

If the White House technology was in the basement, the splendor was on the first floor. As Mrs. Grimsley quickly learned, "the only elegance of the house was concentrated on the East, Blue, and Red Rooms." When Mrs. Lincoln gave state inaugural delegations tours, she showed them the first floor. The rest would have only upset them.

The East Room was palatial in size, on the seedy side of elegant in decor, with "a faded, worn, untidy look" even for an unworldly young man from upstate New York. "Its paint and furniture require renewal," Stoddard said, "but so does almost everything else about the house, within and without." Jackson had given the East Room its four tawny-veined black marble mantels and three cut-glass chandeliers, long since refitted with gas. Inured to the florid taste of the day, Noah Brooks, an old friend of Lincoln's and a columnist for the *Sacramento Daily Union*, informed his distant readers that the ceiling was frescoed "in a very ordinary style," naked putti "sprawling about overhead in a very loose manner," the "unbreeched urchins" looking chilly on a winter's day.

Though they both had towering ceilings and dwarfed any ordinary room, the Green Room and the identically sized Red Room were the smallest White

House parlors. The Green Room, sometimes called the conversational room, was little used, but Mrs. Lincoln loved the Red Room, the living room, she called it. Oversized crimson and gold satin furniture and a grand piano made it seem smaller than it was. In arch Victorian style, it was cluttered with bric a brac, "some of which stuff" was "very ancient," according to Noah Brooks. The candelabras were a gift to John Adams from a Barbary pirate king.

No paintings graced the White House except for a few aging portraits of former residents. Apart from some richly colored hangings, the walls had a kind of "unfurnished bareness." A few works of art had been acquired through the generosity of successive Congresses, most of which had not been generous at all. There was "little to boast of in that line," Stoddard said, "and it is to be hoped that something better will be done hereafter."

The State Dining Room in the southwest corner overlooking the south lawn was sometimes called the Congressional Dining Room, for its usual clientele. Stoddard called it plain and simple and hardly big enough for a head of state. The table ran the length of the room under a great chandelier, and so did Monroe's plateau, a horizontal mirror with a gold-plated rail that glittered under gaslight, but a scarcity of matching, unchipped china made for embarrassing state dinners. A socialite thought the "antique clock and grim candlesticks from the Madison reign" stood stiffly on the two Italian marble mantels.

The house was flush with silver locked up in the steward's cupboard. When the czar's minister to Washington died in 1833, Jackson had bought his serving pieces at the estate sale, complementing Monroe's French knives, forks, and spoons stamped "President's House" with the silversmith's hammer.

Across the hall from the State Dining Room, the Family Dining Room adjoined the pantry and overlooked Pennsylvania Avenue. Perhaps with tongue in cheek, Brooks said it only sat three dozen, but it was not a pretentious room, with upper-middle-class Victorian furniture, family photographs on the mantel, and bowls of fruit on the sideboard. A dumbwaiter hoisted food from the kitchen below.

*　　*　　*

On the dismal second floor, a wide central hall ran the length of the family quarters from the head of the formal staircase at the western end of the house to the office wing on the east, divided by two sets of pocket doors. When they stepped out of their bedrooms, the Lincolns never knew whom they might bump into. The hall was a semipublic thoroughfare.

The furniture had survived generations of neglect. A "degradation" Mrs. Lincoln called it, for "in all humility be it spoken" she "would not have given it houseroom" had she lived "in the humblest cabin." It was fortunate that her husband did not care. His bedroom, bathroom, and dressing room suite in the southwest corner shocked Mrs. Grimsley. "A mahogany French bedstead, split from top to bottom, was the best piece of furniture in it." Connecting bedrooms were fashionable in prosperous homes, and the White House followed the fashion. An interior door joined the president's suite to Mrs. Lincoln's bedroom, and she typically slept in his, unless she was punishing him.

The young Lincoln boys, Willie and Tad, had small bedrooms facing Pennsylvania Avenue. Away at Harvard, their older brother, Bob, seldom used his room over the north portico. Three bedrooms were available for guests. Eight servants' rooms were tucked under the eaves of the attic.

The plumbing was first class. Water had been piped in through hollow tree trunks from a spring in Franklin Square since 1833, and a few discrete water closets had dignified the house since Jefferson's time. Franklin Pierce had installed hot and cold running water in every bedroom, a partitioned flush toilet in his dressing room, and another downstairs in the porter's lodge. The Lincolns must have been pleased. Their Springfield backyard had a pump and a privy. But the plumbing had its flaws. In 1862, Richard Henry Dana, a blueblood Bostonian and the author of *Two Years Before the Mast*, had a chat with Mrs. Lincoln in one of the parlors and found it "smelling of bad drainage."

Marble-topped wash stands with decoratively painted porcelain sinks had been ordered by Buchanan for every bedroom and his dressing room and would soon be installed, with swivel spigots that opened when you swung them out and closed when you swung them back in. Servants kept the towel racks draped with fresh linen. Funded by a hefty $4,420 appropriation, Potomac water would soon be piped in, which would prove to be no blessing.

Adjoining Mrs. Lincoln's bedroom, the oval sitting room was the family's private refuge, the same size and shape as the Blue Room beneath it. The Lincolns called it the library. Stoddard called it "a delightful retreat," especially in summer, when the south portico's overhang gave it precious shade. Prompted by his wife, Millard Fillmore had installed the low, paneled bookcases in 1850 and begun to fill them. Several presidents had added books since then—biography and history, law and religion, Shakespeare and Robert Burns, a few modern novels. In 1862, Buchanan would write Lincoln about some books he had left and hoped to get back, closing with a wish "that you may be more happy in your exalted station than your immediate predecessor."

*   *   *

Mrs. Lincoln bought scores of books for the library at Appleton & Co. and other New York bookstores, including twenty-one volumes of Washington Irving bound in calfskin, eight volumes of Longfellow, *Queens of England*, *The World's Noted Women*, and *Female Sovereigns*. Accounting separately for books to be taken home and books to be left in Washington, the president dipped into his own pocket for $124.25 of a $250 bookseller's bill, the amount of the annual book-buying appropriation. Other purchases followed. *The History of Creation* cost $2.50.

The library was a comfortable, inviting place, with upholstered rockers, a wood-burning fireplace, and a striking river view framed by the pillars of the south portico. Lincoln often met informally there with friends and important callers. His secretaries were welcome, but Stoddard took his borrowed books elsewhere. Lounging in the family quarters did not feel right to him, though Lincoln once found him reading with his feet on the mantle and did not object.

*   *   *

Before the Lincolns moved in, President Tyler's ten-year-old boy had been the only child to live in the White House. Willie and Tad Lincoln, formally Thomas Lincoln in honor of his grandfather, were a novelty.

Everyone loved Willie. Ten years old when the family moved in, full of "boyish frolic," according to Hay, but a studious child "of great promise," Willie spent hours planning imaginary railroad trips, absorbed in his collection of timetables. Mrs. Grimsley adored him, "a noble, beautiful boy," very bright, "methodical, frank and loving, a counterpart of his father, save that he was handsome." On the Lincolns' first Sunday in the Red Room, Willie sat down at the piano to play for the family and some guests until Mrs. Grimsley spoke to him as if Dickens had come up with her name. "No one is without example," she said, "and as your father's son, I would remember the Sabbath day to keep it holy." Willie said he would, and did.

His little brother, Tad, played a more disorderly role, to sharply mixed reviews. "There could be no greater contrast between children," in the opinion of Mrs. Grimsley, who was seven years younger than their mother and probably not thrilled that the boys called her grandmother. If Willie was at heart a quiet reader, Tad was a "merry, spontaneous fellow, bubbling over with innocent fun, the life, as also the worry of the household." Nearly eight years old, he did not know his letters, could not dress himself, and struggled with a speech impediment that baffled some adults and endeared him to others. Willie and

Willie Lincoln, posed in Matthew Brady's fashionable Washington studio. Library of Congress.

Tad called their parents "Maw" and "Paw" in plain western style, but Tad sometimes called his father "Pappa dear" and it came out "Pappa day."

Tad was a kind little boy, Hay said, but "perfectly lawless," with "a very bad opinion of books and no opinion of discipline." Hay tried to keep him out of his father's office, with small success, but often found him uplifting. "Early in the morning you could hear his shrill pipe resounding through the dreary corridors of the Executive residence." Tad made friends of all the servants. A policeman later said, "I wish I could show what a capital little fellow he was."

Many people thought otherwise. With "a bachelor's opinion of obstreperous children," Nicolay could not understand how Lincoln let Tad run through his office whenever he liked, blowing a horn or not, no matter who was there or why. A senator called him "more numerous than popular." When Tad broke one of the vestibule's stately mirrors with a ball, he kicked at one of the shards: "I don't believe Paw will care." When he marched into a meeting beating a drum, Lincoln astonished the room: "My son, can't you manage to make a little less noise?" The meeting went on to the beat of Tad's percussion.

Cerebral though he was, Willie was in on Tad's tricks, often hatched in the attic, where they found a bin of calling cards accumulated since the house was built and made snowstorms of them on the stairway. Elsewhere in the attic they discovered the junction of the bell pull system, yanked all the cords at once, and mobilized a dozen staff. Stoddard said it got them banned from the attic. He did not say the ban was enforced.

Willie and Tad turned the flat White House roof into a fort or the deck of a warship, depending on their game, manned it with neighborhood children, equipped it with a spyglass, and armed it with a log cannon and some old condemned muskets. They played on the south lawn with the servants' boys. "There was no color line there," the butler's son said. There was no class line either. "The bootblacks and other colored boys who peeped through the fence were invited in," and so were the tattered newsboys, black and white.

Stoddard said Tad had "always under his protection" one or more "curs of low degree, famished appearance, and unimaginable extraction." The boys kept a small menagerie in the stable—donkeys, horses, ponies, goats, and a pardoned Thanksgiving turkey, all of which ruined the flowers and infuriated the gardener. A bodyguard said of Tad in 1911, "as I look back over nearly half a century I see him most plainly and oftenest seated in a little wagon, driving a pair of goats through the White House grounds." Sometimes he drove them inside, scattering guests and office seekers.

Neither Willie nor Tad went to school. A Polish pianist gave them piano lessons. Alexander Williamson, a scholarly Scot in his forties, held a govern-

Tad Lincoln, with chin whiskers penciled in by himself. Library of Congress.

ment job in the mornings and tutored them in the afternoons at desks and a blackboard in the State Dining Room. A favorite of their parents (though Mrs. Lincoln had bargained like a fishwife over his pay, he said), Williamson stayed on throughout Lincoln's presidency. He must have been a saint.

*　　*　　*

When Mrs. Lincoln first saw them in early March, the grounds behind the White House had not yet come back into leaf and bloom, but she found them exquisite even then. They were thought to have the look of "a Southern plantation, straggling and easy going." The outbuildings running down toward the Treasury Department included a woodshed, a carriage house, and a tin-roofed, stuccoed stable. The long, low, flat-roofed service wings stretching out from both ends of the White House contained the two original wells, drawn by hand pumps and covered with low brick domes, storage space, domestic service rooms, and the servants' men's and women's privies.

The south front of Lincoln's White House, with the conservatory on the left. Library of Congress.

Franklin Pierce had caused a greenhouse to be built in 1853, when fresh-cut flowers came into vogue, chancing the common wisdom that their vapors were unhealthy. Four years later, Buchanan put an imposing glass conservatory over the western service wing, connected to the house by a narrow, glass-paned passage. A visiting French aristocrat called it simple and unpretentious like the rest of the house, but it was humble only by Napoleonic standards.

Filled with light, warmth, exotic color, and fragrance on a winter's day, it was crowned by a steep-pitched ceiling that drew the eye up to 12 colored transparencies portraying the months of the year. A water heating system supplied the warmth, basins of water produced the humidity, and sunlight came from all directions, spiked with bands of color from above. The fragrant air was scented with lemon and orange trees, hanging baskets of flowers, and tropical blooming vines trained up around a light wooden frame. The gardeners laid out beautifully tended plants in terra cotta pots on green painted tables in massed rows of flowers and eye-catching foliage. There were roses of every color, flowering cactuses of every shape and size, camellias, azaleas, cape jasmines, ferns, spirea, poinsettia, many other flowers, plants and shrubs, ripe strawberries year round, a water lily tank stocked with goldfish, and a treasured sago palm passed down from the hand of Washington.

Mrs. Lincoln could not have been more pleased. She loved flowers dearly and knew how to care for them. She cut them herself for the dining rooms and parlors and arranged them with taste and skill. On most winter days she sent messengers to delighted friends and acquaintances with miraculous gifts of fruit or arrangements of flowers put together by the bouquet man and his assistant, edged with ferns or forget-me-nots in a stiff paper holder.

The Lincolns opened the conservatory to "that portion of the public who might be presumed to be above stealing flowers," Stoddard said, then confined it to family and guests when the presumption turned out to be false. One perfectly respectable woman recalled how she strolled through the conservatory with a friend and "got a few flowers and leaves to press, in memory of the White House," a model for cumulative ruin.

Ironically in view of the pilfering, the conservatory was run by a thief. From his office there, the forty-one-year-old White House gardener, John Watt, managed two dozen helpers and laborers who kept the grounds, painted the fences and outbuildings, raked the leaves, graded the gravel driveways, and tended the conservatory, giving Watt a sizable budget and a choice of opportunities for graft. Appointed in the early 1850s, newly arrived from Scotland, he delighted the Fillmores with his work, but in 1859 the Commissioner of Public Buildings accused him of inflating his bills and doctoring his accounts.

Shocked by an invoice for seed, the Commissioner made him start producing his own, and the jealous Capitol gardener complained that Watt's generous payroll for maintaining the White House walks left them somehow thick with weeds.

Watt charmed Mrs. Lincoln with his knowledge of the flowers, his sycophantic endorsement of her plans for the gardens and the conservatory, and his lovable Scottish burr. She called him "Major Watt" in homage to his title in the D.C. militia. Her entrapment in his corruption came later, and his influence would be profound.

4

A MISCELLANEOUS ASSORTMENT OF LIFE AND CHARACTER

Almost every president but Jefferson had held public receptions once or twice a week between New Year's Day and Lent. Known as drawing rooms or levees, they were open in theory to all and confined more or less in fact to gentlemen and ladies who had been properly introduced to the president or brought a letter of introduction from someone who had. The exclusion was unspoken and self-enforced. In James and Dolley Madison's day, James Fennimore Cooper had said that the "poorer and laboring classes stay away." The degree of exclusivity had ebbed and flowed with the presidents but had never disappeared, certainly not in the Buchanan administration.

Lincoln broke the mold. His weekly public levees were open from the start to any sober person with a smile and a clean shirt, a policy unmatched even in Jackson's day. Anyone could meet the head of state at home, an English writer said, and "it is not high treason to stare him hard in the face."

On Friday, March 8, four days after his inauguration, the "muddy footed world at large" beat its way to his door for his first levee. Though the night was cold, the crowd was overwhelming. Word had somehow spread that no one would be refused. Beginning at eight o'clock, led by "the advance column of the grand army of office-seekers," said the hostile *New York Herald*, a countless horde of Republicans arrived at Lincoln's door "so that he may know them when they call again." The *Herald* was not charmed: "Among these strange faces may be detected something of all the isms and kinks and crotchets of our Northern reformers—spiritualism, free speech, free soil, free men, free love, free farms, free rents, free negroes, women's rights, bran bread and patent medicines."

The barbaric invasion of nobodies swamped the privileged class who typically appeared at levees—government officials, military officers, well dressed tourists, and the social elite, "dying to see how Mrs. Lincoln fills the place of Miss Lane . . . how Madame is dressed, how she looks, how she will do."

Mrs. Lincoln was not a novice hostess, but her ignorance of White House protocol was nearly as profound as her husband's, who insisted on following custom to dispel the myth of his unfitness. He put Nicolay in charge of learning it, made Seward its overseer, and left the First Lady out, which did not please her.

Guided by Seward and the domestic staff, the Lincolns staged their levees by the book and wrote only one new page—admitting everyone who showed up. In 1861, black men and women did not, never dreaming that the president's open door was open to them. Otherwise, "citizens in all sorts of dress" were welcome, said Benjamin French, the marshal of the inaugural parade, "from the finished and perfumed dandy down to the shabbiest of the shabby," from women in the plainest clothes, to ladies who followed fashion and ladies who defied it. Seward's teenaged daughter Fanny shocked French by arriving "*without any hoops on.*" Stoddard thought the crowd made a "miscellaneous assortment of life and character."

For many ordinary Americans, attending a White House function was like landing on the moon. *Morrison's Stranger's Guide and Etiquette for Washington City* included tips that Mr. Morrison thought he should share:

> Gentlemen bathe the whole person frequently. . . . It is sad to see a man, otherwise entitled to respect and esteem, whose teeth are blackened with accumulations of tartar and tobacco juice, whose finger nails are tipped with ebony colored arcs, and whose hair and whiskers give countenance to the popular superstitions regarding witches and nightmares.

Men in need of such advice mingled freely at Lincoln's levees, arriving on foot, in hacks, or on the public horse car line that ran up and down Pennsylvania Avenue. The rich arrived in glistening private carriages that discharged their passengers at the portico and waited to be called for when their owners were ready. To keep traffic flowing, everyone came in by the eastern gate and left through the western.

Portable wooden racks were set up in the vestibule with rows of big square holes that could hold a hat and a folded wrap, each with a number and a ticket. Stoddard watched plain people check their coats and walk into the Blue Room to be hit by "a chilly blast of awe, if not of bashfulness, at finding themselves actually in the White House at Washington," about to take the president's hand. Many asked a servant or a confident-looking bystander the name of some officer or gentleman.

*   *   *

Alcohol had not been served at a public White House event since Jackson did it and regretted it. Nor was there any food. The crowd was always big enough, Stoddard said, without "additional attractions." The superb Marine Band in their bright scarlet uniforms, "The President's Own," played light classical music, popular tunes, and marches near the East Room, where John Adams had them play in 1801. They had played there ever since.

Perfect order was not maintained at Lincoln's first levee. Avoiding a line that stretched out to Pennsylvania Avenue, people climbed in through the windows, and many never got close enough to see him, let alone shake his hand. In a sort of social truce, it was the last time North and South would mingle at the White House for years, "and what a crush and jam it was," Mrs. Grimsley said. Encaged in enormous hoops of whalebone or steel, the ladies nearly filled the place themselves. In pretentious English evening dress, the Republican senator Charles Sumner of Massachusetts appeared for the first time since a South Carolinian beat him senseless with a cane on the Senate floor in 1856. Other swells arrived whose home states ranged from Maine to Louisiana.

The president showed the crowd a genial smile and good color, a reporter said. But even to a fellow westerner who had come partway by sleigh from Webster City, Iowa, he seemed "awkward and ungainly and not at all at home," for the Lincolns were only "plain people from Springfield."

The president shook hands in the Blue Room at the head of the receiving line with his wife to his right and the guests filing in from his left. Following protocol, Mrs. Lincoln addressed the few people she knew and smiled, nodded, or curtsied to the many she did not. It was not the right thing to give her your hand. Behind her stood her sisters and Mrs. Grimsley. It occurred to a brigadier that they could save her from being crowded merely by deploying their hoops. They were simply dressed in comparison to the First Lady, whose diamonds and pearls matched a red silk dress trimmed with lace, and "red and white japonicas in a wreath behind the ears." The papers described her appearance in detail. Whether she liked the *Herald*'s report of "the well-rounded proportions of a wholesome little Western matron" is unknown.

Nicolay and Hay stood with Lincoln throughout the ordeal, which left his right hand all but lame. Discreteely weighed down with weapons, Ward Hill

Lamon played the marshal of the District of Columbia's role, standing at Lincoln's left, taking the name and state of everyone who wished to be introduced. When he knew who they were, he asked them anyway, so as not to embarrass the strangers behind them. He would then present to the president "Mr. Kaufman from California" or "Mr. and Mrs. Smith from Charleston." Lincoln shook their hands from eight until half-past ten, remarking as he pushed them along that he hoped to see California some day, or to see South Carolina back in the Union. To keep the line moving, he often took a gentleman's hand with his right and a lady's with his left.

The Blue Room had been a parlor for Charles Francis Adams Jr.'s family, but it did him no good when he tried to cut the line twice. In the end, he and a friend set themselves "in the main current, and were pushed and squeezed along." Adams scanned the crowd with reluctant respect:

> There they were—the sovereigns; some in evening dress, others in morning suits; with gloves and without gloves; clean and dirty; all pressing in the same direction, and all behaving with perfect propriety. . . . The sight was not pleasant to see, and even less pleasant to participate in; but still good of its kind. Here, as everywhere, the people governed themselves.

With the breath nearly squeezed from their bodies, Adams and his friend came in sight of Lincoln's "tall, rapidly bobbing head" as he shook the people's hands and quickly passed them on, but when people he knew came along, he bent down and whispered in their ears, "in pleasant, homely fashion, though not exactly in one becoming our President." Adams "hurried by as quickly as I could," apparently keeping his ancestry to himself.

Stoddard thought the White House parlors turned into workshops at levees, but Hay said Lincoln enjoyed them and seemed surprised when people consoled him about enduring them. The abolitionist Jane Grey Swisshelm deplored the custom that forced the President of the United States to shake hundreds of hands "as one might pump on a sinking ship," but when someone asked him in a reception line if his handshaking was more tiring than his work, he denied it. "Oh, no, no," he said. "I am pretty strong," and it actually rested him, "for here nobody is cross or exacting, and no man asks me for what I can't give him." Hay watched him laugh when old friends came through the receiving lines, which Nicolay supposed were new and enjoyable for tourists, "but for us who have to suffer the infliction once a week they get to be intolerable bores."

Many people armed themselves with a speech, Hay said, but "unless it was compressed into the smallest possible space" they never got to deliver it. The people behind them pushed it out of them, or the president moved them along with his right hand in theirs and his left pressing their backs. One "little wee bit of a fat man, half smothered in the crowd" stuck his hand into Lincoln's through a fast-closing gap and "wheezed out some choked sentences about freedom, glory, emancipation," before he was borne away.

The evening always ended with a promenade. The president, the First Lady, and any distinguished guests linked arms with a chosen partner, not necessarily of the opposite sex, strode into the East Room as the Marine Band played "Hail Columbia," and walked an oval path for half an hour or so, smiling and nodding at the people along the walls and in the middle, letting everyone have a good look. Lincoln promenaded with Mrs. Grimsley at his first levee and overheard condescension as they passed. "The President bears himself well," one sophisticate said, "and does not seem the least embarrassed."

When the band struck up "Yankee Doodle," the traditional finale that surely annoyed the South, the Lincolns left the room through a path the doormen cleared and walked down the hall and up the grand staircase, signaling the crowd to go home. People rushed the vestibule, waving claim checks at the doormen, and pushed themselves out the door. Some went out swearing over the loss of hats and coats.

A friend wrote Harriet Lane, Buchanan's retired hostess, that the Lincolns' first levee attracted a gay and lively crowd, but only seven ladies of her circle had come. "The great mass" were strangers, "who had not been in the habit of being present on such occasions." The once largely British domestic staff was changing too. A Washington grande dame in Buchanan's time, now a rebel in Richmond, was informed by a friend that "the ensemble of the personnel of the White House has sadly changed, more befitting a restaurant than the House of the President."

*   *   *

The celebrated Harriet Lane was the picture of courtly chic. Queen Victoria had befriended her. A naval vessel had been named for her. When a home-spun congressman winked at her over a glass of wine at a White House dinner and complained about the food, another guest was shocked. "Oh, that's nothing," said Miss Lane, "such things happen here any day. Nobody notices these people from the rural districts."

She could not help but notice the Lincolns. Mrs. Grimsley was gracious enough to say that Miss Lane had left the White House "in a perfect state of readiness," but the same could not be said of its new residents. When Lincoln had made his courtesy call on Buchanan before the inauguration, Miss Lane had been reminded of "Burns," the "tall, awkward Irishman who waits on the door." Burns was the better looking, she said, "but I only had a side view."

Worse than Lincoln's artlessness, Miss Lane had heard that his wife was "awfully Western, loud and unrefined," and Miss Lane did not know the half of it. Sprung from the haughty Todds of Lexington, Kentucky, Mrs. Lincoln had a finishing school education and a shaky sort of French, but her social skills were provincial and her temper was wild. She had often humiliated her husband in fits of public rage. On petty provocation, she had come at him with brooms, a knife, hot tea and coffee, and "very poorly pitched potatoes." Lincoln's law partner William Herndon said she made his life at home "a burning, scorching hell."

Herndon was not unbiased on the subject of Mary Lincoln, whose wrath had scalded him too, and she had her friends and admirers, but many others described her as unbalanced. Women were often shocked by her "outrageous tantrums," unsettling "attacks of what we called in those days hysteria," tastes and habits considered "vulgar and pestiferous beyond description," and a temper that descended to "a species of madness," all of which made their mark on Lincoln's White House.

The president too got poor reviews as the head of capital society. Some said his "uncouth manners, self-taught and partly forgotten" were a precious American archetype, the edges of which were noticeably filed down in his White House years, but Charles Francis Adams Jr. thought his poorly tailored suits betrayed an ignorance of his place. As fine a writer as he was, his spoken English bore the scars of his youth. He heared rather than heard, would git instead of get, told statesmen what he done instead of what he did; but he spoke with simple dignity, and it somehow seemed right for him. A touch of Kentucky grammar with a comic twist of his chin could sharpen a keen remark.

For many capital grandees, his politics were more offensive than the way he held his fork. An antislavery White House had shattered Washington's Southern-dominated hierarchy, Stoddard said, leaving society "semi-chaotic." The Maryland and Virginia aristocrats who led it came from states that had not yet seceded but were pro-Confederate, while the middle and working classes were predominantly loyal. It was "decidedly low" to declare for the Union, and even loyal Southerners began to disappear from Lincoln's levees and shun his wife. Mrs. Grimsley watched in horror as "an element" filled the void whose standing was based on new wealth, but cultivated folk from Philadelphia, New York, and Boston soon displaced them, reinforced by the

Mary Lincoln. Library of Congress.

Lincolns' Western friends, military officers, gorgeously decorated diplomats—notably the pro-Northern Russians and Chileans—and their glamorous wives.

On Saturday afternoons in winter, the First Lady was expected to be "at home" to visitors in the Red Room, primarily but not exclusively women. Stoddard and some of her friends helped her in the receiving line, and the president sometimes slipped in and stood in the back until someone approached him. An Englishman watched him pull awkwardly at one white kid glove then the other. "Mr. Lincoln does not stand straight on his feet, but sways about with an odd sidelong motion, as though he were continually pumping something from the ground."

Like her husband, the First Lady received all kinds of people and let it be known that "decent and clean clothes" were the only standard of dress. Her Saturday afternoon receptions were not as fine as the president's evening levees, where a "glittering crowd" lit by gaslight ignored the hoi polloi, but she set a double standard. "Ladies" should appear in full dress.

The Times of London's William Howard Russell returned to his room at Willard's on Saturday, March 30, to find a lush bouquet and an invitation to her first reception. He arrived late, and only two or three women were there. "The Washington ladies have not yet made up their minds that Mrs. Lincoln is the fashion," he wrote. They missed their Southern friends and sneered at the vulgar Yankees in command of "this preposterous capital." Russell sympathized with her struggle to transform herself "from a condition of obscurity in a country town to be mistress of the White House," but his first impression of her failure was "not diminished by closer acquaintance."

A full three years later in 1864, the small talk she had practiced in a hundred receiving lines disappointed another Londoner: "Do you keep your health, Sir?" "How long have you been in this country, Sir?" "How long do you conclude to remain, Sir?" "And how do you like the country, Sir?" There then ensued "a deep and, to me, embarrassing silence," the Englishman wrote. "At last she spoke again"—"And you keep your health, Sir?' "

He gave her a sweeping bow and moved away politely as she addressed the next man in line: "Do you keep your health?"

Many White House guests thought her charming. Richard Henry Dana thought her a "cross, suspicious, under-bred" woman who "looks like the housekeeper of the establishment," and "a not good tempered housekeeper at that." He was hardly more impressed by her husband: " 'Abe' looks like a man who has brought in something to sell."

William Howard Russell cared less about Mrs. Lincoln's breeding than her vulnerability: "The lady is surrounded by flatterers and intriguers" who snickered behind her back after telling her how fetching she was, a jowly prairie matron looking patently absurd in a debutante's plunging dress and a water nymph's flowered wreath. The polished women she longed to impress laughed her off as "a vulgar doll with foreign frippery," a "mean and vulgar" look, and the air of "a dowdy washerwoman."

Stoddard witnessed a clash of cultures at one of her receptions. Some upper-class women from Boston in sensible high-necked gowns included a "tall, gray-haired, severe-faced lady, in very plain black silk" who studied Mrs. Lincoln's low-cut crimson dress "remorselessly." When some Manhattan socialites arrived in vivid colors "and a fine glitter of diamonds," the Puritans did not mix with the Knickerbockers, of whom they disapproved, and the New Yorkers displayed "sincere reciprocity."

*　　*　　*

On the day after his maiden levee, Lincoln's first diplomatic reception did not go well. Ignoring custom and courtesy, the diplomats failed to arrive together or even in full force, a tacit show of sympathy for the Confederacy. The French minister stayed home, and Mrs. Grimsley thought his British counterpart, Lord Lyons, was only "coldly dignified," an implicit rebuke from a popular bon vivant who would soon be heard to say, "If you're given champagne at lunch, there's a catch somewhere."

The ministers from Holland and Bremen came to dinner at the White House and were not impressed with its occupant. "During the two and a half hours I sat next to him," the Dutchman told his superiors, "I could not discover anything statesmanlike in him. His conversation consists of vulgar anecdotes at which he himself laughs uproariously."

Early on, Nicolay made a list of what to wear on state occasions—black pants (white in summer), white shirt, white cravat, white or straw-colored kid gloves, a black dress suit, or blue with "bright buttons." Seward's State Department gave Nicolay a memorandum of advice that neither he nor the president had required on the prairie: "Avoid the word 'Sir' in conversation when you address a titled person for the first time on greeting him. You may say, 'How do you do Lord Lyons?'" Not all of it sunk in. More than a year later, Lincoln sent his autograph to a British earl's widow with a kind little note that credited the idea to "Mr. Lyon."

Unlike almost everyone else, foreign diplomats did not come directly to the White House on business. They went instead to Seward, though the State Department's memorandum to Nicolay let him know that if a diplomat called in the evening "it is well for the President to go down."

All three of Lincoln's secretaries knew some French, but not enough to handle the foreign diplomats, officers, and tourists for whom it was the common language, or to read European letters to the president. Hay and Stoddard brought a Russian-born French professor to the White House for lessons but soon gave them up for more urgent concerns.

On Wednesday, March 27, Seward presented the minister of the new kingdom of Italy to Lincoln in the Blue Room, letting William Howard Russell stand quietly in a corner. Russell had never seen Lincoln before. The Chevalier Bertinatti arrived in a "cocked hat, white gloves, diplomatic suit of blue and silver lace, sword, sash, and ribbon of the cross of Savoy." Russell thought he saw a smile cross Seward's face and suspected he was thinking of his own rumpled suit. More likely, he was wondering what Lincoln and the chevalier would make of each other.

When the president ambled in, Russell was struck by his swinging arms, big hands and feet, and poorly fitted, wrinkled black suit. He looked like a small-town undertaker, smiled like a country lawyer, and seemed about to shake hands all around until Seward's cold stare and "the profound diplomatic bows of the Chevalier Bertinatti" brought him up short. As Seward introduced the Italian, Lincoln bowed too sharply and listened to Bertinatti read his credentials. With a second bow "still more violent," the president drew his reply from his coat and read it. Then he and the chevalier traded complements and shook hands. Despite Lincoln's awkwardness, Russell "left agreeably impressed with his shrewdness, humor, and natural sagacity."

*   *   *

On March 28, Lincoln read "in cold shock" a stiffly formal note from his general in chief of the army, Winfield Scott, recommending the abandonment to the rebels of Fort Sumter in Charleston Harbor and Fort Pickens in Pensacola, a craven alternative to war. Lincoln would soon tell a friend that had he known the intolerable strains he would face in his first months in office he would not have thought it possible to survive them.

As he grappled with the grim decision to surrender the forts or fight a civil war and wondered if he had the strenght to endure the stress, his wife wrote a friend that their carriage was *"very luxurious,"* and "the pleasure grounds here are exquisite . . . I am beginning to feel so perfectly at home, and enjoy every thing so much. The conservatory attached to this house is so delightful. We have so many choice bouquets."

She had also "formed many delightful acquaintances. Every evening our blue room is filled with the elite of the land, last eve we had about 40 to call in, to see us *ladies*," including her Kentucky cousin John C. Breckinridge, Buchanan's vice president. Soon to be a rebel general, Breckinridge invited Mrs. Grimsley to keep her White House room "when the Confederacy takes possession." A "seemingly merry war of words" ensued, with "an undercurrent of storm and sting."

About a year later, Mrs. Lincoln's sister Elizabeth walked the president into the conservatory in midwinter to turn him from his cares. "How beautiful this is," she told him, the roses so fine, the "exotics" so grand, gathered from every corner of the earth.

Lincoln listened in silence before he replied. "Yes," he said, "this whole thing looks like spring. But do you know I have never been in here before. I don't know why it is so, but I never cared for flowers. I seem to have no taste, natural or acquired, for such things." When Elizabeth persuaded him to cross the street to the park at Lafayette Square, he said he hadn't been there for a year.

*   *   *

The Lincolns gave their first state dinner on the night of March 28 in honor of the cabinet. A White House messenger took an invitation to William Howard Russell, who arrived at seven to be confronted by the wary doorman Edward McManus, "particularly inquisitive as to my name and condition in life." Once satisfied, Edward told Russell where to leave his hat "so that it would be exposed to no indignity."

The Marine Band was playing in the vestibule as Russell approached the Blue Room, where the dinner guests were chatting before they were called to the table. Expecting to be announced, he simply walked in. Mrs. Lincoln seemed conscious of being more than a lawyer's wife and succeeding only to a point, but her manners were an agreeable surprise, and so was the president's aplomb. Russell admired the way he left one group of guests to join another by raising the obligatory laugh at a presidential witticism and moving off "in the cloud of merriment produced by his joke."

Mrs. Grimsley thought the evening fell short of a gay affair, the times being what they were. The women were enormously hooped and the men all in black, with "not a scrap of lace or a piece of ribbon," Russell told his British readers, "except for the gorgeous epaulettes of an old naval officer who had served against us in the last war." General Scott, another feeble veteran of the War of 1812, took ill before dinner and was put to bed upstairs.

If Nicolay followed protocol, as Lincoln had instructed him to do, he told the gentlemen which ladies they would take into dinner, introduced them if they were not acquainted, and signaled the Marine Band to stop the music for "Hail to the Chief" as the president escorted his partner to the State Dining Room, followed by the other paired guests. They were seated from a chart prepared by Nicolay with State Department help, the Lincolns facing each other at the center of the table rather than its head. Nicolay had spent hours writing ladies' names in red and gentlemen's in black, alternating them by gender, accounting for rank and precedence (a task that required careful study), separating combatants believed to be engaged in feuds, starting over when anyone sent regrets.

The table was lavishly decorated with Monroe's figurines, his French silver, his vases filled with fresh cut conservatory flowers and ferns, his gilded and mirrored brass plateau running lightly down the table under gaslight. The napkins, stiffly starched, matched the crimson and white damask tablecloth. The Marine Band played behind closed doors, muting its splendid music for dinner conversation. The meal was privately catered and served "in the French manner," in courses. The main course was fish, neither good nor bad enough for Russell to mention. Several wines were served, and the president's glass was filled for the sake of good manners. He would touch it to his lips but take no more than a sip.

Russell found it all quite unpretentious, there being no liveried staff or displays of ancient plate. John Hay he found "very agreeable and lively." Interrupted by the silence that stilled the room when the president told his stories, Russell heard in the "Babel of small talk round the table" a "diversity of accent" that challenged him.

After dinner, according to form, the gentlemen would have risen and stayed where they were as the ladies retired to the Family Dining Room. The women used the lavatory in the porter's lodge. For the men, the servants brought in cigars, screens, and chamber pots. After half an hour or so, the genders reunited in the Red Room for coffee and conversation.

The cabinet was asked to stay after the other guests left, and heard from their shaken president what General Scott had told him: as a gesture to Virginia and the other Southern states still in the Union, forts Sumter and Pickens should be given up without a fight. The cabinet was stunned. Lincoln got no sleep that night.

*   *   *

The job seekers who descended on Lincoln included a thoroughly unqualified applicant for the counsel's post at Florence, a woebegone writer from Massachusetts named Herman Melville, whose book about a whale had failed. At

Lincoln's second levee, the line to shake his hand wound through the parlors for an hour and a half. "Of course I was one of the shakers," Melville wrote his wife. "Old Abe is much better looking than I expected and younger looking. He shook hands like a good fellow—working hard at it like a man sawing wood at so much per cord." Melville found the scene "very fine altogether. Superb furniture—flood of light—magnificent flowers—full band of music, etc."

Regrettably for the struggling author, the diplomatic post went to someone else, an actual diplomat, refreshingly enough. On the following pleasant Sunday, Melville found himself in Lafayette Park, "opposite the White House, sunning myself on a seat" before he went home to the Berkshires.

On Saturday, April 6, surely lobbied by Mrs. Lincoln, Secretary of the Interior Caleb Smith wrote to Secretary of the Treasury Salmon Chase about the standard $20,000 appropriation for new White House furniture and furnishings that Congress had approved in February. Could it be made available immediately?

Five days later, Mrs. Lincoln wrote to Ward Hill Lamon, the president's armed protector. The subject was William Wood, the shady New York businessman who had given her two fine horses and flattered her from Springfield to Washington: "I trust you will *redeem your promise*," she wrote, and persuade the president to make Wood commissioner of public buildings, the official who oversaw the White House. "I believe him to be a clever man and would make an efficient Commissioner." Lamon replied the same day: he said he had never reneged on a promise to a friend.

5

THE WHITE HOUSE IS TURNED INTO BARRACKS

Before Lincoln took office, Buchanan had ordered plans to defend the capital from a Southern attack. Mindful of the paradox that a buildup of federal forces could provoke one, Colonel Charles P. Stone recruited a local militia instead, stiffened by 640 regular troops who were gradually moved in. General Scott and his staff chose three centers of resistance that a small force could hold until reinforcements arrived. The President's Park and its brick and stone buildings were among them, the White House included.

On Monday, April 8, Lincoln had the South Carolina authorities notified that Fort Sumter would be defended, all but assuring war. Two days later, thirty companies of Stone's militia were inducted into the U.S. Army and assembled on the edge of the White House grounds between the War Department and Pennsylvania Avenue.

Stone took special care to protect the Executive Mansion, but Lincoln had made it clear that the president of the United States must not be seen to *need* protection. On the evening of April 10, troops were positioned in the basement and sentries were hidden in the bushes. No one walking down the driveway would have seen a guard, Stone said, but when anyone entered the grounds "by *any* entrance, he was under the view of at least two riflemen standing silent in the shrubbery, and any suspicious movement on his part would have caused his immediate arrest." That night, a sentry challenged Nicolay and Hay coming back from an evening out.

The commander in chief was not consulted about the details. Stone worked with Lincoln's brother-in-law and house guest, Benjamin Hardin Helm, a West Point graduate. The president was fond of Ben Helm, and the feeling was mutual. A Kentucky Unionist, Helm had come to Washington hoping to rejoin the army, certain that the North and South would not come to blows. Stone introduced him every night to the rotating officers commanding the mansion's defense and gave him authority to summon their troops.

Three days after they were deployed, a Manhattan businessman left a meeting with Lincoln and met newsboys hawking headlines on Pennsylvania Avenue. "Fort Sumter on fire!" they cried, "The barracks burning!"

* * *

The war brought the capital little zeal for the Union. Local sympathy for secession overwhelmed it. A "sort of pall hung over Washington," Stoddard said, and "the gloomiest kind of shadow" fell on the White House.

A quasi-military secessionist group called the Democratic Jackson Association, "Dem. Jack. Ass." to Lincoln's friends at the *Washington Evening Star*, was allegedly tracking his movements and plotting a coup. Scores of women took to their pianos, opened their windows, and played the rebel anthems, "Dixie," "The Bonnie Blue Flag," and "Maryland, My Maryland," literally filling the air with rebellion. You could hardly walk the streets without hearing "Dixie," Stoddard said, until it took on "a weird, spell-like influence." The capital seemed haunted, "and its central, darkest, most bewildering witchcraft works around this Executive Mansion." General Scott wanted to send Mrs. Lincoln and the boys north to safety. She refused to go unless her husband did, knowing that he would not.

On April 15, Lincoln called on the loyal governors to send seventy-five thousand troops to subdue the rebellion. Virginia and three other border states replied with ordinances of secession. Officers from those states started resigning their commissions, and Virginia's armed militia started gathering by the Potomac. In sight of Lincoln's windows, hostile sentinels and artillery appeared on Arlington Heights.

Tens of thousands of Washingtonians fled. "Property could be had for a song," someone said, "even badly sung." A home near the White House had been about to sell for $7,000. When the buyer backed out, the price fell to $2,000, with no takers. A newspaperman watched the city empty out. "Walking on Pennsylvania Avenue in the morning," he said, "I could almost count the people in sight on my fingers."

Crippled with worry about the capital's defense, Lincoln heard what sounded like the boom of a cannon and was shaken. None of the staff had heard it. Convinced that the attack had begun, he walked several blocks to the arsenal and found it unmanned. He questioned passersby on his way back. No one had heard a thing.

Assigned to defend the White House with little means, Major David Hunter approached two Republican killers. The wild-haired, wild-eyed, newly chosen Senator Jim Lane of Kansas, "the celebrated border ruffian and single-hand knife fighter," Stoddard called him, had terrorized pro-slavery partisans with John Brown. Kentucky's Cassius Marcellus Clay, about to leave for Russia as Lincoln's minister to the czar, had fought off a swarm of attackers who disapproved of abolitionists, knifing one to death. Hunter asked Lane and Clay to assemble their friends as an amateur White House defense force.

The results would have been comic were it not for the stakes. "The Clay Battalion," also known as "The Strangler Guard," mustered fewer than fifty men, most of whom had never strangled anyone. Some of the 130 members of Jim Lane's "Frontier Guard" were genuine Western cutthroats, but the fighters were outnumbered by potbellied congressmen, senators, and judges in assorted states of decay, near-sighted editors, and failed politicians in search of jobs. Stoddard called them "a regiment of office seekers" who had rallied to the White House to defend their prospects. The frontier was unknown to many of them. They came from twenty states and the Colorado Territory, and many were past their prime. Elisha F. Wallace, sixty-nine years old, had been born when Washington was president and Washington City did not exist.

With rebel artillery in position to shell the capital, Lincoln's secretaries worked at their desks with a "constant listening for thunder." Scant yards away, militia dragged sandbags and beams to the Treasury Department's windows and doors. Hay consulted Major Hunter about the White House's defense. "He told me," Hay said, "that he would fulfill any demand I should make." He did not say with what.

Rumors hit the Executive Mansion that 1,500 armed men were in Alexandria and others were landing on the Maryland side of the Potomac. Nicolay half expected to be attacked that night. If a small rebel army hit the city there would be little to slow them down, let alone throw them back. "We were not only surrounded by the enemy, but in the midst of traitors." Well informed of its vulnerability, the rebels seemed sure to take the White House on their first free afternoon. Fred Seward, the Secretary of State's son and assistant secretary, saw something good in it all. The office seekers had "scattered at the first alarm."

On Thursday, April 18, the first of ten days of fine weather, Jim Lane's unarmed Frontier Guard marched from Willard's to the White House and formed up in the East Room like the cast of a comic opera. In Lincoln's presence, Secretary of War Simon Cameron presented a sword to Lane and armed his men with new Sharps rifles. Some of those men knew how to use them. Others seemed more likely to shoot one another by mistake than a rebel on purpose. Finding no army belt long enough to gird him, Kansas's other senator, Samuel C. Pomeroy, ran a string from the buckle to the strap, giving the men a laugh. A major on General Scott's staff made an aide of Hay, who recorded it in his diary: "I labored under some uncertainty as to whether I should speak to privates or not."

As Nicolay and Hay looked on, the Frontier Guard struggled through an "exceedingly rudimentary" drill in the East Room "under the light of the gorgeous gas chandeliers" and lay down for the night on the velvet carpet among stacked muskets and open ammunition boxes. "The White House is turned into barracks," Hay wrote. It occurred to him that American troops, if such they could be called, had never camped so luxuriously. With a dubious dose of wit, a sentry stopped the president at the point of a bayonet when he couldn't give the password. Lane's men were loudly amused. And so the Frontier Guard took possession of the President's House.

No one told Colonel Stone. A light in the East Room surprised him when he came to inspect his men. He was still more astonished when he walked into the basement from the south lawn and heard many voices upstairs, mingled with the sounds of men handling weapons. The captain of the guard explained that Lincoln's brother-in-law Lieutenant Helm had said it was all right. Stone went upstairs to encounter a ramshackle army, and Clay explained who they were and what they were doing. "I applauded the good spirit," Stone recalled, but kept his own men in place "until the time came when others than myself were responsible for the safety of the President."

That night, Edward McManus the doorman brought Hay the card of a woman who had come with a female friend to see the president about his safety. Lincoln was in bed, and Hay came down to speak with her. He found her neither young nor fair "to any miraculous extent," but her friend was "a little of both." A Virginian had told her that he and several others would soon do a thing "that would ring through the world." Hay brought the story to the president, who only grinned.

*   *   *

On Friday morning, April 19, according to the *New York Tribune*, the anxious citizens of Washington got up, "found that they were not attacked," had breakfast, and "went into the streets to listen to rumors."

The 6th Regiment of Massachusetts Volunteers, the first to answer Lincoln's call, were changing trains on their way to Washington on that April 19, the anniversary of their forefathers' confrontation with British troops at Lexington and Concord, and replayed it in reverse. Hostile civilians attacked them as they marched through Baltimore. Fighting their way to the depot, they lost several men and arrived with their wounded in Washington late that afternoon, electrifying the city with the news that blood had been shed. The secessionists cut the telegraph wires behind them, burned the bridges, and stopped the trains, cutting Washington off from the north. Many loyal people fled the capital by whatever means they could. The hostile ones stayed.

A friend of Buchanan's called on Lincoln that day. With the White House at risk of capture, he took the time to sign her autograph book: "Whoever in later-times shall see this, and look at the date will readily excuse the writer for not having indulged in sentiment or poetry. With all kind regards for Miss Smith, A Lincoln."

The Frontier Guard returned to the White House that night and exchanged hearsay. Occupying the President's House for the next several days, Stoddard said, the enterprising men of the "office-seekers brigade" were ready to protect him at night and ready to annoy him in the morning, ahead of their competitors.

Jim Lane's company was excused, with orders to return when called, but Clay's remained. Among them was the notorious Count Adam Gurowski, fifty-five years of age—"The Terrible Count," his friend Henry Wadsworth Long-fellow called him. An eccentric condemned in absentia as a Polish revolutionary, Gurowski made his living as a translator at Seward's State Department. Now he made an entry in his diary: "For several days patrolled, drilled, and lay several nights on the hard floor. Had compensation, that the drill often reproduced that of Falstaff's heroes."

As Hay patrolled the White House late that night, Major Hunter and an Italian exile named Vivaldi were asleep on the East Room floor, "and a young and careless guard loafed around the furnace fires in the basement. Good looking and energetic young fellow, too good to be food for gunpowder, if anything is," Hay's diary entry said.

There was no reliable word about the Rhode Island regiment and the well-equipped, well-heeled 7th New York Militia, the elite "Silk Stocking Regiment," who were moving toward Washington's relief. A Frontier Guardsman from Ohio named Clifford Arrick scribbled in his diary too: "Unabated anxiety prevails." The meager White House defense force consoled themselves with rumors. Some Unionist refugees from Virginia reported talk among the rebels that Jim Lane had a thousand savage fighters under his command instead of 130 men of all shapes and ages trolling for easy jobs. The rebels were "in terrible awe" of them. To discourage an attack, the Frontier Guard were told to spread the tale that Lane was about to strike Virginia with a mob of howling frontiersmen.

On Sunday, April 21, Hay in all his snobbery returned from a night out and found Vivaldi and other Frontier Guards pacing the north portico "in belted and revolvered dignity, looking like gentlemen in feature and dress," as if it were a disguise. Incoming loyal Virginians reported that the rebels were in growing "dread of Jim Lane and his John Brown horde," who were thought to be capable of repelling five thousand men. That night a few dozen of them paraded down Pennsylvania Avenue with rifles and enormous navy revolvers, hoping, perhaps, that their "several bayonets" would strike fear in the hearts of Virginians. Not to be outdone, Cassius Clay swaggered into the president's anteroom strapped with three pistols, a Bowie knife, and "a sublimely unconscious air" that reminded Hay of a hero on the cover of a twenty-five cent novel.

Desperate for more help than Clay's, Lincoln stared out his window at the river on April 23, the first hot day of the year, and sent a note by messenger to Gideon Welles: "I think I saw three vessels go up to the Navy Yard just now. Will you please send down and learn what they are?" They were nothing consequential. Two days later Lincoln spotted another ship coming up the river and was told it was an old mail steamer. People passing his open door saw him pace and pause at his windows, talking to no one but himself. "Why don't they come? Why don't they come?"

On April 24, Lincoln welcomed to the White House the demoralized 6th Massachusetts and its wounded men injured by the Baltimore mob. "They came in confused and flushed," Hay said, and "they went out easy, proud, and happy." It is hard to see why. "I begin to believe that there is no north," Lincoln told them. "The Seventh Regiment is a myth, Rhode Island is another. You are the only real thing."

Fortunately, he was wrong. The 7th New York arrived the next morning to a welcome fueled by relief. The route from the North was open, they said. Half a dozen regiments had passed through Baltimore and were on their way. "All is safe now," Private Arrick wrote in his diary. "Everybody thinks so. Everybody says so. Everybody feels so." The traitors across the river had missed their chance. "Twenty-four hours ago they might have seized the Capital. Now all Hell can't take it."

Marching down Pennsylvania Avenue in their smart gray uniforms under bright silk flags, led by a splendid band, the 7th New York passed the White

House in review, 991 armed men, a big number seven on the back of each man's haversack. As a grateful crowd cheered, Lincoln stood on the granite sidewalk with senior officers and his Secretaries of War and State, easily spotted high above the crowd even with his hat off, said the *New York Times*. With a marching salute, the regiment wheeled through the west gate, "thronged with ladies and gentlemen," and down the gravel drive. Mrs. Lincoln sat at an open window with Mrs. Grimsley and some friends. The colonel of the regiment was presented to the president, the men cheered the women and the Lincoln boys, and the women waved and cried.

The 8th Massachusetts and two Rhode Island regiments quickly followed. On April 26, with no further need for a makeshift White House garrison, Jim Lane led the Frontier Guard from Willard's to the East Room. It may have been only the *Star* that thought they made "a formidable appearance." One of their windy leaders bid farewell to the president, whose reply was brief. That night "some Germans" reported what they thought might be pistol shots behind the White House, which the Clay Battalion reoccupied.

Normalcy returned the next day. On the south lawn of the White House, Hay said, the 7th New York's band delighted a gaily dressed, grateful crowd as they strolled safely by, "soldiers loafed in the promenades," and martial music filled the air "with vague suggestions of heroism."

The Frontier Guard were given certificates decorated with an engraving of the White House, signed by Lincoln and the Secretary of War, certified by "General Lane" that the bearer had defended the capital "when threatened by hordes of traitors." Count Gurowski admired the certificates but would not accept one, the Guard having done no fighting. Each man got a whopping $500 for a few weeks of part-time work after Lincoln said he would pay it if the government did not. In its own final act, the Clay Battalion lined up before the south portico and was photographed with civilians in stovepipe hats, one of them very tall, too far from the lens to be identified.

On May 2, the natty Providence Marine Corps of Artillery led its half-dozen horse-drawn cannon past Lincoln and the White House like an undefeated team that had yet to play a game. Behind them came a regiment almost every day, some in conventional uniforms of various colors and trim, others in exotic military dress inspired by the armies of Prussia and the French Foreign Legion. To the tune of splendid bands, Nicolay said, "a magnificent river of steel points glittering down the avenue" past the President's House raised his spirits and encouraged his staff.

For the rest of the war, a pair of uniformed sentries paced a beat before the north portico, starting from opposite sides. Early on they challenged all callers, but caution disappeared with the threat of a rebel attack, and everyone simply walked past them.

Rewarding his brother-in-law Ben Helm, the Kentuckian who had helped protect the White House, Lincoln offered him a paymaster major's commission, a plum opportunity and a path to higher rank. Mrs. Lincoln begged him to accept it and move with her sister into the White House, where Emilie's beauty and charm would make her the belle of the city. Helm went home to think. An admirer would later say he "remained grateful to Lincoln for his kind offer, and even after he had taken the field at the head of Confederate troops he sent felicitous messages to the president in 1861 and 1862."

6

IT IS GOOD TO LOOK AT BEAUTY ONCE IN A WHILE

"There was something almost dreamlike and unreal" about the passing of the crisis, Stoddard said, an illusion of deliverance. The coming of spring gave new life to a city filling up with eclectic uniforms, flags, and military bands. The Rhode Island regiment that Lincoln had thought mythological passed before him in "charming weather," improving Hay's mood. They looked wonderful in their simple uniforms with finely colored bedrolls on their backs. Soldiers of all descriptions filled the streets. Stoddard watched a regiment of lancers ride by under his White House window. Opinion was divided about their value in a fight, but they made a good show. Those "fellows who go ridin' round the streets," a congressman called them, "carryin' a red rag on the end of a stick."

Mrs. Grimsley wrote a friend that she had made some agreeable acquaintances at the White House and "many disagreeable ones, who value themselves and other people only by their laces and diamonds." She thought the excitement had blown over, except for the stir of troops, but Jim Lane dropped by on April 29 and picked out with Nicolay's spyglass a big rebel flag on the roof of an Alexandria hotel. Lincoln did the same with the telescope in his office and gave some visitors a look.

To kill any notion that business would resume in the office-seeking line, a notice appeared in the *New York Times*: The President had suspended all appointments of less than urgent importance, except for military ports and commissions. They easily filled his time as the White House filled up with applicants for commissions. Some were former officers. Others were politicians with no more experience in uniform than an honorary rank in a state militia. Many had no military credentials at all, Stoddard said, just a curious idea "that if a fellow had torn around actively in the presidential campaign" or could run a flour mill he could embarrass a rebel West Pointer at the head of a brigade. One small, well-dressed gentleman came again and again to beg a general's commission from anyone he could buttonhole. He had served in his state militia, he said, his grandfather was an officer in the Revolution, and he really needed the pay. It crossed Stoddard's mind that he was as fit for a general's star as several men who wore one.

It must have seemed to Lincoln that half of the existing officers chasing promotions and commands were in his office. So many made nuisances of themselves that officers soon needed permission to enter Washington. A newspaper said that a boy had thrown a stone at dog on Pennsylvania Avenue and hit three Generals. When asked to make a very young man a paymaster, Lincoln said he would not make the Angel Gabriel a paymaster if he wasn't twenty-one. On a typical day, Nicolay said, the president sat down to a six-inch stack of appointments on heavy paper resistant to pen and ink and signed them like "a laborer sawing wood."

To spare him from consuming whole the endless requests for commissions from influential men, Stoddard briefed them for him, occasionally relieved by Nicolay or Hay. Hundreds of such briefs sat in leaning piles on the cabinet table or were stuffed "rubber-banded" in "this drawer and that." Some made Lincoln laugh. Others made him mad. Politicians after votes and glory thought a military education or experience were optional, even suspicious qualifications for a general.

Chaplains' commissions were pursued not only by the bravest clergy but also by "loose-footed ministers" as Lincoln called them, unemployed pastors who aspired to be majors without "keeping company with a regiment in the field." Stoddard was tasked with screening them, "and a queer set of fellows it brought me in contact with," he said. Some good, pious men were eager to serve, but so were "broken-down reverends" defrocked for incompetence or some discretely labeled "other cause."

As the city clogged up with generals, Hay helped the president receive three Potawatomie Indian chiefs. Their leader, Hay said, dressed for the occasion "in a wonderful style of shabby genteele" and spoke comfortably in English, but the other two were silent, including "a magnificent broad chested, bare armed giant with a barbaric regal adornment of bear claws." Lincoln "amused them immensely" with the two or three Indian words he knew, intelligible to them or not, and amused John Hay by speaking broken English.

"Where live now? When go back Iowa?"

*   *   *

Except for formal clothes at receptions and state dinners, Lincoln's White House wardrobe aimed at nothing but respectability. A "display of gentility" would have been false, Nicolay said, not to mention political poison, and clothing did not interest him. According to Nicolay, "Lincoln never gave a fraction of thought or a moment of care to any question of dress. He followed the ordinary fashion and wore what the tailor, hatter, and bootmaker made for him." He "was not slovenly," Stoddard said, dispensing faint praise, but neither knew nor cared whether he was well dressed. A harsher judge found his wardrobe in "hopeless disorder."

In the office he wore a black cravat and a black broadcloth suit, loose on his six-foot-four-inch frame, sometimes with a black or buff vest. To his wife's dismay, the coat was not replaced when the cuffs wore out. An original touch was the worn pair of carpet slippers, often kicked off, sometimes showing bright blue socks in need of darning. Nicolay said the commander in chief had been known to present himself in a faded dressing gown and frayed slippers only when dignitaries showed up unexpectedly, but the chief of the National Detective Police was called to the White House and found him "in shirt-sleeves and slippers, ready to receive me." After a reporter had him awakened for some news, Lincoln sat in his nightshirt for an hour reminiscing about his boyhood love of canes. "It was a freak of mine," he said. You could never spot a witch without her stick.

He often bowed to his callers. "He doesn't smile when he takes your hand," one said, "he does not ring it like a bell, nor wave it like a flag. He merely takes it, and quietly and silently squeezes it into dough."

His height could be a shock. One caller said he drew himself out like a telescope as he rose, and there seemed to be no chance that his getting up would end. Another watched him rise, "untwisting the kinks of his back" like a genie sealed for centuries in a bottle.

A painter who sketched him at work found him more "indifferent to the effect he was producing, either upon official representatives or the common people" than anyone who ever held office. When he took a seat he wore it, and there was no telling how. He might lean back, throw one leg over the arm of his chair and lay the other on a table. He sometimes conducted meetings crosswise in his chair, swinging both legs back and forth. A female caller said he sat in such "a folded up sort of way" that "one would almost have thought him deformed." Stoddard once came upon him in his office lying on the sofa "with his hands folded over his head and looking as if he did not care two cents for the past, present or future."

In midconversation he would get up and lean against the mantel or stand before the fire with his hands behind him, insisting that his guests stay seated, making them uncomfortable. After he sat down he would get up and pace as he spoke, running a hand through his scarecrow hair. Sufficiently entertained while seated, he would cross his legs, lock his hands over his knees, and rock back and forth in amusement. Enjoying a silent laugh, he could lean back in his chair, shoot his legs forward as if repelled "by some violent process," look at the ceiling open-mouthed, and somehow stay entitled to "profound respect."

His exhaustion was often plain. As two men made a complex case on a matter of some importance, he settled back in an armchair and then down into it, crossed one foot over the other, and closed his eyes, as motionless as if he had fallen asleep; but the moment they finished their plea he sat up and said what they wanted to hear. When trouble came from a messenger as he worked bent over his desk, he bent "even lower for a moment, as if some burden had suddenly grown heavier."

Instinctively self-effacing, he spoke of the White House as "this place" and never of himself as president. Instead he would say, "since I came into this place." A wealthy friend regretted his "provoking humility." Early one morning, the doorman Edward McManus came upon him standing at the front door in an old linen wrapper with "shuffle slippers and blue socks" on his feet, waving and shouting at a newsboy to bring him the paper, "and he didn't have the look of a regular president at all."

Unaffected though he was, nothing displeased him more than uninvited familiarity. In June of 1863, accompanied by other officers, a major slapped him on the knee and asked him for "one of your good stories." Lincoln stood up, turned his back on the man, and with great dignity explained to his embarrassed companions that he often substituted a little story for a long explanation.

The most common impression of his style was a perfectly startling simplicity coupled with simple dignity. Only two classes of people who spent any time with him failed to see the power and goodness in him, Hay said, those who judged him by "a purely conventional standard of breeding" and those so poisoned by hostility that they distrusted their eyes and ears. Despite his country speech and unconventional comportment in a chair, Eastern patricians who expected a clodhopper were often surprised by the impression he made in his office.

George Templeton Strong, a wealthy Manhattan lawyer, had an audience with him in 1861. "Decidedly plebian" the New Yorker sniffed to his diary, though "clear-headed and sound-hearted." He laughed like "a yahoo, with a wrinkling of the nose that suggests affinity with the tapir and other pachyderms; and his grammar is weak." But when Strong returned with a colleague, he raised the president's grade. A barbarian or worse in "outside polish," he was nevertheless "a most sensible, straightforward, honest old codger," the best president since Jackson at least.

Despite his fractured diction, a British writer who came to his office was "quite convinced that the President has many excellent qualities, which will some day or other be recognized and appreciated."

*   *   *

With the White House relieved from fear, there was time to enjoy the grounds, which a guidebook told the public were not to be missed. The simple north lawn and the lush south lawn, sloping gently toward the Potomac with ornamental gardening, vases, and statues, were neatly trimmed. Every spring a livery stable paid to scythe the lawns for hay, and a farmer's sheep cropped the stubble. Since Jackson's day, the lawns had been rolled with watering machines, pierced wooden drums on wheels.

On either side of the south lawn, walking paths curved through the spring-blooming dogwoods, purple redbud trees, and stately old chestnuts. Southwest of the house, concealed by a fence and a brick wall, was an old-fashioned country garden with peach trees and flowers. Mrs. Lincoln picked the strawberries herself. On the opposite side was a gated kitchen garden, screened by ancient trees. The sentry box built in Jackson's day still stood by its gate, with the notable absence of a sentry.

The lawn sloped down to Jefferson's Wall, built of stone at the direction of the third president, which marked the end of the south lawn. Beyond it was only undergrowth and marsh all the way down to the river. The nearest part was the Treasury Park, hardly a park at all but an ungroomed place with an unused half-mile racetrack where the National and Potomac baseball teams scored against each other in the range of 33 to 31. It would later be called the Ellipse.

In season, the scarlet-uniformed Marine Band had given Wednesday and Saturday afternoon concerts on the south lawn since the 1840s, "a sort of outdoor reception accompanied by music." In 1861, Congress added a drum major, an Italian bandleader, and thirty professional musicians, mostly Germans, who played exquisitely and filled the lawn with music lovers. Even the world-weary William Howard Russell enjoyed "the excellent band of the United States Marines" with friends from the British consulate as they strolled the grounds overlooking the tent-covered Arlington hills, watching artillery practice by the river. Music days, the concerts were called. People sat on the lawn and under the trees with picnic lunches. Scruffy newsboys shouted headlines through the crowd.

When Lincoln came out on the south portico with family and guests, the band liked to play his favorite piece, "The Soldiers Chorus" from a Charles Gounod opera. One of a group of invited women noticed that with the bandstand some distance away, "the open air softened the sound till it swept by the group on the portico full of melody and almost sad in its deep tones." The lawn was filled with colorfully dressed women and children, officers and their ladies, and "knots of pretty girls, fresh and blooming as spring flowers, scattered here and there in bright relief against the emerald background." Lincoln turned to his guests: "It is beautiful, is it not? It is good to look at beauty once in a while."

At another concert in May, after a thousand children had passed through the White House to shake the president's hand, groups of soldiers went up to the portico and greeted him, and a little girl offered her lips, which a reporter from the *New York Tribune* watched him kiss "with paternal dignity." As if a bell had rung, every little girl in sight "and some larger ones" rushed the portico, "and for fifteen minutes the President had as much on his hands as one man might desire."

*   *   *

On a hot May 13, the 12th New York came down Pennsylvania Avenue behind the stars and stripes as its marching band played a mocking "Dixie" and "The Bonny Blue Flag," delighting William Stoddard and the crowd "as if a counter spell had been uttered." Northern troops had occupied Baltimore that day. When the band reached the White House they broke into "Maryland, My Maryland," taunting the neighborhood rebels.

On any given day, a rebel spy or two and any number of sympathizers mingled with the crowd in the President's House itself. The commander in chief's home and headquarters were not secure, and Ward Hill Lamon told him so. Telegrams had been sent and received in Washington for fifteen years, but not in the White House. The telegraph was confined to the War Department, where the transmission and receipt of military communications could be supervised, according to Nicolay and Hay. Why it could not be supervised in the White House they did not say, but the inference of insecurity is plain.

Lincoln's walks across the President's Park to the War Department early most mornings and almost every night took him through the turnstile at the edge of the White House grounds. He often went alone and rarely came back before ten. His secretaries could tell from his gait whether the news was good or bad. The brick-paved path was flanked on the Pennsylvania Avenue side by wooded ground. It made a beautiful little park by day, a worried soldier said, "but at night, lighted only by the wavering beams of a solitary gas jet, it was a place of shadows and gloom." A modest brick wall edged the path's southern side, no barrier for any assassin who could step around the telegraph wires stretched between pegs to trip intruders. In a city full of traitors at war, Lincoln's nightly walks through the woods gave thoughtful people fits.

7

INK STAINED AND
WORK WORN

Lincoln staffed his presidency with young men. Nicolay was twenty-nine, Stoddard twenty-five, Hay twenty-two, all of them interested in young ideas, young clothes, and young women. (Only Nicolay was romantically attached, and his letters to his fiancé were full of coy allusions to pretty girls, a dubious choice of tactics.) Nicolay alone was entitled to be called the president's private secretary, and Hay was known to cross the title out on his White House envelopes, but people called him and Stoddard "Mr. Secretary" too.

Stoddard thought Lincoln had chosen his secretaries well. "They grew up under his eye in Illinois, and he knew pretty well what was in them." They were able, hard-working young men, sufficiently educated for their duties, with no Washington ties to anyone but him, and their loyalty was almost blind.

Nicolay's corner office at the southeast end of the building had a connecting door to the president's. When Lincoln was in his office, Stoddard said, "an air of intense suppression" came over Nicolay's. As White House offices went, Nicolay's was as shabby as the rest. Noah Brooks thought the dark mahogany doors, marble mantels, and paneled wainscoting "more suggestive of the days of the Madisons and Van Burens than of the present." The carpet was frayed, the mahogany furniture had been banged up for twenty-five years, and a quarter century of Washington sun had dulled the green curtains that framed the river views to the south and the expanding Treasury Department to the east. The tiny lavatory in a corner by the door was a luxury, installed on Buchanan's orders, the only one in the office wing, presumably shared.

Men too important for the anterooms often waited in Nicolay's office before they got into Lincoln's, sometimes two or three at a time, cutting into Nicolay's day, thumbing through the newspapers he kept on a table. A Southwestern politician-turned-general strutted into Nicolay's office and pontificated to all three secretaries until the president called him in, letting Hay release a laugh. Some canny men lobbied Nicolay directly, skipping Lincoln entirely.

Directly opposite Nicolay's office, across the big, open waiting room, Hay shared with Stoddard the corner office overlooking Lafayette Square. The northeast room, as Stoddard called it, was typically "in full blast" with favor seekers, diplomats, and other important men who preferred its amusing occupants to Nicolay. Lincoln sometimes wandered in for a laugh himself. After hours, Stoddard said, it was a good place to read in and "a good place to loaf in." Hay decorated it tastefully with figures modeled in wax, bas reliefs on the mantel, and engravings on the wall. Law books filled the bookcase.

Identical to Nicolay's office in size and shape, the northeast room's battered furniture made it feel smaller. The sofa and two upright desks in the far corners, old and "somewhat infirm," Hay Stoddard said, "and he now and then sat down at one of them" when he was not in Nicolay's office charming unhappy dignitaries. Stoddard used an enormous table desk with rows of deep drawers and a littered, green cloth top, "ink stained and work worn," that stood against the wall to the right as you walked through the door, "its left elbow toward the fireplace." Stoddard thought of it as "a kind of breakwater" between Nicolay and Hay. To celebrate a gift of pocket knives, Tad and Willie carved it up one day.

The door was always open, and Stoddard watched the human comedy in the waiting room from his swivel desk chair. Some of the comedians popped in. One day Stoddard looked up at a well-dressed man who suddenly loomed over him, his face "all one shine" of hearty confidence.

"Is Old Abe in?"

"If you mean the President of the United States," Stoddard replied, "this is Congress Day," and only senators and congressmen could see him.

Andrew Jackson's chair, presented to him by the people of Mexico, sat opposite Stoddard's desk, an eccentric piece of furniture on rollers, lightly framed in mahogany with a hollow leather seat. It was said to have been Jackson's favorite. Now it was Hay and Stoddard's guest chair. When a fat New York senator dropped into it after trudging upstairs one day, it shot out from under him, drawing laughter from him and his friends.

A connecting door linked the northeast room to the bedroom that Nicolay and Hay shared. A liability more than a perquisite, it made them available to the president twenty-four hours a day. Nicolay told Therena, shortly after moving in, "We have very pleasant offices, and a nice large bed room, though all of them sadly need new furniture and carpets. That too we expect to have remedied after a while." Stoddard lived in a boarding house and later leased a brownstone on Louisiana Avenue where his brother and some friends paid him rent and his sister kept house.

Except for the odd night out at the likes of the Metropolitan Club or Harvey's Oyster Saloon and the frequent availability of a dinner party, Nicolay and Hay took their meals at Willard's Hotel. A political beehive just a five-minute walk away, Willards' was no place for gourmets. An Englishman called it "the huge, noisy hospital for incurables," where 2,500 people might be fed on a given day to the screech of wooden chairs being scraped across the floor. Based on the Londoner's experience, White House secretaries got no special treatment, "for neither senator nor representative, governor of a State nor general in the army, millionaire, merchant, nor roving English dandy is a bit better off or treated with one whit more deference at Willard's than the roughest specimen of a bagman in the dry goods line." Hay told a friend that "an enterprising genius" had opened a little shop under Willard's selling Japanese curiosities "and everybody goes there and gets unmercifully cheated."

*　　*　　*

Lincoln gave Nicolay a level and scope of authority that was understood rather than explicitly defined. Only a few cabinet members had more power, and Nicolay's control over Lincoln's calendar was a formidable tool when the president let him use it. Nicolay told Therena he looked forward to a day when he could read or write a letter "without being haunted continually by some one who wants to see the President *for only a few minutes.*" Stoddard referred to Nicolay as "the bulldog in the anteroom" and put the phrase in quotation marks, suggesting it was commonly used. As the principal White House greeter, spokesman, and buffer, he deflected as many senators, officers, and unaffiliated irritants as he could, but the president was a hard man to manage. When a well-known writer asked Lincoln for five minutes by a slow watch, he gave him ten, "and if you are very entertaining, I'll give you twenty."

People who loved Lincoln had reason to thank Nicolay for protecting him, Stoddard said, and reason to grumble too, a flattering description of a presidential aide.

A newspaperman liked the "methodical, silent German way about him. Scrupulous, polite, calm, obliging, with the gift of hearing other people talk, coming and going about the Capitol like a shadow," never drawing attention to himself, quick to respond to a request, committed to his job, devoted to the president. Years later, in his pointed, taciturn way, Nicolay captured their relationship in a single sentence. "There was never any red tape between us."

Where Nicolay was smart and conscientious with a hidden sense of humor,

CHAPTER 7

Hay was casually brilliant with an open wit. Though the Speaker of the House said Hay had the most impressive grasp on public affairs he had ever seen in one so young, Nicolay told his daughter years later that Hay had laughed through the war but never at it, and made friends effortlessly, while simply getting acquainted was hard work for Nicolay. Their bond was forged by a shared ordeal and a common devotion to the president. Between themselves they referred to him as the Chief, the Ancient, the American, and the Tycoon, after the emperor of Japan.

In August of 1862, while Hay was fending off job seekers in 100-degree heat, Nicolay was in Minnesota on a peacekeeping mission to the Chippewa and sent Hay a teasing letter from Saint Paul, where the hotel smelled of kerosene. "Nevertheless I hear a pleasant babble of girls' voices in the next room and am curious to look further before condemning it." Nicolay wrote next from Fort Ripley, which was not so enticing a spot. He had read about a rebel army near Washington and calculated an even chance that Hay's scalp would be taken before his. "Pray have the rebels removed from their close proximity to *la Maison Blanche* before I get there. I shall need a quiet retreat in which to recover from my Indian scare."

Over time, Hay acquired something close to Nicolay's stature as a buffer protecting the president, and familiarity bred contempt for pomposity. A Pennsylvania congressman spent two and a half hours with him, Hay said, and "didn't talk about himself more than nine tenths of the time."

Young as they were, no task was too important for Nicolay or Hay. Nicolay's role in negotiations with the Chippewa chief Hole in the Day was only one of his distant missions. Hay's included vetting Confederate peace feelers in Canada. When General William Rosecrans proposed to send an officer from Missouri to brief Lincoln on a conspiracy to undermine the government, Lincoln suspected a conspiracy to undermine the Secretary of War and gave Hay a note to take to Rosecrans that instructed the general to tell Hay whatever he would tell Lincoln, which turned out not to be much. To pass the time on the train, Hay said, he "wrote rhymes in the same compartment with a pair of whisky smugglers."

Describing his duties after the war, Hay distinguished them from Nicolay's too modestly:

Nicolay received Members of Congress who had business with the Executive Office, communicated to the Senate and House the messages of the President, and exercised a general supervision over the business. I opened and read the letters, answered them, looked over the newspapers, supervised the clerks who kept the records and in Nicolay's absence did his work also.

He did more than that. Lincoln often took him to the War Department and to Seward's house on Lafayette Square. More personable than Nicolay, Hay worked more smoothly with powerful men. He discussed his eagerness for emancipation with Secretary of the Treasury Chase and his repugnance toward the foreign colonization of freed slaves with Postmaster General Montgomery Blair. He spent evenings at Seward's alone exploring everything from the war and politics to Seward's concerns about his son. At dinner parties and receptions politicians told him what they would not say in public. The abolitionist Massachusetts senator Henry Wilson informed him that the abolitionist Wendell Phillips, Wilson's constituent, was a liar.

Hay filled a place in the president's life that Nicolay did not. Lincoln thought of him as a son and sometimes as a brother. In 1864 he took him to "a sacred concert of profane music" as Hay called it. "The Tycoon and I occupied [a] private box and (both of us) carried on a hefty flirtation with the Monk Girls in the flies."

*   *   *

Stoddard had little contact with Lincoln. He saw him every day and had talks with him now and then, but his duties were almost entirely separate from Nicolay's and Hay's. His post as patent secretary had not been considered equal to theirs, "but my case was somehow understood to be an exception," or so he liked to think. "My special business, year in and year out," he said, "is keeping my mouth shut and forgetting things." His duties were largely clerical, but experience would show that his powers as the master of the incoming mail were considerable, and he occasionally got to play "big Private Secretary" when the other two secretaries were away.

Stoddard found Lincoln always kind and cordial but "generally the most absorbed and unconversational of men." He passed his secretaries in the halls as if they were not there, unless business required speech.

He came to Stoddard's office one night with an invitation in the form of an order: "I am going to the theater to see Hackett play Falstaff, and I want you to come with me. I've always wanted to see him in that character. Come to my room. It's about time to go." It was Hay who typically accompanied Lincoln on his visits to important homes and offices, but Stoddard had his moments. Absorbed at his desk one night, he was startled by a voice at his shoulder. "Leave that and come with me. I am going over to McClellan's house."

When he wasn't helping with the president's mail, Stoddard helped Mrs. Lincoln with hers, an honor that Nicolay and Hay were glad to delegate. Unlike them, Stoddard got along with her, whether out of empathy, expedience, or the instincts of a born contrarian, all of which were in him. He helped her in receiving lines and advised her on many things, but there was never any question that the president came first. When Nicolay and Hay were unavailable for a reception, Stoddard would stand beside the president and "leave Mrs. Lincoln to her own resources."

Rocked by her vicious mail and its false imputations of treason, she had Stoddard open and read every letter that was sent to her, to eliminate the very means of disloyal messages and weed out the vitriol. She asked him to show her nothing he had not read himself, and withhold anything he was not sure she wanted to see, not excepting letters from her sisters. He was told to forward all mail from her other Southern kin directly to the scrap basket.

Never as close to him as each other, Nicolay and Hay were known to call Stoddard "Mrs. Lincoln's Secretary," intending no complement and only half-joking. Years later, Stoddard called the title malicious. Nevertheless, he thought he had a friend in Hay, "a born diplomat if ever there was one," and "a right-down good fellow" with a catching laugh, "always the life of any place he ever got into," much like Stoddard himself. "He and I struck up a kind of queer partnership," Stoddard said. "Neither of us could dance worth a cent," and they engaged an Italian dancing master to improve their romantic prospects. Talented writers both, they wrote for several papers under pseudonyms, stuck religiously to the Lincoln administration's line, and considered it unnecessary to disclose their association with it.

They may have been too much alike. Their egos rubbed against each other, and the friction produced heat. When they read their poetry to each other, Stoddard admired Hay's "a number of sizes more than he did mine." On the other hand, Hay was a novice rider, as Stoddard surely reminded him when he took him out to practice. They both worked crushing hours, but Hay lived on his salary while Stoddard made a small fortune speculating in gold and stocks, largely based on what he saw and heard at the White House. It was perfectly legal, at least as Stoddard described it, and Mrs. Lincoln congratulated him for it, but it irritated Hay, and the rub grew increasingly raw.

If Stoddard's friendship with Hay was challenging, his relationship with Nicolay was "of an entirely satisfactory character," as he coolly put it later. Thirty years after the war, mellowed by the passage of time, he remembered Nicolay as "a very good fellow, and a man of considerable talent," but in 1866, when the workplace wounds were fresh, he assigned to his former boss "a dyspeptic tendency" and "an artificial manner the reverse of popular." Nicolay could say no "about as disagreeably as any man I ever knew."

In time the frictions would tell.

*　　*　　*

Lincoln typically started the day with Nicolay, Hay, or both, looking over letters they had drafted, hearing about the mail, discussing what he wanted done. They often worked together, on and off, into the night.

The daily "caravan of personal petitions" took up much of the secretaries' time, Stoddard said. Lincoln wanted a written brief on every important request, which his secretaries delivered as concisely as they could. He grasped the issues quickly and "needed fewer 'explanations' than any other man I ever knew."

Nicolay and Hay, and Stoddard in their absence, had access to Lincoln day and night, whatever he was doing and whomever he was with, a privilege they exercised sparingly during business hours. They slipped in to have him sign papers as one set of visitors was leaving and another coming in, and interrupted meetings if necessary. They had no set hours, and Lincoln never asked what they were doing with their time. He loaded them with work to their limits or beyond and could hold them "sharply" accountable, Stoddard said. Stoddard never heard him denigrate any of them, despite the inevitable mistakes, but the president was "an unconscious driver" and "unrelentingly exacting," and he came down hard on one of them after someone—he did not know who—gave a letter imprudently to the press.

The secretaries tried to intercept the eccentrics who got past the doorkeepers. Stoddard called the doormen "capable fellows, and it is not often that an out-and-out lunatic can pass by their keen inspection; but they are not infallible and there are many kinds of insanity," too many to keep out. "Lunatics and visionaries are here so frequently," Nicolay told Therena, "that they cease to be strange phenomena to us." The best way to handle them, Nicolay said, was to act as if they made sense. One simple-looking man came to Nicolay about the war. "I am commissioned from on high to take the matter in hand and end it," he said. He intended to lead two thousand men to Richmond to commit Jeff Davis and his circle to an asylum, and no earthly power was competent to stop him, but he preferred presidential authority. Nicolay said the president was too busy to see him, but he was free to proceed on his own responsibility, and he went away satisfied. When Hay turned away another deluded caller, the man let him know to whom he spoke: "I am the son of God." Hay replied that Lincoln would be glad to meet him if he returned with a letter of introduction from his father.

One afternoon a woman came to Stoddard neatly dressed in mourning and "not ill-looking," with "the saddest face you have seen for many a day." She wanted to see the president. "They have robbed me of my rights," she said softly. "I want my rights." Attractive and subdued as she was, there was something off about her, poor soul, and Stoddard answered her gently. "The President is very busy with the war."

"So he is," she said. "Busy about the war. I forgot that. But I want my right. A divorced widow's right." She promised to return and hurried away, gentle "even in her madness."

Cabinet members sent Hay their delegated parts of the president's annual message to Congress, which Nicolay carried up to Capitol Hill every December. No president had read one in person since Jefferson discontinued the practice, thinking it smacked of the crown. Nicolay took other messages up on horseback or even by horse-drawn streetcar, a democratic form of transportation shared with senators, generals, and pickpockets; but he usually took "the Executive Cab," pulled by two strong horses, in order to get there quickly, Stoddard said, "and not be robbed on the way." Hay took lesser communications to Congress when Nicolay was unavailable.

Whoever brought the president's messages to the House and Senate was formally announced and earned the permanent privilege of both floors. It was therefore a memorable day, Stoddard said, "I think it was in the latter part of '61," when neither Nicolay nor Hay was around to deliver one. Without waiting for the president's coach, Stoddard paid his own cab fare and appeared at the portals of both houses, where the doorkeepers formally announced that the president's private secretary had arrived with a message. Stoddard would never forget it. "That was me."

Nicolay and Hay, not the White House messengers, delivered the most important, sensitive documents and messages to senators, cabinet secretaries, and assistant secretaries, and exchanged ideas with many of them. They were typically shown in as soon as they arrived, for as Stoddard said with mock importance, "a President's Private Secretary could not be detained one moment in an anteroom."

The secretaries worked on patronage with mixed success. In March 1861, Nicolay wrote to his former boss Ozias Hatch, to whom Lincoln often deferred on local appointments. Perhaps an awkward squabble over the Springfield Post Office could be resolved by giving it to Mrs. Lincoln's cousin Mrs. Grimsley. "I think the President would be pleased to have the riddle solved in that way." It wasn't.

Nicolay and Hay engaged the president frankly on sensitive issues—how to transform emancipated slaves into free men and women, whether the European cotton trade should flow through American ports, the politics of the rebel peace overture. When Lincoln had business with important, distant men, military or civilian, he often sent Nicolay or Hay to deliver his instructions and bring back what they learned. They sat in on presidential meetings, covered luminaries' weddings and funerals, joined the president on carriage rides to army camps, fed news to newspapermen, filtered their messages to the president, and filtered them back. When Congress was in session, Nicolay said, an overload of trivia kept him anxious, annoyed, and overworked.

*   *   *

Lincoln wrote his own speeches. According to Noah Brooks, he liked to compose in pencil in an armchair on a piece of stiff white cardboard on his knee, erasing and revising as he coaxed out his thoughts. To test a speech's rhythm, he would read it aloud to himself. To make it clear to audiences of every degree, he would read it to a White House servant, and again to one or more secretaries, with gestures and facial expressions, making adjustments along the way, seeking advice and not always taking it. "Nothing sounds the same when there isn't anybody to hear it and find fault with it," he told Stoddard, who replied that he didn't know if he cared to criticize the president's work. "Everybody else will," Lincoln said.

Notwithstanding Nicolay's diligence, Hay's charm, and Stoddard's wit, many White House regulars were not fond of any of them. People accustomed to deference did not respond well to instruction, snobbery, or cheekiness. Great men who had strolled unannounced into Buchanan's office whenever they felt the urge now heard from some nobody in his twenties that the president had no time for them, a point of view that chafed.

Lincoln's friend Noah Brooks chafed in print. "These three secretaries are all young men," he told the *Sacramento Union*'s subscribers, "and the least said of them the better, perhaps." As close to Mrs. Lincoln as he was to the president, Brooks called Nicolay, also in print, "The grim Cerberus of Teutonic descent who guards the last door which opens into the awful presence" and "has a very unhappy time of it." Less "flintiness of face" would serve the president better, for before they saw Lincoln, the waiting room crowd learned to like him or not "according to their treatment by his underlings." Nor was Brooks keen on Stoddard or Hay. "The President is affable and kind, but his immediate subordinates are snobby and unpopular."

A Pennsylvania politician with a grudge against Nicolay claimed that Lincoln was urged to fire him more than once and let him stay out of nothing but kindness, for Nicolay was "a good mechanical routine clerk" and "utterly inefficient as the Secretary of the President." The *Chicago Tribune*'s city editor called Hay "a beardless boy" and complained that "Mr. Lincoln has no private secretary that fills the bill and the loss is a national one." After Lincoln sent Hay to South Carolina, a colonel met him at a picnic, "a nice young fellow," the officer thought, "who unfortunately looks about seventeen and is oppressed with the necessity of behaving like seventy." The colonel amused himself watching "Mr. Hay laboring not to appear new mown."

None of it troubled Lincoln, who swiftly dismissed generals and officials who disappointed him but trusted Nicolay and Hay implicitly and revealed himself to them on the issues and personalities of the day. By 1862, he was close enough to Hay to speak of the "dreadful cowardice" of George McClellan, his general in chief of the army.

*   *   *

Part of the White House was a family residence, Stoddard said, "but all the rest, including the reception rooms, was merely a workshop" and "a remarkably silent workshop, considering how much was going on there. The very air seemed heavy with the pressure of the times, centering toward that place."

For Lincoln it was a melancholy place, fleetingly relieved by the odd amusing moment, a chat with a genial secretary, a romp with his little boys, or a visit from a friend. On the last day of August 1861, Seward brought his sixteen-year-old daughter Fanny to the White House after Sunday dinner. Fanny thought the library or Lincoln's office, she was not sure which, was "awfully hot with gas and a wood fire," and "Mr. Nicolay" came in, "whom I liked quite well." The president showed off his kittens "playing in one of the grand halls. Mr. L seems quite fond of them. Says they climb all over him."

Play never lasted long. Stoddard walked the president back to the White House from Seward's in the rain one night after a depressing review of the war. Watching from the porter's lodge, Edward McManus opened the door before they reached it, wringing his hands with "a comicality on his face, ready for speech." When he saw the president's eyes, all the fun died out of his own.

On March 29, 1861, Nicolay complained of a thicket of work "almost impossible to get through." After a month in Washington, "the daily mounting of the treadmill" had denied him a single hour of sightseeing. By January 5, 1862, it was worse: "Life here at this time—even in its best phase . . . promises little else than weariness and disgust at the end of each day's task." Even after the "abomination of desolation" fell on the city in August 1862 after Congress adjourned, Hay said his work could fill twenty-four-hour days. On February 21, 1864, it seemed to Nicolay as if the pressures of his job were growing "day by day. I am beginning to doubt my ability to endure it a great while longer."

He envied Hay a mission to Florida "in metaphorical clover while we poor devils are eating the husks of hard work in the national pigsty."

*　　*　　*

Stoddard said Lincoln's own day was "a continual stepping from one duty to another." He sometimes escaped to a borrowed desk by a window in the War Department's telegraph office, where the optional distractions included Pennsylvania Avenue and a prosperous tribe of spiders in a windowsill web, preserved and protected by the keepers of the cipher room.

In January 1862, Edwin Stanton was sworn in as Lincoln's new Secretary of War in his salt-and-pepper chest-length beard, his wire-rimmed spectacles, and his pitiless stare. Hay soon begged Nicolay to stop telling people he could wrangle favors from Stanton: "I would rather make the tour of a smallpox hospital." As grim as a witch trial judge, the Secretary of War was one of the few men in Washington who could work as hard as the president, and even Stanton's assistant secretary, Charles Dana, was struck by Lincoln's stamina. "Night after night he would work late and hard without being wilted by it, and he always seemed as ready for the next day's work as though he had done nothing the day before." He unburdened himself to a friend one night: "You can see the fix I am in. I am kept here every night until nine to twelve o'clock and never know when I can leave." Even when he did, rest escaped him. "While others are asleep, I think. Night is the only time I have to think." He slept with one eye open, he said. "I never close both, except when an office-seeker is looking for me."

Young Julie Taft, the neighborhood child of a former judge, often came to the White House with her brothers to play with Willie and Tad. Lincoln treated her like the daughter he never had. More than half a century later she remembered walking into the library, greeting him in his armchair with a dog-eared Bible in his lap. He took her hand and squeezed, and stared out the window at nothing until her arm ached. Then he spoke like a startled man: " 'Why Julie, have I been holding you here all this time?' He released me," Julie recalled, "and I went off to find the boys." On another afternoon, as Julie read in the library by a window, he stood and gazed at Virginia with one hand on her shoulder and the other on the window, then paced the room with his head hung down and his hands behind his back, sighing now and then. "And crying a little," Julie recalled, "I slipped out in the darkening twilight."

Stoddard said Lincoln rarely troubled his Secretary of the Treasury (he did not pretend to be a financier), left foreign affairs to Seward, and let the attorney general alone. But the War Department seemed to open "right into his room."

CHAPTER 7

Absorbed in the catastrophe that threatened the nation's life, he learned to delegate other things. Seward's private secretary, George Baker, brought him State Department documents to sign. In the first few months, he studied every page. "I never sign a document I have not first read." Then he started having Baker read them to him, and later just to summarize them. By 1864 he was saying, "Show me where you want my name."

The White House knew no weekends. Saturday was just a slightly shorter workday, and war had no Sunday, Stoddard said, but the Sabbath brought "a faint suggestion that it was meant to be a day of rest." The public was excluded, the offices were quiet, and work got quietly done. Stoddard was a weekly churchgoer but Nicolay and Hay were not. Stoddard once heard them say that they meant to go some day (with more bravado than accuracy—they were not so impious as that). But if the president was at church, the office might be empty on a Sunday morning as the secretaries took precious time off.

Most of the servants had the whole day free, for as one of them said, President Lincoln was a God-fearing man. He needed the rest that the Sabbath brought too, but he worked on Sunday when it was necessary and sometimes when it was not. When he went to the Smithsonian to hear the editor Horace Greeley speak, he told another listener that the speech was intriguing, and he'd like to take the manuscript home and read it carefully some Sunday. On quiet Sundays in the office, he enjoyed a casual chat with his secretaries, and his face would go dark when a messenger announced some obnoxious politician. A woman was pleased when Congressman Isaac Newton arranged to introduce her to the president on a Sunday, Lincoln having said that Sunday was the only time he had to himself. She seems to have missed the irony.

As Stoddard worked at his desk one peaceful Sunday morning, Hay came in and stood by the open door, gleeful about some story. He had only started telling it when they both collapsed in laughter, drawing Nicolay across the hall to make Hay start again. While the three of them were laughing, Lincoln appeared and dropped himself into Andy Jackson's chair, throwing one leg over the other. "Now John, just tell that thing again." It was even better the third time. "Down came the President's foot from across his knee, with a heavy stamp on the floor, and out through the hall went an uproarious peal of laughter." Hay was about to go on when the doorman Edward McManus interrupted, "washing his hands and looking penitent." The Secretary of War was in the president's office, he said, and a pall fell over the room. Stanton never came on Sunday except with terrible news.

"There was something all but ghastly" in the death of Hay's story, Stoddard said. "The shadow came back to Lincoln's face, and he rose slowly, painfully, like a man lifting some enormous burden. He even seemed to stagger as he walked out." Hay was staggered too. "There was no more laugh nor story in him, and he and Nicolay went over to their room."

*   *   *

Lincoln was an early riser, and Noah Brooks thought he spent his best two hours before breakfast, reading, writing, and studying. Before the workday began, he would try to relax in the library for a few precious minutes at the oversized table in the center of the room, with Shakespeare, the Bible, or the latest comic punditry on politics, society, or the war. Seward usually walked over to discuss whatever was new until the president was called to breakfast, where he went if there was nothing catastrophic to keep him. Henry Bellows, who spent much time with him as the head of the Sanitary Commission, a private organization authorized by Congress to aid and comfort soldiers and sailors, said his meals were often irregular, cold, and hurried.

Mrs. Grimsley said, "Only repeated protests brought any degree of regularity" to them. Mrs. Lincoln invited a repertory cast to breakfast and would send a servant to tell the president they had company. Sam Galloway, a former Ohio congressman, was a regular. Lincoln would come to the table looking awful, sit down with a bare nod to Sam, and tell his wife, "Mother, I do not think I ought to have come." Then Sam would share a joke, knowing that his face would lighten, and Lincoln would tell a little story over an egg, toast, and coffee. His barber shaved him after breakfast, Bellows said, and because he was so considerate, the razor was generally applied "when *it was convenient for the barber*," not the president of the United States.

Then he typically walked over to the War Department for the morning's telegraphed news and returned at about ten to admit the day's procession. When Mrs. Lincoln was home, he left the shop for the Family Dining Room for lunch. Hay said he rarely took more than a biscuit, a glass of milk, and whatever fruit was in season.

Little Julie Taft often saw him reading in the library after lunch, "sometimes in his stocking feet with one leg crossed over the other, the unshod foot slowly waving back and forth, as if in time to some inaudible music." Annoyed by the indelicacy, Mrs. Lincoln might order a servant to fetch his slippers.

Afternoon carriage rides with his wife, sometimes replaced by a horseback ride, were his only daily outings. Mrs. Lincoln hardly ever went to his office, but servants delivered her summonses when he worked past their carriage time. One lovely afternoon while he was in a meeting, she sent for him several times, then told the servant to tell him he *had* to come. The president left the meeting with a comic display of submission.

The Lincolns dined between 5 and 6, usually with friends. The president was "very abstemious—ate less than any one I know," Hay recalled. "Drank nothing but water—not from principle, but because he did not like wine or spirits." There was no dressing for dinner in the Family Dining Room, whether friends were invited or not. Lincoln came to the table directly from his office, typically a little late, sometimes later.

When Mrs. Lincoln was out of town, as she often was, he worked through whatever the servants brought to his office—breakfast, lunch, and supper. When a group of callers apologized for sending in their cards at dinnertime, the president put them at ease: "Oh, no consequence at all." Mrs. Lincoln was traveling, "and when she is away I generally browse around."

Despite Cornelia Mitchell's culinary skills, the president disliked fine dining. A White House waiter said, "Lincoln could eat as much ham and cabbage as any man who dug in the dirt. He ate cornbread too, and wasn't ashamed to own it." Mrs. Lincoln knew what he liked and what was good for him, and made sure he got it. He often barely noticed. His sister-in-law Elizabeth watched him chew mechanically, deep in thought, tasting nothing. At breakfast one morning, Noah Brooks remarked that milk was not a common drink for a western man. Lincoln looked at his glass as if for the first time. "Well, I do prefer coffee in the morning," he said, "but they don't seem to have sent me in any."

Before the dinner table was cleared, congressmen and senators began showing up in his office. He typically spent his evenings there, often in conversation with friends. With them he was "the riskiest of story tellers," Hay said. He sometimes spent an hour in the Red Room after dinner, chatting with Mrs. Lincoln's guests in what Hay called "his armor of dignity and reserve," or relaxing with friends of his own, or listening to music. He enjoyed classical music but preferred sentimental ballads. Alone with him in the White House, Ward Hill Lamon sang tear-jerking songs on the order of "The Lament of the Irish Emigrant."

Lincoln's opportunities for rest were rare. Hay later said that on rare occasions the president would shut his door and see no one. Sometimes he would go out for a lecture or a concert or a play. Other than that and his afternoon rides he allowed himself almost no recreation.

Almost every night, he walked to the War Department at nine or ten, came back to chat with his wife, and went to bed between ten and eleven unless the war or urgent business demanded more of him. When his burdens kept him awake, he might come to Nicolay and Hay. "I would be awakened by someone seating himself on the side of my bed," Hay said, "and Lincoln's voice would say, 'Lie still, don't get up. Would you mind if I read to you a little while?' " To avoid "the dull pleasure" of laughing alone, he would share his favorite humorists, like "Petroleum V. Nasby" or "Private Miles O'Reilly," the wry English poet Thomas Hood, or his Scottish counterpart Robert Burns, the dialect corrupted with Lincoln's rustic twang.

Once his mind had cleared, he would "start for the door and on down the dark corridor," Hay said. "The candle carried high in his hand would light the disheveled hair as the President in flapping nightshirt, his feet padding along in carpet slippers, would disappear into the darkness."

8

THE REPUBLICAN QUEEN IN HER WHITE PALACE

The North was a nation of farmers, mechanics, and frugal Yankee merchants who disapproved of opulence, and the Executive Mansion's grandeur, such as it was, set a trap for every president. Seated at a White House dinner, gold-plated spoon in hand, an opposition congressman had threatened Martin Van Buren with his own utensils. All he had to do to enflame his constituents, the politician said, was to hold up one of these.

Nevertheless, almost every president and first lady had upgraded the house to a greater or lesser degree and tried to repair the damage done by hard use. In Buchanan's time, Harriet Lane had added $22,000 worth of gilded furniture, a piano, some new gas chandeliers, and drapes for the formal rooms. Mrs. Lincoln meant to surpass them all, to make the Executive Mansion what it ought to be, and to show the ladies of Washington that they had misjudged her taste and style. It would cost her husband more than money.

He endorsed the continued work on the splendid new Capitol dome, despite its wartime consumption of resources. If the work went on, he said, the people would know that the country would too. The refurbishment of the White House might have struck him the same way, had he thought much about it, but the commissioner of public buildings presided over renovations, the job was still open, and the president had other things on his mind.

On May 12, 1861, the commissioner's sphere being "very near the lady of the house," Mrs. Lincoln again asked Ward Hill Lamon to persuade her husband to appoint William S. Wood, who had flattered her from Springfield to Washington, capped with the gift of a fine pair of horses. The other candidates, she said, were "very unsuitable, deficient in intelligence, manners, and it may be, morals."

She wrote from New York, where she had gone with one of her nieces and Mrs. Grimsley as soon as the rail lines reopened after the rebels' isolation of the capital. Ladies did not travel alone, and her husband was otherwise engaged. Her escorts were the unimpeachable Colonel Robert Anderson, the hero of Fort Sumter, and the highly impeachable William S. Wood, who showed her around the city and stayed in the same hotel, an indiscretion that made the rounds. With a civil war less than one month old, Mrs. Lincoln hit the shops on The Ladies' Mile hard, and everybody knew it. She could not step out of a carriage without reporters at her elbow. She would spend several days in New York, one newspaper said, shopping and recovering from "the arduous cares and duties of the White House," and was "purchasing quite extensively." And so she was.

Given the ceaseless beating that the White House endured, Congress routinely provided $20,000 for furnishings and $6,000 for improvements and repairs to be spent in a four-year term. Mrs. Lincoln spent it all in a few manic days, intoxicated by nearly everything the delighted merchants showed her. The haul included gilded mahogany furniture upholstered in French satin, bales of imported wallpaper, a stupendous velvet carpet for the East Room, a rosewood grand piano, and many other treasures. To replace the mismatched settings on the presidential table, she settled on seven hundred pieces of hand-cut Dorflinger glassware, a 208-piece dessert service, and 190 pieces of double-gilded, royal purple Haviland dinnerware, each piece wrought with the seal of the United States.

Mrs. Lincoln's embellishment of the White House would have been defensible, even admirable, had it not overlapped with a civil war, but her personal shopping was a scandal. She so admired the Haviland china that she bought a duplicate set of her own, with her initials in place of the American eagle. Among other personal adornments, The Ladies' Mile yielded two black lace shawls at $650 each and one of cashmere at $1,000. White House doorkeepers earned $600 a year. Stopping in Philadelphia, the First Lady ordered nearly $7,000 worth of luxurious odds and ends at William H. Carryl & Bro., "Importers and Dealers in Curtain Materials and Trimmings of Every Description." Judging by the wealth she was lavishing on the place, the *Philadelphia Dispatch*'s New York correspondent surmised that "Mrs. President Lincoln" had "no apprehension that Jeff Davis will make good his threat to occupy the White House in July."

Newspapers all over the country started vilifying her as no first lady had been vilified before, exaggerating what needed no exaggeration, a sport that would entertain the press for four years. They "pounced upon her like buzzards," said the *Chicago Tribune.* "They flew in at the windows of the White House. They pursued her from the blue room to the boudoir." With the country at war with itself, Mrs. Lincoln had gone shopping.

To put her acquisitions together, she engaged John Alexander, whose family business on Pennsylvania Avenue had been redoing the White House since Dolley Madison's day. For months, Alexander and his men took the house apart, covered it with scaffolding, and put it back together again, scrubbing windows, mirrors, and floors; replacing wallpaper, carpets, and drapes; adding cornices, moldings, and gold leaf. The house reeked of paint and rang with hammers and saws. "Two coats of pure white paint on the outside renew its right to be designated the 'White House,'" said the *Daily Alta California,* a San Francisco paper. Monroe's classic furniture, too fine and valuable to discard, was freshly varnished and reupholstered in crimson satin, "tufted and laid in folds on the back, rendering a modern appearance."

The obnoxious gold spoons were replated. So were the dessert knives and sugar tongs. More gas pipes were run through the walls, more valves were put in, old chandeliers were refinished, and new ones were installed, along with 1,600 feet of gilded molding and a bluestone walk. Carved mahogany furniture from Carryl's of Philadelphia was uncrated and carried into bedrooms the public would never see. Sheepskin rugs went down by the beds. White lace curtains went up on the windows, letting people look out but not in. The *Alta California* thought the library, predominantly green, had been "chastely and not extravagantly refurnished," but Mrs. Lincoln wrote a note on a bill for wallpaper, presumably to explain its unchaste bottom line: Mr. Carryl had been "particularly desired" to select "the richest style."

The First Lady's interests did not run to art. After the walls were redone in extravagant French wall coverings—a "heavy velvet cloth paper of crimson, garnet, and gold" for the East Room—the same dead presidents went back up over them. From time to time inspirational paintings supporting the war were exhibited temporarily, but the White House was no gallery.

*   *   *

The renovations were barely underway when the president hosted his first diplomatic dinner on June 7. Nicolay and Hay absorbed the State Department's guidance, Mrs. Lincoln made do with what she had, and she did a splendid job. The Washington *Evening Star* called it "the most brilliant affair of the sort that has ever taken place at the Executive Mansion." Harriet Lane's wax fruit and plaster of Paris flowers gave way to stunning flowers fresh from the conservatory and the grounds, festooning the tables and chandeliers.

The Lincolns and their lingering prairie houseguests "entirely forgot we were expected to be embarrassed," Mrs. Grimsley said, and enjoyed it all immensely—the diplomats' decorations, their wives' "exquisite court dresses," and the gay conversation, for "diplomats do not dine with the solemnity common to Americans." Effusive toasts were made, decanters were passed, and "elaborate snuff boxes" were exchanged, a custom not practiced in Springfield. Everyone adjourned to the Red Room, and the diplomats retired diplomatically.

Before the renovations were done, Nicolay and Hay's offices were freshly papered, carpeted, and curtained, but the new chief attraction in Nicolay's was a five-foot Viking mace. On its way to the Smithsonian it distracted high-placed favor seekers waiting for Lincoln's ear.

Mrs. Lincoln told a historian that she had elegantly redone the president's office, which was only half true. The seedy rug was trashed, replaced by a dark green carpet with buff-colored diamonds; new green wallpaper with gold stars went up on the walls; the woodwork got two coats of paint; and silk bell pulls were hung by Lincoln's chair to call the staff and signal the doorkeeper that he was ready to start or end a meeting. (Stoddard could tell he was "fire mad about something" when the bell rang long and hard.) But the faded green horsehair seating stayed, "stately, and semi-comfortable," and so did the old-fashioned desks and the battered tables and chairs, no doubt by Executive order. The bookcases were still "sprinkled with the sparse library of a country lawyer." The *Alta California*, smitten by the sumptuous work in the rest of the house, said the president's office "is very neatly papered but should be better furnished." It resembled "the dingy old room" he had occupied in Springfield as president-elect, but "Mr. Lincoln don't complain."

Apart from leaning on the mantle a photograph of John Bright, a crusading Member of Parliament bent on egalitarian reform, Lincoln added few personal touches to his office. He had fought Democrats all his life, but he left over the wood-burning fireplace the drab old portrait of the Southern-born Andrew Jackson that Buchanan had put there. No stronger defender of the Union had ever been president.

Lincoln's office was no ceremonial stage but a cluttered place of work, as he comfortably let everyone see. On May 2, 1861, Lieutenant Robert Gould Shaw, a privileged young Bostonian fated to win posthumous glory at the head of the 54th Massachusetts Colored Infantry, dropped in with a friend. Shaw had heard of Bob Lincoln at Harvard, he told the President, and had little else to carry the conversation. He soon informed his parents that Lincoln's desk was "perfectly covered with letters and papers of every description." Not one of the White House's thirty-one rooms was devoted to files. The president and his secretaries kept their papers in their offices. Though "reckless of all order," Lincoln quickly found whatever he needed, including the latest books of rustic humor, kept handy on a corner of his desk, in which he found "the excitement and relief which another man would have found in a glass of wine," said the editor of the *New York Times*.

On any given day, you could tell which theaters of war were active by the exposure of their maps in the president's office. On April 30, 1861, Hay walked in as some generals and high officials were leaving, and found "the great map of Virginia, newly hung and fronted by conscious-looking chairs. The air is full of ghastly promises for Maryland and Virginia."

As the war dragged on, the office filled up with maps—spring-loaded maps on wall-mounted rollers, maps spooled on dowels in standing wooden racks, folios of maps behind the sofa, maps spread out on the tables, maps leaning against the chairs, maps on Lincoln's writing desk. A lithographic slave map showed the density of human property in shades of black to gray, letting estimates be made of the slaves who would flee to the Union's armies as they took the South. Lincoln tracked the opposing armies on maps laid out on a table, using pins with blue and gray sealing-wax heads. Tad once used them to "make a war map of Willie," Stoddard said, producing noise and "rapid movements" on both sides.

The cabinet had sat for decades at the long mahogany table in the middle of the room. Probably made for Jefferson, it was sometimes bare and sometimes draped with a green baize cloth like a billiard table. It was the only broad work surface in the office, and Lincoln often left it cluttered with papers, maps, and books, around which the cabinet met and over which they peered. When the cabinet was not sitting, its graceful chairs of curved-backed oak were offered to surplus guests.

A hand-me-down upright desk with alphabetically labeled pigeonholes blocked the interior door to the anteroom like a barricade. Stoddard thought it looked like something from an old furniture auction. Lincoln sometimes worked there, or spread himself out across the cabinet table, or wrote at a little desk between the windows overlooking the tents and fortifications dotting Arlington Heights. His worn leather armchair was disreputable enough for a new cabinet member to notice: "I should think the presidential chair of the United States might be a better piece of furniture than that." Lincoln took a look. "There are a great many people that want to sit in it," he said, "though I'm sure I've often wished some of them had it instead of me."

When his backwoods cousin Dennis Hanks came to see him, he found him at "an old desk worth about six bits."

*   *   *

Cabinet members had instant access to Lincoln, and Seward strolled in from the State Department several times a day with the careless lack of pretense typical of the true aristocrat and "the easy familiarity of a household intimate," Stoddard said. "He went into the President's room the other day with the knot of his cravat nearly under his left ear, and carrying an unlighted cigar in his hand."

The cabinet met in Lincoln's office, ordinarily twice a week. When he wanted them on an unscheduled day he would send a note to Seward or have Hay dispatch messengers. The president's secretaries came in and out with documents but never stayed. Lincoln often paced as he spoke and listened, and every man sat where he pleased, some at the table, some not. "I have seen one stretched on the sofa with a cigar in his mouth," Stoddard said (almost surely Seward), "another with his heels on the table, another nursing his knee abstractly, the President with his leg over the arm of his chair, and not a man of them in any wise sitting for his picture."

Except for Seward, they tended to be a solemn bunch, but their meetings could be entertaining. One caller waiting in Nicolay's office while the cabinet

Lincoln, his cabinet, and General Scott in the president's office. Library of Congress.

met in Lincoln's heard laughter next door as if they were enjoying a rollicking good time. Attorney General Bates once brought a placard he had gotten in the mail describing the presidential qualifications of one T. W. Smith of Philadelphia, and they were of "a stunning order." The sign drew the antici- pated laugh and was pinned up in a conspicuous place, where it stayed for several days. P. T. Barnum was ushered in one afternoon with "Commodore Nutt," two-and-a-half-feet tall in elaborate naval regalia, a featured performer in Barnum's Thumbiana and Lilliputian Opera under a regal $30,000 three- year contract. A newspaper called him "Barnum's $30,000 Nutt." He demanded to know whether it was the Secretary of the Treasury who was spending all the taxpayers' money, but when Stanton owned up that it was he, the Commodore forgave him.

*   *   *

Removed from shiny objects in Philadelphia and New York, Mrs. Lincoln panicked when the bills came in. The $20,000 budget for four years of fur- nishings had been overspent by nearly $8,000 in a few weeks, not to mention her insatiable personal shopping on credit. Unable to bring herself to tell her husband, she made frantic and pointless attempts to scrape the money up. Hay rejected her plea to apply the White House stationery fund to her debt. The dairy cows' milk was traditionally sent to hospitals, and "the whole city felt scandalized to have it haggled over and peddled from the back door of the White House." Even Stoddard, Mrs. Lincoln's only ally on the office staff, was taken aback when she "proposed to sell the very manure in the Executive stables, and to cut off the necessary expenses of the household."

In sheer desperation, she blurted her predicament to John Watt, the light- fingered White House gardener, who showed her how to solve it. Major Watt taught the First Lady of the land how to forge expense authorizations, pad the payroll, buy drapes through the kitchen account, and otherwise redecorate the books. Everyone did it, he said, and no one would be the wiser. Within weeks, Buchanan's steward was gone, replaced by Watt's wife. Merchants connived with Mrs. Lincoln to overbill the government to cover her personal purchases and even to give her cash. Watt would later admit that silver costing $6,000 was booked for regilding light fixtures.

On May 31, unaware of her fraud on the government, the president sur- rendered to his wife and named the confidence man William S. Wood com- missioner of public buildings. She was said to have locked herself in her room until he did. Lincoln's future Supreme Court appointee David Davis found he appointment incomprehensible. Lincoln replied that it would ruin him. True or not, the word was passed in high places that Wood had cuckolded him. An anonymous letter on "the scandal of your wife and Wood" warned the president that libels about their conduct would "stab you in the most vital part." Wood took the job, subject to Senate confirmation that would never come, and promptly authorized Carryl's of Philadelphia to procure wallpaper for the Executive Mansion "of such character and quality as Mrs. Lincoln may direct."

More common than speculative talk of adultery, flagrant rumors that Mrs. Lincoln was a rebel sympathizer, or even a spy, were flatly false. Raised in Kentucky, with four half brothers and three brothers-in-law in the Confederate army, she was despised in the South as a traitor and mistrusted in the North as a Southerner. Her talented dressmaker and confidante, the remarkable Elizabeth Keckly, was a former slave, an independent businesswoman, and one of Washington's most sought-after "modistes." Mrs. Lincoln showed Mrs. Keckly scant sorrow when her youngest half brother, Alec Todd, was killed in battle at twenty-three: He had made his odious choice, she said, and the rebels would hang her husband and perhaps his wife if they could.

But she wept for Alec in private. Just over half her age, he had played with Bob Lincoln as a child, and his death broke her heart. Another rebel half brother had already been killed, and a third would eventually follow. The loss of her brothers caused her pain, but she truly despised their cause.

*   *   *

At half past five on June 1, 1861, a pleasant Saturday evening, a crowd "bright with uniforms" was enjoying the Marine Band on the south lawn when the brisk sound of musketry drifted across the river. The crowd rushed down to Jefferson's wall to look, and Nicolay took a spyglass to the roof. It was only Northern soldiers practicing, but there was reason for anxiety. The first skirmish of the war had been fought before dawn at Fairfax Courthouse, less than twenty miles away. Two weeks later, another was plainly heard in Washington.

Ordinary life went on, and so did the White House social calendar, which reassured the city and oiled the gears of government. More business was done over the dinner table, Stoddard said, "and in the glare of the gas-lights" at receptions, than on Capitol Hill. Invitations to White House affairs had always been presidential currency, and so they remained.

In Lincoln's White House as in others, politics demanded a high tolerance for low bedfellows, but a certain class of men was barred from the dining rooms and parlors even if it was necessary to receive them upstairs. By title alone, cabinet ministers, Supreme Court justices, and diplomats were suitable guests, but the same could not be said for a senator or a congressman whose status as a gentleman was in doubt. "A man might be able to carry the hundred and first ward of Babylon," Stoddard said, but "not be just the person you would like to see dancing with your wife."

It was therefore no small thing that Mrs. Lincoln drew around her a clique of polished men with reputations for indifferent morals: "My *beau monde* friends of the Blue Room" she called them. On most evenings, all of them were male, and her husband was not among them. It was enough to spread the whiff of scandal in itself, exacerbated by their sordid histories. On the face of things, they were drawn to the bright discussions of politics, art, and books, but some were forging credentials as White House insiders to put to profitable use. Mrs. Lincoln was warned repeatedly that they were not respectable. In past administrations, blackguards, rakes, and fallen women had stayed away from the White House, as the lower classes did. "The poor knew they would feel out of place, and the immoral were barred by public opinion." Not by Mary Lincoln.

One of the friends she welcomed to the President's House was a well-bred slug by the name of Henry Wikoff (pronounced Why-koff). Born in Philadelphia, expelled from Yale as a boy, reviled on two continents as a man, "the Chevalier Wikoff," as he liked to hear himself called, had bounced around high society as a sort of professional cad, "by what means few could tell," a newspaperman would say. "That awful creature Wikoff," William Howard Russell called him, "an unclean bird" in the opinion of John Hay, who thought it an "enduring disgrace to American society that it suffers such a thing to be around."

After his wealthy fiancé called off their wedding in 1851, Wikoff had kidnapped her in Italy in a curious bid to change her mind and been jailed for it in Genoa. His lurid account of *My Courtship and Its Consequences* had raised the desired stir and made the intended sales. Affecting "an air after the English manner," the chevalier "mingled with society of every shade and grade," spreading "the gossip of courts and cabinets, of the *boudoir* and the *salon*." If his mores were not Victorian his politics were not Lincolnian. Cashing in on his notoriety as a felon, he had published in 1861 a letter to Prime Minister Palmerston commending slavery, insisting that Northern meddling with it justified secession, and declaring that Lincoln had "no apparent claim to so great a distinction" as the presidency.

No discerning lady would have let him past her door. It was child's play to charm his way through Mrs. Lincoln's. With a little stylish flattery at an open reception or two, he quickly became her Master of Ceremonies, a disgusted critic said. "No one went so early but this person could be seen cozily seated in a chair as if at home, talking to the ladies of the White House. None called so late but they found him still there." Respectable guests started taking the precaution of asking Edward the doorman if Mr. Wikoff was in, as he nearly always was. Mrs. Lincoln was sufficiently indiscrete to wait for him in Willard's lobby, the crossroads of Washington City, where she helped him put on his gloves and showed him to her carriage. People talked, and so did the press.

Other patrons of Mrs. Lincoln's black sheep salon included Congressman Daniel Sickles, later General Daniel Sickles, who had kept a mistress while serving as a diplomat in London and presented her to Queen Victoria. His sexual liberalism ended where his pretty young wife's began. In 1859, he shot her lover to death on Pennsylvania Avenue within pistol range of the White House and got away with it on a plea of temporary insanity. It was said that Mrs. Lincoln let herself be seen with him when no other respectable woman would have done such a thing.

William A. Newell, a virulently nativist former governor of New Jersey, was a member of Mrs. Lincoln's salon. So was Oliver S. Halsted, an arms merchants' lobbyist. The poet Nathaniel P. Willis, the scandalously effeminate editor of the popular *Home Journal*, revered Mrs. Lincoln in print as the "Republican Queen in her White Palace," which Willis haunted alone, leaving his wife at home. Senator Charles Sumner, another Blue Room regular, was a pompous, humorless Bostonian who affected English clothes and a bit of an Oxford accent. "I have never had much to do with bishops down where we live," Lincoln told a friend, "but, do you know, Sumner is just my idea of a bishop." The senator lounged about the Blue Room with Mrs. Lincoln by night and schemed to unseat her husband by day.

Mrs. Lincoln's letters were all but silent about the suffering that consumed her husband in the vortex of a civil war. Victories, defeats, and casualties went all but unnoticed, blotted out by luxuries, amusements, and social intrigue. On October 6, 1861, a note to a friend said nearly as much about the war as her letters ever did: "If we could accomplish our purpose without resorting to arms and bloodshed how comfortable it would be—But that is impossible. . . . The diplomatic corps have returned to the city, quite a number of strangers are daily coming in, and our 'blue room' in the evenings is quite alive with the 'beau monde.'" After Mrs. Grimsley returned to Springfield, Mrs. Lincoln let her know that a gentleman called "the Cap" had been over for dinner, "as refined and elegant as ever," and Governor Newell and Halsted "are frequently here, *as who is not?*"

* * *

Mrs. Lincoln scaled back on the public fits she had thrown in Springfield, but the White House saw its share. An occasionally reliable servant named Thomas Stackpole, a burley, rough-looking man, said he saw her attack the president: "Struck him hard—cursed him—damned him," but her temper did not always cow him. A New Yorker was with him in his office when "a big Indianan" came in. "She wants you," the servant said.

"Yes, yes," Lincoln said, and stayed where he was.

The Indianan returned. "I say she wants you!" Silently unmoved, the president finished his meeting.

And yet he humored her. As Mrs. Keckly got her ready for a reception, he typically asked her which women he could speak to, and proposed some nominees. She rejected two one night as he fumbled with the buttons on his gloves. "Well, mother, I must talk with someone. Is there anyone that you do not object to?"

"I don't know as it is necessary that you should talk to anybody in particular."

"But, mother, I insist that I must talk with somebody. I can't stand around like a simpleton and say nothing. If you will not tell me who I may talk with, please tell me who I may *not* talk with."

"These are the ones in particular," she replied, putting three off limits, including the Secretary of the Treasury's twenty-one-year-old daughter Kate Chase, "the prettiest Kate in Christendom." Hay had formed the opinion that the effort Miss Chase devoted to pushing her father toward the presidency, which did not endear her to Mrs. Lincoln, left her time to be "only a little lovelier than all other women."

Much of capital society despised the First Lady's self-indulgence. In the agitated view of Dr. Robert K. Stone, the White House physician, "Mrs. Lincoln was a perfect devil." Dr. Stone's wife thought her "insane on the subject of money." The *Cincinnati Commercial* called her "a fool—the laughing stock of the town, her vulgarity only the more conspicuous in consequence of her fine carriage and horses and servants in livery and fine dresses, and her damnable airs." The livery was imaginary. The rest was not. A *New York Tribune* correspondent was convinced that she visited the military hospitals, as she often did, to feast on the flattery and attention, a view not confined to men.

The pioneering newspaperwoman Mary Clemmer Ames was passionate on the subject:

> While her sister-women scraped lint, sewed bandages, and put on nurse's caps and gave their all to country and to death, the wife of the President spent her time in rolling to and fro between Washington and New York, intent on extravagant purchases for herself and the White House. [As if] there were no national peril, no monstrous national debt, no rivers of blood flowing she seemed chiefly intent upon pleasure, personal flattery and adulation; upon extravagant dress and ceaseless self-gratification.

Her sister Elizabeth called her "the most ambitious woman I ever saw." She "spurred up Mr. Lincoln, pushed him along and upward—made him struggle and seize his opportunities." She said more than once, to more than one person, that she had married him because he would be president, "for you can see he is not pretty." Her enemy William Herndon, Lincoln's former law partner, said she prodded him into the White House like a toothache that tormented him night and day.

The servants called her Madam, as in "Madam expects you in the Red Room." She had grown up commanding slaves in her father's Kentucky home, and Stoddard said she was the absolute mistress of everything in the White House but the office wing. In a letter of reference for his coachman Ned Burke the president said, "I take no charge of the servants about the house," but the word was out that the First Lady did not know how to oversee a great house and was too proud to ask. The word about town was that some of the servants were leaving to "live with gentlefolks."

Marshall Ward Hill Lamon had originally taken charge of them, assisted by his wife, but Lamon had "no more tact than a drill sergeant," Stoddard said, and overplayed his hand. Mrs. Lincoln turned him out in less than two weeks.

Some of the domestic staff were offered bribes for overheard information and insisted years later that none of them succumbed. Stoddard called them loyal to the president and the Union, but more servants turned over during Mrs. Lincoln's White House reign than any other. According to her ally Noah Brooks, who surely heard it from her, they included "suckers who grew rich [!] on the pickings and stealings from the kitchen garden and conservatory, and who had spies in every room of the house." She cleaned them out, Brooks said, in "a terrible scattering of ancient abuses which once accumulated downstairs." She may not have gotten them all. Nicolay would discover in September 1864 that his gold watch was missing from his dresser drawer.

Nonetheless, two old black servants spoke years later about how good Mrs. Lincoln was to the help, with plain equivocations: "She had her ways, but nobody minded her, for she would never hurt a flea, and her bark was worse than her bite." When she was not sick with her dreadful headaches or worried about something (no rare exceptions), she was said to be a pleasure to work for. Some of the domestic staff's descendants said "the old folks loved Mary Lincoln with a love that went with them to the tomb, and they thought of her as second only to the Emancipator."

Mrs. Lincoln hired women to do plain sewing by the day. Rosetta Wells, a seamstress descended from slaves, made and mended the family's clothes and hemmed their linens. Mrs. Wells was a talker, and Tad was fond of her. In the manner of the day when addressing older black women, he called her Aunt Wells and liked to watch her search for the spectacles she had pushed up under her headscarf. Mrs. John Brooks often joined her in her sewing. Tad would hide their needles, then tell them where they were and run away laughing.

Mrs. Lincoln was engaged about the White House as most women were in a wealthy home. She supervised the housekeeping, wrote letters at her desk, and typically went down to the conservatory to tell Major Watt, the gardener, what she wanted done and how. She was "all over the kitchen," a servant said, and could put on an apron and cook. She knew how to choose meats, prepare vegetables, and bake bread, and the steward, cook, and waiters "*knew* that she knew."

The servants liked the president. One said in old age that he treated them "like people" and would "laugh and say kind things." Noah Brooks said he let them bear no hardship he could lift. He was fond of Peter Brown, a freed slave who had been the White House butler since the Buchanan administration, managing the kitchen and waiting at table. Brown's son Robert shined shoes around the Treasury Department and the White House, ran errands, did odd jobs around the kitchen, and played with the Lincoln boys. When his father brought him to the president's office, Lincoln rubbed his head and called him a handsome boy. Years later, Robert said it made him so angry he wanted to hit him, but was smart enough to duck away.

Noah Brooks told his readers in 1863 that "the President has succeeded in getting about him a corps of attaches of Hibernian descent whose manners and style are about as disagreeable as can be," except for Charlie Forbes, variously described as a footman, valet, or messenger, depending on who was watching. Charlie often looked after Tad, and befriended him.

After Lincoln ran into his coachman, Ned Burke, one morning and asked

9

THIS IS A
GOD-FORSAKEN HOLE

In the winter of 1862, the English novelist Anthony Trollope found the White House "nice to look at" but built on marshy ground and so unhealthy that few who lived there escaped life-threatening disease. "Men desert such localities," or at least do not congregate there, Trollope wrote. "But the poor President cannot desert the White House. He must make the most of the residence which the nation has prepared for him."

Nicolay and Hay deserved sympathy too. When they moved into the White House in March, they had found it disappointing but comfortable. June made them wonder if it was habitable. After one intolerable afternoon, William Howard Russell, another newcomer, told his diary that the sun was not much hotter in India than it was that day. On July 20, Nicolay drank three pails of ice water in an afternoon.

"It is very warm," Stoddard said in a rare burst of understatement, and the open windows let in heat instead of a breeze. Back in town from New York, George Templeton Strong declared that, "of all detestable places, Washington is the first." The tropical humidity came in second to the "mosquitoes, and a plague of flies transcending everything within my experience." Two blocks from the White House, they "blackened the tablecloths" at Willard's "and absolutely flew into one's mouth at dinner." The green louvered shutters on the south-facing White House windows blocked the sun but not the bugs. Working in coats and ties, Lincoln and his staff had a choice of afflictions. They could open the windows and be bitten to distraction or keep them shut and be steamed like heads of broccoli.

And then there was the smell. Not far below the south lawn, within sniffing range of the White House, sat the noxious Washington Canal, an abandoned commercial waterway bearing "floating dead cats and all kinds of putridity" that "crept and soaked through the city . . . reeking with pestilential odors." Animal carcasses big and small floated by with the odd human corpse. Decaying plants and beasts left "at low water a sickening mass of corruption into which all the sewers of the city empty." When a breeze wafted up from the south, the Marine Band's White House concerts were touched with the scent of canal.

Poison was suspected when everyone but the servants fell ill in the summer of 1861. Mrs. Grimsley said "it proved to be only an over-indulgence in Potomac Shad, a new and tempting dish to western palates." The key word may have been Potomac. Tens of thousands of troops encamped by the river had fouled it and spread disease.

Three weeks after the Lincolns moved in, Willie and Tad contracted measles, a mild case of a potentially fatal illness. Mrs. Lincoln was alarmed but had no aptitude for nursing. The boys disliked the maid who attended them, and Mrs. Grimsley was cajoled to step in. Their father would make his way to the sickroom for lunch and a cup of tea, stretch out on the couch, and read to them aloud or regale them with memorized poetry until a messenger called him back.

Stoddard thought the mortality that plagued the White House every summer crawled up from the mold in the basement, but clouds of pestilent mosquitos blew in from the marsh adjoining the Smithsonian and the mudflats on the Mall, "that great slope of grass and weeds and rubbish between the White House grounds and the Potomac," where the half-built Washington Monument overlooked hills of trash and unsuspecting cattle grazing by a reeking slaughterhouse. The Potomac deposited "such material as any decent river might wish to be relieved of," Stoddard said. Its fumes drifted into the White House on the southern breeze.

Cholera took its toll from May through November. Typhoid and smallpox had their seasons. Doctor Stone went through the White House, office by office, early in the smallpox season: "Have you been vaccinated? Glad of it! Very glad of it! But it will do no hurt to repeat. I'll shut the door for a moment. Take off your coat and bare your arm." At one time or another, deadly illness gripped the president, both of his little sons, and all three of his secretaries. Whenever one of the staff fell ill and left for a while to recover, the others absorbed his work and sent him cryptic notes in their private slang. Nicolay's daughter summed it up years later: "This is a God-forsaken hole. Keep out of it as long as you can. We can get on quite well without you."

When Hay came down with "Potomac fever" during the summer of 1861,

Stoddard nursed him and took up the slack. It was then that Stoddard learned the private secretary's job.

*   *   *

On June 19, as Lincoln watched from an upstairs window, an enormous military observation balloon was towed down Pennsylvania Avenue and moored for a demonstration on the White House lawn. Flabbergasted Washingtonians had never seen such a thing before, including the President of the United States. "A balloon is now floating nearly over the President's house," said the breathless *Boston Transcript*. "A bugler was just sent up and the strains of the bugle grew clearer and more distinct as he mounted."

Toward the end of June, workmen put up over the bandstand on the south lawn a pavilion of blue and white striped canvas with a circus tent roof and a flagpole in the middle rising twenty or thirty feet above it. On a Saturday afternoon, surrounded by the 12th New York Infantry and dignitaries including Benjamin French, the president raised the pavilion's flag, which had flown from a naval vessel in a minor engagement. Too old and infirm to walk or stand, General Scott stayed seated on the south portico like an aged Roman god.

Lincoln worked the halyards and the flag rose smartly until it snagged on the metal ring where the pole ran up through the tent. The president tugged hard and yanked it through, but some stars and stripes tore loose with an ugly rip. When the breeze took the severed flag, artillery boomed, the Marine Band played "The Star Spangled Banner," and French "felt a sorrow I cannot describe." The omen cannot have been lost on Lincoln.

A few days later, the landscape architect Frederick Law Olmsted wrote a letter to his wife after a cool morning walk with a friend through the White House grounds. He had just suspended work on Central Park to serve on the Sanitary Commission. The capital was a city of flies, "far worse than Staten Island in fish time," he said. Contemptuous of their bumpkin president, Olmsted's friend had mocked him casually to his face as if he were some local character: "I saw the President this morning walking hastily with two or three other loafers to the War Department," Olmsted said.

> He looked much younger than I had supposed, dressed in a cheap and nasty French black cloth suit just out of a tight carpetbag. Looked as if he would be an applicant for a Broadway squad policemanship, but a little too smart and careless. Turned and laughed familiarly at a joke upon himself which he overheard from my companion en passant.

That night, a famous songstress just back from Italy entertained Mrs. Lincoln's guests in the Red Room, singing at the piano in a shawl, luring the president downstairs when the finale drifted into his office. Someone asked her to play for him and she did, "having laid off the shawl from shoulders that no South would ever have seceded from." She sang Bellini's "Casta Diva," loosely translated as "Virgin Goddess," to the president's delight.

Deeper music drifted in from the south lawn as the uniformed band and singers of the 8th New York performed a serenade. The president stepped out with his guests and looked up at the stars in a city almost free from artificial light. What the *New York Times* called The War Comet of 1861 was low on the horizon, trailing an immense feathered tail. With a look of prophetic dignity, Lincoln put one hand on a friend's shoulder and pointed with the other. An onlooker said, "I really thought I had seen nothing in my life more like an historic apparition. I looked on—the band played on—then the music ceased."

*   *   *

On the first Independence Day of the war, Pennsylvania Avenue was "red, white, and blue with flags," and a four-mile parade of twenty-three New York militia units, over two thousand diversely uniformed men, passed the White House in delightful weather for an hour and a half. Some marched with fifes and drums, others with brass or coronet bands, one with highland kilts and shapely legs. The crowd cheered them all. As the president, his cabinet, and his senior officers saluted from a stand under a huge flag, a tall, handsome woman dashed up to him out of the crowd and curtsied. He reached out and took her hand, and she ran back before anyone else had moved. An assassin could have done worse.

A regiment of immigrants called the Garibaldi Guards thrilled the crowd in their bright red blouses and wide-brimmed feathered hats. In the continental tradition, every company marched with its vivandiere, a female provisions vendor, and every man had flowers or a sprig of evergreen tucked into his jacket, hat, or musket. As the vivandieres saluted, the soldiers tossed their garlands toward the reviewing stand in "a perfect shower of leaves and flowers" that covered the cobblestoned street. "It was unexpected," Nicolay said, and "strikingly novel and poetical."

In less than three weeks, many of the young volunteers who marched past the Lincolns that day would be killed or maimed near Bull Run, an obscure Virginia stream just twenty miles south of the White House. As the president lost sleep over the coming collision, his wife wrote a letter to a friend: "I wish

I could hand you over the magnificent bouquet just sent me. The magnolia is superb. We have the most beautiful flowers and grounds imaginable, and company and excitement enough to turn a wiser head than my own. . . . There are so many lovely drives around Washington and we have only *three* carriages at our command."

*   *   *

Lincoln convened a council of war in the Blue Room. A few days later, the officers spread their maps on a table in the library before the president, the cabinet, and Nicolay, and final preparations were made to attack the rebel army at Manassas, Virginia, a single day's march from the White House.

At or about that time, a young officer named Oliver Otis Howard, a future founder of Howard University, forgot his junior place at a conference in Lincoln's office and volunteered an opinion. Seward disagreed and indicated sharply that freshly minted colonels should be seen and not heard. As Howard recalled years later, his superiors stared him down in a tight lipped silence. When the moment had passed and the generals were absorbed in a map, Lincoln rose casually from his chair, slipped around to Howard, who had slinked to the far side of the room, and "put his arm about his young officer, giving him an affectionate pat and a look of tender sympathy, then stole back to his seat." Howard never forgot it. "I loved Lincoln from that hour."

Three days before the Battle of Bull Run, William Howard Russell watched Lincoln cross Pennsylvania Avenue in the midsummer heat by the partly built Treasury Department, "striding like a crane in a bulrush swamp among the great blocks of marble" in an oddly cut gray suit with a soft felt hat on the back of his head, "wiping his face with a red pocket handkerchief." Two days later, with rumors popping everywhere, Benjamin French saw him at the War Department "in a common linen coat" and straw hat, maneuvering through the crowd "without looking to the right or left, and no one seemed to know who he was." He had no escort at all.

As the battle was fought in oppressive heat on July 21, the dull, distant rumble of artillery drifted up from the south to the White House on a quiet Sunday morning and continued throughout the day. Lincoln bore the stress with no visible effect and went to church. When he returned, an aide of General Scott's reported that the battle was won, and the president took a carriage ride. While he was gone, Seward rushed in with a telegram and told Nicolay and Hay that it was lost. Lincoln came back, took the news in silence, and went to Scott's headquarters.

Walking through the President's Park on his way back with Nicolay, he met an old friend who asked him for the news. "These war fellows," he replied, "are very strict with me, and I regret that I am prevented from telling you anything, but I must obey them, I suppose, until I get the hang of things." Surely, his old friend said, he could say whether it was good or bad. Lincoln grasped his arm and leaned down close to his ear. "It's damned bad."

Fear shook the White House into the night. Mrs. Grimsley was told that the rebels were on their way and the city was about to be shelled. "It was a time of intense anxiety," she recalled. "And can you wonder at it?"

Politicians who had driven out to watch the battle as if it were a game began to straggle into the White House around midnight. Like most of the rest of the household, Lincoln was up all night, stretched on a sofa in his office, taking panicked men's reports of chaos, of barely escaping with their lives, of the rebels right behind them. He took notes and asked questions, paced the room and read dispatches.

A miserable, drenching rain fell the next day as broken regiments waded back through the mud on Pennsylvania Avenue. From a State Department window, Seward's son looked down at the motley crowd, in and out of uniform, shuffling past the White House. Benjamin French called them stragglers "in all shapes." There were "some without hats, some without shoes, some with two guns and some with none," some wounded, many convinced "that the rebels would soon be upon us and take our city." William Howard Russell noticed that a "pale young man" had lost his sword, "for the empty sheath dangled at his side."

The rebels did not come, but the dead had not been fully buried when the Philadelphia merchant William H. Carryl, Mrs. Lincoln's purveyor of "curtain materials and trimmings of every description," billed the government the shocking sum of $6,858.80 for sumptuous bits of this and that, ranging from a bedstead with "elegant satin side rails," to 21½ yards of "rich ornamented fringe," to a pair of "rich, elegant," custom-made carpets.

A White House messenger brought the president's courtly friend Senator Orville Hickman Browning of Illinois a bouquet with a note from the First Lady letting him know he would have a friend in her if he helped confirm William S. Wood as commissioner of public buildings. The assistant secretary of the Interior told Browning "a great deal of scandal about Mrs. Lincoln."

* * *

Six days after the disaster at Bull Run, the White House was thrown open for a Saturday evening levee, perhaps to show that order had been restored and the government prospered. William Howard Russell noticed that most of the people who jammed the hot reception rooms did not put on airs or neat clothes. Some privates in hobnailed shoes and coarse gray militia uniforms stood timid at the edge of the Blue Room, cowed by surroundings more luxurious and women more elegant than they had ever thought about until they were coaxed in. Lincoln exuded confidence in the receiving line. Soldiers, politicians, and reporters who saw a lively White House and took the commander in chief's steady hand would tell others.

It was business as usual in the office. Within a week of Bull Run, a Lincoln crony named Henry Whitney skipped the waiting room crowd and was warmly received. When Seward came in, Lincoln teased him in front of Whitney, which did not charm the Secretary of State. Other important callers arrived after Seward left. Lincoln told them he was busy, and turned back to Whitney, asking about amusing characters they had known in Illinois.

A general sent in word that he had to leave town that evening and needed to speak to the president first. "I suppose I must see him," Lincoln said. "Tell him when I get through with Whitney I will see him." He was not through in time. The general left "declaring that the President was closeted with 'an old Hoosier from Illinois, and was telling dirty yarns while the country was quietly going to hell.'"

*   *   *

On Thursday, August 1, Mrs. Lincoln wrote a friend that "the Prince and suite are expected in Washington, and on Saturday we dine them at 8 o'clock p.m. Very different from home. We have only to give our orders for the dinner, and *dress* in proper season." The prince in question, Napoleon Joseph Charles Paul Bonaparte, not quite forty, a nephew of the late emperor, had brought an entourage to America with the perfectly sensible goal of avoiding a duel in France. Close to his cousin, the Emperor Napoleon III, the prince was an important guest. The emperor was undecided about recognizing the Confederacy, and Seward wanted to please him.

The prince had just arrived from New York and so had George Templeton Strong, who found Washington "hotter and more detestable than ever. Plague of flies and mosquitoes unabated." Declining an invitation to stay at the sweltering White House, the prince lodged in Georgetown at the French minister's hilltop home. The lack of rain was fortunate, despite the heat and dust. In a typical summer downpour, a foot of muddy water could flow into Pennsylvania Avenue from its dirt cross streets, "not thick enough to walk on nor thin enough to swim in," the *New York Herald* said, and yet it could have been worse. The avenue being paved, you could touch bottom there. After the storm was over, the receding flood would decorate the street with "the unconsidered trifles swept out of saloons, shops, and houses." A few days after Napoleon's visit, William Howard Russell waded past the White House "in a current that would have made a respectable trout stream." He had managed to catch the curbstone, he said, and lived.

Mrs. Grimsley wrote a letter on the day the prince arrived: "Today Mary has a large dinner-party for the Prince Napoleon and suite. There will be no ladies present except Mary and myself. I wish it was over." And so, it seems, did the prince, who arrived with his retinue at noon, in a blanket of humid heat, to be introduced to the president. One of Napoleon's aides, Lieutenant Colonel Camille Ferri-Pisani, judged the White House "a rather nice palace, located in the most secluded section of Washington and surrounded by a beautiful garden." There ends the complementary part of his review.

No one opened the door. To the prince's sheer astonishment, "one goes right in as if entering a cafe." The only Lincoln on hand to greet Napoleon was little Willie, playing serendipitously in the vestibule. In a letter home to Paris, Colonel Pisani assured his superiors that he would not condemn a head of state for simple habits. "I cannot, however, prevent myself from noticing that it is illogical to live in a great palace and not to have a doorman," overlooking the possibility of a negligent doorman.

Pisani thought the Blue Room was magnificent, but the furniture, though luxurious, was in poor taste." The prince and his royal retinue waited unattended for fifteen minutes and were about to turn around and leave when Seward showed up in a straw hat, uncombed hair, and no tie, "or rather his tie was so narrow that it does not deserve to be mentioned." The prince was reminded of a schoolmaster.

Maurice Sand, an artist taught by Delacroix, son of the novelist George Sand, was one of the prince's companions. When Lincoln ambled in, painfully ill at ease, he was holding white kid gloves, which Sand astutely inferred had never been worn and never would be. Despite his coarse American beard, Sand thought he made a good appearance and was not without grace, but the unforgiving prince thought the president had the bearing of a bootmaker. He was "badly put together," the prince confided to his diary, and comically naive, "an Illinois lawyer after first having been a carpenter, I think."

After Lincoln shook all the French hands, Pisani feared the interview would end right there, for the president simply looked at them. "Mr. Lincoln gained a few more minutes by asking the Prince to sit down and by sitting himself, the whole affair being done with a great moving of chairs." Then they sat and stared at one another, and Pisani could see that the prince enjoyed the cruelty of his silence. Lincoln finally took the risk of speaking of the prince's father and proved himself confused about which Napoleonic brother his guest was the son of. The president's small talk was uninspired. How did his visitors like America? It was very warm. Napoleon spoke excellent English but silently amused himself watching his host suffer. "After ten minutes of this," he wrote in his diary, "I grow bored and leave."

The newspapers announced that Napoleon would dine at the White House that evening. Late that afternoon, enjoying the Marine Band's Saturday concert on the south lawn, Nathaniel Willis, the poet of Mrs. Lincoln's salon, glanced up and noticed the president sitting at his open window and wondered whether he had time to dress for dinner. Despite the sullen heat, he was wearing a gray suit coat, his knees pulled up to his chin, reading documents and listening to the music, apparently unaware that the public could see him. Willis had just pointed him out to friends when he moved to a different chair, had a cloth draped around his neck, and was shaved. As the barber shook the cloth out the window, Lincoln combed his hair, put on a black coat and white tie, and disappeared.

The prince and his people were shown into the Blue Room before the Lincolns came down. As the Marine Band tucked into "Yankee Doodle," the French were shown onto the south portico and displayed to the star-struck crowd. Napoleon's breast was "a flame of decoration," Mrs. Grimsley said, with one hand stuck in his waistcoat. The resemblance to his uncle was strong, and he worked on it, haircut and all. Whether Seward or Lincoln, Nicolay or Hay were behind this bit of theater on the White House stage, it signaled imperial friendship toward a Union freshly whipped at Bull Run.

The French returned to the Blue Room, and the Lincolns came in with their son Bob, down from Harvard for the occasion, joined by Mrs. Grimsley, Nicolay, and Hay. The cabinet soon appeared, along with the French and British ministers, another diplomat or two, some senators, and the doddering General Scott, leaning on the arm of the young celebrity General George McClellan. "History waiting on prophesy," Lincoln remarked to Mrs. Grimsley, "memory upon hope."

Lincoln led the procession into the State Dining Room with Mrs. Grimsley, followed by the prince and Mrs. Lincoln. The French tongue predominated at the table, but according to McClellan, who had studied at the French military academy, he sat beside a diplomat "who labored under the delusion that he spoke our native language with fluency," while the prince spoke English "very much as Frenchmen do in the old English comedies." McClellan no doubt spoke French as comedians did in Paris when impersonating Americans.

Not once but twice, the Marine Band played the "Marseillaise," the revolutionary anthem that the emperor had banned, as Seward knew but the German bandmaster did not. The prince came graciously to the rescue: "Mais oui, je suis Republicain en Amerique!"

General Scott told Lincoln he had dined with every president since Jefferson, and the last should be judged first. To Mrs. Lincoln's sure delight, the prince gave her soiree some self-referential praise. "Paris is not all the world." His diary told a different story. "Mrs. Lincoln was dressed in the French style without any taste. . . . Bad dinner in the French style."

Mrs. Lincoln submitted its cost to the crooked White House gardener John Watt, who billed it to the Interior Department at $900, a year and a half's wage for a White House watchman and a stunning sum of money for a bad French dinner. Even the shady William Wood, Mrs. Lincoln's anointed commissioner of public buildings, refused to endorse the bill. The Secretary of the Interior balked too after discussing it with Seward, who had given the prince the same dinner on the following night, with the same number of guests, provided by the same caterer, for $300. Watt covered the bill with invented purchases of plants and supplies, which Mrs. Lincoln certified.

As her resident poet, Nathaniel Willis, passed the White House soon thereafter, he noticed Willie Lincoln playing with a boy on the sidewalk as Seward drove in with the prince in an open carriage. Seward doffed his hat to Willie "in a mock heroic way," and Napoleon followed suit. Playing along with the game, Willie removed his cap and bowed from the waist to the prince and the Secretary of State. The carriage drove on to the portico, and Willie "went on unconcernedly with his play."

Judge Taft, the neighbor whose children played with the Lincoln boys, found it hard to believe that "within three miles of the City, deadly enemies are ready to cut our throats."

10

THIS DAMNED
OLD HOUSE

On August 9, Nicolay surrendered to poor health and exhaustion and took a short vacation while Hay did both their jobs in the "searing boiling maddening" heat, as William Howard Russell had it. Nicolay's breezy letter from Newport, Rhode Island, rubbed it in on Hay. "Voila l'experience du premier jour! I have listened to a stupefying sermon, taken a refreshing and invigorating bath in the surf, and got an introduction to two pretty young ladies. Altogether I think the pros rather have it."

In less than a week, Hay took a break of sorts too, accompanying his friend Bob Lincoln, his nemesis Mrs. Lincoln, and the prim Mrs. Grimsley to the Jersey shore, leaving Stoddard in charge of the shop with the renovations underway. Hay returned to work when Mrs. Lincoln reinvaded Manhattan, and answered Nicolay's letter. The White House was "a damp oven" with nothing new to tell. "An immense crowd that boreth ever. Painters who make God's air foul to the nostril. Rain, which makes a man moist and adhesive. Dust, which unwholesomely penetrates one's lungs. Washington, which makes one swear."

Lincoln took no vacations. The closest he ever came was a visit to West Point in the summer of 1862 and the occasional excursion to army headquarters in Virginia on the presidential steamer *River Queen*. Urged by a friend to get away and clear his mind, he admitted he needed a rest, but a vacation would do him no good. His burdens traveled with him.

He did enjoy an evening now and then with friends, in his office, the Red Room, or the library. Joining one such casual gathering, an Englishman was stunned by "the terms of perfect equality on which he appeared to be with everybody." The other men occasionally called him "'Mr. President,' but the habit was to address him simply as 'Sir,'" as gentlemen commonly did with one another. The Londoner thought he looked worn and depressed, but for "a sparkle of dry humor about his eye," and he left most of the talking to the others. Seward ribbed him when cigars were lit. "I have always wondered how any man could ever get to be President of the United States with so few vices," Seward told their English visitor. "The President, you know, I regret to say, neither drinks nor smokes." Lincoln called it a doubtful complement and told a story at his own expense about men with no vices having few virtues. The Englishman found the conversation unrestrained in a stranger's presence to a point beyond his understanding.

*   *   *

A committee of the House of Representatives had learned in early August that Mrs. Lincoln's toady William Wood had corrupted himself as commissioner of public buildings. They reported it to the president, who permitted him to resign. On September 7, Lincoln nominated Benjamin French to succeed him.

Lashing back at one accuser, Wood insisted that the gardener John Watt was disloyal to the Union and kept dishonest accounts, which panicked Mrs. Lincoln, his co-conspirator. On a hot September 8, she jumped to Watt's defense in a letter to Secretary of the Interior Caleb Smith:

> I much regret that Mr. Wood still pursues the attack, and tries to bring the charge of dishonesty upon Mr. Watt who in all his accounts with us has been rigidly exact. Circumstances have proved that Mr. Wood is the last man who should bring a charge against any one . . . he is either deranged or drinking.

By way of preemptive defense, Mrs. Lincoln added that Wood might say *anything* "against those who tried to befriend him when he was so undeserving."

She also said that French would vouch for Watt, and told French that day that she was satisfied with his appointment, which he noted in his diary with a hint of foreboding: "I hope and trust she and I will get along quietly." By the end of the month they had made a bad start. He told her in a letter, instead of face to face, that no funds were available to repaper the White House. When the money freed up, he wrote a note on a wallpaper bill: "as selected by Mrs. Lincoln and not by Com. Pub. Bdgs."

On September 9, browbeaten by his wife, Lincoln made Watt a first lieutenant in the 16th U.S. Infantry, an odd appointment for a gardener, who kept, still more oddly, his White House post. The First Lady wrote the Secretary of

War with thanks for Watt's commission but said he preferred cavalry, to be sure he remained on special White House duty. The connection between horsemanship and horticulture was not made clear. Mr. Wood had made false charges against Watt, Mrs. Lincoln said, and she hoped, with palpable anxiety, that the secretary would do what she asked, "this morning."

On his way to the State Department that day, Lincoln walked through the south grounds during a concert, quite unnoticed according to William Howard Russell, and received an unsettling document from Congressman John F. Potter, who chaired the House committee investigating Wood. The committee had been informed, no doubt by Wood, that Lieutenant Watt, the doorkeeper Edward McManus, and the watchman Thomas Stackpole had made disloyal remarks. Tipped off to Watt's strange commission as an officer, the committee thought it stranger still that he had called Jeff Davis the best man in America.

Mrs. Lincoln wrote Congressman Potter, ignoring Stackpole and McManus but shocked to hear Watt called a traitor. The charge, she said, was an invention of Wood, "now proved to be a very bad man, to my own knowledge, who does not know what *truth* means." Watt had "found out much about *him*," and Wood must have supposed that Watt had brought him down.

In the president's office the next day, Lincoln handed Potter's report to French and called Watt in to defend himself. French was inclined to believe Watt's denials. Neither Stackpole nor McManus were questioned, and nothing came of it all.

In times to come, Mrs. Lincoln recommended Stackpole for jobs, helped him start a business, and got him appointed White House Steward. The Superintendent of the Old Capitol Prison claimed that Stackpole used Mrs. Lincoln's influence to get wartime trading permits, which he sold to an arch secessionist, "an idler in good clothes." It was said that when word got back to the president, he blamed his wife's "partial insanity." David Davis, his Supreme Court appointee, had thought Mrs. Lincoln deranged since the 1840s. The judge was convinced she was "a natural born thief"; that "stealing was a sort of insanity" for her.

While their bedrooms were being beautified, the Lincolns stayed in the opulent room overlooking Pennsylvania Avenue where Buchanan had put the Prince of Wales, "the stately guest room," the First Lady called it in a letter to a friend. A woman by he name of Piatt, half of a fashionable couple who had traveled to Washington with the Lincolns for the inauguration, was coming again, and Mrs. Lincoln would receive her upstairs, delighted to show off the family quarters. "I must mount my white cashmere," she wrote. Mrs. Piatt "spoke last winter of the miserably furnished rooms. I think she will be astonished at the change."

*　　*　　*

Nicolay wrote Therena when the heat broke in late September. As if to celebrate, he had spent $24 on a sofa and $18 for six chairs. "It begins to feel a little more as if civilized people could live here—a proposition which seemed to me very doubtful during the summer months." The prospect of living at all was no sure thing. With the president's spyglass, a huge rebel flag could be seen from the White House, flying from Munson's Hill overlooking Bailey's Crossroads.

Frederick Law Olmsted was back in Washington and kept his wife informed: "I just now walked after dinner into the President's grounds where on the lawn the Marine Band (Germans) were playing exquisitely" a duet from a Verdi opera. "It was all very fine" except for some dragoons, "as dirty and as rowdy as you ever saw any laborers after a muddy day in the park." Mrs. Lincoln was on the south portico looking down on the crowd like a queen with "that insufferable beast Wikoff" as if they were a couple. She chatted and nodded with him constantly. "If he had been the king he could not have carried it off better." Wikoff was "the most perfect picture of stupidity and dullness: a great ass and nothing else." To entertain his wife, Olmsted sketched the chevalier in his top hat, muttonchops, and monocle.

In "silvery weather" a few weeks later, Olmsted joined his Sanitary Commission colleagues in Lincoln's office and liked him better, as cognoscenti often did on close inspection.

> He appeared older, more settled (or a man of more character) than I had before thought. He was very awkward and ill at ease in attitude, but spoke readily with a good vocabulary, and with directness and point. Not elegantly, "I heered of that," he said, but it did not seem very wrong with him and his frankness and courageous directness overcame all critical disposition.

To men who saw a classical education as a condition of serious thought, Lincoln showed no interest in hiding his ignorance of dead languages, and repartee with intellectuals who quoted them did not unsettle him. When a British antislavery orator accompanied by American sophisticates sent in their cards, he engaged them in his office on emancipation and the meaning of the Civil War. After one of the Americans turned to the Englishman and recited a

Latin maxim, the president leaned forward in his chair: "*Which*, I suppose you are aware, *I* do not understand." On their way down the hall to the service stairs, which wound through the porter's lodge and let Lincoln move through the house unseen, as he liked to do, he told the Englishman, "Your folks made a rather sad work of this mansion when they came up the Potomac in 1812. Nothing was left of it but the bare walls."

The war was never far from Lincoln's desk, but he never had uniformed aides and learned what he could of the fighting from whoever came to hand. When the six sole survivors of a harrowing special mission were presented to him in his office, he shook all their hands, asked them shrewd questions, and bantered with them by name like a friendly farmer.

*   *   *

Still new as commissioner of public buildings, French told his brother what a plum job it was. It came with a salary of $1,800, and the job he had given up paid $200 more, but he had made his son his messenger at $1,000 a year and enjoyed certain perquisites like bouquets from Mrs. Lincoln and waves of pretty women who tried to flirt him into hiring their relatives. But then there were his interviews with 'The Republican Queen' who plagues me half to death with wants with which it is impossible to comply, for she has a keen eye for the dollars!" In simple recompense there was "honest old Abe who calls me 'French' and always tells me a story when I go to talk with him." When French said the White House basement was home to generations of rodents, Lincoln suggested a ferret, "one of those little fellows that drives away the rats." Better yet, French might distribute teams of ferrets around the departments, "for there are rats everywhere."

In October the East Room was stripped of its carpet and wallpaper under French's oversight. Crated sofas and chairs were unloaded at the Washington depot, hauled down Pennsylvania Avenue in wagons, and stacked in their crates in the halls. Expecting imported fabrics, paper, and carpets, Mrs. Lincoln had the president ask Treasury Secretary Chase to let her orders coming in from Europe go untaxed.

Then came a new run of trouble. French told Secretary of the Interior Caleb Smith that there were insufficient funds to pay William H. Carryl's invoice for the frills Mrs. Lincoln had bought in Philadelphia, and a White House gatekeeper named James Upperman told Smith that Watt, the gardening cavalrymen, had defrauded the public treasury. Naming names, dates, and figures to the penny, Upperman said Watt had authorized payments to a White House cook, coachman, fireman, and laborers for services not rendered and

Benjamin French. Library of Congress.

flowers, manure, and the use of a horse and cart not delivered, all of which presumably ended up in his pocket. Smith broke the news to French and Lincoln, who promised to decide soon what to do.

On a gray October 26, Mrs. Lincoln sent a messenger to Smith with a pitiful plea of mercy, not innocence. Watt had come to her that morning.

> He says he will ever be deeply grateful to you if you would *today* attend to some business, which he says he has spoken to you about. He expresses great friendship and gratitude to you, and if you will *kindly* release him from his present trouble he promises and I *know will keep his word*, that you will not be embarrassed by him again and will be too happy to serve you henceforth in any way. Very sincerely, your friend Mary Lincoln

Smith wrote to Seward the next day. Watt insisted that the disgraced William Wood had jimmied the accounts, Smith said. Watt had told Mrs. Lincoln it was all right and proper, and she had no idea to the contrary. Smith "would be glad to have her relieved from the anxiety under which she is suffering." Duly relieved, she returned to the shops in New York that very day, shadowed by the *Tribune* and the *Herald*.

Smith interviewed Watt, French, and a White House laborer, but not Upperman, and dropped the whole thing. Outraged by the whitewash, Upperman complained to a Senate committee chairman (a member of the president's Republican Party), cited unexamined witnesses by name, and got nowhere. "The thing's a swindle but this is the wife of our President," a Senate *Democrat* said, "the first lady in this land, and we only disgrace ourselves by this exposure."

Lincoln covered the government's losses personally, but word of the scandal got out. William Howard Russell had heard by November that the "Scotch gardener" was by Mrs. Lincoln's influence a U.S. Army Lieutenant attached to the White House "to superintend ye cooking," that the government had been charged for White House servants and charged for them again as if they were "laborers on ye grounds," and that Wood had been cashiered for refusing to charge Napoleon's dinner to Watt's manure account. Some newspapers flattered Mrs. Lincoln shamelessly while others "deal in dark insinuations against her loyalty, Union principles, and honesty." She was loyal to her husband but vulnerable to scheming sycophants "and has permitted her society to be infested by men who would not be received in any respectable private house in New York." The distinguished Boston historian George Bancroft would soon be told that "Madame wished a rogue who had cheated the government made a lieutenant: the cabinet thrice put the subject aside" until the president finally acted on it after Mrs. Lincoln slept in a separate room for three nights straight.

On November 10, Hay wrote to Nicolay, away on a western trip:

> Hell is to pay about Watt's affairs. I think the Tycoon begins to suspect him. I wish he could be struck by lightning. He has got William & Carroll [William H. Carryl] turned off and has his eye peeled for a pop at me because I won't let Madame have our stationary fund. They have gone to New York together.

Mrs. Lincoln's only friend among the secretaries was in a more cheerful mood. All of the new curtains, carpets, and furniture were in, Stoddard said, leaving the house of the chief magistrate no longer out at the elbows. That night, as if in celebration, blue, green, orange, and red fireworks shot up from Blenker's Germans' regimental camp across the river, in sight of the White House windows. Lincoln and Hay watched the Germans pass by in a torch-light parade marking McClellan's appointment as general in chief, the decrepit General Scott having finally shuffled into retirement.

Later that week, on a cold day of fast falling leaves, Lincoln disposed of Watt in a letter to the adjutant general: "Lieut. Watt who, I believe, has been detailed to do service about the White House is not needed for that purpose, and you [should] assign him to his proper place in Regiment." The Senate soon revoked his commission, and Lincoln advised the Treasury Department comptroller:

> [O]nce or twice since I have been in this House, accounts have been presented at your bureau, which were incorrect—I shall be personally and greatly obliged to you if you will carefully scan every account which comes from here; and if in any there shall appear the least semblance wrong, make it known to me directly.

* * *

"There was little gaiety in the Executive house" in Lincoln's day, as Hay would have it. "It was an epoch, if not of gloom, at least of a seriousness too intense to leave room for much mirth." In fact there was plenty of mirth in the wartime White House, and more throughout the city, and the secretaries plunged in. Nicolay called New Year's Day "the arrival of the gay season" until Lent ended most of the gaiety. In a single week in February 1863, he and Hay found time for a White House reception, three other receptions, five parties, three "dancing parties," and two "hops" at Willard's and the National Hotel.

"After that there will be little or nothing going on in the forty days during which pious people are supposed to go 'into the wilderness.'" Among many other invitations, Nicolay saved one from "the young ladies of the 'National'" who asked him to "a private 'Hop' in their drawing room."

In 1864, Lent did not slow Nicolay down: "I think I have been out at something or other every night since its beginning." In 1865 he wrote Therena on February 14: "Hard work and hard party-going together have pretty well used me up so that I feel quite stupid today, and generally disgusted, and dissatisfied with myself and everybody about me."

Mrs. Lincoln welcomed friends to the White House almost every night, and professionals entertained larger gatherings. Essayists, actors, and poets delivered readings, and many singers performed, from an operatic diva to a celebrated Indian maiden to the famous Hutchinson Family Singers. So did comic lecturers and novelty acts. Commodore Foote and his sister the Fairy Queen, two miniature entertainers drawing sellout crowds in the odd current rage for such things, delighted the Lincolns' guests.

Indifferent to the static arts, Lincoln was moved by music. Except for an opera enjoyed in New York and fiddled western fare, he had never heard great music and took every chance to hear it now. The brilliant Marine Band captured him. As they played at a White House levee, he encountered Elizabeth Peabody, a Boston abolitionist, in the Green Room. "Is not that music *beautiful*," he said. Minutes later "Hail to the Chief" stopped him cold. "Oh *is* not that *beautiful*?" Mrs. Peabody thought it "pervaded every fiber" of his being.

After the Lincolns took Tad to a nine-year-old Venezuelan piano prodigy's concert they invited her to play in the Red Room. "I almost forgot to be cranky under the spell of their friendly welcome," she recalled years later, but she remembered soon enough and complained that the stool was unfit, the pedals beyond reach, the action too hard, and the piano too badly tuned to be played. (So did the Hutchinson Singers, who substituted their own melodeon.) Lincoln patted her cheek and persuaded her to play on as her father choked with embarrassment and apologized in broken English until they were out the door.

Stoddard dismissed the critics who condemned "premeditated enjoyment" in a civil war. The occasional White House entertainment, high and low, preserved the mental health of the hosts and guests alike. In November 1861, after a Saturday evening stage performance, the celebrity magician Hermann the Prestidigitator entertained a hundred White House guests. According to William Howard Russell, Hermann drew a "'brilliant throng,' as a collection of rowdies is generally styled by Shaw of the Herald," but Russell's opinion of the First Lady deteriorated during the evening:

Poor Mrs. Lincoln. A more preposterous looking female I never saw. She aped the airs of le monde last night and hid herself behind her gauze curtain, peering out now and then only, and she was clothed in ye royal ermine whilst ye jail bird Wikoff hovered around in attendance.

General Samuel Heintzelman stayed until nearly midnight. Other officers and cabinet ministers mixed with the ladies, according to Benjamin French, who was glad to see Lincoln amused and relaxed. Hermann was generous enough to reduce some tricks to slow motion to show him how they were done, and McClellan deepened his contempt for the man who had just raised him up to the army's highest place: "The most striking feature of the performance," the general informed his diary, "was that the Magician asked the President for his handkerchief—upon which that dignitary replied promptly, 'You've got me now, I ain't got any.'"

On November 28, the Lincolns dined at home with friends on their first White House Thanksgiving, a holiday that Russell had learned was "celebrated by immense drinking and fighting."

On December 7, while Nicolay was writing to Therena, Mrs. Lincoln sent him a message inviting him, Hay, and Stoddard to dinner, "a startling 'change of base' on the part of the lady, and I am at a loss at the moment to explain it." But "as etiquette does not permit anyone on any excuse to decline an invitation to dine with the President, I shall have to make the reconnaissance, and thereby more fully learn the tactics of the enemy."

*   *   *

Less than a month after avoiding culpability for a conspiracy to commit fraud, Mrs. Lincoln was deep in another White House scandal. On December 3, the *New York Herald*, often hostile to the president, published parts of his annual message to Congress, hours before it went to Capitol Hill. Someone had taken it from his very desk and wired it to Manhattan. Suspicion fell on Wikoff, who was known to be close to the *Herald* and had already been brazen enough to send Lincoln a note suggesting he give the *Herald* an advance copy and cheeky enough to write it on White House stationary.

Hauled before a congressional committee on February 10, 1862, Wikoff admitted he had wired part of the message to the *Herald* but would not say how he had gotten it, and was locked up for his chivalry in the Old Capitol Prison. As a reporter named Ben Perley Poore later said that the inference that Mrs. Lincoln had given it to Wikoff was strong and grew stronger when Dan Sickles, the lawyerly member of her salon, turned up as the Chevalier's counsel and "vibrated between Wikoff's place of imprisonment, the White House, and the residence of Mrs. Lincoln's gardener, named Watt."

In the end it was Watt who took the blame. Poore described his story with the derision it deserved. Watt said he had wandered up into the second floor library from his gardening, "being of a literary turn of mind," saw the president's message on a table, picked it up and read it, and "having a tenacious memory," repeated it word for word to Wikoff the next day. For anyone who knew the interplay between Wikoff, Sickles, Watt, and Mrs. Lincoln, it was plain that she had given it to Wikoff, protected by Watt, in a cover story hatched by Sickles.

The congressmen who controlled the investigating committee again let it go, sparking widely accepted rumors that Lincoln had convinced them to spare him disgrace. He never again shared anything with his wife that he did not want the world to know.

*   *   *

On Saturday, December 7, a few days after the scandal broke on the president's stolen message, Benjamin French attended his first of Mrs. Lincoln's receptions as commissioner of public buildings and presented her in the receiving line, a part of the job that he disliked. He would soon like another part less.

A few days later, at Mrs. Lincoln's urgent request, French came to her with a miserable headache and spoke with her in the library. Distraught at having shattered the renovation budget with Carryl's bills—bad news that her husbnad did not yet know—she pleaded with French in tears to tell the president that federal budget overruns were ordinary (as indeed they were), and Congress should be asked to cover this one as it typically covered others. French must not say she had sent him. If he got her out of trouble she would never get in again, and would not spend a cent without him.

Nicolay and Hay had let her steep in her own hot water. French grit his teeth and pulled her out. When he broke the news to Lincoln, who had spent next to nothing on a few bare essentials for his office, the president exploded. It would "stink in the nostrils of the land" for the commander in chief to exceed a $20,000 budget buying "flub dubs for this damned old house" while "poor freezing soldiers" could not have blankets (an allusion to a scandal over shoddy bedding supplied by corrupt contractors).

Lincoln *swore* he would never let the government pay the shortfall. He would pay it first himself. When French denied any involvement with Carryl or his bill, Lincoln rang for Nicolay.

"How did this man Carryl get into this house!"

"I do not know, Sir."

"Who employed him?"

"Mrs. Lincoln, I suppose."

"*Yes*. Mrs. Lincoln. Well I suppose Mrs. Lincoln must bear the blame. Let her bear it. I swear I won't." Did Nicolay have Carryl's bill? Yes he did, and he fetched it. It itemized the First Lady's purchases. The words *elegant* and *rich* predominated.

Lincoln read some of the entries aloud: " 'Elegant, grand carpet, $2,575.' I should like to know where a carpet worth $2,575 can be put."

"Probably in the East Room," French surmised.

"No, that cost $10,000, a monstrous extravagance," Lincoln said. The house was furnished well enough when they moved in, "better than any one *we* ever lived in!" It was wrong to let *one cent* be spent at such a time. Had he not been "overwhelmed with other business" he would never have allowed it. "But what could I do? I could not attend to everything."

French watched him pace and vent and say "many things that I will not undertake to recall." It was "not very pleasant, to be sure, but a portion of it very amusing."

In a violent storm on the day before Christmas Eve, French had a long, dark talk with two senators about "the extravagance at the President's house." One was a founder of the Republican Party, and particularly incensed about it, but in due course the whole thing faded away, along with any notion of Lincoln paying the overage himself. Congress took care of it quietly.

*   *   *

On Christmas night, the Lincolns gave a dinner for old friends and the president's secretaries, and William Howard Russell preserved some impressions of his first American Christmas: "People very gay going to church, boys firing crackers. Cavalry patrols in street, men drunk."

In the meantime, some of the president's friends, led by Matthew Hale Smith of the *Boston Journal*, bore down on the Chevalier Wikoff and unmasked his fraud. The evidence showed that some powerful men in New York had hired him to go to Washington, ingratiate himself with Mrs. Lincoln, collect information upon which they could trade, and help the *Herald* undermine her husband.

Smith took a friendly senator to Lincoln on a February night and said he had something sensitive to say. Lincoln led him to Nicolay's office, asked

Nicolay to excuse them, and locked the door behind him. After showing the president some newspaper clippings about Wikoff that sullied Mrs. Lincoln, Smith described what the chevalier was up to, named his co-conspirators, and said he was downstairs entertaining the president's wife as they spoke. Lincoln asked Smith to wait, took the clippings, and left the room energetically. "The scorpion was driven from the mansion that night."

11

MY PUBLIC
OPINION BATHS

Every president since Washington had been more or less accessible to any prosperous citizen who had a good reason to see him. Even the merely curious might get in with a letter of introduction from an influential friend, but the poor knew better than to ask, and the standards for admission tightened over time. Beginning in Polk's day, callers without appointments signed a register in the porter's lodge, the doorman took their cards, and the president decided whether to admit them. Unless you were rich or powerful, Buchanan was a hard man to see.

Lincoln made himself available to virtually every sane man or woman who came to see him, and some who were not so sane. A doorman once told him that people were on the south lawn, waiting to be admitted. He went to the window and looked. "Turn them in. Turn them in," he said, reminding the doorkeeper of what an old farmer used to say to him: "Tom, pull down the bars and turn in the cows."

While waging a war with existential consequences, Lincoln's staff reckoned he spent three-quarters of his time seeing people, most of whom wanted something, from a daughter of the late John C. Calhoun hoping to visit her son in a prisoner-of-war camp to an enterprising ragman who wanted to follow the Army of the Potomac and pick up its castoff clothes, both of whom got their wish. Endless streams of favor seekers and autograph seekers joined new waves of job seekers as "strolling parties of gaping sightseers peered into the corners and examined their dresses in the mirrors of the parlors and the East Room." Only the family quarters were off limits, and all that kept them sacred was a set of pocket doors. People were known to slide them back and wander down the hall as if they were buying the place.

A Republican senator from Maine sniffed them off as an "ill-bred, ravenous crowd," and friends urged Lincoln to stop indulging them. Determined to see them all, one annoyed supporter said, he excluded or delayed the ones who deserved his time. Senator Henry Wilson of Massachusetts, a former shoemaker and no elitist, chastised him for it. He replied with a sad little smile: "They don't want much and they get but little, and I must see them."

An English author found it "perfectly astonishing." In a chat with a Canadian editor who marveled at it, Lincoln raised its status to a feature of "our form of government, the only link or cord which connects the people with the governing power, and however unprofitable much of it is, it must be kept up." The head of the Sanitary Commission said Lincoln left most of the governing to his cabinet, and focused on what interested him. "He had a notion he was a servant of the people and that he was there to hear their complaints and he spent his time at it."

Throughout the Civil War, the beleaguered commander in chief spent much of his day like a Tammany Hall alderman, meeting his constituents, listening to their complaints, delighting or disappointing them in one-to-ten minute increments, depending on their mission, their attitude, and his mood. People of all descriptions and many states of grooming dropped by to ask a favor, air a grievance, dispense a bit of advice, or simply shake his hand. Hay watched them gather early outside the White House before the doors were opened, hoping "to get the first axe ground," and saw them "put out, grumbling, by the servants who closed the doors at midnight." Lincoln sometimes "had literally to run the gauntlet through the crowds" to have lunch with his wife. How he and his secretaries got anything done at all was a wonder to Hay.

With no guard to stop them, people intercepted him on his way in and out of the White House and lurked along his route to the War Department, thrusting papers in his hands, barking for his attention like beggars in the street. One favor seeker of obscure local prominence badgered him in the vestibule with great proofs that he had put him in office, followed him and Hay to the War Department, making his case as he went, waited until they came out, and walked them back again, chattering all the way. Lincoln turned to him at the door with what Hay called "that smile that was half sadness and half fun."

"So you think you made me President?"

"Yes, Mr. President. Under Providence, I think I did."

" 'Well,' said Lincoln as he opened the door and went in. 'It's a pretty mess you've gotten me into, but I forgive you.' "

Callers high and low—aspiring entrepreneurs, unemployed laborers, Senator Stephen Douglas's pretty widow—expected help and advice on their personal affairs. An impoverished Michigan widow faced with losing her little home to a mortgage of a few hundred dollars brought her four young children to the president by every imaginable conveyance. "In her simple mind," Stoddard said, "she had no doubt of his boundless wealth, or that once he heard her story he would pay off the mortgage." He put his name at the top of a subscription for her relief, which drew the required contributors, and muttered to Stoddard as he signed it. "Children and fools, you know."

The constant strain of seeing suffering he could not relieve and hopes he could not fulfill wore him down, Hay said. He could usually do no good for honest men and women in need, and it burdened him. A Missouri man with a boy in the army asked the president if he could avoid his Confederate brother in battle. A woman who had spent her little means to travel many miles to ask him to discharge her soldier son for no exceptional reason must be heard, he said, even if "I cannot interfere and can only see her and speak kindly to her." His attention to simple folk was extraordinary. When a wire arrived from one John Milderborger of Peru, Indiana—"Can I speak with you if I come? Answer quick."—Lincoln replied the same day: "I cannot comprehend the object of your dispatch. I do not often decline seeing people who call upon me; and probably will see you if you call."

He was more selective with bigger fish, and broke or delayed appointments with powerful men. When a leading senator arrived with two prominent abolitionists, they found themselves in the anteroom with a woman and her child. "She now and then wept but said nothing. The President saw her first, and she came out radiant." The Russian minister wrote home to Saint Petersburg that Lincoln was a good man but the intriguers who had put him in the White House had made it a club and worried the life out of him with demands and complaints until he told the commiserating Russian that his friends afflicted him more than his enemies. When Edward McManus brought important men's cards to him, Lincoln spoke freely about why he would or would not see them, inadvertently educating the cagey Irish doorman about whether he could trifle with them or not.

Stoddard said the President's House lost its charm for many callers when the president was away, delighting his overworked secretaries. "The entire White House, without him in it, is only a shell, a sort of perfunctory headquarters, from which the life has departed, and we and the ghosts have all the eastern wing of it to ourselves." The crowds also shrank when Congress adjourned. Otherwise they filled the place nearly every day but Sunday, when Lincoln's friends came to ask a little favor or bring a cousin whose neighbor's sister needed one.

Almost no one was turned away, but people waited hours for a minute with the president and sometimes days. After being told he was too busy to see them, many lingered anyway, hoping to catch him on the fly. Senators and congressmen waited too, taking his secretaries' time. Like cabinet members, the Republic's second officer was admitted whenever he came, which was not often. Stoddard did not recall "that I ever saw Vice President Hamlin at the White House, though he may have been there a few times for all that." The Speaker of the House came next in priority, then senators, then congressmen, in the order in which they sent in their cards. A dozen or so might be fuming in the anteroom at any one time. "While they waited," one accomplished politician said, they often heard Lincoln's laugh, "in which he was sure to be joined by all *inside*, but which was rather provoking to those *outside*."

The Prussian Louis Burgdorf kept the door to Lincoln's office and did other things too, for $50 a month. Lincoln called him Louis. He had been the White House steward until Buchanan demoted him. Apart from the inescapable Edward McManus, Louis was the only servant who stood out for Stoddard: "German, crusty, pragmatical and pertinacious; proud of his position and authority, and little tolerant of interference; but trustworthy, and, on the whole, capable." In 1863, Lincoln wrote his Treasury Secretary Salmon Chase a note about Burgdorf that implies a certain closeness among the three of them: "Please give Louis, whom you know, an audience of a few minutes." In November 1864, as Lord Lyons and Count Mercier, the British and French ministers, were getting ready to leave, Lincoln did not try to keep them. "Louis Bergdorf had been making secret signs to him through the half open door for the last half hour that Mrs. Lincoln and the children would have cold turkey for their Thanksgiving dinner if he didn't cross over to the other side of the building."

Burgdorf often waved people into Lincoln's office and pointed them to a corner while the president finished with others. One of them said, "I do not think that he knew I was there." Some friends and important men simply walked into other people's meetings. In the very act of being introduced, Lincoln asked a sister-in-law of Nathaniel Hawthorne and Horace Mann to sit to one side as a servant announced another important caller over her shoulder. She waited until the man left. After a pleasant chat, the delivery of a telegram let him ease her out: "You see how it is."

Lincoln developed a tactic to dispose of minor officeholders who came to him for no other reason than to regale their constituents with what they had told the president and the president had told them. "Lincoln would size up such a man in half a minute" and get rid of him just as quickly. Before his visitor had said much of anything, Lincoln would tell a little story, shake the man's hand as they laughed, and turn back to his desk, "and the politician would find himself leaving the White House more than satisfied with his call, which had lasted two minutes instead of two hours."

Even important people shared his time as he did two things at once. Several cabinet members found him with "his head on the back of one chair, his legs resting on another, his collar and cravat on the table," talking with them while he was shaved. When the assistant adjutant general took a ticklish issue to his desk at the end of the day, the president "was seated with his feet on a chair, a towel round his neck, while his servant was shampooing his head." Lincoln told the officer, "Just fix it any way you think best."

Noah Brooks could see how people absorbed in themselves "broke down his courage and his temper" and "exhausted his strength." He spoke of "the great flood gates" that opened on him every day, every man and woman wanting something, resenting the time he wasted on the others. From "the senator seeking a war with France down to a poor woman seeking a place in the Treasury Department they darted at me with thumb and finger, picked out their special piece of my vitality, and carried it off." They left him with a feeling of "*flabbiness*." The only physical change he ever ordered at the White House was the erection, shortly before his second inauguration, of a partition across the south side of his anteroom, denying a window to the waiting herd but creating a passage that let him move between his office and the family quarters unseen.

The *Albany Evening Journal* reviled the "White House bores" who could not be bolted out, driven off, or bluffed. The "Honorable Jonathan Swellhead come all the way from Wisconsin," the Reverend Dr. Blowhard, and the Committee of the Synod of the Seek-No-Further Church had traveled many miles to be heard, and they would not be heard in brief. "They belong to the class of bores who make long speeches." There was "no shaking them off until they have had their say" and abused the patient grace of the President of the United States.

Some only wanted comfort in a terrible time, and that he freely gave. To his pleasure, others only wanted to shake his hand, like a white-haired gentleman who brought his daughter to see and honor him. The very young son of a prominent man came merely to say that "all the boys in my school are for you," and was still telling friends in 1913 how Lincoln told him to grow up to be a good man and a good American. Before making time for a political leader, Lincoln spent half an hour with a mute young woman who spoke with pencil and paper. "That girl had no favor to ask," he told the politician, "but she will live happier all her life because she met the President."

Several evenings a week, friends like Brooks and Browning dropped by for a cup of tea. Sitting with Browning after dinner, Lincoln once rang a servant to bring him a volume of poetry, then sent for another. After an hour and a half, Browning was ready to leave, but the president asked him to stay. A waiting room crowd was "buzzing about the door like bees," he said, ready to strike as soon as Browning left.

Orders to exclude every caller did not apply to Browning, who was not above bringing bees. When he came one night with a bill forming "New Virginia" from the western part of the old one, he brought some friends to meet the president. Other important callers did the same. The novelist Anthony Trollope was told that anyone could walk in and see the president, "but that, I take it, is not considered to be the proper way of doing the work." A distinguished man should be asked to bring him in and introduce him. But "I found that something like a favour would be incurred, or that some disagreeable trouble would be given if I made a request to be presented," which Trollope chose not to do.

Lincoln was not always patient with his visitors. Stoddard said blasts of petulance could erupt from "an overtaxed brain." When a caller asked him to lend his name to a business, Lincoln sprang from his chair and demanded to know if the man took the president for a broker. When a disappointed job seeker called him unjust, he took him by the collar and physically threw him out. When someone told him it would be very easy to do a certain thing, he said, "Oh, I know that, and so it would be 'very easy' for me to open that window and shout down Pennsylvania Avenue, only I don't mean to do it just now." When Browning told him that a supposedly loyal woman who had lost her slaves to the army wanted "a sufficient number of negroes" from the government's pool of escapees to work her farm for wages, he said he would rather throw up. He would rather take a rope and hang himself.

There were times when mere civility was too much. On what must have been a hard day, he turned away a woman whose husband had been imprisoned for disloyal conduct. She told him he would help her if he knew the circumstances. "No I would not," he replied. "I am under no obligation to provide for the wives of disloyal husbands." Then he asked her coldly if her husband had the consumption. She said that he did not. "Well," Lincoln said, "it is the only case. Nearly all have the consumption." Outright cruelty was not beyond him. When two gaunt Irish women in despair begged him to release their imprisoned draft-resisting husbands in Pennsylvania, Lincoln not only denied them but also mocked their brogues.

Perhaps on an easier day, while his old friend Joshua Speed sat watching in his office, he looked weary as two simple women asked him to free another Pennsylvania draft resistor, the son of the one and the husband of the other, one of twenty-seven men already imprisoned for fifteen months. Lincoln had an officer bring in the papers. It was a bad case, the officer said, and a lenient sentence. Staring out the window, speaking as if to himself, Lincoln said "these poor fellows" had suffered enough. "So now, while I have the paper in my hand, I will turn out the flock." The younger woman ran across the room and tried to kneel at his feet. He took her by the elbow. "Get up, get up," he said impatiently. "None of this." When the older one said quietly that they would meet in heaven, he took both of her hands in his and led her kindly to the door.

After they had left, Lincoln drew his chair next to Speed's by the fire. "Speed," he said, "I am a little alarmed about myself; just feel my hand." It was cold and damp. He pulled off his boots and put his feet to the fire. The heat made them steam. Speed said he was overworked. "How much you are mistaken," he replied. "I have made two people happy today. I have given a mother her son and a wife her husband. That young woman is a counterfeit, but the old woman is a true mother."

He sometimes concealed his generosity. When another elderly woman asked him to free her son, a rebel she had sheltered before he was caught, she gave him her word that the boy would have no more to do with the rebellion. "Your word," said Lincoln dryly, "what do I know about your word?" Then he scribbled the order on the back of her application. "Now I want you to understand that I have done this just to get rid of you."

* * *

Lincoln often admitted for an hour or so at a time as many people as his office could reasonably hold, hearing them out in turn, responding in front of the others in a civics lesson of sorts. The Beggars' Opera, he called it. Some of them edged their way to the back of the room, Hay said, "and leaned against the wall, hoping each to be the last, that they might in tete-a-tete unfold their schemes for their own advantage or their neighbor's hurt."

In 1909, half a century after the fact, an observer of one such session published a revealing recollection of a gated railing between Lincoln and his callers that his secretary opened and closed, one petitioner at a time. No such barrier existed, but the memory of the event made it seem as if it did.

Lincoln walked in looking haggard and sat at his desk, his field stubble hair looking as if he had been running his hands through it. A nervous man handed him a document that the president started to read with "short-shanked spectacles" on the end of his nose. He paused and peered deeply into the man's face before he read on. Then he gave him another piercing look, put the paper down, and spoke sharply to him.

"What's the matter with you?"
"Nothing."
"Yes there is. You can't look me in the face. You have not looked me in the face since you sat there. Even now you are looking out that window and cannot look me in the eye." He flung the paper into the man's lap. "Take it back. There is something wrong about this. I will have nothing to do with it."

The rest of the group got a warmer welcome. Lincoln heard them out patiently and granted their favors when he could, always softening a refusal with advice.

A Chicago lawyer who had known him for years got a look at his makeshift hearing room and the testiness that could darken it. Lincoln drew up to the fireplace when the lawyer arrived, put his feet on the andirons, and enjoyed a talk about friends as the doorkeeper handed him cards. Then he had their owners brought in together, retaining his casual pose and asking his friend to do the same.

The first was a local Virginian seeking a pardon for a servant, once his slave, who had stolen $30. In a mellow frame of mind, Lincoln accepted his caller's claim that the thief was "a good fellow" sorely tempted and unlikely to sin again. "I guess we will have to let him out."

The next man changed his mood. He had brought a mirrored device attached to the barrel of a gun that he claimed would let a soldier aim it from a rifle pit without exposing his body. Lincoln watched a demonstration closely—"if your looking glass works, it is a very good thing"—and suggested he take it to the War Department. The man said they had already rejected it, but did not test it fairly. "Well," said the president, his patience suddenly gone, "do you want me to test it?"

"Oh no," the man replied. He wanted the soldiers to do so.

"Ah," said Lincoln, "what you want then is a license to go down to the Army and peddle your looking-glass machine among the soldiers, is it? Good day, Sir."

Halfway to the door, the man turned around. "Mr. President, there is a lady outside here, Mrs. Dr. Walker, who wished me to say to you that she desired to see you."

"Well," replied the president, "you have said it."

Stoddard said the office wing was typically full of anxious men, "generally with mouths full of tobacco" and "not of the first order," and only one or two women, who were treated no more generously than the men, sometimes less so if Lincoln suspected that men had sent them. But some of Stoddard's colleagues were sure that the president was vulnerable to women, especially mothers, and helpless prey for a woman with a child. He once heard a baby cry in the anteroom, had the doorman bring in the mother with her infant, and pardoned her condemned husband on the spot. As she left the office sobbing, prayerful with relief, the doorman said, "Madam, it was the baby that did it." Stoddard said he disliked seeing people, women especially, for whom he had done a favor, "like saving a life for them or that sort of thing."

Kind as Lincoln was, manufactured cheer was not in him. He never told his callers how delighted he was to see them, unless he was, or how good he thought they looked, unless he did. He would come directly to the point: "Well, what can I do for you?" or simply, "Well?"

The scent of government contracts brought a well-dressed swarm of bees, which Lincoln diverted elsewhere. In 1863, he sent Cornelius Vanderbilt Jr., "son of the Commodore," to the quartermaster general of the army. "He comes with a business proposition to you," Lincoln's note said. "Please give him a fair and respectful hearing, and oblige him if consistent with the service."

Like a pretty girl smiling at a sailor, Lincoln could show no interest in any man without risking a proposition. In 1863 he complemented an actor named James Henry Hackett after seeing him play Falstaff and invited him to the White House, where they passed a pleasant evening discussing Shakespeare and Hackett's reminiscences about Sam Houston, Davy Crockett, and other past admirers. The acquaintance had what Hay called the usual sequel. Walking into Lincoln's office one night, Noah Brooks told him that Hackett was in the anteroom. Lincoln sighed. He had hoped the actor had left, he said, for here was an example of the cost of casual friendship in this place. Hackett wanted something, and "What do you suppose he wants?" "Well, he wants to be counsel to London. Oh dear."

Some favor seekers were more artful than others, and some made a living at it. A tall, black-eyed, black-haired lady in black silk had built a reputation as a cultured lobbyist of sorts, gracefully securing pardons and other good things. She would come to the White House with elegant companions simply to show them around, Stoddard said, and "somehow or other her field of operations is made profitable."

*　　*　　*

The seemingly unpardonable waste of the president's time as a court of common pleas had its compensations.

Dispatched to the White House in 1862, an aide to General in Chief of the Army Henry Halleck joined the lawyers, landlords, and laundresses who filled the anteroom. As Halleck's aide arrived, the President of the United States was coaxing out the door an insistent old woman who was not prepared to go. "I am really very sorry, madam, very sorry," he said. "But your own good sense must tell you that I am not here to collect small debts."

After Lincoln showed him in, the astonished young officer was startled enough to say that not one in ten people who came to see Halleck got in. The rest were sent to subordinates and went away content. That was all very well for the military, Lincoln said, but politicians who moved in high circles were inclined to forget that "they only hold power in a representative capacity." The time he spent with "the average of our whole people" was the best-spent time of his day. Whether their requests were frivolous or not, they kept him in touch with the people from whom he came and to whom he must return. He called his little talks with the common man and woman "my public opinion baths." They were not always pleasant "in all their particulars," but they were "renovating and invigorating" as a whole, and they helped him see his duty.

It was not sheer waste, Hay said. Lincoln learned something from most visitors, and they sometimes raised his morale, especially with tales of military heroism, which he often absorbed like a child. He learned a great deal from office-seeking insiders, promotion-seeking officers, and experts of all kinds. Many went away surprised that they had given him more than they took. He often asked, "What are people talking about?" In an age without polls, even their prejudices informed him.

He also understood that he endeared himself politically to the family and friends of his visitors throughout the North who would soon shake the hand that shook the hand of the President of the United States.

*　　*　　*

Lincoln welcomed clergymen who came to his office to counsel, exhort, admonish, or rebuke him, all of which he patiently let them do. "The latch string is out," he told Ward Hill Lamon, "and they have the right to come here and preach to me if they will go about it with some gentleness and moderation."

Except for the ones who assured him that God was on the Union's side of the killing, a presumption he found ungodly, he treated them all respectfully, Quakers in particular. There were Quakers in his ancestry, and Stoddard thought he was drawn to them by a commonly held misimpression that they were unusually honest and "his strong sense of the humorous and appreciation of the quaint and odd," which they seemed to share. "Going into his room this morning to announce the Secretary of War," Nicolay said, "I found a little party of Quakers holding a prayer meeting around him, and he was compelled to bear the infliction until the 'spirit' moved them to stop."

From a Committee of the General Synod of the Evangelical Lutheran Church to the self-described spokesmen for the Israelites of New York, religious delegations surrounded him and read their resolutions on almost every issue, from abolition to the uneven observance of the Sabbath in the military, to God's plan for suppressing the rebellion. Nicolay thought it odd that so many bright people had so little common sense. Lincoln endured it like a saint. After a spokesman for the Presbyterian General Assembly read long resolutions that must have been tedious beyond belief, he said that they encouraged him. When a clergyman came alone to his office one day, Lincoln shook his hand, offered him a seat, assumed a patient air, and finally said he was ready to listen. "Oh bless you, sir," the pastor replied. "I have nothing special to say." He had only called to pay his respects. Lincoln stood up and grasped both of the minister's hands. "I am very glad to see you indeed. I thought you had come to preach to me!"

He often welcomed secular delegations like the one from the National Academy of Sciences, which he had signed into existence. On the morning of March 13, 1862, a Massachusetts whip manufacturer's representatives arrived to present him an ivory-handled, gold-banded whip and invited a knot of tourists to join them, no doubt because Nathaniel Hawthorne and another well-known writer were among them.

To Hawthorne's amusement, random citizens lounging about the White House attached themselves uninvited to the hybrid set of whip makers and wordsmiths and were ushered with them into the anteroom, where another eclectic assortment latched on, some in workmen's clothes. When the president sent word that he was late at breakfast, his visitors were shown to his office, where the secretaries of War and the Treasury were waiting too. By then, Hawthorne wrote, "we formed a very miscellaneous collection of people, mostly unknown to each other, and without any common sponsor, but all with an equal right to look our head servant in the face."

Lincoln ambled in and greeted the whip makers' congressman, who must have been pleased to show them that the president knew him, as Lincoln surely knew he would be. With "a comical twist of his face," Lincoln joked about his breakfast and shook hands all around. If he gave the international literary celebrity any more or less attention than the rest, Hawthorne did not record it. Even for the author of *The Scarlet Letter*, there was "no describing his lengthy awkwardness, nor the uncouthness of his movement," which seemed somehow familiar, "as if I had been in the habit of seeing him daily, and had shaken hands with him a thousand times in some village street." He was dressed in shabby slippers, an old frock coat, and unbrushed matching pants, "worn so faithfully" that the suit had become a second skin. He looked as if he had just gotten out of bed. Free of any pretense, he "had a kind of natural dignity quite sufficient to keep the forwardest of us from clapping him on the shoulder and asking for a story."

The commemorative whip was presented with remarks that Hawthorne found "shorter than the whip, but equally well made," something about using it on the rebels. Lincoln accepted it as a tool of peace, and his visitors left delighted, only regretting that they had not seen him fold his legs, "which is said to be a most extraordinary spectacle," or heard one of his stories that "would not always bear repetition in a drawing room, or on the immaculate page of the *Atlantic*." Indeed the *Atlantic* thought Hawthorne's tale insufficiently immaculate to print, and purged the best parts.

Lincoln saw small delegations like the whip makers in his office, letting them fan out around him. Bigger groups were received in the East Room and often comprised "a deputation asking an impossibility or a committee demanding an impertinence." One Sunday evening, Lincoln greeted some Boston abolitionists led by Wendell Phillips, who had publically called him "a first-rate second-rate man." New Englanders with a cause were not known for their humor, and Lincoln entered laughing. That morning, he said, his sons had let him know that the cat had produced kittens and the dog had delivered pups, "so the White House was in a prolific state," which failed to charm the Bostonians. "The hilarity disturbed us," one of them later said, but their Puritan glares quickly softened, for "it was pathetic to see the change in the President's face when he resumed his burden."

When a large group of men and women promoting blue laws against alcohol called on Lincoln, Hay said they "filed into the East Room looking blue and thin in the keen autumnal air." Hay's coachman, "about half tight," looked them over with "complacent contempt and mild wonder." Lincoln endured three "blue-skinned damsels" impersonating Love, Purity, and Fidelity, and an orator who insisted that the army drank so much whiskey as to bring down the curse of the Lord on the Union forces. If such a curse there was, Lincoln said, he thought it was unfair, "as the rebels drink more and worse whiskey than we do."

Later that month, Senator Jim Lane, who had led the Frontier Guard in the dark days of April 1861, returned with seventy rough Republicans from Missouri and Kansas, most of them steeped in mob violence and not happy with their president. When the doormen barred the press on the prescient orders of Lincoln or his staff, a newspaperman let the doorman Edward McManus know he was speaking to an editor. "Oh yes," Edward said. "Editors, of all persons," were not to be admitted.

Lane's angry men fanned out along three sides of the East Room, more remarkable for their grit than their intelligence in the opinion of John Hay, who sized them up as an "ill combed, black broadcloth, dusty, longhaired and generally vulgar assemblage of earnest men." Lincoln gave them more than two unpleasant hours. After their spokesman read a bill of particulars, the president replied politely without a hint of cringe. They peppered him with questions, complaints, and demands, marginally respectful at best, which he cut down one by one. They did not leave happy, but they left. Hay seems to have wondered if they would.

12

BRIGHT JEWELS AND BRIGHT EYES

F our bands of music gave a White House serenade on the war's first New Year's Eve, a prelude to the open house that every president since Jefferson had hosted on New Year's Day. No exception was made for the war, another demonstration of normality.

On the warm New Year's morning of 1862, thousands of eager citizens in their best winter clothes lined Pennsylvania Avenue and enjoyed an annual ritual, cheering the procession of dignitaries who came to greet the president. Arriving under a portico unusually bright with flags and two coats of fresh white paint, the cabinet were admitted first with their elegant wives and guests, followed by the diplomatic corps with their emerald stars, scarlet ribbons, and gold lace. Next came the sober Supreme Court, then scores of brilliant officers in brass-buttoned dress-blue uniforms and gold-braided epaulets. After taking Lincoln's hand in the Blue Room, almost all of them fled the house ahead of the public crush that the mansion had been fortified to receive.

According to the *New York Times*, the splendid new carpets were "neatly covered with a tasteful cloth to protect them from injury," and the circular sofa in the center of the Blue Room was replaced with President Tyler's formidable marble table, a sort of Alamo behind which the Lincolns could retreat to hold off the crush. When the gates were opened at noon, the public rushed the portico "like a mob bent on plunder." Once inside, they abruptly turned respectful, passing into the Blue Room through a double line formed by the Metropolitan Police in their blue coats and caps, for the first time in White House history.

To old Washingtonians, the crowd was full of new faces, some of them known to the police, who extracted thieves and prostitutes when they could. Orville Browning had his pocket picked nonetheless.

As the Marine Band played in the vestibule, a New Year's Day tradition, Nicolay and Lamon presented the sovereigns to the president, who kept them moving. Only family, friends, and guests could linger in the Blue Room. Attended by Stoddard and some friends, Mrs. Lincoln nodded and smiled and only gave her hand to senior officials and the ignorant common citizens who did not know better than to offer her theirs. Dressed in beaded buckskin, Kit Carson's successor as New Mexico's Indian Agent gave her a striking blanket figured in red, white, and blue, five months' work for a Navaho woman. After passing through the line, people left on a carpeted ramp pushed out through a floor-to-ceiling window.

That night, the president gave the traditional White House dinner for the cabinet, the Supreme Court, the diplomatic corps, and special friends on Capitol Hill. Indulging a bit of vanity, Nicolay sent Therena *Frank Leslie's Illustrated Newspaper*'s woodcut of Lincoln shaking hands at the reception, "in which you will discover accurate and elaborate portraits of John and myself." He mistook it for *Harper's Weekly*.

*   *   *

Having made a showplace of a third-class hotel, Mrs. Lincoln was eager to show it off, especially to the doyennes who tittered behind her back. At his own expense, the president was expected to give costly state dinners during the winter, but his wife overcame his reverence for precedent and convinced him that a series of receptions for invited guests would be cheaper and more democratic than "stupid state dinners," for which, not incidentally, Seward and Nicolay controlled the guest lists.

Her husband accepted her plan, and she staged what came to be known as the Grand White House Party of 1862. Washington had seen nothing like it. Seward's State Department had advised the president that parties, if given at all, must be informal or "accidental." Mrs. Lincoln's was neither, with predictable results. "La Reine," said Nicolay to Therena, had accomplished what Seward had feared. "Half the city is jubilant at being invited, while the other half is furious at being left out in the cold." According to a Washington socialite, it "increased her personal unpopularity to an intense degree."

Social climbers lusted for "free tickets to 'the Greatest Show on earth,'" Stoddard said, and hundreds left unsatisfied were bright with jealous rage. Great Northern newspapermen begged invitations from Nicolay and Hay, who gave Stoddard the job of saying no, "perhaps because it was disagreeable and I was young."

Nicolay called in Stoddard as Mrs. Lincoln was about to give invitations to two of her pet New Yorkers who were waiting downstairs with reporters from the *Herald* and the *Spirit of the Times*, both of them hostile to Lincoln and eager to come to his party. The tickets were in Nicolay's hand. He did not want to give them up and could not convince Mrs. Lincoln to withhold them. Stoddard would have to work on her. Here was an example of how "all the ugly part of it fell on me," Stoddard thought. He took the tickets to the Red Room, where Mrs. Lincoln and her sycophants were smiling, and asked to speak to her alone. He let her see his anger and told her that the men she was about to reward had been abusing her and her husband as if they were pickpockets. "They can't have the invitations."

"Of course they can't," she said. She walked back and told them that Mr. Stoddard had "absolute charge of this business. I am sorry, of course, but I must abide by his decision." Stoddard had an "interesting little mill" with them in the vestibule, but Mrs. Lincoln "never really went back on me," as he later recalled, "and was wide awake to any attack upon her husband." Nicolay and Hay were stunned by his little victory.

*   *   *

On Sunday, February 2, Mrs. Lincoln was preparing for her party on a bright, bracing day with the snowy streets in awful shape when Senator Sumner took Ralph Waldo Emerson to the White House. Willie and Tad were in Lincoln's office, and a barber was cutting their hair, which he "whiskeyed" when he was done, getting it in their eyes. Willie said Seward could never guess what the boys had been given. Seward bet a quarter that he could. A rabbit? A bird? A pig? They told him he was wrong, and he handed Tad the quarter before Willie said a rabbit it was. According to Emerson's journal, Willie sent "a mulatto" to find the president, and the boys disappeared.

Emerson formed a better impression of Lincoln than he had hoped, frank and plain spoken, with a lawyerly mind, "correct enough, not vulgar, as described, but with a sort of boyish cheerfulness" of the storytelling kind one enjoyed at a Harvard reunion. Kentucky bred as he was, Lincoln said he had once heard Emerson suggest in a lecture that "a Kentuckian's air and manners seem to say, 'Here I am; if you don't like me, the worse for you.'" Emerson liked his style. "When he has made his remark, he looks up at you with great satisfaction, and shows all his white teeth and laughs."

As Lincoln and Sumner discussed a Maine sea captain named Gordon, Emerson could see that the president was a match for the senator, who wanted Gordon executed for his conviction as an African slave trader. Lincoln said he was not yet satisfied and would look at the evidence again. For Emerson, his gravity was a pleasant surprise.

Lincoln let Gordon hang, with a two-week stay to prepare himself. "In granting this respite," his order read, "it becomes my painful duty to admonish the prisoner that, relinquishing all expectation of pardon by Human Authority, he refer himself alone to the mercy of the common God and Father of all men."

* * *

On Wednesday, February 5, Mrs. Lincoln's fabulous party made history, and the slush kept no one away. Young boys "anxious to gain a penny" kept the neighborhood sidewalks clear. At thirty years of age, Theodore Roosevelt Sr., a friend of Hay's and the father of a three-year-old boy, was flattered to be there. "I find that but six men under fifty are invited," he told his wife, and no general less important than a division commander. Roosevelt's only complaint was the swarm of police, who kept gawkers off the portico as the guests came in.

The cabinet was there, and so were Bob Lincoln, many generals, senators and congressmen, almost every diplomat in town, Cyrus McCormick of the revolutionary reaper, and scores of "dazzling beauties," according to a rapturous newspaperman, including Kate Chase, who had even caught Emerson's eye. One reporter said Ms. Chase was "tastefully attired in a mauve silk," another that she made her entrance "bewitchingly in white silk." No doubt they inspected Miss Chase more closely than the color of her dress. An older, less bewitching lady had forgotten to rouge one side of her face.

The affair was rigidly formal, Stoddard said, and although it was called a ball there was no dancing, which Lincoln had vetoed as a concession to civil war. Unlike the plan Mrs. Lincoln had sold her husband, there was nothing democratic about it and nothing cheap. The guests showed their invitations at the door and were led to the second floor, where coats and hats were checked and bedrooms were opened as dressing rooms for the women, a thoughtful way to show them off. The gentlemen took the ladies down the ceremonial staircase in "the height of fashionable extravagance." Some women from small towns were said to be disappointed by the men in funereal black suits but consoled by a dozen uniformed generals and the plumed diplomatic corps. McClellan struck heroic poses flanked by his glamorous French aides, the comte de Paris and his brother the duc de Chartres. The Marine Band played opera in the hall.

The president wore a black suit and a pleased if uncertain expression. His wife made her entrance with flowers woven into her hair, an expensive array of pearl jewelry, and a low-neck white satin gown trimmed with black-and-white ribbon and black lace, half mourning for Queen Victoria's Prince Albert. Apparently ignorant of the latest fashion, Oregon's senator James Nesmith wrote his wife the next day that the "weak-minded Mrs. Lincoln had her bosom on exhibition and a flowerpot on her head."

Lincoln greeted his guests near the center of the newly finished East Room, which the *Chronicle* judged "in exquisite taste, with a monster carpet, equal in beauty to ancient tapestry." Woven in velvet in a single piece, the carpet was 100 feet long and 48 feet wide. Mr. Carryl of Philadelphia had designed it himself and supervised its weaving in Glasgow on the only loom in the world that was big enough to produce it. One smitten critic compared its figures and colors—"the most ornate and beautiful surprises of vases, wreaths, and bouquets of flowers and fruit pieces"—to the night sky, "where the beauty of one star is lost in the combined grandeur of the whole." Its background of pale sea green put another admirer in mind of transparent ocean waves "tossing roses at your feet."

The East Room's huge mirrors reflected "the gay and varied crowds who filled it—jewels in a rich casket." The parlors were bright with the conservatory's bounty of fragrant evergreens, exotic plants, and exquisite bouquets. Several young couples were spotted in the Red Room, "oblivious of all that was transpiring around them."

At eleven o'clock, the party was just getting started as the Lincolns promenaded ceremoniously through the parlors, a kaleidoscope of "bright jewels and bright eyes." The elegant Blue Room had required no renovations, except for a new rug, but fresh carpeting, curtains, and paper had much improved the Green Room. Everything in the Red Room was new, but for Gilbert Stuart's full-length portrait of Washington, saved by Dolley Madison when the British burned the place in 1814. Senator Browning's daughter was on the president's arm, Mrs. Lincoln on the senator's. Stoddard took a ribbing from Seward for his "awful international blunder" of leading the Secretary of State and the diplomatic corps through the wrong door into the vestibule.

New York's society caterer Henri Maillard set a storybook supper in the State Dining Room, whose doors were thrown open at eleven to a dazzling display. Monroe's silver mirror ran the length of the table past a magnificent candelabra; enormous vases of flowers fresh cut in winter; a pair of cornucopias on a shell held up by mermaids under a crystal star; kneeling cupids spreading a chain of flowers; confectionary displays of a ship under sail, an ancient warrior's helmet, Jackson's mansion, and a pagoda; a cake and sugar fort filled with candied quails; a basket of tropical fruits on a pedestal supported by swans; the goddess of liberty over "a simple but elegant shrine"; a four-bowl fountain held by water nymphs; and "twenty or thirty ornaments of cake and candy delicately conceived and exquisitely executed."

The buffet included oysters, pate de foie gras, aspic of torgal, patti giblets a-la-enaisanz, canvass back ducks, filet de boeuf, stuffed turkey with truffles, partridges and quails, charlotte-russe a-la-paisienne, fruit glace, orange glace, biscuit glace, competes, bon bons, and "fancy cakes." Neither the reporters nor their readers knew what half of it was or how it was pronounced, but all of it flashed by telegraph to a nation whose sons lived in mud and ate hardtack. Putting it far too lightly, Stoddard later said there were "murmurs of impropriety" over news about public servants feasting and preening in the President's House as they ran a catastrophic civil war. Even more would have murmured, he said, if the Lincolns had let the winter pass without improving the capital's social life, a thin rationalization at best.

The leading guests promenaded in the East Room after dinner, and the fun went on until three. As the Marine Band closed with "The Girl I Left Behind Me," it occurred to at least one guest that many a fine young man had enjoyed his last romance. Nicolay called the evening "a very respectable if not a brilliant success," but distasteful nonetheless. "A lamentable spirit of flunkeyism pervades all the higher classes of society," he told Therena, who "worship power and position" and covet "social honors and recognitions," and "their vanity has been tickled with the thought that they have attained something which others have not."

Unbeknownst to the guests, "by way of an interesting *finale*," two servants "much moved by wrath and wine, had a jolly little knock-down in the kitchen, damaging in its effects to sundry heads and champagne bottles. This last is strictly entre nous."

*　　*　　*

While the guests enjoyed the party, Willie Lincoln was ill upstairs. He had suddenly gone feverish on the day of Emerson's visit, almost surely from drinking water piped in from the Potomac. Mrs. Lincoln's friend and dressmaker Elizabeth Keckly nursed him at his bedside, assisted by the aged White House servant Mary Dines, who drafted letters for her fellow escaped slaves at their Seventh Street camp. "Poor old Aunt Mary," Lincoln called her. Mrs. Lincoln wanted to cancel the party but the president thought not, after the White House physician assured them that Willie was improving. He turned much worse as the guests arrived.

Dr. Stone was called for again and again and saw no cause for alarm, but Mrs. Keckley watched Willie grow "more shadowlike," and childhood shadows were often fatal. Mrs. Lincoln slipped away repeatedly from the party to hold his hand and worry, her triumph turned into a nightmare. The music wafted up to Mrs. Keckley "in soft, subdued murmurs, like the wild, faint sobbing of far off spirits."

Willie survived the night but did not improve. Days passed, Stoddard said, and the shadow took over the house, while "some who understood its meaning went about as if they did not wish to make a noise in walking." Nicolay said fear for Willie's life consumed his father's mind until Tad went feverish too and was brought into the sickroom. Attorney General Bates found the president exhausted by worry, pacing the room as his little boys fought for their lives, escaping to his office and coming back again.

The scandal over Wikoff's theft of the president's message to Congress erupted during the deathwatch. So did widespread outrage over "the recent brilliant *fete* at the White House," as the *Sunday Mercury* called it. Mrs. Lincoln complained with good cause that the same social avatars who had urged her to take "that heartless step," as she quickly came to see it, condemned her for it now. "I have had evil counselors."

Benjamin French thought the party had been magnificent, "and the President will pay for it *out of his own purse*," but hostile newspapers ripped the Lincolns for dreadful taste and judgment. A Cincinnati paper thought "the condition of the nation too humiliating to inaugurate a carnival at the Government mansion." Others published "The Lady President's Ball," a poem passed around by wire about White House revelers nibbling delicacies while a dying soldier chokes on sickening broth. The uproar was not confined to Democrats. The scandalized Republicans included a Massachusetts congressman: "With equal propriety might a man make a ball with a corpse in his house."

The outrage was not unanimous. Mrs. Lincoln's friends at the *Herald* commended her for restoring the White House and excluding from her splendid soiree the "swarm of long haired, tobacco chewing and tobacco spitting abolitionists, whose presence, both physically and morally, was contamination."

On February 20, just after 5 p.m., Nicolay was dozing on his sofa when the president walked in. "Well Nicolay, my boy is gone, he is actually gone," he said, then burst into tears and fled to his office.

His wife was convulsed for weeks, in bed in the care of friends, convinced that God had punished her for the sin of vanity. Her sister Elizabeth came from Springfield. The Lincolns sent their carriage for Senator and Mrs. Browning, who stayed a week. Dorothea Dix, the head of the army nursing corps, sent a nurse named Rebecca Pomeroy to care for Tad, who was still in danger. Lincoln called Mrs. Pomeroy one of the best women he ever knew. Scores of wounded boys made do without her.

The White House was draped in black, "contrasting strangely with the gay and brilliant colors of a few days before." Willie was laid out in the Green Room with a storm beating at the windows. After the Lincolns had taken their leave of him (Mrs. Lincoln never entered the room again), the servants came in and cried. Faced with the president's suffering, cabinet members, diplomats, and generals fought for composure at the funeral in the East Room. Mrs. Lincoln could not bear to come.

Lincoln hovered over Tad, who was not declared safe for days. The president shut himself off on Thursday, a week after Willie's death, and again on the Thursday after that. His office was closed for weeks. After he started doing business again, he put on his marble mantel a picture that Willie had painted of an Illinois landscape. He was said to show it to visitors "pathetically." After Tad recovered, he kept him at his side almost constantly, and coped.

* * *

Mrs. Lincoln could not. Three months after the funeral she told a friend, "I can scarcely command myself to write." There were no White House social events for the rest of 1862, and the First Lady wore black until 1864. The White House was like a tomb, she said, and it pained her to be in it. But even her friend Noah Brooks understood that "the black shadows rested on many another American home," and her unremitting grief was considered unseemly. A socialite who despised her said she mourned "according to her nature." Instead of being drawn to other mothers weeping over sons, or led to minister to them, "She shut herself in with her grief, and demanded of God why he had afflicted *her*! Nobody suffered as she suffered. The Nation's House wore a pall, at last, not for its tens of thousands of brave sons slain, but for the President's child."

While Willie's death was still a fresh wound, a congressman called on Lincoln with two colleagues and found him dignified and cordial in his grief. "The rain poured down in torrents," the congressman told his wife, "and the wind wailed around a sorrowful mansion." While waiting in the anteroom, the congressman had noticed incredulously that someone had drawn whiskers on a white marble bust of a Secretary of State from a clean-shaven era.

"The little fellow that is gone did that," the doorkeeper said. "He got up on a chair and said, 'what was a man as had no whiskers?' "

*   *   *

A few weeks after Willie died, the corrupt White House gardener John Watt came to Lincoln's friend Orville Browning with the watchman Thomas Stackpole and asked him to find Watt a different federal garden to till. Then Stackpole returned alone. Watt was a bad influence on Mrs. Lincoln, he said, and ought to be sent far away. Unless "a new leaf turned over at the White House," he said, apparently intending no pun, "the family there would all be disgraced."

Stackpole said Watt had told the First Lady how to pay private expenses with public money, and helped her do it. Eventually, it had been necessary to tell the president, who was "very indignant" (putting it mildly) and repaid what had been filched. Watt's wife was White House stewardess in name only, Stackpole said. Mrs. Lincoln took her $1,200 salary, bought silver plate for herself, charged it to the government for repairing White House plate, and told her husband it was a gift. It was she, not Watt, who gave Lincoln's congressional message to Wikoff. She continued to meet Wikoff in the White House, arranged by Watt, after Lincoln barred him. "He told me many other things which were painful to hear," Browning told his diary, "which will result in the disgrace of the family at the White House, unless they are corrected."

Less than a year later, Watt approached the editor of the *New York World* and proposed, for a consideration, to expose Mrs. Lincoln's corruption and swear that her relations with certain men were indecently improper. He said he could produce a letter from her on concealment of their schemes. The editor told the paper's owner that "Watt is a low fellow" but "shrewd and smart and thinks that he ought to be well paid for his document, to which he will make oath."

*   *   *

By the end of March, a month after Willie's death, the president had recovered his poise, Tad had begun to run around again, and Benjamin French had a talk with the Lincolns as commissioner of public buildings. In a rather cryptic letter, French told his brother that part of the interview was funny, but the president looked careworn and Mrs. Lincoln wept:

> I shall try to do my duty to both, *if I can*, but it is a task. The President is the very soul of honesty, honor and openness of heart. Mrs. Lincoln is—Mrs. Lincoln and nobody else and like no other human being I ever saw. She is not easy to get along with though I succeed pretty well with her. If I ever see you again I

will amuse you with my yesterday's experience. I dare not put it on paper even
to you.

In a letter to Nicolay, who was in Kentucky, Hay showed Mrs. Lincoln no
sympathy, despite the loss of her child: "The enemy is still planning a campaign in quiet. She is rapidly being reinforced from Springfield. A dozen
Todds of the Edwards breed in the house."

Sure enough, a few days later, Hay informed Nicolay that Mrs. Watt had
suddenly quit as White House stewardess and Mrs. Lincoln had pressed him
for the salary. "I told her to kiss mine," an indelicate translation of what must
have been a slightly more polite refusal. Hay wrote to Nicolay again the next
day. Mrs. Lincoln's friend Stackpole had come to him with a scheme involving
her animal fodder budget:

> The devil is abroad, having great wrath. His daughter, the Hell Cat, sent Stack-
> pole to blackguard me about the feed of her horses. She is in "a state of mind"
> about the steward's salary. There is no steward. Mrs. Watt has gone off and there
> is no *locum tenens* [no stand-in]. She thinks she will blackguard your angelic
> representative into giving it to her, which I don't think she'll do it, Hallelujah!

Hay's aunt, Mrs. Milton Hay, a figure to be reckoned with in Springfield,
was visiting him at the White House. When she called on Mrs. Lincoln, a
servant said the First Lady "was in one of her moods and would not see
anyone." Hay wrote again to Nicolay: "Things go on here about as usual.
There is no fun at all. The Hellcat is getting more Hellcattical day by day."

*   *   *

After Willie died, Tad was even more the mansion's "chartered libertine," as
Hay would call him, indulged in every way. He knew what an office seeker
was and would ask them what they wanted, how long they had been waiting,
and how long they proposed to stay. The "noisome horde" fawned on him,
Hay said, hoping for some advantage, but were treated with cool contempt
and turned into his "grinning servants and toadies." Tad stood at the foot of
the stairs and charged them a nickel to climb it "for the benefit of the Sanitary
Fund" until the staff put a stop to it. He bought a sidewalk gingerbread woman's inventory, marked it up under the portico on a board over two sawhorses,
and pocketed the job seekers' change.

Glad as he was to exploit the White House jackals, Tad was kind to the
powerless. He often petitioned his father for some widow or pitiful private
he found in the anterooms, Hay said, "dragging his shabby protégés into

the Executive presence, ordering the ushers out of the way, and demanding immediate action from headquarters." According to Hay, Tad's interventions were not so frequent as to lose their charm, and his father rarely denied his pleas for the underclass. The secretaries called them Tad's clients. One day he brought some ragged street children to the kitchen to be fed, and the steward turned them away. The White House was government property, not a charitable institution. Tad appealed to his father, who agreed that "the kitchen is ours."

On the Monday after Easter, neighbor children rich and poor rolled colored eggs down the sloping south lawn. One of the president's chairs was set out to make it easy for Lame Tommy, one of Tad's less fortunate friends. A contestant recalled in old age that there were "always plenty of little Negroes" to eat the eggs that broke.

Tad liked honest work. Lincoln once asked the chief engineer of the Washington fire engine *Hibernia* to pump water from a White House well, "which Tad will show." When a group of distinguished callers left the president's office and found a boy on the portico helping workmen put up scaffolding, they shook his hand and asked his name. "Tom," he replied, a grownup name for an aspiring grownup.

13

NOT AN AMERICAN
CRIME

O n Friday, April 11, 1862, Congress passed a bill abolishing slavery in the
District of Columbia. On the following Monday night, Bishop Daniel
Alexander Payne of the African Methodist Episcopal Church presented his
card at the White House. He had come to urge the president to sign the bill
and could not have known how he would be received. No one had heard of a
black man in such a place for such a reason. Lincoln greeted him in his office,
gave him a seat by the fire, and warmly introduced him to two friends, Carl
Schurz, his just returned minister to Spain, and Elihu Washburne, a powerful
Illinois congressman.

After Payne made his case for the bill, Lincoln said some gentlemen had
urged him to veto it that very day. He evoked divine guidance and did not
commit himself. Two days later he signed the bill.

It was a groundbreaking move to take counsel from a black man in the
White House, but Lincoln had welcomed Payne as if it were an ordinary
thing. The bishop had led his denomination in Washington for years but had
been to the President's House only once before. The slaveholding President
Tyler had treated him coldly when he preached at the funeral of Tyler's valet,
but Lincoln had received him "as though I had been one of his intimate
acquaintances," Payne said, "or one of his friendly neighbors."

On the morning of May 4, Hay went riding with Nicolay. The redbuds
were in bloom on the White House grounds, and the foliage had "that fresh
and yellowish-green tint that makes a spring landscape so bright," but spring
ran afoul of Mrs. Lincoln. Later that month, three months after Willie's death,
Hay wrote her a note, the preferred form of Hellcattical communication,
knowing she had decreed a year of mourning. The Secretary of the Navy
wanted to know if she objected to the Marine Band playing on the south lawn.

If not, they would start the next day. The concerts were a long tradition and provided some relief from the war, and Mrs. Lincoln replied immediately, deploying the royal we: "It is our *especial* desire that the Band does not play in these grounds this summer. We expect our wishes to be complied with."

Hay tried a fallback position: "I communicated your answer to the Secretary of the Navy, Gideon Welles. He says he will be governed in the matter by your wishes. He requests me to ascertain whether you have any objection to the Band playing in Lafayette Square."

"It is hard that in this time of sorrow, we should be thus harassed," Mrs. Lincoln replied. "The music in Lafayette Square would sound quite as plainly here. For this reason, at least, our feelings should be respected." And they were.

Twelve months later, after hundreds of thousands of mothers had lost their sons, the First Lady insisted on stopping the music for yet another year to mourn hers. Welles said the people should not be denied again, and delicately advised the president not to turn a private sorrow into a public deprivation. Lincoln said his wife insisted on it, at least through the Fourth of July, though the concerts might be staged in Lafayette Square. In the end, Welles said, the President told him to use his own judgment.

The concerts resumed on June 13 in Lafayette Square. Three days later, Mrs. Lincoln returned from a shopping trip to Philadelphia, which did not interfere with her mourning, and requested from Welles for a friend "the small appointment of assistant Paymaster in the Navy. . . . I am sure you will not refuse me this trifling courtesy."

On June 21, as commissioner of public buildings, Benjamin French signed an invoice for Irish linens and the like, bought by Mrs. Lincoln, and noted on its face that he had authorized their purchase after she assured him "they were absolutely necessary."

*   *   *

On Independence Day 1862, some veterans of the War of 1812 made an old men's march across town to the White House, where Lincoln made appreciative remarks. After working most of the day, Nicolay told Therena he had never had so dull a Fourth of July. The little boys on Pennsylvania Avenue had exhausted their firecrackers in the morning and could not afford to reload, leaving the streets inappropriately calm.

Nicolay and others were concerned about more serious attacks. In the previous fall, Massachusetts's governor John Albion Andrew had brought three constituents to the White House after dark. The doorman said Lincoln was out but would return. Killing time while they waited, they wandered through public and private halls, upstairs and down. Many rooms were open and lit, but the only signs of life were two pairs of children's shoes outside a bedroom door. The governor and his friends chose a room that suited them until the president returned, heard their voices, and joined them.

Any well-dressed assassin with a bogus governor's calling card could easily have done the same, had any deception been necessary. In hot weather, the president's office door was literally open, an acquaintance said, "and anyone could go in unannounced. I was accustomed to doing so." An entrepreneurial gunsmith exposed Lincoln's ludicrous vulnerability even when his door was attended: "On my arrival at the White House I was ushered immediately into [his office], with my repeating rifle in my hand, and there I found the President alone."

You had to get by two languid doormen before you got to Lincoln during the day, a newspaperman said, one at the front door, another outside his office, "but they did not consider it necessary to be vigilant after office hours, and I often walked into the White House unchallenged and went straight up to the private secretary's room adjoining his own without seeing any person whatever." The doors stayed unlocked well after dark, when Lincoln often worked with no one but a messenger dozing in the anteroom. Hay's friend on General Halleck's staff said he often thought as he walked into the White House how exposed Lincoln was, that if anyone attacked him in his home or office there would not be a single armed man to overcome. Although "we would have been puzzled to give a good reason," Stoddard said, the secretaries worked uneasy at night, keeping one ear cocked for "the footstep in the hall."

Lincoln was even more vulnerable in the President's Park. Any stroller on the White House grounds might come face to face with him alone. A teenaged clerk found himself "within ten feet of the President as he came out to mount his horse. . . . I could have stepped three paces and touched him." Finding children playing on the portico, Lincoln leafed through their schoolbooks while they gathered around him as if he were their father. In October 1862, two astonished privates on leave found him leaning against a tree on the grounds, deep in thought as he "cut at the grass with his cane." They gave him a startled salute, and he blessed them. A sentry told them he often came out alone in the early evening to read and walk.

He dismissed his friends' fears. "If I have business at the War Department, I must take my hat and go there." He would be careful, he said, but he had to do his job. He saw hundreds of strangers every day. Surrounding him with guards to fend off assassins would only put the idea in their heads. No matter how well he was protected, anyone who wanted to kill him, including a rebel agent, if such "is within the purposes of this rebellion," could trade his life for his, "and do you think the Richmond people would like to have Hannibal Hamlin here any better than myself?" The vice president had been an anti-slavery zealot since the 1840s. "In that one alternative, I have an insurance on my life worth half the prairie land of Illinois."

He refused a military guard when he went to church or a play. People would be discouraged to think he needed one, he said. He often left the White House at night to walk to the theater or a cabinet minister's home with a single unarmed companion less rough and ready than himself. His wife told him how she worried. "All imagination," he would say.

The head of the War Department guard said Lincoln walked over there every night in an old gray shawl, with no more protection than a "shockingly bad hat" and "a worse umbrella." In all his fierce authority, Secretary of War Stanton issued orders that when the president came alone—and he seldom came any other way—he would not return unescorted. One rainy night he waved his escort off: "I have my umbrella and can get home safely without you." They would not let him go, they said, for they dared not defy Mr. Stanton. "No," Lincoln said in mock dismay, "I suppose not," for Stanton would have them shot inside of twenty-four hours.

Lincoln's vulnerability increased in the summer of 1862. To avoid the heat and mosquitoes, the family moved to a cottage on the grounds of the hilltop Soldiers' Home, a refuge for disabled veterans in rural northwest Washington. After breakfast every day, the president was driven to the White House by an unarmed coachman and returned in the late afternoon. He sometimes rode horseback both ways, passing through woods alone.

Late that summer he succumbed to his friends. Ward Hill Lamon, William Hanna, and Leonard Swett accused him of reckless negligence. Apart from the physical risk, Lamon had been telling him for a year that eavesdropping traitors infested the White House and no one should get upstairs without sending up a card, a precaution his predecessors had taken. "Somebody must do something," Swett said. Would he leave it to the three of them to make some arrangement? Lincoln told a general that assassination was "not an American crime," but a guard might relieve their anxiety.

On Stanton's orders, Company A of the hard-fighting 11th New York Cavalry, known as Scott's 900, mostly from New York City, encamped at the Soldiers' Home. When the president went to and from the White House and the Lincolns took their rides, twenty-four cavalrymen in jackets of yellow-trimmed blue rode with them on black horses with drawn sabers on their shoulders, riding two by two. When Lincoln rode horseback, Tad often came along "with his cape flying in the wind," his pony keeping up at his father's side. They drew some curious looks from passersby like Walt Whitman, a longhaired author of immoral poetry who earned his bread as a government clerk and watched Lincoln pass dozens of times. "We have got so that we always exchange bows," Whitman wrote, "and very cordial ones."

His cavalrymen were soon devoted to him, their regimental historian said, though they could not help but see "certain defects," an intriguing evasion. As close as Lincoln grew to some of them, he resented their "espionage" and complained, perhaps literally to deaf ears, that he could not hear his wife over the din of a hundred hooves and two dozen rattling scabbards and was more likely to be shot by an accidental discharge of one of his protectors' carbines than captured by a squad of rebel cavalry. They were under standing orders to go to their stable on K Street after they reached the White House, to keep them out of sight.

Nonetheless, mounted pairs of Scott's 900 were posted at the mansion's carriage gates, and sentries with bayoneted muskets protected the adjoining walk-in gates, "so that things begin to look more like war," Stoddard thought. The protection turned the White House into "a pretty carefully guarded head-quarters in these days, for some unexplained reason."

Lincoln told Noah Brooks that he "worried until he got rid of it."

*   *   *

Nicolay wrote Therena on a hot Sunday night. "The gas lights over my desk are burning brightly and the windows of the room are open, and all bugdom outside seems to have organized a storming party to take the gas light." It was only just possible to endure. "The air is swarming with them, they are on the ceiling, the walls and the furniture in countless numbers, they are buzzing about the room, and butting their heads against the window panes, they are on my clothes, in my hair, and on the sheet I am writing on." The plebian gnats, the patrician roaches, and the diplomats from the Musquito Kingdom were "maddened and blinded" by the light, and flew into the flames "to be swept out into the dust and rubbish by the servant in the morning," a minia-ture tableau of the folly of human humbugs, who "even in this room" went buzzing around the light and power of the government.

In the thick heat of August, Lincoln welcomed five clergymen to his office. Far from the usual routine, the event made White House history, for the group was "a Committee of colored men" selected by their churches and civic organizations at Lincoln's request. No president had ever invited black people to send delegates to the White House to discuss a proposed policy, but the policy was repugnant to most of them, the formation of "Negro colonies" in Africa or Latin America.

The same new law that had freed Washington City's three thousand slaves over Lincoln's signature had authorized him to spend $100,000 to help them go voluntarily to Haiti, Liberia, or whatever foreign country he might select. He wanted to know their leaders' thoughts, and to let them know his. He told them that colonization alone could neutralize the "great physical difference" that disadvantaged both races. The blacks endured horrific wrongs, but even when freed they were not treated equally, and were it not for "your race among us" there would be no civil war. It was best for both races to separate. Many black people might rather stay, he said. "This is—I speak in no unkind sense—an extremely selfish view of the case." White Americans were unwilling, "harsh as it may be, for you free colored people to remain with us."

The Chevalier Henry Wikoff, cover of *Vanity Fair*, August 16, 1862.

Well intentioned though Lincoln's support for colonization may have been—a lifeboat for free blacks and freed slaves in the event of an ugly white backlash against the impending emancipation—it produced an explosion of indignation from black leaders and white abolitionists across the north, with a smattering of support from some, including the chairman of the delegation that had heard it. The president's embarrassment was not confined to his colonization scheme. A fawning caricature of Chevalier Wikoff, Mrs. Lincoln's ousted master of ceremonies, graced the August 16, 1862, cover of *Vanity Fair*, bowing in laughable clothes.

*   *   *

Three members of the delegation of black ministers who had gone to see the president belonged to the Social Civil and Statistical Association, the "SCSA," which collected statistics on black schools, businessmen, and property owners to show that they thrived in freedom and deserved citizenship, and to undermine Lincoln's colonization policy. Its president, William Slade, held one of the most prestigious jobs available to a man of African descent. He was the second ranking servant in Lincoln's White House.

Respected by the president's secretaries, Slade was variously called his messenger, valet, manservant, and "mulatto doorkeeper," but his title was White House Usher, equivalent to an English butler. Though he and his wife owned and lived in a boarding house at 464 Massachusetts Avenue, Slade had a room in the White House basement, stayed overnight with his family in bad weather, kept a set of keys, and knew every consequential person in town.

Second in rank only to the steward, who oversaw the household's accounts and operations, Slade bossed all the servants, as one of them later said. According to John Washington, the black historian who collected their memories, he supervised their work, arranged the food and service, helped serve at dinner parties, and prepared special dishes. When large entertainments exceeded the staff's capacity, Washington said, kitchen help and waiters were brought in "from among the colored men who worked for other officials and knew just how to handle things under the joint supervision of Cornelia Mitchell," the "colored cook," and Slade, a light-skinned Virginian "of distinguished Southern ancestry." Slade's wife, Josephine, a fellow White House employee, was close to Mrs. Lincoln. Tad was taken to their boarding house to play with their daughter and sons, "a real boy in the midst of real boys and girls, white and colored."

In addition to leading the SCSA, Slade was president of "The Convention," an association of black churches and civic organizations; an elder at the

William Slade. Library of Congress.

prestigious 15th Street Presbyterian Church, which many White House servants attended; a friend of Frederick Douglass; and a raconteur. John Washington said the "colored people who served him" gave Lincoln "an example of what freedom would accomplish" and showed him how productive and independent black men and women could be. Slade surely influenced that view.

The president enjoyed trading stories with him into the night, "somebody to loosen up on," another servant said. He often knew Lincoln's thoughts and plans before his secretaries did, particularly on slavery. The president would try his ideas and rhetoric on him. "William, how does that sound?" Only then would he try them on Nicolay and Hay. There was shrewdness in this, as he searched for words to move everyone, black and white, formally educated and not. When the Emancipation Proclamation was published, Slade said he already knew every word.

On August 17, 1862, Lincoln broke the White House color barrier again and welcomed "a committee of colored ministers of the Gospel" who had come on their own initiative seeking leave to serve black troops. He handed them a note to be shown to the officers they encountered, directing that they be given every accommodation consistent with military operations, the language he used in any order involving civilians.

When leaders of Washington's black community wrote to Secretary of War Stanton, praising him for endorsing the city's "colored regiments" and proposing to help choose their officers, William Slade's was the lead signature. To supplement the petition, Slade wrote a private note to the President of the United States.

*   *   *

In the last days of August 1862, Robert E. Lee won a second rebel victory at Bull Run, reprising the panic in Washington that had followed the first. Pennsylvania Avenue filled up again with ambulances and carriages bringing in the wounded, and again the rebels did not come. They marched into Maryland instead, where McClellan led the Army of the Potomac to meet them.

With Lee uncomfortably near the Soldiers' Home, Lincoln accepted his first substantial infantry guard after an honorable show of resistance. Two companies of the 150th Pennsylvania Volunteers, the elite "Bucktail" regiment, pitched their tents by the Lincolns' cottage. The deer tails on their hats were trophies of their marksmanship. As the weather turned cold and the family moved back to the White House, two different Bucktail companies went with them. One encamped beneath the south lawn, the other on the War Department grounds. When a soldier got careless one night, a musket ball passed through Mrs. Grady's house on 15th Street, stopped by a wall near a lucky young woman.

For the rest of the war, Bucktails paced the sentries' beat before the north

Colonel Tad Lincoln. Library of Congress.

portico. Mrs. Lincoln's many kindnesses to them included a midnight meal when the sentries were relieved. Tad hung out in both their camps, "in which," a Bucktail said, "he seemed to have a weighty sense of proprietorship." He learned every man's name and came home to his mother black with campfire soot. The Pennsylvanians commissioned him their honorary colonel and had a uniform made, which he wore in formal photographs as solemn as McClellan's. He signed at least one letter "Col. Tad Lincoln."

A few days after McClellan turned Lee out of Maryland at Antietam, Hay came to Stoddard with a sheet of paper in his hand and an odd look on his face. "Stod," he said, "the President wants you to make two copies of this right away. I must go back to him." Stoddard put his head down and worked mechanically until he realized what he was copying and stopped. It was Lincoln's final draft of the Emancipation Proclamation in the president's own hand. Stoddard finished his work, brought the copies to Hay for delivery to the House and Senate, and slipped the original in a drawer. Perhaps no one would think to retrieve it. In the fullness of time, Hay came back and got it.

*   *   *

The Pennsylvania Avenue horse car line ran every three minutes past the White House stop, but some of its patrons, many of them in uniform, had to wait much longer for an omnibus with a sign: "This Car Exclusively for Colored People."

The south side of the Avenue, halfway to Capitol Hill, was known for cheap variety shows and a row of experienced embalmers whose war-driven business could be measured by the coffins stacked on the sidewalk. On her way to Mrs. Lincoln's reception on a damp, cloudy Saturday, a Michigan woman watched "30 or 40 little negro bootblacks" weaving through the crowd behind a fifer and drummer luring patrons to "some low theater."

On the smart north side of the street, ladies on their way to the Blue Room dipped their hooped silks in "slop water" running down the alleys into the curbs. Soldiers were everywhere, loitering about the hotel and restaurant doors in assorted embellishments of uniform. Every fifty yards or so, a mounted cavalryman kept watch "over the dust and a few vagabond dogs" and intercepted riders exceeding the speed limit. On any given day the Avenue was lined with organ grinders, sidewalk soap venders, telescopes trained on the Capitol and the White House at so much per view, a man hawking toy wooden bugs on elastic strings.

People strolling past the President's House enjoyed "a pleasing succession of kaleidoscopic effects." Fresh brigades on their way to the front marched in crisp new uniforms to the beat of regimental bands, bright flags snapping in the wind, led by cavorting freed slaves, skirted by mounted officers dashing to and from the War Department. Creaking mule-drawn wagon trains heavy with weapons and ammunition jolted down Pennsylvania Avenue, rutting its rounded cobblestones until they "sank under the weight of war." Muted by a little distance, depending on the direction of the wind, the almost constant din of carriages, hacks, and carts "mixed up in inextricable confusion" could be heard in Hay's office and the Family Dining Room.

*   *   *

In mid-December, Lee and Stonewall Jackson decimated the Army of the Potomac at Fredericksburg, and the loss of over thirteen thousand Northern lives hit Lincoln like a hammer: "If there is a worse place than hell I am in it." As the slaughter was described to him in his office, he "groaned, wrung his hands," and paced the room, "saying over and over again, 'What has God put me in this place for?'" In the press and on Capitol Hill, angry men wanted him out of it.

Three days before Christmas, the president had regained his composure and showed Captain John A. Dahlgren, the chief of naval ordinance, a little packet of gunpowder in his office. "Well, Captain," he said, "here's a letter about a new powder" with a sample that left too much residue when fired. "Now I'll show you." He took a sheet of paper, sprinkled it with powder, brought it to the fireplace, picked up a coal with the tongs and blew on it, depositing specks of charcoal on his nose. Dahlgren thought how peaceful he was, how easily diverted from the critics he had just been damning. He put the coal to the powder "and away it went." Then he smugly displayed the residue.

Mechanically inclined and attracted to any new weapon that might shorten the war, he welcomed eccentric men who brought him all sorts of improbable arms and gear, which he forwarded to the staff, Stoddard said, "until my room looked like a gun shop." Some changed the war, like the model of an ironclad gunboat that sat on the mantel there. Others were White House jokes. When someone brought in a cavalry saddle with "new features all over it, and in it, and under it," Lincoln examined it intently and left it in his office until someone took it to Stoddard's, where it lasted for a while as a conversation piece. A prototype piece of chest armor was a table ornament for weeks after Lincoln approved it, subject to its inventor strapping it on and letting riflemen have a go at him.

Not all White House judgments on new weapons ideas were sound. A cast iron ball filled with gunpowder, to be thrown by hand and "burst on striking and scatter bits of iron in all directions" was "a horrible thing for close combat," Stoddard said, "but of no practical use" unless the rebels stood still and let it be thrown at them. It served as a White House paperweight. When a visionary raised the notion of "an ironclad balloon to carry heavy guns" he raised a good laugh. Lincoln spent an hour in the basement with a model "air boat" on a pivot attached to a clockwork propeller and pronounced it "curious but not useful." He did think well of the clever new code that the Signal Corps practiced on the grounds, sending wireless messages over substantial distances by holding or waving flags in designated positions.

Knowing Stoddard was the White House marksman, Lincoln walked him down to test new firearms in the Treasury Park, the junk-strewn field beneath the south lawn where an "old pile of lumber as large as a small house" was getting older. It may have been that very eyesore that let an Englishman say of Washington City that some of its great public buildings stood in tawdry settings, as if the British Museum had "suddenly migrated to the center of an exhausted brickfield, where rubbish may be shot." At half past six one morning, Lincoln grabbed a prototype rifle, handed Stoddard a musket with a new fitting, walked him down to the lumber pile, and started a shooting match that supported one of Stoddard's rare critiques of the commander in chief: "He never was a first rate shot."

On two consecutive evenings in the "waste fields," Lincoln spent an hour firing a new Spencer rifle with Spencer himself, "a quiet little Yankee," Hay said, who joined them at their makeshift range. According to Hay's ranking, Spencer was an expert shot, loading and firing seven rounds in less than thirty seconds with "contemptible simplicity and ease," Lincoln was only fair, and Hay embarrassed himself. Watching the weapon kick, a cocky passerby advised the president that "a gun ought not to rekyle. If it rekyled at all, it ought to rekyle a little forrid," which Lincoln enjoyed quoting.

As Lincoln stood by in the Treasury Park one day, an inventor demonstrated a compound for burning fortifications. Boards were set up, the stuff was thrown against them, and the president pulled a handful of grass from the flaming ruin. "That's very curious indeed," he said. "Very interesting. Now can't you invent something to burn bricks, mortar, earthworks, or even green grass? Up to this date, our armies find no difficulty in burning wood."

14

BUNDLES AND BALES

Every day but Sunday, the Prussian Louis Burgdorf climbed the stairs to the northeast room with a locked leather mail pouch and dumped its nubby contents on the green felt top of Stoddard's massive desk. Sometimes several hundred letters fell out, sometimes a few dozen. Stoddard pegged the average at 250. Battles and controversies brought more. Far from dreading the barrage, Stoddard could not imagine a more interesting place beyond a battlefield than the White House correspondence desk, bombarded with "the brutalities, enmities, and infamies of the President's letter-box," for the White House mail was "a very curious department of American literature."

Ruthless pruning was required to keep it from overwhelming everything else, "and it had to be swift work." The greater part of the mail—the rustic advice and prophecies, the religious diatribes, the offers to deal the president into money-making schemes, the dead weight of sheer obscenity (some of "the foulest blackguards on earth" had the president's address)—went directly into Stoddard's willow wastebasket, a destination he wished Dante could have seen "before he completed his list of limbos." Like the poet's gates of Hell, its rim was an edge "from which no traveller returned."

Soon there were two willow baskets on either side of Stoddard's desk, swallowing up the damned, spilling drifts of litter on the floor. Letters from amateur generals and fireside politicians were generally long and their lives were "generally short, owing to the handiness of the willow baskets." So were malevolent harangues. Storming into Lincoln's office with a violent screed, Stoddard got himself laughed at. Mere malice was too common to be noticed.

Death threats were taken more seriously. Nearly every mailbag brought a cold, unhinged, or precautionary threat against Lincoln's life. Some of the ugliest were addressed to his wife. Forbidden to show them to the Lincolns or even to mention them, Stoddard gave them to Nicolay, who shared them with the War Department and the president, who kept a heavy folder of them in his pigeonhole desk. One sketch of a man on a gallows arrived with a bit of verse, if such it could be called: "Two posts upright/One beam crossed tight/ One rope pendant/Abe on the end on't." Bad as the poetry was, Lincoln said, the likeness was worse, but whoever had composed it had done his best in literature and in art.

Before the war stopped regular mail delivery from the Confederacy, Hay had not been surprised by the venom the South spit in, but the ignorance in high places astonished him. It was disturbing to see the names that common Southerners called the president, but "harrowing" to see an officer and a gentleman from Georgia call him a "godam ole foole."

Mingled with the vitriol was "the rant and drivel of insanity." Stoddard was convinced that "when any man goes clean crazy" he sits down at once and writes a letter to the president. The Angel Gabriel sent four pages a day, and claimed "to dip his pen in blood, which looked altogether like an inferior article of red ink." Several of the twelve Apostles stayed in touch. A patriot sent advice composed and signed by a committee of the founding fathers, all of them long since dead. Many spectral correspondents had not learned to spell on the other side.

On a typically crowded day, a well-dressed man watched Stoddard turn mail into trash as he waited to see Lincoln. After a moment of speechless horror he exploded. Surely the president did not know that "a mere boy, a *boy* I say!" was keeping his mail from him. To educate the man, Stoddard read aloud from a few of the rants he was trashing, including "a horrible thing from an obscene, idiotic lunatic," and told his guest that "if he insisted on the President's giving time to such things he must take them in himself, as I was forbidden to do so." The gentleman commiserated with the boy on the depths to which "beastly men can sink."

Some amusing bits of lunacy escaped the willow wasteland to be passed around the shop, including an earnest letter from a man who proposed a cross-eyed gun with two barrels pointed in opposite directions. Armed with such a weapon, a cross-eyed regiment could clear rebels from both sides of a river at once, and "I'm cross-eyed enough to be colonel of it." Stoddard took the letter across the hall to Lincoln. The president thought there was about as much in it as some of his generals gave him. A letter from P. T. Barnum must have reached him too. Secessionists had grown so scarce in New York, the showman said, that he could not find one to display.

After Stoddard disposed of the trash and passed around the amusements, about half of what was left consisted of honest requests or reports that should have been sent elsewhere. Stoddard referred such letters to the proper departments, often with a note on the letter's face that conveyed the president's positive, negative, or noncommittal remarks, unbeknownst to the president. In a ticklish case, Stoddard might consult Nicolay or Hay, but he made it his youthful business to conjure what Lincoln would do, "and my decision was never found fault with except in a few cases, and in these I was approved, as I remember it."

Complaints reached Lincoln that Stoddard was wielding minor powers of the presidency, but he never interfered. "I concluded he was satisfied even with the willow basket," Stoddard said. Occasionally, Stoddard used "the power of the paper-cutter" for more important ends. He once manipulated the flow of correspondence to let a woman-and-child killer hang without passing on to the president some petitions from influential men for a pardon. When Lincoln detected what Stoddard had done he did "no more than look sidewise at me."

Stoddard marveled at the number of citizens who thought they had a right to Lincoln's personal services. A Westerner wrote and asked the president to go down to the patent office to see what was holding up his application. A man who had lost a lawsuit sought advice about an appeal. All such requests were bound for the willow wastebasket.

Requests for Lincoln's autograph were common, and commonly failed to get past the secretaries, though Hay tried his hand at forgery, making collectors happy without interrupting the president. Augustus N. Dickens of Chicago, Charles's brother, sent for an autograph in 1864. Whether he got Lincoln's or Hay's is unknown.

The secretaries reviewed "bundles and bales" of pleas for federal jobs "of every name and grade," and referred the best ones to the appropriate departments, accompanied by written briefs. They troubled the president with next to none of them. Though Lincoln was patient as a clock with respectful job seekers who took the trouble to see him in person, he spent almost no time on those who merely wrote, perhaps more concerned about having citizens believe they had his ear than giving it.

Letters from public men and ordinary citizens who actually deserved an answer went to Hay, who vetted them for the president. "At first we tried to bring them to his notice," Hay said, but he had time for only a few, and "at last he gave the whole thing over to me, and signed without reading them the letters I wrote in his name." Hay learned to keep a straight face when minor politicians inquired if Lincoln had read their letters to the cabinet. The ones he wrote for the president's signature were often more polished than the ones Lincoln wrote himself, though not as shrewd. After the war, Hay told several friends that it was he, not Lincoln, who had written a famously eloquent letter to a woman in Boston after the White House was told, falsely as it turned out, that she had lost five sons in battle.

On July 19, 1862, Lincoln sent a letter to an editor of the *New York Tribune*, who suspected such shenanigans. "You are in error," it said, "if you suppose any important portion of my correspondence escapes my notice. Every thing requiring my action or attention is brought to my notice." The letter did not define "important" or disclose that Hay had written it.

Though Lincoln was kept informed of the drift of his mail, only a small part of it got past Hay to the president's desk, briefed and assessed by a secretary who thought it worth his time. Lincoln once sent a fifteen-page letter from the president of the University of Michigan next door with a note asking Nicolay to "run over this and tell me what is in it." He assured a few close friends that envelopes from them marked "Private" would come to him unopened, but spared himself a letter from a congressman who had lost his seat and was given a third-tier job in poor compensation. "I understand my friend Kellogg is ill-natured," he wrote on the envelope, and "therefore I do not read his letter." Had he done so he would have proved himself right.

Lincoln probably read more telegrams than letters, as he hung about the War Department Telegraph Office waiting for news from the front. A well-connected Philadelphian often wired advice. When the know-it-all inquired whether one general was "dumb enough" to punish another for a misstep, Lincoln composed a hot reply, then told the telegrapher, "I guess I will not send this. I can't afford to answer every crazy question asked me." After that, the telegraphers had a word for such messages. "Crazygrams" they called them.

*   *   *

Apart from drafting letters for Lincoln's signature, Nicolay and Hay often wrote to generals and high officials directly, and what they wrote could be pointed. Replying to a self-anointed peacemaker whose only credentials were his Colorado gold interests, Hay advised the mining mogul that "it is necessary for me to use a certain discretion in the choice of letters to be submitted to the personal inspection of the President. In order to avoid a further waste of time on your part, I have to inform you that your letters are never so submitted." Guessing that it would take him half an hour to detect the sarcasm, Hay wrote an outraged state senator that the president would not have authorized a troop movement that had inconvenienced his constituents had he known it would pass through the senator's district. Hay would have added that the senator might consider spelling "solemnly" with an "n" had Lincoln not thought that a bit too much.

Hay's estimate that Lincoln wrote half a dozen letters a week suggests that he was not privy to them all, since Lincoln wrote many more. Rarely dictating, he composed them by hand or told a secretary what he wanted to say and reviewed a draft. He was wary about putting things in writing at all, and said more than once that it was better to regret having failed to write a letter than to write one he wished he had not. His Illinois friend and advisor David Davis, whom he put on the Supreme Court, said the president had written him not a word since he took office. He did write letters of recommendation, one for a physician who had "operated on my feet with great success, and considerable addition to my comfort." A White House employee named Calvert seemed like "a very faithful, worthy, and gentlemanly young man."

Lincoln sometimes wrote a nasty letter, marked it "Not Sent," and stuck it in a file, venting steam without harm. In one such draft, he told General Ambrose Burnside that a message from the general "makes me doubt whether I am awake or dreaming." In another he answered a long harangue from the wife of a prominent man in search of a federal job: "It is difficult for you to understand what is nevertheless true, that the bare reading of a letter of that length requires more than any one person's share of my time," and the actions she demanded were not among "the legitimate duties for which I am supposed to be placed here." According to Nicolay and Hay, some such letters "slept undisturbed" until they were found decades later.

Other barbs went out as written, exposing the stress that provoked them. Francis Preston Blair, Lincoln's close advisor, sent him a pompous note from one William Alexander of New York defaming General Nathaniel Banks, which fetched a taut reply: "I would like to know who is the great man Alexander, that talks so oracularly about 'if the president keeps his word,' and Banks not having 'capacity to run an omnibus on Broadway.' How has this Alexander's immense light been obscured hitherto?"

Lincoln wrote slowly, carefully, and legibly, had his secretaries make copies when he wanted them, and sometimes made his own, filing some of them in his alphabetized pigeonholes. He often scribbled orders on odd scraps of paper, envelopes, or whatever came to hand. He did not keep a letter book, which might be carried off, he said, though it would have made "a back load."

Never fussy about pens, he used common wooden holders with steel points but preferred a little barrel pen made in England by Gillott. By the end of his time in office, he kept them in a small brass rack with a broken end.

His secretaries had to buy their own pens and every sheet of paper that did not become an official document. Congress had not increased the $250 annual appropriation for White House stationery since John Adams spent his, but it pushed the wartime figure to $1,000 in 1862. Engraved White House bond was common enough for Nicolay to use for rough drafts, or at least to discover halfway through that rough they were. He kept them in his files, crossed out and interlineated.

The elegant White House stationery was made of fine stock. Long letters were written on a single sheet of paper in a choice of two sizes, folded in half to make four pages of 8 by 10 or 5 by 8 inches, ruled with light blue lines like a school examination book. "Executive Mansion" was engraved in gothic type in the upper-right corner, with "Washington, ———— 186" beneath, the date and year to be filled in. The upper left corner was embossed with the manufacturer's mark, "A. P. Lawrence/Extra Fine." Similarly engraved, shorter notes were written on unlined 8 by 5 inch stock, with no embossing.

Envelopes were engraved "from the President of the United States." After March 1864, when Congress authorized it, they were franked with his signature, or Nicolay's or Hay's. Nicolay's letters were sealed with dark red wax impressed with the presidential seal—an eagle in a circle and 35, or later, 36 stars; or with "Private Secretary to the President" around the rim. The Postmaster dated and marked them "Washington/Free."

Like all things diplomatic, letters to heads of state—condolences to Queen Victoria on the death of her mother, an equivocal response to the tycoon of Japan's request to extend a treaty deadline—were drafted for Lincoln's signature at the State Department and uniformly addressed to Great and Good Friend, whether the recipient was the czar or the king of Siam, whose offer of a gift of elephants was graciously declined. Lincoln asked Congress where to put the more portable presents that came with the Siamese letter—a jeweled sword and scabbard, a pair of ivory tusks, and a photograph of the king and his daughter, all consigned to the collection of curiosities at the Department of the Interior.

The mail delivery wagons brought domestic gifts too, a dozen terrapins from a loyal man in Virginia, the late Henry Clay's snuffbox sent by his son, shirt studs carved from pipestone by a judge's young daughter in the South Dakota Territory, a tub of fall butter, a salmon trout, and a "share ticket" for repairing Faneuil Hall signed by John Hancock and an ancestral Abraham Lincoln, mailed by a Hancock descendant. White rabbits arrived for the Lincoln boys, and beautifully quilled moccasins for their father. "He put them on and grinned." On behalf of the United States, he accepted $868 from a "penitent supplicant" who had come by it "in a dishonest manner" and returned it "by the influences of the Holy Spirit."

Some gifts were hand delivered. When a painter brought a portrait of the president, Lincoln declared it the best he had seen, because it was the ugliest. The artist "was rather taken aback for a few moments, but went away perfectly satisfied."

When anonymous supporters from New York sent assorted wines and liquors, Mrs. Lincoln took Stoddard to the basement, where the intoxicants had been left. Neither she nor the president enjoyed wine, and she was sure he would not allow it in the house. Stoddard laughed and said the gentlemen seemed not to have left anything out. A note of thanks should be sent to the forwarding address, and the goods should go to the hospitals, to be left to the doctors' and nurses' discretion, which Mrs. Lincoln did.

She had no such qualms about gifts sent from China in 1861, an elegant caddy of tea and a set of rice paper books of gorgeously painted flowers, birds, and costumed courtiers. Supposedly rescued from a burning palace, the books distracted her boys from the measles. "Unfortunately," Mrs. Grimsley recalled, her cousin accepted too many personal gifts, but "Mr. Lincoln was not in this respect 'worldly wise' and Mrs. Lincoln could not anticipate the storm of censure which fell upon her." The loot included a silver-plated sewing machine inlaid with pearls and enamel, a fabulous tablecloth from Constantinople, drifts of silk and embroidered fabric, a gold and enamel brooch set with forty-seven diamonds, and pins with twenty-seven more. Adorned with $2,000 worth of laces, Mrs. Lincoln told a woman at a White House reception that "she hardly felt it right to wear them in these times, although they were a present."

Buckingham Palace sent a slice of the Prince of Wales's wedding cake to the homes of heads of state, including the White House, which it reached "in due season," according to Noah Brooks, "but rather dry."

*   *   *

Lincoln told Brooks that he didn't read the newspapers; he skirmished with them. After a short time in the White House he broke an old habit of absorbing several a day and had Stoddard write morning news and editorial digests, a laborious task in dip pen and ink, especially since the output went unread. Stoddard gave it up after two weeks. The secretaries read the major papers from Chicago, Saint Louis, Cincinnati, and the big Eastern cities and kept Lincoln apprised of their editorials, though he was typically uninterested in their predictable bloviations.

The big Washington dailies—the *Chronicle*, the *Republican*, and the *Star*—
were put on his table, and Nicolay said he read the major news, but Hay said
he rarely opened a newspaper unless Hay called his attention to something
special. Even then he often said, "I know more about that than any of them."
The war news generally reached him before it reached the press, and his
public opinion baths exposed him to "rival interests," Hay said, with "one
informant naturally correcting the error or extravagance of another."

The White House subscribed to the papers it needed, and dozens of lesser
ones came in free, which got no closer to Lincoln than the servants who
snatched them up. Most of their editors marked key items in colored ink to be
sure they reached the president. "They did not do so," Stoddard said. He
tossed them on a pile near his desk after a glance at the color-coded bits,
which Lincoln never saw.

All of that said, Lincoln understood the power of the press. He never gave
a press conference or a formal interview, but chatted with newspapermen in
his office and instructed his gatekeepers to bring him their cards and messages
immediately, however he might be engaged, cabinet meetings included. When
Stanton refused to discuss a victorious battle, reporters hurried to the White
House and Lincoln admitted them immediately. "I know what you have come
for. You gentlemen are keen of scent, and always wide awake." He pointed
them to chairs, laid his long legs on a table, summarized the facts from a sheet
of paper, added thoughts of his own, and accepted their thanks as they dashed
to the telegraph office.

According to Stoddard, a well-known reporter had enjoyed special access
to Lincoln despite his paper's hostility to the administration until a rumor got
back to the White House that he was repeating a vulgar pun that Lincoln had
shared with a cabinet member. The president called him in, and he waited by
Stoddard's desk, "a jolly fellow, full of wit," but after being called into Lincoln's office he left "with unusual haste," and he did not leave jolly.

War correspondents came to Lincoln's office from the front, sometimes with
word from his generals. When a reporter returned from the dreadful Battle of
the Wilderness with Grant's message—"There will be no turning back"—the
president kissed his forehead.

Lincoln resented Joseph Medill, the hostile owner of his home state's *Chicago Tribune*, and refused to see him at the White House when he called four
times in a month. Nicolay soon got a letter from a spokesman for the *Tribune*
who noted that it was mailed to Lincoln every day and asked if he read it,
having heard that he did not. Nicolay replied that *he* kept the paper on his
table and examined it regularly, as did the Western men who happened by.

The president read the news in the Washington dailies but rarely looked at others "for want of leisure to do so." Nicolay would keep reading the *Tribune*, "reserving only the privilege of finding as much fault with it as it finds with the Administration."

Nicolay and Hay spoke with newspapermen who could not get in quickly to see Lincoln. Whitelaw Reid, already important in his twenties as an editor of the *Tribune*, was an almost daily visitor. He was close to Hay and Stoddard, who enjoyed his bright, good cheer, Stoddard said, as he hailed "me or John to ask us for any news or to tell us what we did not know."

The occasional Southern newspaper and the Northern papers that quoted them, including the anti-Lincoln *New York World*, were brought to Hay, who shared them with the president when he thought they might interest him. In April 1864, "loafing into my room," Hay said, Lincoln "picked up a paper and read the *Richmond Examiner*'s attack on Jeff Davis. It amused him. 'Why, the *Examiner* seems about as fond of Jeff as the *World* is of me.'"

15

LIKE SO MANY GREENHEAD FLIES

The New Year's Day reception of 1863 was the first White House social event since Willie's death. Everyone knew that Lincoln would sign the Emancipation Proclamation that day, and thousands wanted to be in on it. In Indian summer weather, the police and the Bucktail guards were overwhelmed by a crowd so dense as it neared the door that a man who had been punched could only swear he would retaliate "if I could get my hand up."

For people jammed under the portico there was no escape. Every few minutes, the door was shut to consume "a new mouthful," then opened for another. Ladies' hoops were bent or broken, a congressman's coat was ripped, a tearful young woman's bonnet was crushed, and a Bucktail with a musket that everyone knew was useless pleaded uselessly with the crowd. "My gosh gentlemen. *Will* you stan' back? You can't get in no faster by crowdin'. Oh, I say, *will* you stan' back?" Noah Brooks looked on as "the gay and festive crowd responded by flattening him against a pilaster."

A line of polished coaches inched up the gravel drive bearing Washington grandees who could not be seen to arrive on foot, but no one got in ahead of the sovereign people. A brigadier general who expected to be saluted and escorted inside learned otherwise, and so did a group of cavalry officers, "glorious in lace and jingling spurs," who galloped under the portico and were beckoned to the back of the line.

Once inside the President's House, the digested chunks of humanity were instantly civil. Brooks watched them straighten their clothes at the back of an orderly line as if they were at the post office. At Mrs. Lincoln's request, a dismounted detail of Scott's 900 checked their coats for weapons, a task that the cavalrymen thought beneath them. At the end of the reception line, Marshal Lamon presented several thousand citizens to the president, who smiled, shook their hands, and looked straight through them. Brooks had been his friend for years, and Lincoln did not see him as he looked him in the face. His eyes were in the Blue Room and his mind was somewhere else, perhaps on the signal event of the nineteenth century and its unforeseeable consequences.

After three hours of handshaking, the president went up to his office to sign the Emancipation Proclamation. There were a few invited witnesses but no ceremony. He massaged his aching hand for minutes before Nicolay gave him the pen. His signature would be examined forever, he said, and he would not have it waiver. Then he signed his name slowly and looked up and smiled. "That will do."

A black minister joined the celebration on the White House grounds. "Men squealed," he said, "women fainted, dogs barked, white and colored people shook hands, songs were sung, and by this time cannons began to fire." Nothing like it "will ever be seen again in this life."

*   *   *

When Orville Browning arrived to go riding with the Lincolns that afternoon, the First Lady let him know that a spiritualist named Mrs. Laury had delighted her with "wonderful revelations" about Willie "and also about things on earth." Topping less distressing news, Mrs. Laury had disclosed that every member of the cabinet was an enemy of the president and had to be dismissed.

Men and women claiming contact with the dead had materialized in disturbing numbers in upstate New York in the 1840s, rapping tables and ringing bells. By the 1850s, spiritualists were exploiting grief everywhere, and the fraud spread predictably with the trauma of war. The mystics who haunted the White House mail convinced Stoddard that "there are very badly conducted insane asylums in the other world."

Mrs. Lincoln's dressmaker, Mrs. Keckly, who had lost a son in battle, introduced her in her grief to spiritualism, and the First Lady hosted several séances in the Red Room. The famous spiritualist Nettie Colburn's claim that the president attended two of them has the ring of truth. Three years after the death of his son, Lincoln asked an army officer, "Do you ever find yourself talking with the dead? Since Willie's death, I catch myself every day involuntarily talking with him as if he were with me." Some of his adversaries jumped on rumors that the President of the United States was conversing with disembodied souls. One pamphlet bore the subtitle, "The Nation Demoralized and Its President a Spirit Rapper."

Thirty years later, Nicolay tried to dissuade a Lincoln biographer from believing it: "I never knew of his attending a séance of spiritualists at the White

House or elsewhere [a weak denial], and if he ever did so [even weaker] it was out of mere curiosity, and as a matter of pastime, just as you or I would do." The notion that Lincoln was a spiritualist was "almost too absurd to need contradiction."

"Lord Colchester," the self-styled illegitimate son of an English duke, a ruddy-faced mystic for hire whose affinity for spirits ran to whiskey as well as ghosts, warned Mrs. Lincoln late in the war that her husband was in danger, which may have been divined from an evening with his drinking companion John Wilkes Booth.

*   *   *

Queen Victoria's social mores prevailed in Lincoln's White House, excepting his wife's salon. After Mrs. Lincoln invited a niece and her hasband, a man named Baker, she confided to a friend that it was whispered about town that Mrs. Baker got up at daylight and "rode out with a *gentleman* in a close carriage, leaving her husband in bed, miserable, silly man!" Respectable dinner guests said goodnight at eleven, but the voice of Mrs. Baker was heard at 2 a.m. "with gentlemen in the library, on the same floor with the President's apartments, the latter disclaiming against such proceedings."

It had snowed on the evening of January 8, 1863 when the socially prominent Virginia Woodbury Fox, who kept a lively diary, was driven to the White House for tea with Mrs. Lincoln and found a young officer from Boston with Robert Lincoln, enjoying his Harvard vacation. Brazenly enough, the officer "played with Tad on the sofa—at home!" When Mrs. Lincoln mentioned the snow at Harvard, Mrs. Fox said the Cambridge boys "improved it by going to Boston to see the pretty ankles," an allusion to toe-length skirts being lifted above the slush. Hadn't Robert told her so? Mrs. Lincoln said he wouldn't dare. Mrs. Fox discretely left out the Harvard boys' name for a snowy day. "I did not call it, as they did, 'leg day.'"

On the afternoon of Friday, February 13, Robert came into his mother's room as Mrs. Keckly braided roses in her hair over a low-cut pink silk gown. Mrs. Lincoln and her son spoke in a style that the president had never heared in the woods.

"You are at leisure this afternoon, are you not, Robert?"
"Yes, mother."
"Of course, then, you will dress and come downstairs."
"No mother, I do not propose to assist in entertaining Tom Thumb. My notions of duty, perhaps, are somewhat different from yours."

In the end Robert came down.

Some crowned heads of Europe had received Charles Sherwood Stratton, a tiny native of Bridgeport, Connecticut, better known as General Tom Thumb, P. T. Barnum's brightest star, and Mrs. Lincoln's friends had convinced her to welcome him as he passed through Washington City on a wedding tour with his two-foot-eight-inch bride. The First Lady had already sent a gift of Chinese screens inlaid with gold, silver, and pearls, and selected about fifty lucky guests for the White House reception of the year. Three prized tickets were assigned to Benjamin French, who was sorry to learn that "the stupid headed servant went to the Capitol, and not finding me there, did not come to the house, so I did not get the invitation. It was a *dern* shame."

Grace Greenwood, a groundbreaking female reporter, was there. "Rather to my surprise," she wrote, so was "the high-toned and austere Secretary of the Treasury," Salmon Chase. She watched him arrive early, "as if in boyish haste to see the show," with his exquisite daughter Kate and her "certain entangling charm." For Miss Greenwood, the scene took on a touch of the bizarre as the tiny Mrs. Stratton, in her wedding dress and two-yard train, walked the length of the East Room to the Lincolns on her husband's arm. The president took her hand "as though it were a robin's egg, and he were fearful of breaking it" and presented the little couple to the First Lady with none of the mock deference that "a lesser man" might have shown.

As the Strattons promenaded around the East Room, Lincoln watched them pass with "a smile of quaint humor" and "a gentle, human sympathy" for the happiness of "this curious wedded pair—come to him out of fairyland." Tad served cake and ices and told his mother that Mrs. Stratton would look just like her if *she* were small, which seems unlikely to have pleased her.

French told his sister that the next day's public reception "was a *crusher*." Mrs. Lincoln surmised that many people came expecting to see the diminutive celebrities, who had already moved on. But the joy had worn off a few days later when French spent a half hour with Lincoln. "He certainly is growing feeble," French thought. As the president wrote a note, his hand shook like an old man's. He had just had his fifty-fourth birthday. French said he needed rest. He said it was a pretty hard life for him.

It was hard on Stoddard too. A near-fatal illness hit him in the spring, perhaps another gift of White House water. It took him weeks to regain half speed.

*   *   *

On Friday, March 27, on a diplomatic mission in "disgustingly bad weather," fourteen Comanche, Apache, Kiowa, Caddo, Cheyenne, and Arapaho chiefs were led into the East Room and seated in full regalia in a semicircle on the floor. The surrounding invited guests included the cabinet; the British, French, Prussian, and Brazilian ministers; and their wide-eyed children and wives.

Stoddard thought the chiefs were an imposing group of men. Yellow Wolf, a Kiowa, wore a Thomas Jefferson Peace Medal around his neck. He said it had been given to his ancestors. Among the Cheyenne were Standing in the Water and War Bonnet. Pricked Forehead spoke for the Comanche, Poor Bear for the Apache. One chief wore leggings trimmed with bits of scalp he had taken from the ninety-three men he had killed. Less than half of the scalps were black. The others came in all shades.

Plains Indian chiefs in the conservatory, Nicolay standing in the center, Mrs. Lincoln at the far right. Library of Congress.

When the chiefs were well settled, Lincoln walked in and shook their hands. A Cheyenne named Lean Bear asked to be heard through an interpreter. "Our wigwams are not so fine as this," he said, "they are small and poor." He asked for the great chief's wisdom on what his people should do about the encroaching whites. He would keep his young men in check unless they were attacked, he said, and stay out of the white man's war.

According to the *Daily Morning Chronicle*, the chiefs received Lincoln's interpreted reply with "evident signs of satisfaction." He informed his attentive guests that "we pale-faced people think that this world is a great, round ball, and we have people here of the pale-faced family who have come almost from the other side of it to represent their nations here . . . as now you come from your part of the round ball." A globe was wheeled in, and the Smithsonian Institute's secretary pointed out Washington City and "their own country" and dispensed some geophysical science.

Then Lincoln gave Lean Bear his advice. "I can see no way in which your race is to become as numerous and prosperous as the white race except by living as they do, by the cultivation of the earth." Then he pointed out what he called another advantage of the white man's way. "Although we are now engaged in a great war between one another, we are not, as a race, so much disposed to fight and kill one another as our red brethren." Before the chiefs went home, handsome peace medals and certificates declaring them friends were distributed.

Less than two years later, as seven hundred Colorado Territorial cavalry approached a Cheyenne village that flew an American flag, Lean Bear rode out with his peace medal on his chest to show them Lincoln's certificate. They shot him from his horse and killed him on the ground. In what became known as the Sand Creek Massacre, War Bonnet and Standing in the Water died defending scores of women and children who were shot or hacked to death. Some were eviscerated alive.

*　　*　　*

In the first days of May 1863, Robert E. Lee and Stonewall Jackson surprised Fighting Joe Hooker at Chancellorsville and devastated his army, upsetting his plans to take Richmond. It was the South's greatest victory of the war. On Tuesday, May 5, Nicolay wrote a friend in Springfield, revealing how little the White House knew. "We have but little information beyond what you will find in the newspapers up to date."

At three the next day, Noah Brooks and Dr. Anson Henry, a house guest, were chatting in the library when Lincoln came in with a telegram in his hand and shocked his friends with his striken look as he stumbled to a chair, his face like the gray wall behind him. The Army of the Potomac had returned to its starting point north of the Rappahannock, and the pontoon bridges were up. It was sugarcoated news of defeat. Lincoln got up, locked his hands behind his back, and paced. "What will the country say? Oh, what will the country say?" Then he suddenly left the room. Dr. Henry burst into tears, not so much from the news, Brooks thought, as the sight of Lincoln's face. As

Brooks looked out a window, a carriage came up in a driving rain, and Lincoln and General Halleck got in on their way to Hooker.

The office work went on after a fashion, Stoddard said, "very much as things are done in any other family when there is a coffin in the house." When Lincoln returned the next day, his office was closed to everyone but messengers, cabinet members, senior senators and congressmen, and summoned officers.

Stanton and Halleck left together at about nine, leaving Lincoln alone in his office. Stoddard worked into the night to clear his desk, knowing that the next day's mailbag would bring "the wails and the mourning" and demands from homes and offices to account for another lost battle and its dead. More than a third of the mail was a "measureless denunciation" already, laced with "piteous pleas for peace." Stoddard was in his office and Lincoln was in his. There was not another soul in the office wing. Both of their doors were open, "for the night was warm."

In a silence so deep that Stoddard could hear his watch tick when he checked it, a repetitive creaking came from across the hall as Lincoln paced alone. The pacing stopped past midnight, and "the sudden silence made one put down letters and listen." Then it started up again. Stoddard went home at three without looking in. "It would have been a kind of profanity" to intrude. At the top of the stairs he paused and heard the "sentry like tread" continue.

Stoddard returned before 8 a.m. to find Lincoln in his office with nothing to show that he had left it. He was eating a hearty breakfast at the cabinet table, and he spoke to Stoddard cheerfully. Beside him was a draft of his orders to Hooker, preparing the next campaign.

The use of "colored troops," which Lincoln had been reluctant to endorse, may have been part of what he had pondered the night before. On June 1, a few days later, a committee of New York's Church of the Puritans came to his office and asked him to mobilize ten thousand "colored men of the country." Lincoln told them he would gladly receive not ten thousand black troops but ten times ten thousand, a striking change of position.

On his way to work on a Sunday, months thereafter, Stoddard paused before the White House as one of the first black regiments marched down Pennsylvania Avenue, "a fine looking body of men," Stoddard thought, but "a somewhat doubtful experiment." Seward came along, smoking the habitual cigar, and stopped to watch too. As the two of them turned toward the house, Stoddard asked him what he thought. Seward took his cigar from his mouth and slowly replied without looking up, as if he were talking to himself. "It grows. It grows."

After Stoddard went up to his office the regiment came back the other way and passed beneath his window. Someone told Lincoln, and he came across the hall to look. "Well, Mr. President," Stoddard said, "what do you think of that?" With his lips compressed and his eyes half shut, an expression "habitual to him when thinking," Lincoln turned back to his work. "It'll do," he said. "It'll do."

On June 22, after checking in at Willard's Hotel, a pair of distinguished envoys of the Governor of New York made two failed attempts to see the president. They had heard the hotel barkeeper propose a bet that Robert E. Lee, now marching through Pennsylvania, would enjoy his Fourth of July dinner at Willard's.

With Mrs. Lincoln's backing, Stoddard had been preparing an Independence Day celebration to be watched from a grandstand on the Mall. "The White House seems a furnace," he said, and with Lee so close to the city its people were again full of fear. An ebullient general gave Stoddard an infantry division, a unit or two of cavalry, and some towed artillery for a parade. "Give you a band of music too," he said. "Flags! Hurrah! Pitch in!" Stoddard the presidential secretary was bullish on America, and Stoddard the Wall Street speculator "went wildly short of gold in New York."

After the fourteen-block-long parade delighted the crowd, Stoddard gave a catered dinner for distinguished guests. In the middle of it all, news of twin victories at Gettysburg and Vicksburg came "tumbling in," he recalled, and "the price of gold was tumbling at a rate that made my dinner bill of small account."

Tuesday, July 7 saw a celebratory White House serenade. Unprepared to speak, Lincoln delivered an awkward address with a flat beginning, soon to be improved: "How long ago is it—eighty odd years" since this new nation began?

* * *

On July 18 Hay wrote to Nicolay, who had gone west to negotiate with the Utes, and taunted him with White House debauchery. Hay and Bob Lincoln had enjoyed "a fearful orgy here last night on whiskey and cheese. The house is gradually going to the bad since you left."

In a lighthearted mood the next day, Lincoln scribbled some atrocious doggerel about Gettysburg and made a gift of it to Hay, who "ran the Tycoon through one hundred court martials" in a "sitting of six hours!" Lincoln's buoyancy was fortunate for scores of lucky men whose sentences were reviewed, including a 1st Colorado cavalry deserter: "Let him fight instead of being shot," Lincoln said, as he did on any thin excuse; but for every commuted death sentence, another took its place. Hay would soon tell Nicolay, "I daily hold the Tycoon's nose to the Court Martial grindstone."

The Judge Advocate General came to Lincoln's office every Friday to review death sentences, making him dread the day. Hay helped him through it, and for what seemed like the longest time, Stoddard was assigned to brief clemency pleas, many prepared by poor, barely educated men and boys. Lincoln decided as many as a hundred in each prolonged ordeal. Cutting off a Thursday chat, he turned a friend out of his office. "Tomorrow is butcher's day, and I must go through these papers and see if I cannot find some excuse to let these poor fellows off."

Hay said Lincoln lost no sleep letting murderers or rapists die, or men who had gone over to the rebels, but his softness on deserters and sleeping sentinels maddened his generals, and so did his empathy for boys who ran under fire. "Leg cases," he called them. He said he was none too sure what he would do in their place. "It would frighten the poor devils too terribly to shoot them." As he spoke one day with a chaplain, the wind blew the sound of musketry across the river. He got up from his chair, walked to the open window, and turned back with damp eyes. "This is the day when they shoot deserters. I am wondering whether I have used the pardoning power as much as I ought."

Learning from a constituent that her nineteen-year-old boy would be shot the next day for sleeping on guard, an upstate New York congressman who had served with Lincoln in the House took the next train for Washington and talked his way past a doorman who led him to the president's bed after midnight. "Well," Lincoln said, "I don't believe that shooting him will do him any good." He wrote out a telegram in his nightshirt, roused a messenger, and told him to send it from the War Department and stay until its receipt was acknowledged. When the man did not return, Lincoln went over himself until the acknowledgment arrived. "Now you just telegraph that mother that her boy is safe," he told the congressman, "and I will go home and go to bed. I guess we shall all sleep better for this night's work."

*   *   *

In the summer of 1863, Stoddard had only partly recovered from his illness and two new men were brought on to help Nicolay and Hay, a Swiss immigrant named Gustave Matile, "the Gustav" as Hay was soon calling him, now the youngest of the professional staff, and a lawyer named Nathaniel S. Howe, now the oldest.

Born in 1841, the Gustav had studied law with Abram Wakeman, a member of Mrs. Lincoln's salon, and was seemingly unimpressed by proximity to greatness. "I may not remain in public office very long," he told a friend rather pompously six months later, "for I find that my experience in law matters is getting rusty." Hay was in no position to blame him. Returning from a rest in Rhode Island and a commencement speech at Brown, Hay found Washington City "as dull as an obsolete almanac."

Howe was brought in as a clerk requisitioned from the Department of the Interior, the old bureaucratic shell game. A native of Haverhill, Massachusetts, he was no mere scrivener. He had been a judge and a state senator and needed a job after failing as a lawyer. Far more accomplished than Lincoln's secretaries had been as White House novices, Howe was in good odor with Hay, who wrote to Nicolay on August 7 in torturous heat and humidity: "The Tycoon is in fine whack, I have rarely seen him more serene and busy," and Howe "is better than Stod, as he is never stuffy and always on hand."

Stoddard said after the war, "I never had a better or more faithful friend than John Hay, as his many letters testify." But some of Hay's letters say otherwise. From Hay's point of view, Stoddard had begun to see himself as a Wall Street wolf with a hobby as a White House secretary. "Stod is more and more worthless," Hay told Nicolay in September. "I can scarcely rely upon him for anything." In October, Hay got "a more than usually asinine letter from Stoddard who is in New York stock Jobbing and writes to me pretending he is working for the election."

$$* \quad * \quad *$$

In 1845, the autobiographical *Narrative of the Life of Fredrick Douglass, An American Slave*, made an international celebrity of its author, a self-educated, articulate, charismatic escaped slave, the most famous abolitionist in the country. On a hot day in August 1863, Douglass went to Lincoln with Senator Samuel C. Pomeroy, who had bivouacked in the White House as a Frontier Guard with a belt strung around his belly in 1861.

Lincoln was sprawled in a chair with his legs out, surrounded by books, papers, and secretaries. "The room bore the marks of business," Douglass said, and everyone seemed drained. Douglass was concerned about how he would be received. "I was an ex slave, identified with a despised race, and yet I was to meet the most exalted person in this great republic," but Lincoln put him at ease. He rose and offered his hand as Douglass was introduced, and lit up "as soon as my name was mentioned." Lincoln interrupted as he started to explain who he was. "I know who you are, Mr. Douglass. Mr. Seward has told me all about you. Sit down. I am glad to see you."

Douglass said he was soliciting black recruits for the army, no longer an easy task since the word had gotten out that they were unfairly treated. Lincoln gave honest answers to every point he raised, not all of which he wanted to hear. Douglass admired his candor, "the first great man that I talked with in the United States freely, who in no single instance reminded me of the difference between himself and myself, of the difference in color."

*   *   *

"The yellow leaves on the trees in the President's grounds look golden in the radiance," Stoddard wrote in October, "and even the somber evergreens in Lafayette Square appear more cheerful than usual." In fine autumn weather, General James Garfield, not yet thirty-three, was brought to Lincoln's office to recount his heroism at Chickamauga; Tad was photographed on the grounds on a South American pony, the gift of an ambitious colonel; and the three thousand walking wounded of the Invalid Corps limped past the White House in ten sky-blue battalions armed with muskets or sabers and pistols, depending on their mutilations. "A number of the officers had but one arm and many were lame and the men as a general thing looked rather pale and not able to stand much fatigue." Some of them did light work around the White House.

On November 4, the Lincolns returned from the Soldiers' Home, and a carter hauled nineteen loads of furniture back down Pennsylvania Avenue for the First Lady. Later that month, to Lincoln's delight, Colonel Charles Halpine, an Irish-born friend of Hay's, described for the *New York Herald* a White House visit attributed to his comic alter ego, "Private Miles O'Reilly," commencing with

> a great scene of handshaking at the door between Private O'Reilly and Edward McManus, the chatty old gray-haired gentleman from Italy—where O'Reilly knew him—who has kept watch at the gate through five administrations; and who is now assisted by Thomas Burns, also from Italy, who has outlived the storms of two reigns. It was "God bless you Miles," and "God bless you kindly Edward," for as many as ten minutes, the handshaking being fast and furious all the time.

On November 18, Lincoln left Washington to dedicate a military cemetery, taking Nicolay and Hay. As he often did when he traveled, he took William Johnson too, the part-time black valet rejected by the servants in 1861. The president sent a note to Johnson's employer, the Treasury Department librarian: "William Johnson goes with me to Gettysburg. A. Lincoln." Neither Nicolay nor Hay were sufficiently moved by his speech to take memorable note of it William Johnson may already have heard it.

The president felt an illness coming on at Gettysburg, which worsened on the train back to Washington. William, as Lincoln called him, kept a cool, wet towel on his face to ease his fever and made him as comfortable as he could. On Thanksgiving Day, the president was in bed with varioloid fever. A milder form of smallpox affecting people who had already had the disease or been vaccinated, it was quite enough to kill. Barely able to move, Lincoln told Dr. Stone he had thought of a consolation: "It cannot in the least disfigure me." He soon came up with another. "Now I have something I can give everybody."

The White House became a smallpox hospital, Stoddard said, and the job and favor seekers disappeared overnight. A "penetrable quarantine" began at the front door. You could get past Edward McManus by displaying a vaccination scar, only to confront "the impassible Mr. Nicolay." The White House was strangely quiet, which Stoddard could not enjoy as he considered the risk to Lincoln's life. "It is impossible not to calculate the consequences, and to remember all you know" about Vice President Hannibal Hamlin. In a letter to Colonel Halpine, alias Private Miles O'Reilly, Hay took it typically lightly, the odds of a deadly outcome being low: Lincoln was "too sick to read and not well enough to object to anything. So I had him at my mercy and read him into a fever."

As Lincoln improved and slowly started working in bed, Edward came to Stoddard, a smallpox survivor, and told him that the president wanted him. "He understands that you are proof against infection." Lincoln was sitting up, "half-amused." He was fine, he said, and had never been worried; the rest had done him good. Perhaps he could work in a smallpox ward and discourage visitors. Then he gave it a second thought. "Well no. They'd all go and get vaccinated" and "come buzzing back around me like so many greenhead flies."

On December 2, he was well enough to do some business but not to attend the ceremony capping the Capitol dome with the Statue of Freedom, chosen before the war by Senator Jefferson Davis. Lincoln's full recovery took a month. As he gradually returned to work, he was not above using disease to ward off bores, one of whom had settled in for a long discourse when Dr. Stone happened by. "Doctor, what are these blotches?" Lincoln asked, holding up his hands. Stone played along and told him what they were, and his caller beat a barely polite retreat as Lincoln urged him to stay.

William Johnson, too, contracted smallpox, typically transmitted by prolonged contact with an infected person, especially during the onset of symptoms. With the White House draped in mourning for Caleb Smith, the late Secretary of the Interior, the *Chicago Tribune* was about to report an epidemic spawning "great terror" in the capital when its Washington correspondent found Lincoln counting greenbacks in his office. It "is out of my usual line," he said, "but a President of the United States has a multiplicity of duties not specified in the Constitution or acts of Congress." William Johnson could not draw his pay, being "very bad with the small pox," and Lincoln had collected it for him. *He* had not infected William, he said, "at least I think not." He was dividing William's pay as William had wished, putting part of it in an envelope, which Lincoln signed, sealed, and labeled "very carefully."

In a day or two William was dead. Lincoln retired two loans he had cosigned for him, paid to bury him in what was later called Arlington Cemetery, and had a gravestone carved.

Like William Johnson, Solomon James Johnson, not a relative, cut Lincoln's hair and beard, and the president got him William's Treasury Department job with a note to Secretary Chase. "This boy," said the note (Johnson was a black man in his twenties) "would like to have the place made vacant by William Johnson's death. I believe he is a good boy and I should be glad for him to have the place if it is still vacant."

*   *   *

On the afternoon of September 22, 1863, Lincoln's Supreme Court appointee David Davis had dropped by his office and found him distraught over the death at Chickamauga of his Confederate brother-in-law General Ben Hardin Helm, who had helped protect the White House in 1861. "I saw how grief stricken he was," Davis said, "so I closed the door and left him alone."

Helm's widow, Mrs. Lincoln's pregnant half-sister Emilie, "a wonderfully bright and prepossessing woman," had gone to Atlanta for the funeral and asked General Grant for a pass to get home to her mother in Kentucky. Grant refused, and Emilie's mother asked Lyman Todd, the Lexington postmaster and Mrs. Lincoln's cousin, to ask the president. Lincoln sent the pass.

In early December, when Emilie reached Fort Monroe, the Union stronghold at Hampton Roads, Virginia, on the flag of truce boat, she declined to take the oath of allegiance required to disembark and asked to go to Washington on parole. Years later she would say she could not desert the cause her husband and brothers had died for. Aware of her family connections, federal officers wired Washington for instructions, and Lincoln dispatched a terse reply: "Send her to me."

The youngest and prettiest of Mrs. Lincoln's sisters, "a pathetic little figure in her trailing black crepe," Emilie brought a daughter and described her arrival at the White House in her diary.

> Mr. Lincoln and my sister met me with the warmest affection, we were all too grief-stricken at first for speech. I have lost my husband, they have lost their fine little son Willie, and Mary and I have lost three brothers in the Confederate service. We could only embrace each other in silence and tears. Sister and I dined intimately, alone.

They spoke of the happy past and avoided the unspeakable present. After dinner, Mrs. Lincoln had the parlors lit in gaslight for her sister to see and took her to the mansion's best guestroom, overlooking Pennsylvania Avenue, even though Willie had died in it. Buchanan had fitted it up it for the Prince of Wales, and Mrs. Lincoln and Carryl's of Philadelphia had improved it again with a magnificently carved rosewood and walnut bed, crowned with an eight-foot headboard and a canopy under a gilded half coronet. The purple bed hangings seemed "gloomy and funereal" to Emilie, "though brightened with yellow cords." The curtains reversed the colors, yellow with purple trim.

While Emilie lived in the White House she watched her sister cheer the president, which he needed. As Emilie came across the room to greet her one morning, Mary dropped the newspaper she had been reading and held out her arms pathetically.

> "Kiss me Emilie, and tell me that you love me! I seem to be the scapegoat for both North and South!" Then suddenly, as if she had thrown off a dark cloak and stood revealed in a gay costume, she held her head up and smiled. I was marveling at the transformation but instantly understood the cause as Brother Lincoln's voice came to us, "I hope you two are not planning some mischief."

Their antithetical loyalties left the president as tongue-tied with Emilie as his wife, but deeply sympathetic to her loss. "She and Brother Lincoln pet me as if I were a child," Emilie told her diary, "and, without words, try to comfort me." The sisters wept together with clasped hands over their dead little brother Alec.

In a moment alone with Emilie, Lincoln told her he was worried about Mary, that "her nerves have gone to pieces." Emilie said she feared that "if anything should happen to you or Robert or Tad it would kill her." The president shook his head. "Stay with her as long as you can."

That night Mary knocked at Emilie's door and asked to come in, smiling through swollen eyes. There was hope and comfort when a loved one died, she said, "and if Willie did not come to comfort me I would still be drowned in tears." Emilie recorded what Mary said in her diary.

"He lives, Emilie!" she said with a thrill in her voice I can never forget. "He comes to me every night, and stands at the foot of my bed with the same sweet, adorable smile he has always had. He does not always come alone. Little Eddie [the brother who had died in childhood before Willie was born] is sometimes with him, and twice he has come with our brother Alec. He tells me he loves his Uncle Alec and is with him most of the time. You cannot dream of the comfort this gives me. When I thought of my little son in immensity, alone, without his mother to direct him, no one to hold his little hand in loving guidance, it nearly broke my heart."

Emilie found it chilling. "Sister Mary's eyes were wide and shining and I had a feeling of awe as if I were in the presence of the supernatural. It *is* unnatural and abnormal. It frightens me."

General Dan Sickles, the friend of Mrs. Lincoln's salon who had represented Wikoff as his legal counsel, called on her with New York's Senator Ira Harris the next day. Lincoln was in bed with his illness. Sickles had left a leg at Gettysburg, where he had nearly cost the North its victory, and he spoke to Emilie Helm in a tone better heard than described. He had told Senator Harris that Emilie might have news of his friend, the rebel general John C. Breckinridge, he said. When Emilie said she had none, Harris spoke "in a voice of triumph."

"Well," he said, "we have whipped the rebels at Chattanooga, and I hear, Madam, that the scoundrels ran like scared rabbits." Emilie stared him down. "It was the example, Senator Harris, that you set them at Bull Run and Manassas." Mrs. Lincoln changed the subject, but Harris turned to her sharply. "Why isn't Robert in the Army?" She blanched and straightened her neck. "I have insisted that he should stay in college a little longer," she said, "as I think an educated man can serve his country with more intelligent purpose than an ignoramus."

Harris stood and pointed at her. "I have only one son and he is fighting for his country!" Then he bowed low to Emilie. "And, Madam, if I had twenty sons they should all be fighting the rebels."

"And if I had twenty sons," Emilie replied, "they should all be opposing yours." She hurried from the room and her sister overtook her, put her arms around her, and let her cry on her shoulder. That night Emilie confessed to her diary, "I forgot that I was a guest of the President and Mrs. Lincoln at the White House."

The angry pair of Yankees had reached the portico and started down the stairs when Sickles stopped abruptly, stumped back up the steps, and demanded to see the president. Lincoln came down from his sickbed, and Sickles repeated what his sister-in-law had said. Lincoln's eye twinkled. "The child has a tongue like the rest of the Todds." Sickles was not charmed, and slapped a table hard. "You should not have that little rebel in your house."

Lincoln drew himself up quietly. "Excuse me, General Sickles, my wife and I are in the habit of choosing our own guests." They needed no advice on the matter, and "the little rebel" had come because he had ordered it.

In all her time at the White House, Lincoln spoke with Emilie only once about her husband: "You know, little sister, I tried to have Ben come with me. I hope you do not feel any bitterness or that I am in any way to blame for all this sorrow."

It was "the fortune of war," Emilie said. Her husband had loved him, and was grateful for his offer, but he had to follow his conscience. "Mr. Lincoln put his arms around me, and we both wept."

The president almost begged her to move in and comfort Mary, despite the incalculable cost of a rebel in the White House with a reelection campaign in the wings, but Emilie demurred. "I feel that my being here is more or less an embarrassment to all of us," her diary says, "and I am longing for Kentucky and mother."

Before she took her little daughter home, Emilie watched Tad play host to the girl, showing her photographs on a rug by the fire. "This is the President," he said.

His cousin shook her head. "No, that is not the President, Mr. Davis is President."

"Hurrah for Abe Lincoln!" Tad said.

"Hurrah for Jeff Davis!" the little girl said.

Tad appealed to his father, who took a child on each knee. "Well, Tad," he said, "you know who is your President, and I am your little cousin's Uncle Lincoln."

On December 14, Orville Browning came to the White House with a friend who wished to have a rebel brother-in-law released as a prisoner and committed to his custody. In no position to object, Lincoln told Browning that Emilie was in the house, "but he did not wish it to be known."

He took a chance that day. Writing an oath for Emilie to sign "in presence of Almighty God" that she would support the Union and all lawful proclamations as to slaves, he gave her a pass to Kentucky, with "protection of person and property, except as to slaves, of which I say nothing," and a pardon consistent with his proclamation of amnesty for all repentant rebels who swore loyalty.

As Emilie left the White House, Lincoln looked at her hard. "Little Sister, I have known you all your life, and I never knew you to do a mean thing. I know you will not embarrass me in any way on your return to Kentucky."

*　　*　　*

The imperial Russian fleet arrived that month, lying off Alexandria in a show of support for the Union, a shot across the bows of Britain and France. A few days after Emilie's departure, Lincoln welcomed the officers to an afternoon in the East Room, excluding the common man and woman in czarist style. Benjamin French thought the reception was "the most brilliant I ever attended, because it was the only one where the mud stained people did not mingle with the court dresses, epaulettes, shoulder straps, etc." The "magnificently uniformed" Russians were "exceedingly polite and *stiff* in their manners, as all foreigners appear to be to us free-and-easy 'Yankees.'" Hay had met them at the home of Gideon Welles and left with mixed impressions. "They have vast absorbent powers and are fiendishly ugly."

On a bitter cold December 25, Hay had "a lonesome sort of Christmas. I breakfasted, dined and supped alone. Went to the theater and saw *Macbeth* alone. Came home and slept alone."

New Year's Day 1864 began just as glum, but the sun broke through, "and a cold wind soon froze up the streets and made the walking good." Indifferently groomed on the best of days, Seward led the diplomatic corps into the Blue Room in their "gold lace and toggery," striking Noah Brooks "like a molting barnyard fowl among peacocks." But the diplomats drew the usual appreciative gasps from the citizens lined up for the show despite the wind. They were excited enough to crowd the police line, Stoddard said, but orderly, curious, and eager to shake the president's hand.

Ward Hill Lamon brought two young women from Springfield who were visiting him and his wife. "Old Abe merely shook my hand and I passed on," one of them wrote in her diary, but "Madam was very gracious" and "we had the honor of walking round the east room with her. A band of music played very finely and the scene was a very pretty one."

*　　*　　*

Shocked by Lincoln's vulnerability after he removed his cavalry guard, Ohio's governor David Tod had caused 108 picked horsemen to be recruited to form the 7th Independent Troop of Ohio Volunteer Cavalry, assigned to protect the

White House and other key points in Washington, a mission not disclosed to them until they reached the capital in December. Mounted on black horses, dashingly called the Union Light Guard, they had expected glorious work and were disappointed and even ashamed to find themselves on "parade soldier" duty guarding the president, who consented reluctantly. Nothing like cavaliers, their ranks included farmers, teachers, an artist, a shoemaker, a stonecutter, a watchmaker, two dentists, and four "colored cooks."

Quartered in barracks just south of the Treasury Department, the Union Light Guard had little to do. A noncommissioned officer and a half-dozen privates, uniformed but unarmed, kept unobtrusive order at receptions. A mounted detachment escorted the Lincolns on their afternoon rides. In two-hour shifts, facing pairs of cavalrymen sat their mounts at the White House gates twenty-four hours a day. To give them some relief from the boredom and the cold, the corporal of the guard blew a police whistle every half hour, signaling one man at each gate to change places, riding across the lawn, crossing in front of the house, followed by the other two.

Having watched the procedure with interest, Tad asked to examine the corporal's whistle one night, then ran into the house to a second-floor window and blew it. He kept it up for half an hour, "to the bewilderment of the sentinels," who enjoyed the extra exercise and may not have been bewildered. To make amends, Tad brought the corporal a bowl of punch smuggled out of a state dinner.

In their ample free time, the Union Light Guard groomed their mounts and polished their tack, earning the horses more attention than their riders in the opinion of one of the men, but a jaded English tourist was not impressed when he joined some other "loungers" on the steps of the north portico and watched Lincoln's carriage arrive, escorted by what must have been the Union Light Guard. The Englishman mistook them for the Invalid Corps. "The animals on which they rode had four legs," he said, "and an odd tail or two, and more or less the shape and manner of a horse, and I suppose were intended for horses, but barely fit the definition of one." The riders were less presentable still, "mud-spattered, and threadbare as an Irishman's coat." They bore no resemblance to the Queen's Life Guard, and the president's "tumble-down" coach could not have been mistaken for hers. "It might have been centuries" since it was washed or painted, and "no decayed cabby" would have put his head in the coachman's hat. "The Constitution has some queer provisions. I wonder if it compels the President's coachman to brush his hat the wrong way."

At least one member of the Union Light Guard shared the Londoner's appraisal of Lincoln's everyday coach. It was "about on a par with the average street hack, and his team would be called common plugs anywhere." They had started their useful lives as the presentation pair given to Mrs. Lincoln in 1861, a handsome but fragile breed, and had grown so "thin, worn out, and badly groomed," Stoddard said, that people had started to talk. Lincoln may not have noticed, but Walt Whitman did. "The equipage is of the plainest kind," he wrote, "only two horses, and they nothing extra."

With the Union Light Guard at the White House gates, resting drawn sabers on their shoulders, another Englishman walked into the White House "quite unmolested and unannounced." The guardsmen had no apparent security role, and seemed "merely to prevent a block among the carriages, and had nothing to do with pomp or state. Their attire was as ragged, their boots as muddy, their horses as ungroomed, and their hair as unkempt as usual."

One of their junior officers had been court martialed for "tormenting cattle," among other obscure offenses. To discourage a small herd of dairy cows from "running at large in the lot at the rear of the President's House," he had ordered some troopers to tie buckets, pans, and tin cups to their tails.

On Monday, January 4, a letter to Lincoln arrived and was saved. It may have been the first of its kind of 1864. "Your days are numbered," it said. "You have been weighed in the balance and found wanting. You shall be a dead man in six months from date December 31, 1863. Thus saith the good Spirit. Joseph." A few weeks later, a "fair, plump lady" from Dubuque burst into a cabinet meeting and announced that she wanted a look at Lincoln, who gallantly replied that he had the best of the exchange. The unimpeded access to the president and his cabinet was not as amusing.

On a foggy night, Lincoln asked Noah Brooks to walk with him to the War Department. As they left the family quarters, he took an iron-studded cane from a collection in a corner, looked around with mock concern, and spoke in a comic whisper. "Mother has got a notion into her head that I shall be assassinated, and to please her I take a cane when I go over to the War Department at nights, when I don't forget it."

As they walked in the dark down the path, Brooks thought he saw a menacing figure lurking among the trees. Lincoln took it in and teased him about his anxiety, then spoke to him more earnestly. "I long ago made up my mind that if anybody wants to kill me, he will do it. If I wore a shirt of mail and kept myself surrounded by a bodyguard it would be all the same." An elaborate guard would merely tell his enemies that he feared them, and challenge their ingenuity. He thought he was safest among the people, and his best protection was to show he was not at risk.

*   *   *

In January 1864, Hay was appointed assistant adjutant general with a major's rank and pay, which lightened the White House payroll. Nursing silent thoughts of a Senate seat, he left for two warm months in Florida to help build a government capable of readmission to the Union. Less than a week later, Nicolay let him know there was trouble in the winter White House.

Mrs. Lincoln was insisting on excluding Rhode Island's Senator William Sprague and his wife from a state dinner, a snub that would damage the president over the First Lady's petty jealousy of the lovely new Mrs. Sprague, none other than the former Kate Chase. Nicolay brought the issue to Lincoln, who overrode Mrs. Lincoln's veto, producing "such a rampage as the House hasn't seen for a year, and I am again taboo." Poor Stoddard had "fairly cowered at the violence of the storm, and I think for the first time begins to appreciate the awful sublimities of nature." Between themselves, Nicolay and Hay started calling the First Lady "Her Satanic Majesty."

There was more. Mrs. Lincoln barred *Nicolay* from planning and attending the dinner and "fished around with Stod" about getting *him* to take over the role. Nicolay instructed Stoddard to say he did not know how, and even if he did, it was Nicolay's place, and Stoddard "*could* and *would not* do anything in the premises." Stod followed his orders, and Mrs. Lincoln decided to "run the machine" herself.

On the very day of the dinner, Edward McManus came upstairs with the Madam's apologies. She needed Nicolay's help and hadn't slept for a night or two. Nicolay thought she was happier "since she cast out the devil of stubbornness." The dinner came off fine, and Nicolay told Hay that "Her S Majesty" had been defeated.

Benjamin French, who wrestled her almost daily as commissioner of public buildings, had soured on her too. No longer regarding her as "a curiosity" but an "excellent lady," he compared her to a hyena. When French made the mistake of managing the domestic staff directly rather than through the First Lady, his power "went to grass," Stoddard said. Her receptions were wearing him out. "I guess you never saw a man rising 63 who was so bedeviled with all sorts of matters as I am," he told his brother, "the American Empress demands my personal presence for two hours every Saturday and three every alternate Tuesday—and no vittles and drink given!" To add expense to injury, the fresh kid gloves she insisted he wear to each event cost him "$2.25 per pair! Isn't it awful!"

Newly remarried as a widower, French expected more trouble as he and the Empress outdid one another in insincerity:

Mrs. Lincoln has recently fallen to flattering me, must look out. At the last "Matinee" before yesterday she talked about my elegant wife, her dignity of manner, etc. I wound up by saying she looked like a queen. Yesterday she told me I was growing young, and "no wonder" she said, "with such a beautiful young wife." I think she wants the White House refurnished!

After two years of abuse by job seekers, partygoers, and tourists, the 1861 renovation was already dented and bruised. When Nicolay gave a tour to a couple from home, the wife's oohs and ahs

> were truly fresh and interesting, and almost enough to make me forget for the moment what an ill-kept, inconvenient, and dirty old rickety concern it really is, from top to bottom. I wonder how much longer a great nation, as ours is, will compel its ruler to live in such a small and dilapidated old shanty and in such a shabby-genteel style.

Later that year, Congress considered replacing it. With ample good cause, the White House was thought to be unhealthy, "inadequate and inconvenient for its purpose," crowded by neighborhood growth and on its way back to decrepitude. A new presidential residence might be built in a quiet suburb, "handsome, spacious and modern in its appurtenances," with the White House delivered to the State Department as a workplace and a stage. "Perhaps when the war is over," a *Boston Journal* columnist hoped, "and the national debt has been paid, a building will be erected worthy of the name of Executive Mansion."

*   *   *

A young English girl wrote home in February having spotted a celebrity at Willard's—"Walt Whitman, with his long hair on his shoulders, is here." She arrived at Mrs. Lincoln's Saturday afternoon reception at one o'clock, "an hour for bonnets and morning dress." The driveway was full of carriages, elegant men and women chatted in the Green Room, and "the air was pleasant with the scent of flowers." A boy on the staircase was "doing his best to upset the gravity of the servants." When Mrs. Lincoln spoke to him, he answered politely and behaved. "I think they called him Thad."

Lincoln was shaking hands in the Blue Room, seldom expanding on "How do you do?" until the English girl came up to him. "He looked so kind that I forgot to be frightened." She told him her people were with him "heart and soul," which cheered him, and inspired a pro-British response. Then she curtsied to Mrs. Lincoln, stepped away from the president, and "watched him with all my eyes." Looking anxious and careworn, he beat one glove slowly against the other and smiled now and then, chatting "like a person who hears that what he is saying is good, and a little enjoys it." He did not look like "a very cultivated man, but you knew he was *great*."

It was a common European perception, seeing past his awkwardness to his character. Lincoln was "unused to society," said Lafayette's grandson after a White House levee, and looked "just the same as he must have appeared while felling trees in Illinois. But I must add that he dominates everyone present and maintains his exalted position without the slightest effort."

Later that winter, another White House racial bar came down. "I shall never forget the sensation produced at a levee by the appearance of two tall and very well dressed Africans among the crowd," Stoddard said, "a practical assertion of negro citizenship for which few were prepared." The black men courted no special attention, but the president greeted them warmly. An author of children's and religious books saw no sign that he knew they were black. It was thought to be the first time in history that "colored men" attended a White House reception, and yet Lincoln treated it as "an ordinary occurrence, much to his credit and renown." Stoddard was glad that the two brave men had come. He thought they had done it well, whatever their intentions had been, and some remarks overheard in the startled crowd were "as good as a play."

Making an unwitting mockery of its name, the *New York Freeman's Journal* told its subscribers that "filthy black niggers" now jostled white people, even ladies, in the President's House; but before a year had passed, racial integration at White House levees was old news. A military hospital nurse watched Lincoln merely nod to people in a receiving line who "gazed at him vacantly as if he were part of the furniture." To "the lowly, to the humble, the timid colored man or woman, he bent in special kindliness."

16

CRAZY AND POETRY

Francis Bicknell Carpenter was a handsome thirty-three-year-old portrait painter from upstate New York with sweptback hair and a close-trimmed beard. A Philadelphian named Edward Dalton Marchant had already spent three months at the White House painting the signing of the Emancipation Proclamation, but Mrs. Lincoln wanted better results. On Christmas Day 1863, she told Carpenter that the president had endorsed his proposal to produce a life-sized painting of Lincoln's first reading of the Emancipation Proclamation to his cabinet.

Carpenter made his way to Mrs. Lincoln's Saturday reception on February 6, 1864. Despite filthy weather, the streetcars were "crowded to suffocation" as they unloaded at the White House stop. Scores of private carriages rolled through the gates between the mounted sentinels of the Union Light Guard, resting naked sabers on their shoulders with no thought of using them. Two more cavalrymen sat their horses before the portico, taming the crowd.

A servant standing in the vestibule pointed people in the right direction, and Carpenter took his turn in the reception line. When he introduced himself to the president, Lincoln stood up straight in a parody of self-importance. "Do you think, Mr. Carpenter, that you can make a handsome picture of *me*?" Getting started on the spot, Carpenter asked to see him after the reception in his office, where the proclamation had been signed and the painting would be set.

Lincoln's desk was strewn with papers as he seated the eager painter. "Well, Mr. Carpenter, we will turn you loose in here, and try to give you a good chance to work out your idea." Carpenter would sketch as Lincoln worked, and paint his vast canvas in the State Dining Room. He was drawing within the week and sent the president to Mathew Brady's photographic studio for an ambrotype. Carpenter would work at the White House for six months, absorbing what he saw, befriending Bob Lincoln and Hay. With open access to Lincoln's office, except for the most sensitive meetings, he sketched unobtrusively in a corner. When the president worked alone he seemed to forget the artist was there. If a caller eyed Carpenter warily, Lincoln would brush it off. "Oh you need not mind him. He is but a painter."

Lincoln brought people down to the State Dining Room to watch him paint. As Carpenter described his work, Lincoln discussed its subject, sitting on the end of the table, swinging his long legs, running a hand through his hair. Mrs. Lincoln fretted over the painting's enormous size. "What puzzles me is what on earth we are ever going to do with it."

As Carpenter drew late one night in the president's office, Lincoln, Nicolay, and Hay returned from the opera and gathered in the secretaries' bedroom. When Lincoln's laughter drew Carpenter in, Nicolay was sitting in a chair with his boots off, Hay was in bed, and the president was leaning over the footboard, laughing "like a schoolboy" about some misadventure of Hay's, which Hay repeated to Carpenter without being coaxed.

*   *   *

Nicolay told Hay about a shortage of help: Stoddard was sick again, and "Congress sends up a hungrier swarm of gadflies every morning to bedevil the President and to generally retard and derange business. My subs [the clerks Matile and Howe] are not yet well broken in and I must necessarily give everything my personal supervision." Only partly recovered from his most recent illness, Stod said, "I was down with the typhoid fever. It was a pull of weeks and I got up too soon, only to go down again."

Yet another overqualified clerk was appointed to the Interior Department and assigned to White House duty. Edward Neill, a forty-year-old graduate of Amherst College and the Andover Theological Seminary, was a Presbyterian minister, the author of a *History of Minnesota*, a father of Saint Paul's public schools, a founder and former chancellor of the University of Minnesota, a former State Superintendent of Public Instruction, and the recent chaplain of the First Minnesota Volunteer Infantry and the United States Military Hospital of Philadelphia. He made for a weighty clerk.

"I was appointed to read and dispose of all letters addressed to President Lincoln," he said, "and commissioned a secretary to sign land patents," Stoddard's old job. But Neill's responsibilities were broader. He drafted correspondence for Lincoln and Nicolay and decided which incoming letters the president should see. When Nicolay and Hay were away, Neill stepped into their duties. On his way out of town in July, Hay wrote Neill a note that summed up the heart of the secretaries' mission: "Refer as little to the President as possible. Keep visitors out of the house when you can. Inhospitable, but prudent."

The incoming mail had expanded from one daily bag to two, and the Prussian Louis Burgdorf, who delivered it, lacked social skills: "A man would come through the door before me with a leather mail-pouch," Neill said. "He would unlock the pouch, pour out its contents on the table, and go out again without saying a word." The quality of those contents had not improved. "Good and true men without foresight" sent twenty or thirty pages about what they would do in Lincoln's place. Schoolgirls sent the president their photographs in exchange for his. "College students afflicted with the autograph mania stormed him with requests for his signature."

The slot on the correspondence desk labeled "Crazy and Poetry" must have been full. A "messenger of the King of Kings and Lord of Lords" found time to write from New Zealand. A married man in love with a young girl promised to take her to church every Sunday if the president sent him a divorce. An applicant to West Point admitted he was nearsighted and "did not possess a form like Appolo" but had read in *Plutarch's Lives* "that some of the ancient heroes were deformed."

A curious letter came from Canada, sent by a deserter who had been to church and wanted to surrender. He would walk around the White House grounds on a certain day and hour, wearing a distinctive coat. Neill asked a messenger to look for him, and he appeared on schedule. Looking as if he had suffered, the man told Neill he was willing to die for his crime. His letter went in to the president, who sent it back with a note returning him to his regiment with his service extended by the length of his absence.

There was no break in court martial reviews. When the assistant adjutant general asked Neill about the status of the papers on a soldier who had killed a man, Neill went to Lincoln, who pointed at his desk. "There they are," he said, "tell him they are still in soak." The officer came back in two weeks. The condemned man, who had pleaded insanity, should be hanged or pardoned, the officer said. Lincoln rifled through a case stuffed with papers, found the physician's report "without the slightest difficulty," and read its last sentence to Neill: "Although I cannot pronounce the person insane, he certainly is peculiar." It was enough to spare him the rope.

*   *   *

On Tuesday, February 9, Lincoln spent the morning on court martials while Carpenter sketched him. Late that night Nicolay wrote to Hay:

Put crepe on your hat. Tonight at about 8:30 while Cooper [a coachman] was gone to his supper, the stables took fire and burned down. The carriages and coupe alone were saved—everything else went—six horses, including the President's, ours, and Tad's two ponies are "gone where the good horses go." The heaviest loss really falls on Cooper. He reports to me that he had $300 in gold and about $100 in bills in the room in which he slept. All this even including what few clothes he had is of course gone, as no one ever heard of any coin ever being recovered after a fire. Poor fellow!

Cooper was sure it was arson. He had not been away an hour, and the gas could not have started the fire. Mrs. Lincoln had dismissed her coachman, Patterson McGee, that very day, Nicolay said, "and Bob, who is here, suspects him of the work."

Nicolay's flip response to the burning of the animals, including his own, clashed with Lincoln's. A telegrapher leaving the War Department had seen smoke rising from the south grounds and run back to wire the engine house above 17th Street. A fire bell was rung, but a neighbor said the Bucktails "stood around and did not take their hands out of their pockets." Lincoln ran hatless from the house, chased by a corporal of the Union Light Guard. When he reached the boxwood hedge enclosing the brick stable, he "sprang over it like a deer," asked the soldiers if the horses were out, demanded to know why not, tore at the door with his hands, and was on his way into the flames when they pulled him back.

Just as it occurred to a soldier that the fire could have been set to draw the president out and assassinate him, a gentleman in the crowd stepped up. "Mr. President," he said, "this is no place for you," and walked him arm in arm to the house with the captain of the guard, who ordered an extra cavalry detail. When the corporal who had chased him went inside, Lincoln was in the East Room, looking at the burning stable. "He was weeping." Tad explained that his father had tried to save Willie's pony.

Lincoln asked Congress for a new stable the next morning, and a $12,000 appropriation was on his desk in two days. He wanted "a substantial, convenient, well built stable, with no money thrown away in ornamentation or extravagance," and he wanted it fast. The carriages, the new horses, and their hay were outside in midwinter. As for the stable's location, the president asked French to consult Mrs. Lincoln. A new site was chosen near the old one, and salvageable brick, stone, and wood were reused. "I received all sorts of advice," French said, "indeed all sorts of contrivances to get some of that $12,000 into pockets of people who could not aid me to the amount of a picayune." After a noble effort, French brought the stable in at $2,000 over budget.

On February 15, in a hand so exquisite it could have passed for engraving, Nicolay wrote Thaddeus Stevens, who chaired the House Ways and Means Committee, asking Congress to replace the horses lost in the fire and subsidize the carriage that delivered the president's messages. Through February 1, the carriage, harness, and horses and almost three years of feed and coachman's wages had cost a whopping $3,060.49. Nicolay had covered some of it from Executive Office funds but paid more than half of it himself—$1,742 in three years from a $2,500 salary.

Eventually, Congress did the right thing, which was something like an aberration. Necessary but unauthorized White House expenses, Stoddard said, were always eked out somehow, but Nicolay and Hay "were always calling for more and not getting it, like so many Oliver Twists."

The fire left only a passing cloud on the winter social scene. On Tuesday evening, February 23, George Bancroft, an intellectual celebrity in fierce white muttonchops who had written a popular history of the United States, attended a White House levee. Lincoln had met him in 1861 and recognized him in the receiving line. "He took me by the one of his hands," Bancroft said,

and trying to recall my name, he waved the other a foot and a half above his head, and cried out, greatly to the amusement of the bystanders: "Hold on—I know you, you are—History, History of the United States—Mr.—Mr. Bancroft, Mr. George Bancroft," and seemed disposed to give me a hearty welcome— expressing a wish to see me some day apart from the crowd.

A friend of Bancroft's wanted Lincoln's autograph on a copy of his Gettysburg speech and, finding him so agreeable, Bancroft asked for it. He promised to send it and did, improving the historian's impression of the house's current occupant.

As February melted into spring, the Lincolns' neighbor Judge Taft heard "the drums beat at dead of night" as thousands of new troops streamed over the Long Bridge into Virginia.

*   *   *

On the night of March 8, two middle-aged officers walked up the White House steps and into the weekly levee. Watching from the portico, the corporal of the guard saw nothing remarkable about the undersized officer with the reddish-brown beard, but he knew a major general's stars when he saw them, and "the slight purplish tinge" of a uniform worn hard in the field. Someone said it was Grant.

Lincoln had sent for Grant, the North's greatest military hero, the cele-brated victor of Shiloh, Fort Donelson, Vicksburg, and Chattanooga, about to be made general in chief of the army. As the president manned the receiving line in the Blue Room, "a certain movement and rumor in the crowd" let him know that Grant had arrived. The two famous men had never met, and they greeted each other warmly with a modest sort of mutual deference. A circle of star struck gawkers kept a respectful distance. "There was hesitation, a degree of awkwardness in the General," according to Gideon Welles, and the receiv-ing line stopped moving.

People rushed the Blue Room as the news of Grant's presence spread, and Seward walked him by the hand to the East Room. The corporal of the guard had followed Grant in with some privates, who "formed a sort of football wedge," the corporal later said, and forced a path through the crowd. Designed to deflect saber cuts, not excited ladies and gentlemen, one of the corporal's brass shoulder plates broke off against Grant in the scrum. People clapped as he passed through the Green Room. Cheers rocked the East Room when he reached it.

Seward had the general climb up on a crimson sofa, to be seen and shake hands without being crushed by his admirers. Noah Brooks thought he looked scared: "It was the only real mob I ever saw in the White House," Brooks said. Grant was not the only one who scaled the furniture. When the tumult subsided after an hour or so, he was "quietly smuggled out" of the East Room. The stately Gideon Welles had never left the Blue Room; the hubbub had struck him as unseemly; but even Uncle Gideon was not immune to celebrity. When Seward and Grant returned to the Blue Room, flushed with the exertion of battling the crowd, "Seward beckoned me," Welles's diary says, "and intro-duced me and my two nieces."

After the doormen herded the crowd from the house, Lincoln led Grant to the Red Room to prepare for the next day's ceremony promoting him to Lieutenant General, a rank only Washington and Scott had held. Handing him a copy of the four-sentence speech he had planned, Lincoln suggested that Grant compose a short reply to read aloud, unaccustomed to public speaking as he was. He should say something to quiet his rivals' jealousy, Lincoln said, and complement the Army of the Potomac, which was going under his command, and discuss his remarks with Stanton.

*　　*　　*

On the next afternoon, a messenger told Neill to look out the window "and I would see General Grant." In civilian clothes with his young son, he was walking away from the White House, where Lincoln had assembled the cabinet, General Halleck, and Grant's chief of staff for the ceremony. Nicolay had felt Grant's pain as he struggled through his penciled reply, which contained not a hint of Lincoln's suggestions. Nicolay wondered whether he ignored the president's advice after consulting Stanton, "or whether, with his deep distrust of Washington politicians, he thought it wise to begin by disregarding their suggestions." It would not be the last time.

On Saturday, March 12, Lincoln made him general in chief of the army and invited fifteen generals to a celebratory dinner, but Grant left the city early, pleading the press of duty. "Gentlemen," Lincoln told the others, "this is the play of *Hamlet* with Hamlet left out." In his office months later, Lincoln told Stoddard that Grant was "the quietest little fellow you ever saw. . . . I believe two or three times he has been in this room a minute or so before I knew he was there." Apart from his terse dispatches, his results were the only tangible evidence that he was anywhere at all.

Admiral David Farragut escorted Julia Grant to a levee not long thereafter. The Lincolns received them in the Blue Room, overcrowded, Mrs. Grant thought, with "beautiful women and brave men." Farragut suggested a retreat to the Green Room and lowered his voice. "The commonality go there." But as soon as they joined the commoners, "a hundred or more of the belles and beaux of Washington" followed.

*   *   *

At a Saturday reception in March, a Baltimore City councilman sang the popular song that began, "We are coming Father Abraham, 300,000 more." According to Benjamin French, everyone joined in the chorus, "everyone who could sing." The writer of the song, "a middle-aged, farmer-looking man," was taken to Lincoln's office and sang it for him and his secretaries and a room full of statesmen and officers.

French was in need of the diversion. He had been having "a glorious fight with that prince of purity—that pattern of propriety—that white-headed, white livered, lying scoundrel, on whose forehead God has written 'Miserable Fool' and who encumbers this earth under the name of John P. Usher," also known as the Secretary of the Interior. Lincoln had sent French a nasty note accusing him of instigating legislation to detach the commissioner of public buildings from Interior Department control and expand his power and patronage. French's reply reeked of panic. It was Usher who had been intriguing, French said. The legislation was a Senate committee's.

"My own impression is that the President will not make much capital by removing me," French told his brother, "because there is an *inside* as well as an *outside* to most things, and watches and some other delicate movements become injured at much exposure!" The allusion was to Mrs. Lincoln. "Abraham is not a fool!"

Within the week, Mrs. Lincoln wrote A. T. Stewart, the prince of Broadway merchants, thanking him for his patience with his unpaid bills and asking him, as "an especial favor to me," to stay patient for two more months. "I deeply regret that I am so unusually situated and trust hereafter to settle as I purchase." She expected in due course to order a black India camelhair shawl, she said, a maharini's extravagance.

Her husband had no notion of her debts. As Nicolay and Hay worked into the night on Saturday, April 30, with Grant and Lee about to collide in epic combat, Lincoln wandered in, laughing over Thomas Hood's poetry, unaware, Hay thought, that his long bare legs and his nightshirt sticking out like an ostrich tail were funnier. "What a man it is!" Hay thought, tied to the fate of the world's biggest army, yet with such "simple bonhomie and good fellowship" that he came to them from bed to share "one of Hood's queer little conceits." Two days later, the *Herald* reported one of his wife's conceits. All day long and late into the evening, Mrs. Lincoln had "ransacked the treasures of the Broadway dry goods stores."

The president sat twice in his office for Mathew Brady's lead photographer where he would sit in Carpenter's painting, at the end of the cabinet table in a wooden armchair. Brady's four-lens camera left four separate images on a glass plate, each taken from slightly different angles from which stereographic images could be made. Carpenter crowed in his diary: "Succeeded very well!" At least until the photographer crossed Tad.

Besotted with Washington stage productions, Tad had decided he wanted his own theater, and was quickly gratified. Under his supervision, the White House carpenter James Haliday, one of his particular friends, built a stage with curtains and theatrical paraphernalia in the sliver of vacant space over the north portico. Tad and a friend named Perry Kelly, the only actors, played their lines to servants and sentries. Tad was beside himself with joy.

When Brady's man needed a closet for a darkroom, Carpenter led him to Tad's theater without consulting Tad, who locked the door with the chemicals inside and would not give up the key. Sitting for his photographs, his father spoke quietly without leaving the chair. "Tad, go and unlock the door." Tad took the key to his mother's room instead, and Carpenter could not coax him out. Lincoln got up and soon returned with the key. He had not reproved the boy much, he said, for Tad "thought his rights had been shamefully disregarded." His father clearly thought so too.

Disappointing news soon arrived of Mrs. Lincoln's sister Emilie, the rebel widow who had stayed at the White House in December. She had smuggled home in her baggage close to her weight in quinine, the only effective treatment for malaria, "a veritable bonanza to the Southern Army." Adding insult to ingratitude, she was said to have bragged about outwitting her "too credulous brother Lincoln." The president wrote a general in Kentucky that the pass he had given her to get her home protected her from nothing at all. Long after the war, she denied that she had sworn an oath of allegiance or betrayed her sister and brother-in-law "after I arrived in Kentucky," a meaningful qualifier perhaps.

Mrs. Lincoln's Southern relatives were barred from the house, and her Alabamian half-sister Martha was the first to know. Toward the end of April, Martha sent her card in to her sister, who refused to see her. She tried again and failed again. The president sent her a pass to return to Selma through the Union lines but refused to declare her thirteen trunks immune from search. After word got back to him that she had shown off the pass and "talked 'secesh' at the hotel," she sent two friends to him to ask him to immunize her bags. He refused the first and told the second that if Martha "did not leave forthwith she might expect to find herself in the Old Capitol Prison."

In the first week of May 1864, the terrible Battle of the Wilderness left more than twenty-five thousand young Americans dead, wounded, or on their way to pestilent prison camps. Carpenter came upon Lincoln, "clad in a long morning wrapper," pacing the narrow passage to the center window over the north portico, "his hands behind him, great black rings under his eyes, his head bent forward upon his breast." Carpenter had painted several presidents and other burdened men, but Lincoln's, he said, was "the saddest face I ever knew. There were days when I could scarcely look into it without crying." On the morning after the battle, the Speaker of the House watched him pace the same way and echoed Carpenter nearly word for word: "I thought his face the saddest one I had ever seen." An hour later he was making congressmen laugh, burying his fears and theirs.

As Grant cut a bloody path south, the trees came abruptly into leaf on Saturday, May 7, and Washington was "suddenly in summer." At the first Marine Band concert on the White House grounds since Willie's death, Lincoln called for three cheers for Grant and his armies instead of a speech. At another concert that spring, Carpenter was sitting in the Blue Room as Lincoln stepped onto the south portico. When the crowd cheered and shouted for a speech, he bowed and excused himself, stepped back into the room, and stretched out on a sofa. "I wish they would let me sit out there quietly and enjoy the music," he said. Hay was glad to have the concerts back, which drew a checkered crowd. "Some good women and some not so good."

On a bright May morning, the Sunday school children of Washington passed under the north portico with banners and flowers as Lincoln stood at the center window with friends, remarking now and then on a little face that struck him as he smiled and bowed to the children in their Sunday clothes. They cheered him "as if their very lives depended upon it."

*　　*　　*

In 1842, Charles Dickens had called Washington "the head-quarters of tobacco-tinctured saliva," and reported that President Tyler's White House was not spared the "desire to spit incessantly," an "exaggeration of nastiness." By 1864, Mrs. Lincoln's refurbishments had endured two years of expectorated abuse. Legions of unclean men tracked in mud and manure, ground it into the East Room's sea green carpet, and overshot the spittoons. Instead of fouling the rugs, other men and women cut them up. Souvenirs "the size of a man's hand" were sliced from carpets, fresh flowers were snatched from vases, lace flowers were cut from drapes, and carved mahogany scrolls were carved from chairs. A soldier was caught skinning a damask sofa. Stoddard said one "relic-worshipping vandal, male or female, cut nearly two feet in length out of a nearly new silk window curtain." The boldest receiving line memento hunters had snipped the very buttons from Mrs. Lincoln's gowns.

One or two watchmen patrolled the house, but the vandals worked in teams, one diverting the watch while another performed the surgery. An officer was caught standing guard while two women took his knife to the crimson brocade of a chair. The wreckage puzzled Lincoln as much as it upset him. "Why should they do it? How can they?" Mrs. Lincoln could not be blamed for demanding repairs.

The London *Daily Telegraph*'s correspondent seemed not to notice the carnage, having little regard for "the plain and not very handsome mansion known as the White House" to begin with. Even after the renovation, the wallpaper was "spasmodic" in his view, the carpets loud, and the curtains "of violent hue." The purportedly tasteless decorator had conspired with "some shoddy upholsterer," and the parlors resembled something between "the waiting room at a railway terminus, the drawing room of an hotel, and the foyer of an opera house. You can tell, at a glance, that nobody lives here; that people are only passing through." The citizens who passed through a levee impressed him no more than the house. "The sovereign people was here, and had not taken the trouble to have its boots cleaned." The faces in the crowd were "full of purpose; energetic faces, determined faces, cunning faces, but not pleasant faces to look upon."

For several consecutive evenings in May, Julia Ward Howe, who had written the words to the "Battle Hymn of the Republic," read her essays at the White House for the Lincolns' invited guests. Hay was enthralled with them, except for the piece on "Moral Trigonometry, whatever that may mean."

On May 21, Hay said, the Unionist Arkansas Congressional delegation "was lying about my office in an orphaned sort of way most of the morning, oppressively patronized by Stoddard, who wants them to recommend him for Marshal of the State." Stoddard would go to Arkansas for two months in the fall, intent, like Hay, on a political career in a reconstructed state.

On an evening in early June, one "Jeems Pipes of Pipesville," a mock rural humorist, the president's favorite kind, gave a Red Room performance fresh from a Washington stage. His "comic imitations" included a stammering man, which brought such a laugh from Lincoln that Carpenter heard it next door. "I once knew a man who invariably *whistled* with his stammering," Lincoln told the entertainer, and mimicked the unfortunate man. "Now if you could get in a touch of nature like that, it would be irresistibly ludicrous." The comedian "mastered it to the President's satisfaction."

Later that month, Nicolay was away on a hot summer night when Hay let him know that "Madame is in the north and the President has gone today to visit Grant. I am all alone in the White pest-house." Malaria was about to shake his buttons off, Hay said, as "the ghosts of twenty thousand drowned cats" drifted in from the canal.

*   *   *

On the same day that Lincoln abandoned the idea of a Central American colony of black Americans, he authorized Saint Matthew's Colored Sunday School to hold its Fourth of July picnic on the grounds at Benjamin French's request. To Hay's elitist eyes, the "Negroes of Washington were very neatly and carefully dressed and the young girls like ill-bred boarding school maids." Their race was not always apparent. "There were many of both sexes perfectly white and blue-eyed." Washingtonians white and black filled rows of benches set up around a speakers' platform, applauding student recitals on the Declaration of Independence and oratorical chestnuts like "The Sufferings of the Poor." Others picnicked under the trees or strolled the grounds in pairs. Swings were hung from branches and enjoyed by young and old.

A veteran of Chancellorsville and Gettysburg was amazed. "A stranger would imagine himself in the palace gardens of Haiti," he said, and marvel at "the dignity assumed by these freedmen. They address one another as Mr. and Miss, though only servants," and "barbers and waiters sport ivory-headed canes." Doleful "contrabands"—former slaves who had escaped in uniform from service in the Confederate army as laborers, drovers, and cooks—seemed to banish themselves from the crowd. "Amidst the fun I saw groups of contrabands in butternut sitting in melancholy mood along the curbstone, as if they thought themselves an inferior order of negro."

17

I HAPPEN TEMPORARILY
TO OCCUPY THIS BIG
WHITE HOUSE

On his last day at the White House, in July 1864, Carpenter came across the president leaning on an iron fence on the path to the War Department, listening to a plain-looking man explain some difficulty. A knot of people gathered as Lincoln heard him out and studied his face. When the man had said his piece, the president asked him if he had a blank card. He searched his pockets anxiously until a gentleman offered one. Lincoln sat down awkwardly on the curb, wrote a simple order to "examine this man's case," and handed it to him with instructions on where to take it. Passersby smiled at the President of the United States, squatting on the sidewalk, scribbling on a card, unaware of the attention, utterly exposed to anyone who happened by.

As the summer went on, a drama in several acts played out on the question of his safety. When the family moved back to the Soldiers' Home for the season, the assistant adjutant general ordered the Union Light Guard to move too, and Lincoln was told they would escort him to and from the White House if he wanted them. "I believe I need no escort," he replied in a little note, "and unless the Secretary of War directs, none need attend me." He surely knew that Stanton *would* direct, as Stanton promptly did.

On that same hot Saturday, moving up from the Shenandoah Valley with a rebel army of ten thousand men, General Jubal Early pushed a small blocking force aside and marched on Washington. With Grant on the offensive in Virginia there was nothing between Early and the White House but a ring of lightly manned forts. Early's little army was too small to hold the capital but big enough to burn it, denying Lincoln a second term and encouraging his successor to accept an independent South.

According to Hay's diary, Sunday was a "rather quiet day" at the White House, a remarkable thing with an enemy army in an outlying neighborhood. Hay thought there was more excitement about it in New York than in Washington. Before the day was out, rebel artillery rattled his windows, but war, Hay thought, was the capital's "natural food and ceased to affect her."

Late that night, with the Soldiers' Home almost within Early's grasp, a carriage brought a message from Stanton urging the president to bring his family back to the White House. Lincoln was not pleased, but back they went. Nicolay was away, leaving Hay without a roommate, and a little after midnight, Bob Lincoln came in and got into bed, saying Stanton had called the family in.

*　　*　　*

In the fierce heat of Monday, July 11, Lincoln went out with his escort to Fort Stevens on the 7th Street road near a house called Silver Spring, a cabinet member's country home. Rebel skirmishers shot at the parapet where he stood, the only time an American commander in chief, or the Union Light Guard, was ever under fire. Lincoln returned at about three as Hay looked out his window: "I can see a couple of columns of smoke just north of the White House. It is thought to be Silver Spring in flames." Working at their desks, Lincoln's secretaries heard cannonading all day, but Neill said business was done as if the closest rebel was in Richmond. That night, the Executive Mansion's Bucktail guards were scraped up with other odds and ends and sent out to face the rebels. Lincoln was "in very good feather," Hay said, and seemed not the least concerned about anything but bagging Early's army.

As Union reinforcements arrived on Tuesday, the muffled thunder of artillery rolled over the White House again, leaving "newsboys coining money over the excitement," an officer said. The people of Washington showed no sign of alarm, the officer thought, "except being subdued as children in a thunderstorm, listening and waiting for the issue. It seems funny to hear the rumbling of street cars mixed with the rumbling of hostile cannon."

Lincoln returned to Fort Stevens, where an officer fell mortally wounded a few feet from his side. Facing more resistance than they had hoped to find, the rebels withdrew and were not aggressively chased, to the commander in chief's displeasure. Before he returned to the Soldiers' Home, Hay asked him if he had any news. Early was back over the Potomac, Lincoln said, but General Horatio Wright had stopped his pursuit, "for fear he might come across the rebels and catch some of them."

*   *   *

A California congressman by the name of Cornelius Cole, a Republican friend of the president's, said that after Early's raid Lincoln still "came and went like any ordinary businessman and laughed at the fears of his friends," but "I determined to change things, so I called at the White House and as usual walked in and upstairs to the President's office unchallenged." Indeed, Cole said, "anyone could go in unannounced." The congressman asked his friend why he had no sentry at his door. None was needed, Lincoln said. When Cole had walked in, the president had been working at his desk with his back more or less to the door, left open in the summer heat. Cole had approached him easily from behind, "and anyone else might have done the same."

A few weeks later, as Lincoln rode out to the Soldiers' Home alone on an August night, someone took a shot at him. No one would have known, were it not for a cavalryman of the Union Light Guard who found the president's hat in the road with a bullet hole in the crown. Lincoln waved the incident off. Some farmer must have emptied his gun coming home from a hunt, he said (just happening to knock the hat off the President of the United States), and nothing should be said.

At or about the same time, a rebel spy named Thomas Conrad later claimed, he was tracking Lincoln's movements from a bench in Lafayette Square in a plot to capture him on his way to or from the Soldiers' Home. "I had company in plenty," the spy recalled. The square was full of tourists gawking at the White House, which made him inconspicuous. According to his memoir, the plot was foiled by the appearance of the Union Light Guard, which had not always accompanied the president before, as his ruined hat showed.

Lincoln's political life was in jeopardy too. With the presidential election in sight, Lee had maneuvered Grant into stagnant trench warfare in Virginia, General William Tecumseh Sherman had stalled in Georgia, and Thurlow Weed, the Republican political mastermind, told the president his reelection was "an impossibility." Making everyone more miserable, a "subduing and oppressive" heat enveloped the White House, Nicolay said, and there was "literally no escaping from it day or night."

Mrs. Lincoln faced a different kind of heat. Influential men were helping her fend off her creditors, but she broke down and told her friend and dress-maker, Mrs. Keckly, that if her husband were defeated, "I do not know what would become of us all." She was $27,000 in debt, "of which he knows nothing." It was $2,000 more than his annual income. "To keep up appearances, I must have money," she said, and Mr. Lincoln was "too honest to make a penny outside of his salary," leaving her no choice but to run on credit. If he stayed in office she could keep him in the dark, but the bills would come in hard with his defeat. As Mrs. Keckly listened, "something like a hysterical sob escaped her."

On August 19, Lincoln sent his coachman to a boarding house to bring Frederick Douglass to his office for another talk about recruiting. Douglass was letting him know that more slaves would escape and join the army if they were better treated when Nicolay announced that the Governor of Connecticut had arrived. Minutes later, he interrupted again. The governor was in the anteroom. "Tell Governor Buckingham to wait," Lincoln said, "for I want to have a long talk with my friend Frederick Douglass."

A few months later, Lincoln met with a Pittsburgh editor and physician who asked him to appoint black officers to lead black troops. The president sent Stanton a note: "Do not fail to have an interview with this most extraordinary and intelligent black man." Earlier he had asked Stanton to "see L. H. Putnam, whom you will find a very intelligent colored man." The stories such men brought home, that Lincoln had treated them with respect at the White House, must have had a productive effect.

Welcoming them to his office and seeking their advice was a groundbreaking move fraught with political risk, but Lincoln never invited any black leader to breakfast, lunch, or dinner, or to join him for a concert on the south portico, or even to take tea in the library. To do so would have been bold, perhaps even incendiary, but not unthinkable. Secretary of the Treasury Salmon Chase "had welcomed me to his home and his table," Douglass said, "when to do so was a strange thing in Washington, and the fact was by no means an insignificant one."

Tradition barred presidents seeking reelection from giving speeches, but Lincoln continued to address regiments and serenaders on the White House grounds, where newspapermen helped him reach voters. On August 22, he thanked the hard fought 166th Ohio before they left for home and reminded them what it had all been for, surely aware that he was addressing their families and friends. "I happen temporarily to occupy this big white house," he said. "I am a living witness that any one of your children may look to come here as my father's child has. . . . The nation is worth fighting for, to secure such an inestimable jewel."

*　　*　　*

That day, Nicolay submitted Neill's resignation as an Interior Department clerk and had Charles H. Philbrick appointed to fill the vacancy. Philbrick was coming but Neill was not going. Philbrick got Stoddard's old title, and Neill got another, the bureaucratic shell game replayed.

Philbrick had befriended Nicolay and Hay at the Illinois Secretary of State Ozias Hatch's office in Springfield and had taken over as Hatch's clerk when Nicolay went to Washington, having mastered the rigorous classics curriculum at Illinois College. A classmate called him an able man "of generous impulses." A female admirer thought him "a sweet little fellow . . . short and rather stout" with "light hair and bright blue eyes with a small nose and the sweetest mouth I almost ever saw . . . quite bashful but intelligent . . . a real true honest young man." A year younger than Hay and a fellow bon vivant, Philbrick had lent him $122.75 in 1861, a substantial sum. After Prince Napoleon's White House visit, Philbrick had gotten a letter from Nicolay and Hay that must have been entertaining. He detected in the letter the influence of the state dinner's wine, and wished in his reply that "you would write after every dinner, for in vino veritas and fun too."

Having reached out to Massachusetts, Switzerland, and Minnesota for their other junior clerks, Nicolay and Hay reached back to Illinois for Charlie Philbrick. It is hard to see why. A few days before the inauguration, Philbrick had written Nicolay to explain that a letter of recommendation he had written for a friend was

> intended more to please him than to affect you. I don't want you to consider that I am as deeply interested in his success as perhaps the letter would indicate. I don't like to be one thing at one time and another at another, but you know I was very much urged to write and write strongly.

Six days after the war began, Philbrick had written Nicolay that "the rolling of drums" at Springfield's recruiting offices had attracted fifty companies of young men. "I have a strong desire to go [unmarried and twenty-three as he was], but a number of things conspire to keep me here." They were still conspiring a year and a half later when Hay wrote to Nicolay about a trip to Springfield: "Charlie Philbrick is going to Hell by a large majority. He was hideously drunk all day and all night while I was there. Something must be done to reform him or he is gone up."

By August 1864, Charlie seemed to have cleaned himself up. The frictions between Hay and Stoddard, who had come back from Arkansas and was thinking about returning, had worn their friendship out, and Hay wrote to Nicolay about replacing Stoddard with Charlie. Stoddard had been "advertising himself" in the Western press. "His asininity, which is kept a little dark under your shadow at Washington, blooms and burgeons in the free air of the West." Hay had told Stoddard, angrily Stoddard said, that "he considered me a kind of miracle of hard work and that I could do more without showing it than any other man he had ever seen," but "abused me also for being 'statuesque' and always inclined to strike attitudes and take positions." Now Hay let Nicolay know that a substitute could be had.

> Charlie Philbrick is perfectly steady now, I am told. I saw him when last in Springfield and he was straight as a string. If you make it proper at your end of the line I am very sure you could not get a man more thoroughly discrete and competent. He made a most favorable impression on me when I saw him—all of one evening. The subject was not mentioned by either of us.

Whether the subject was a White House job or the state of Charlie's sobriety is unclear, but Charlie was on his way to Washington. He found a place to live at 284 G Street, a few blocks from the White House, "in the family of some decayed Virginian gentry," Hay said. Years later, Charlie was remembered as polished, courtly, charitable, and modest. "A better hearted and more genial friend and companion never lived than Charlie Philbrick." Sadly, however, "his was a checkered life, with more shadows than sunshine—shadows that enveloped all who held him dear."

Oblivious to his future, Charlie feasted on oysters by the half-bushel while the White House was repainted, and Hay wrote to Nicolay urging him to extend a trip to New York. Lincoln thought he needed the rest, Hay said. "Besides, you can't imagine how nasty the house is at present. You would get the painters' colic in twenty-four hours if you came home now. Politicians still unhealthily haunt us. Loose women flavor the anteroom."

Sherman's capture of Atlanta in early September turned Lincoln's political fortunes around, and Phil Sheridan's triumph over Jubal Early in the Shenandoah Valley in September and October all but ended any threat to a second term. Learning of Early's defeat, Lincoln "shut up shop for the rest of the day," and Stoddard, the inside trader, treated Nicolay and Hay to dinner at his club, which must have pleased and annoyed them.

Stoddard soon left the White House for good as Lincoln's U.S. Marshal for Arkansas, and Nicolay shared his fears with Hay: "John! What'll we do with the Madam after Stod goes?" Stoddard said his goodbyes to the president and Mrs. Lincoln, had a final chat with Nicolay and Hay, and walked all over the house "for a last glimpse of every room." The only mementoes he took were the antique latchkey that Edward McManus had given him and a residue of typhoid fever.

*   *   *

Mrs. Lincoln was criticized "for having a certain class of men around her," Mrs. Keckly said, but insisted she was using them to help reelect her husband. "I will be clever to them until after the election," she told her friend, then "drop every one of them, and let them know very plainly that I only made tools of them. They are an unprincipled set, and I don't mind a little double-dealing with them." The president, she said, knew nothing about it.

He did know what a risk she was. He told Orville Browning that he lived in constant fear that she would disgrace him. Always antsy, Benjamin French wrote his sister on September 4, 1864, two months before the election: "Rumors are about that the Democrats are getting up something in which they intend to show up Madam Lincoln. Thank Heaven I know no more *of my own knowledge* of her doings than anyone else—indeed I do not *know* that she has ever done a wrong act." French hoped that "such an ungallant and mean conduct as an attack on a *woman* to injure her husband" would do the attackers more harm than good.

Opportunities for such attacks accumulated, centering on Mrs. Lincoln's pet New Yorkers. After the war, Lincoln's Supreme Court appointee David Davis thought the proofs were "too many and too strong against her" to deny. On September 7, Lincoln gave the coveted post of collector of customs in New York to Simeon Draper, a real estate baron and a frequent White House dinner guest. Judge Davis later said that Draper paid the First Lady $20,000 to help him get it. If so, it was a sound investment. The collector enjoyed $20,000 in "pickings and fees" alone, a handsome salary, control over 1,200 jobs, and the profitable privilege of selling captured cotton. Draper later combined intimidation and the offer of a job to persuade the felonious gardener John Watt to drop an extortionate threat to expose Mrs. Lincoln's corruption.

The first lady threw a semipublic fit until her husband appointed as naval agent in New York the publisher of the *Evening Post*, Isaac Henderson, who had given her diamond jewelry and was later indicted. She was overheard on Pennsylvania Avenue telling the president she would roll around the sidewalk unless he gave some man the office he wanted.

Lincoln awarded in succession the prized positions of postmaster of New York and surveyor of the port of New York to Abram Wakeman, another friend of his wife's, who had welcomed him to her Blue Room salon and asked for his silence "about the 5th Avenue business," a cryptic allusion to something left unsaid. According to Gideon Welles, Wakeman felt that "all is fair and proper in party operations . . . and supposes that everyone else is the same." On September 23, Mrs. Lincoln confided a burden to him: her husband was "almost a monomaniac on the subject of honesty." Given his salary, she said (more than five times his prior income as a prosperous lawyer), "I have had to endeavor to be as economical as possible, more so than I have ever been before in my life. It would have been a great delight to me to have had the means to entertain generally as should be done at the Executive Mansion."

Economical in fact as well as in theory, Lincoln often walked over to the Treasury Department to see Levi Gould, a clerk whose office overlooked the White House. He "sat down beside me" to buy war bonds, Gould recalled, and "counted out what money he could spare from his salary."

*　　*　　*

On the morning of October 29, the famous freed slave preacher and abolitionist "Sojourner Truth" reached the White House from her Battle Creek, Michigan, home to see Lincoln before she died. The aged "Libyan Sibyl" came with a friend. It was no longer remarkable that two other black women were among a dozen people in the anteroom when the president admitted them all together. Sojourner Truth simply waited her turn to speak, and was pleased to see that "he showed as much kindness and consideration to the colored persons as to the whites." One of them was sick and could not pay her rent. Lincoln listened closely and told her how to get help.

When he turned to the Libyan Sibyl, her friend told him, "This is Sojourner Truth, who has come all the way from Michigan to see you." He rose, gave her his hand, and bowed. She compared him to Daniel in the lions' den and said she had never heard of him before he was president. He smiled and said he had heard of her often before that. When she called him "the best president who has ever taken the seat," he said he expected she referred to his proclamation, but Washington and several other presidents "were all just as good, and would have done just as I have done if the time were right." Then he pointed to the Potomac. "If the people over the river had behaved themselves, I could not have done what I have; but they did not, and I was compelled to do those things." He signed her autograph book "For Aunty Sojourner Truth, October 29, 1864, A Lincoln." He was later displeased to learn that she came back a few months later and was not let in.

Walt Whitman came by to speak to his fellow poet John Hay about getting a pass home to New York to work for Lincoln's reelection. In the office wing he saw the president speaking warmly with a gentleman who seemed to be a dear friend. He did not interrupt, missing his chance for a chat.

*   *   *

In the fall of 1864, Lincoln told Ward Hill Lamon that Count Adam Gurowski, the Polish revolutionary veteran of the amateur White House guard of 1861, was haunting the grounds, and "he is dangerous wherever he may be." His friend Henry Longfellow had found him explosive. Emerson had met him "growling" at the State Department, where he came to work as a translator in a bell-shaped hat and a long blue veil. Seward had recently fired him. He was said to be "almost a madman when in passion," small, stout, and hideous, "disfigured by a pair of green goggles" that hid a missing eye. Gideon Welles ran into him lurking near the White House and did not enjoy it. Gurowski was "a creature of violent impulses and hatreds," Welles said, particularly contemptuous of Lincoln, with "a strong but fragmentary mind." For three months that fall, unbeknownst to the president, Lamon slept every night at the White House with his weapons and brought other guards.

There were other reasons for unease.

As the White House tutor Alexander Williamson colorfully said, Washington City was full of "vagabonds, vampires, and harpies of every description." Packs of bitter rebels still in tattered uniforms wandered freely about the city. Some were paroled prisoners; others were deserters. Noah Brooks said you could not walk the streets without seeing "squads of these sad-hued, ragged, and haggard mean whites, who slouch along in hangdog style as if they were ashamed to look one in the face."

Men in better clothes loitered on a Pennsylvania Avenue corner near the White House by an unmarked building with closed shutters known as Joe Hall's, which barred plebian patrons from its card tables and roulette wheel. The loiterers included a tall man with spectacles, a drab, loose-fitting overcoat, and a Southern drawl who called himself a Union man from Kentucky and actually held a commission in the Confederate army. The authorities lacked proof enough to arrest him, but the provost marshal did his best to keep rebel spies off the White House grounds.

Not every threat was politically motivated. Almost any polite lunatic could get within inches of Lincoln, and some showed up at his desk. One reasonable-looking man explained in the president's office that it was he who had been elected to it. Touting her qualifications for a job at a military hospital, another caller told him she could see disease with her spirit eyes. "You know rather too much for a hospital," he said.

Even Lincoln had finally had enough, convinced, perhaps, by the vitriol spilled in the election campaign and the hat shot off his head. On November 3, a week before the election, four Washington City police officers were detailed to the White House. Nearly four years into his wartime presidency, with madmen loose in his house, angry rebels on Pennsylvania Avenue, and a half-crazed count lurking dangerously on the grounds, it was the first real round-the-clock guard that Lincoln had ever had, and a poor one at that.

Sergeant John Cronin oversaw the policemen assigned to the White House—John Parker, Andrew Smith, Thomas Pendel, and Alfonso Dunn (variously spelled). They reported to Marshall Lamon, who had asked for the detail and introduced them to the president and his secretaries. They were quite the accomplished crew. Cronin had been reprimanded for intoxication and charged with a bad arrest. Dunn had been absent without leave and written up for violent language and fighting in a police station. Pendel had been accused of needless violence and dereliction of duty. Parker had threatened a superior and been charged with larceny, sleeping on duty, refusing to help a black soldier attacked by thugs, patronizing a brothel, and cruelty to animals. They made a fair sample of the underpaid, poorly trained, ill-regarded Washington City Police, and several were soon replaced with comparably distinguished men.

No announcement was made of their appointment, another sign of Lincoln's discomfort with it. The *National Republican* reported nonetheless that policemen had been assigned to the White House to protect it from vandals and thieves, a story that credulous readers may have swallowed.

No longer would Lincoln walk about town with no one more intimidating than John Hay. An armed plainclothes policeman would stick to him like his coattails. He seemed to fear it impugned his courage. Tom Pendel, one of the new policemen, was chatting in the porter's lodge with his colleague Alfonso Dunn, the coachman Ned Burke, and Edward McManus when the president walked in: "Which one of you gentlemen will take a little walk with me as far as Secretary Stanton's house? He is sick in bed and I want to see him." Pendel volunteered. As they left, Lincoln said, "I have received a great many threatening letters, but I have no fear of them."

"Mr. President," Pendel replied, "because a man does not fear a thing is no reason why it should not occur."

"That is a fact," Lincoln said.

He hated being on his guard as much as being guarded, and it saddened him. He insisted that his protectors keep their pistols hidden, and chat with him as they walked by his side like a friend, not behind or in front of him like a guard. They would walk on his right on his way to the War Department, on his left going back, keeping between him and the trees. George McElfresh, a replacement White House policeman, said Lincoln talked with him as they walked "as if I were a member of the family" and was "always good and kind, as he was to every attaché of the house."

With occasional variation, two policemen were on duty from eight to four, a third from four to midnight, the fourth from midnight to eight. The day men had the door to the president's office and joined him when he left the house. The night guard stayed close when he was up and patrolled the family corridor while he slept. "We were all armed with revolvers," said William Crook, another dubiously qualified policeman, who replaced one of the original four. As Lincoln worked late one night, he took off his shoes, crept up to the anteroom, threw the door open, and told the startled guard, "I wanted to see how you would spread yourself."

McElfresh often took the night shift. One night Mrs. Lincoln asked him if he was alone. He was. "Who was in charge?" "Sergeant Cronin." "Tell him I want to see him tomorrow." When the Sargent reported to her, she asked him to put a second man on night duty, and a second man was posted.

When Crook had the midnight-to-eight watch, Lincoln bid him good night by name, as he surely did the others. Crook felt close to the people asleep in a great house as he stayed awake to protect them. When the president went to bed, Crook sat in a chair by his door, listened for unusual noise, and occasionally got up and paced. "I could see every inch of the whole length of the corridor," he said, "which was so lighted that no shadows could even partly conceal any one who might try to slip through it." He never saw Lincoln ruffled. When messengers woke him up, he "received the message and the messenger kindly."

Tad was often waiting in the vestibule when Lincoln and his guard stayed late at the War Department. His father would sweep him up and carry him to bed. Tad was fond of McElfresh and walked him to the theater in advance when the president planned to go. The policeman explained what they saw on the way, McElfresh later said, "and generally had candies, so he liked to go with me." When Lincoln arrived at the theater, McElfresh would sit outside his box and admit no one, friends of the family included, until he took their cards to the president and was told to let them in.

McElfresh grew tired of the duty, he said. "I have often regretted that I asked to be relieved."

* * *

Favors were done for White House servants touched by the war. Lincoln asked a general to approve a soldier's furlough. "The father of the boy is a domestic in my service." Nicolay told the Assistant Secretary of War that Thomas Cross, a worthy "colored servant in the Executive Mansion," needed a pass to Savannah for his nephew "(also colored)," and should get one.

In March 1865, all four White House policemen were drafted. William Crook got the president to exempt him and Andrew Smith that very day. Unburdened by any legal authority, the First Lady certified that the others were "detailed for duty at the Executive Mansion by order of Mrs. Lincoln," which kept them out of the army. It was not the first time that members of the White House staff were plucked from harm's way. Lincoln's coachman Ned Burke was exempted from the draft, which the *National Republican* reported, undercutting the president's appeal to every home and business to sacrifice for the cause. Nicolay hired a substitute when he was drafted in 1864, a lawful thing to do if not a noble one. The president hired one too. They met at the White House, where Lincoln told his proxy he hoped he would be "one of the lucky ones."

In 1861, early on, Stoddard served three months on militia guard duty around the city with a few hours' leave to "make flying visits to the White House." Later he felt half ashamed to be struggling with the mail instead of the rebels, and sometimes more than half.

Nicolay confessed his guilt to Therena as early as September of 1861:

> This being here where I can overlook the whole war and never be in it—always threatened with danger and never meeting it—constantly worked to death, and yet doing (accomplishing) nothing, I assure you grows exceedingly irksome. . . . It's a feeling of duty and not one of inclination that keeps me here.

On a mission to South Carolina in uniform in 1864, Major Hay became the only member of Lincoln's staff to come under hostile fire. The sight of exploding shells tearing men apart subdued his sense of humor. So did "the wicked little whistle" of shrapnel whizzing past his head.

*   *   *

On Tuesday, November 8, a rainy election day, Noah Brooks found the White House deserted, and Tad pulled his father to a window to watch the Bucktails vote for him. That night, Hay said, he and Lincoln "splashed through the grounds to the side door of the War Department where a soaked and smoking sentinel was standing in his own vapor with his huddled up frame covered with a rubber cloak." Late into the night, they monitored the election returns over a fried oyster supper at the telegraph office with friends.

At half past 2 a.m., some Pennsylvanians showed up with a band of music to celebrate Lincoln's reelection, and he went to a window to reply. Hay thought he extemporized unusually well. Ward Hill Lamon followed Hay home to his room, accepted his offer of some blankets and a shot of whiskey, declined his offer of a bed, and went down the hall to the family wing, where he rolled himself up in his cloak and lay down by Lincoln's door, "passing the night in that attitude of touching and dumb fidelity," as Hay was moved to record it, "with a small arsenal of pistols and Bowie knives around him. In the morning he went away, leaving my blankets at my door, before I or the President were awake."

On Wednesday, November 9, at work on the morning after the election, Neill saw Lincoln's office door ajar and went in to congratulate him at his desk. The president thanked him kindly, put his spectacles on his head, and chatted. Neill noticed a condemned soldier's record in front of Lincoln. It occurred to him that he worked for a man who returned uncomplaining to his least favorite task on the morning after his triumph. Lincoln did not forget the least of their brethren. Early that morning, he sent a message to French: "If Commissioner of Public Buildings chooses to give laborers at White House a holy day I have no objections."

When the Lincolns moved back from the Soldiers' Home, Mrs. Lincoln took a lieutenant of the Union Light Guard aside. She was worried that assassins had hidden in the White House, she said. For several nights, half a dozen dismounted cavalrymen patrolled the halls and the family quarters. Their reliefs slept on couches and the floor.

If Mrs. Lincoln had ever had a plan to drop her shady friends after her husband's reelection, it did not survive his victory. Less than two weeks after he won, she was happy to tell a friend that "the White House has been quite a *Mecca* of late." She thought herself fortunate to retire at 11, and the unscrupulous Abram Wakeman was no discarded tool. In January 1865, she told him about a quarrel with her husband, and he advised her to drop it. "I have taken your advice," she replied, and "we have had quite a little laugh together, most fortunately," for their marriage had been peaceful, "notwithstanding our opposite natures" and the strains of White House life.

The *serpents* that have crossed our pathways will be remembered by both of us with *horror* in after years. The communication made [to] you this morning will I am sure, always be sacredly guarded by you—As *scenes* are novelties with us, I felt strangely disposed to tell you. Thank Heaven, the storm has cleared away and I shall ever, even in jest, take especial pains not to provoke discussion, lest *forbidden subjects* might be introduced.

That last enticing thought would forever be a mystery for everyone but Abram Wakeman, who dined "most informally" with the Lincolns the next day.

Her husband's reelection had not changed Mrs. Lincoln's shopping habits any more than her choice of friends. Her neighbor Judge Taft often saw her carriage parked in front of some merchant's door, its driver and footman with gold bands and cockades on their hats so that no one could mistake them for ordinary men, "while Mrs. L sits in her seat and examines the rich goods which the obsequious clerk brings out to her."

*   *   *

Library of Congress, Nicolay papers.

Nicolay was shooting ducks and talking politics in Illinois when Charlie Philbrick let him know on November 12 that Hay had been misbehaving. "Dear Nicolay: You see above what time and the lack of your kind superintendence has done for our once noble young Major Hay." A friend had sketched Hay in his dissipation the night before, Philbrick wrote, "and I grieve to say it is a too faithful semblance of the unfortunate young debaucher." Charlie hoped that Hay would reform. "For a while he did well and studied French assiduously but the literature which he chose I fear was not of the right kind and corrupted him." The likes of *Confessions d'un Boheme* were "not pious books suited for the young."

Nicolay had hardly returned to Washington from his ducks in Illinois when he fought another round with the First Lady: "About three days of the week have been taken up with a row with my particular feminine friend here," he told Therena, "but I have gotten through it without any serious damage, or even loss of temper."

On December 10, Lincoln welcomed to the White House the *Harper's Weekly* artist Thomas Nast, whose political cartoons would later roast Tammany Hall's Boss Tweed, and Marshal Lamon wrote the president a note: "I regret that you do not appreciate what I have repeatedly said to you in regard to the proper police arrangements connected with your household and your own personal safety. *You are in danger.*" He should accept Lamon's resignation if he did not believe it. He had gone to the theater with no one but Senator Sumner and a diplomat, "neither of whom could defend himself against an assault from any able bodied woman in the city . . . I have played low comedy long enough, and at my time of life I think I ought at least to attempt to play star engagements." Lamon tried Nicolay too: "I may be unnecessarily frightened about Mr. Lincoln's personal safety—but I assure you I think I have good reasons for my uneasiness about him. See that he don't go out alone either in the day or night time."

A few days later, the near destruction of the rebel Army of Tennessee near Nashville made it all but inevitable that the North would win the war. Late that night, Stanton brought the news to "the tall, ghostly form" of Lincoln in his nightshirt with a candle in his hand at the head of the second-floor landing.

*   *   *

A few days after Christmas, Mrs. Lincoln dismissed after fifteen years of service the doorman Edward McManus, that "inexhaustible well of incident and anecdote concerning the old worthies and unworthies," Stoddard called him. She had asked him to notify the newspapers about a reception at once. A half-hour later he had not yet complied, and she told him it was his last day at the White House. He did not take her seriously and smiled a "sickly" smile, but serious she was, and the president did not intervene. The true reason for Edward's dismissal will never be known. Mrs. Lincoln called him a serpent, suggesting some betrayal, most likely a secret revealed.

His replacement was one Cornelius O'Leary. The painter Francis Carpenter called O'Leary a boy, perhaps because he was young, perhaps because he was a servant. An opposition newspaper said Mrs. Lincoln had put him in Edward's place for a share of the cash he took selling pardons for rebel prisoners, for which he too was dismissed when the president was told.

Edward moved to Manhattan and started talking, which worried Mrs. Lincoln. She wrote to Abram Wakeman in February: "I am more shocked than ever that any one can be so low as to place confidence in a discarded menial's assertions, the game of espionage has been going on to a greater extent than we have imagined—If the 'Heavens fall,' E shall never be restored." Already contriving a response should any important listener take Edward seriously, she claimed that Nicolay thought he was deranged. "I have suspected it for some time. . . . Please burn this note." Wakeman's loyalty may be judged by the note's survival.

Mrs. Lincoln asked Tom Pendel, one of Tad's favorites, to resign as a White House policeman and take Edward's place as the head doorman. Acting at her request, French gave Pendel a written police force appointment and sent him to Lincoln to get it signed. Tad got him in: "Tom Pen, give me that paper. Come in now to papa's room."

"It is tolerably quiet here," Charlie Philbrick told Ozias Hatch, "the mob have vacated for the Holidays but we are nonetheless busy in preparing material for them to grind out when they start their mill again next week." The White House was not Charlie's idea of fun. Nicolay and Hay were no longer the carefree chums he used to enjoy, and the workload was uncongenial: "Hay does the ornamental," leaving "the main labor" to others, Charlie wrote. Nicolay was "gloomy on account of physical and mental trouble." If Charlie could only trade some of his extra body weight for some of Nicolay's "indifference and industry," they would both make a good bargain.

18

AND EVERYTHING
SEEMED TO WEEP

The White House doors were opened for the New Year's Day reception of 1865 on a frozen January second, the first having fallen on the Sabbath. Still in half mourning for Willie in purple silk with black velvet trim, Mrs. Lincoln stood with Tad and one of his friends at a window where the crowd in line could see them. Ward Hill Lamon told Nicolay that senators and members of Congress who had not been specifically invited had made their resentment known.

And so did a poorer class. Diverse groups of "colored people" gathered on the lawn for the first time in the history of New Year's Day, the *New York Independent* reported, some beautifully dressed, some "in tattered garments," others in "the most fanciful and grotesque costumes." They had come to test the limits of Lincoln's liberality. When the first "colored woman presented herself" in the reception line, the *Boston Recorder* said, the president took her hand, "and Mrs. Lincoln gave the invariable bow," but when a second and third appeared, the first lady sent word to the door to mingle no more black with white. The former could be admitted at the end.

As the stream of white men and women diminished, several blacks approached the portico cautiously. Others followed when no one stopped them. The *Recorder* called it "a colored levee at the end of the white one." Exhausted after two hours of handshaking, Lincoln rallied when he saw them. "They laughed and wept, and wept and laughed" and blessed him as he welcomed them one by one. Walking home on Pennsylvania Avenue, the *Independent*'s correspondent heard "fast young men" curse the president for admitting them, but the celebrants' delight rang in the reporter's ears and drowned the profanity.

Brilliant as the historic reception had been, Lincoln soon wrote to the president of the B&O railroad, concerned about having enough coal to make gas to keep the White House lit. The railroad man reassured him.

Three and a half years after buying hundreds of pieces of custom-made china, Mrs. Lincoln telegraphed a merchant: "We must have the China tomorrow—Send what you have. Our dinner comes off Monday, and on Saturday the articles must be ready for use here." The next day she wired again: "What is the meaning that we do not have the China."

The meaning of other things consumed the president. Sherman had taken Savannah in December, but few details were known. The first of the general's subordinates reached the White House soon after New Year's Day, when a junior officer gave his card to the office doorkeeper, who "shook his head and pointed to the crowds." Congressmen were waiting, he said. The young man asked him to bring in his card and wrote on its face that he came from Sherman. The doorkeeper returned in no time and showed him in. Lincoln was standing at a mirror shaving himself.

> He paused a moment, came to me with a droll look, heightened no doubt by the half-lathered, half-shaved face, gave me his hand, and asked me to take a seat on the sofa, saying, as he returned to the mirror, that he could not even wait till he had finished shaving when an officer from Sherman's army had come.

Chatting as he made himself presentable, Lincoln toweled his face, took the young man's hand in both of his, sat down beside him, and drained him of all he knew.

*   *   *

With a boxer's build and a fighter's disposition, the twenty-six-year-old army veteran William Crook had replaced Tom Pendel as a plainclothes White House policemen in January. "I had never seen President Lincoln, or any other President," he recalled, and the first White House levee of 1865 was a startling introduction. "The women looked like gorgeous flowers" in their swaying hoop skirts, gaily colored, with braided wreaths in their hair and low-cut bodices, escorted by handsome officers and extravagantly dressed civilians. "The spectacle awed me at first," Crook said. "It was generally considered a brilliant affair. I know it dazzled me."

Standing outside the Blue Room by the vestibule's portable bins for hats and coats, Crook had been ordered to allow no outer garments in Lincoln's presence, a new precaution against hidden weapons. Several women passed the bins with their fashionable cloaks on their backs, but none resisted Crook's requests to check them until Kate Chase Sprague raised her pretty chin to the humble Billy Crook.

"Do you know who I am?"

Crook confessed that he did not.

"'I am Mrs. Senator Sprague,' she announced, as if that were final." Her celebrity and her looks intimidated even Crook, despite his two years in the army, but once he explained his orders, Mrs. Senator Sprague quite graciously complied.

Standing in the reception line but elsewhere in his thoughts, Lincoln failed to recognize the sculptor William Swayne, who had done a plaster bust of him. He "seemed to be in a deep study," Swayne thought, "so I merely turned away quite crestfallen." Then the president repeated something resembling Swayne's name, beckoned him back, and grasped his hand again. "You're the man who made a mud head of me." He had sat for other sculptors, Lincoln said, but Swayne was the best of the lot. The sculptor was pleased to hear it, especially since bystanders heard it too.

Crook faced the president and watched the hands and face of every man and woman who approached him, especially the hands. Having Lincoln's life in his own novice hands made him anxious. Apart from an occasional glance at the president, he later recalled, "I kept my eyes on one couple after another; first being sure that their hands were in plain view, and that they held nothing unless it were a fan or a handkerchief," on which he locked his eyes.

The levee ended at eleven, and the Lincolns chatted briefly with guests before they withdrew upstairs. The president retired to the library, shadowed by Billy Crook, and Mrs. Lincoln went to her room. Some people lingered downstairs for an hour.

After they had gone, Lincoln put on his hat and his rough gray shawl and went down the service stairs with Crook. They slipped out through the basement, a surreptitious route to the War Department. Alone with the president for the first time, Crook fell in behind him, acutely aware that he stood between the commander in chief and danger, but Lincoln waved him up beside him and "began to talk to me in a kindly way, as though I were a bashful boy whom he wanted to put at ease." It felt like an intimate moment, and it put Crook at ease with a sense that he had a friend. "The White House never awed me again."

*   *   *

On January 15, Lincoln spoke in his office with Noah Brooks about the death of the venerated orator Edward Everett. Many people thought Everett's two-hour speech at Gettysburg had eclipsed the president's simple remarks. After "looking round the room in his half-comical fashion, as if afraid of being overheard," Lincoln suggested that Everett was "very much overrated."

Just then, the cards of the eminent Harvard naturalist Louis Agassiz and his congressman were brought in. "Agassiz!" Lincoln said. They had never met, and the president was excited to see him.

Agassiz and Lincoln were lost in mutual awe, each enamored of the other's eminence in a field in which he was a keenly interested amateur. To Brooks, "the President and the savant seemed like two boys," eager to ask ignorant questions, "not quite sure of each other. Each man was simplicity itself." Lincoln asked the professor how he studied, how he wrote and delivered his lectures, how his audiences differed in different parts of the country. These were things not in Agassiz's books, Lincoln explained to Brooks later, and "the other things are." When Agassiz asked if Lincoln had ever given lectures, the president said he had outlined one. "I think I can show, at least in a fanciful way, that all the modern inventions were known centuries ago." Agassiz urged him to finish and deliver it. Lincoln said he had the manuscript somewhere, and would pick it up "when I get out of this place."

After the scientist left, Lincoln turned to Brooks. "Well, I wasn't so badly scared after all! Were you?"

*   *   *

Dreading a new wave of office seekers as his second term approached, Lincoln asked a senator to spread the idea that no office should change hands without good cause: "It seems as though the bare thought of going through again what I did the first year here would *crush* me." But the mob that took Washington for the March 4 inauguration made the first one seem small. At least twice as many people turned out as in 1861, when the capital had been gripped with fear. Now it was flush with certain victory. The morning was dark and rainy, turning the streets into brooks, but "bunting and flags made the city gay with color, the lawns of the White House were dotted with tents," and celebrating citizens and soldiers were everywhere. After the sun broke through, said Gideon Welles, "the day was beautiful, the streets dreadful."

The Union Light Guard escorted Lincoln's coach from the Capitol to the White House. As they turned onto Pennsylvania Avenue, a cavalryman said years later, "I noticed the crowd along the street looking intently, and some were pointing to something in the heavens, toward the south. I glanced up in that direction, and there in plain view, shining out in all her beauty, was the planet Venus." Lincoln noticed too, a marvel at that time of day. Would the omen be good or bad?

* * *

Half the people in town seemed to shove their way into the White House for the inaugural reception. When the northeast gate swung open at seven that night, only pedestrians and private carriages were let in, no hacks or riders, and the line of gleaming coaches ran three-quarters of a mile. An English lady who came in Seward's carriage could not get through the portico and was nearly crushed when she tried. The Union Light Guard and the Bucktails tried to manage the crowd on the outside, uniformed policemen inside. People in distress had to be passed over the heads of the crowd. It was odd that no one died. From the heart of the many-legged beast, a tall naval officer waved and shouted to a cavalryman. "Can't you get us out of this?" With him was Admiral Farragut, sixty-three and "utterly helpless."

Bob Lincoln was there in a fresh captain's uniform, a junior member of Grant's staff. Walt Whitman watched the president shake five thousand hands but resisted the temptation to add one, for Lincoln looked "as if he would give anything to be somewhere else." For this he could not be blamed as he grasped the sovereign hands at the heroic rate of twenty-five a minute, just over two seconds each. A little boy brought by his parents would never forget how Lincoln stopped the line "to take the little, timid fellow's hand and speak a few words." The memory was still warm in 1924.

Frederick Douglass came with a friend, knowing that no one of his race had ever attended an inaugural reception. Now that they were on the battlefield and emancipation was spreading, he thought it was "not too great an assumption" to join the line of citizens high and low. "I had for some time looked upon myself as a man, but now in this multitude of the elite of the land, I felt myself a man among men."

It did not last long. Douglass was told at the door that instructions had been given to admit no colored persons. But when Lincoln was informed of Douglass's exclusion, an order came through to welcome him to what he later described as a "perfect sea of beauty and elegance." As Douglass approached him, Lincoln's face lit up, and he spoke in a booming voice intended to be heard. "Here comes my friend Douglass." As he took Douglass's hand, Lincoln said he had seen him in the crowd as he gave his speech, and asked what Douglass thought of it.

Douglass begged off, saying thousands of people were waiting. But the president insisted. "Mr. Lincoln," Douglass said, "it was a sacred effort."

Douglass later learned that no order barring blacks had been issued. The police were following custom, "as dogs will sometimes rub their necks, long after their collars are removed, thinking they are still there."

The curmudgeonly Gideon Welles thought the reception was not "brilliant, as the papers say it was," but the public stood in line for two hours to get in. Among them were "some rough people" who looted the place for relics, unimpressed by its aura or its guards. When it was over, the formal rooms looked "as if a regiment of rebel troops had been quartered there—with permission to forage." Some arrests were made, and the doors closed at eleven, disappointing a line still stretching to the street.

* * *

As Lincoln's second term began, his wife maneuvered with Noah Brooks to get Nicolay out as private secretary and Brooks in. They could have saved the trouble. Nicolay had thought about leaving for months and had made up his mind to go. Lincoln nominated him as counsel to Paris at a handsome $5,000 a year, and the Senate confirmed him the same day. He let Therena know he would leave in the spring and would ask her to go with him. Hay was going too, as secretary of the Paris legation. In the meantime, they prepared the office for their successors.

As Neill opened Lincoln's mail late in February, there was something about a death threat that unnerved him. It came from Gloversville, New York, in a clear and confident hand: "God knows I have hated you," it began, "but God knows I cannot be a murderer. Beware of the ides of March. Do not, like Julius Caesar, go to the Senate unarmed. If I did not love my life, I would sign my name." Neill took the letter to Hay, who shrugged it off with an observation that "any villain" could get into the president's office, slit his throat, and be gone before anyone knew.

Clinically exhausted, Lincoln held a cabinet meeting in bed. Having won his last election, he could safely repel the job seekers who swarmed once again to his door, which he "rigidly" closed at three. A young woman brought her three small children on March 21 and was told that the president was in a cabinet meeting. She led them into the East Room and sat them down on the floor. Her husband had been killed in battle, she said. She had come to leave his children. "Mrs. Lincoln gave humane directions."

Two days later, glad to be out of the frying pan on an overnight family steamboat trip to Grant's Virginia headquarters, Lincoln dreamed that the White House had burned down (an intriguing metaphor) and made the mistake of telling his wife. Mrs. Lincoln wired Mary Ann Cuthbert, the new White

House stewardess, in charge of all the servants and the household accounts, and instructed her to reply "as soon as you receive this and say if all is right at the house." Mrs. Lincoln followed up with a wire to a doorkeeper the next day: "Ask Cuthbert why my telegram of yesterday has not been answered. Reply immediately."

On the last day of March, Hay wrote his brother that he was eager "to give my place in the Executive Office to some new man," being "thoroughly sick of certain aspects of life here, which you will understand without my putting them on paper." He had almost been ready to go home when Seward offered him Paris. Anxious about the change of command, Charlie Philbrick wrote to Ozias Hatch: "I don't know who will be in George's place. Hope someone good for otherwise I won't stay. Mrs. L will try to put in her favorite, Mr. Brooks, a newspaper man—What the President may think has not yet transpired."

In poor health, Nicolay left for a little warmth and relaxation in Charleston, Savannah, and Havana. He never saw Lincoln again.

*   *   *

At noon on Monday, April 3, word reached the White House that Lee had abandoned Richmond and the rebel capital had fallen. Artillery fired eight hundred salutes in Washington City. "Bands of music, apparently without any special direction or formal call, paraded the streets and boomed and blared from every public place." Arranging to illuminate every public building with gaslight displays, French had never seen the like of it. "In getting into the street I found all the population apparently about half crazy."

That evening, Mrs. Lincoln convened her salon, from which the Chevalier Wikoff was gone but not forgotten. Baron Gerolt, the kindly Prussian minister to Washington, close to John Hay, shared a recollection of bunking on an Atlantic crossing with Wikoff, who had asked him repeatedly what Lincoln thought of his book about kidnapping his fiancée. Mrs. Lincoln and Senator Sumner looked at one another and laughed.

On Tuesday, April 4, the White House was bright with flags and bunting, and Mrs. Lincoln invited friends to celebrate Richmond's fall. Carpenters nailed tiered strips of wood to the windows of every building on President's Square and lined them with candle stubs saved for the purpose. The War Department was decked with unlit lime lights as color-infused fireballs were positioned on its lawn. At nightfall, men with matches were stationed at every window, and a small brass band came out on Stanton's balcony over a transparent eagle with "Richmond" in its beak. At the sound of a signal trumpet, the band struck up "The Star Spangled Banner," and "as if by magic, the windows of twelve buildings were suddenly ablaze, while columns of red, green, and blue transparent smoke floated across the front of the War Department. So promptly was each match applied that spectators wondered what mechanical process—like lighting gas jets by electricity"—had caused it.

Charlie Philbrick may have enjoyed himself too much. Hay wrote him a frosty note two days later: "I must insist that you shall be more regular in your attendance at the office . . . June will come before any progress is made in the work of preparing the office for the new secretary."

Lee surrendered on Sunday, April 9, Charlie's birthday. The war was not over but as good as won. The news reached Lincoln that night. At daybreak on a rainy Monday morning, another cannonade concussed the White House windows and roused the residents of Lafayette Square. According to Noah Brooks, some "raced around in the mud to see what the news was" and some "would be glad when Union victories were done with, or celebrated somewhere else." A crowd sang "The Star Spangled Banner" on the White House lawn as the president had breakfast. Minutes later, Neill said, "a procession with a band of music arrived while I was conversing with the President, who told the messenger to tell them that he would address them that evening."

"The streets, horribly muddy, were alive with people," Brooks wrote, "cheering and singing, carrying flags and saluting everybody, hungering and thirsting for speeches." An impromptu parade of over two thousand men marched to the White House with musicians and patriotic airs, firing six-wheeled howitzers on the way. They filled the north lawn and shouted for the president, who had written a note to Stanton: "Tad wants some flags. Can he be accommodated?" Apparently he could, for Tad waived a captured rebel banner from a White House window, delighting and igniting the crowd. Lincoln told them he would speak the next night and would have nothing to say if he dribbled it out now. He asked the band to play "Dixie" and explained, "I always thought that it was the most beautiful of our songs," and the attorney general had given his opinion "that we have fairly earned the right to have it back." The president left the window as the first note played. "Yankee Doodle" came next.

On the following night, the White House was lit again, bonfires burned, and a fresh crowd filled the lawn. Mrs. Keckly dressed Mrs. Lincoln and looked out a window at "a black, gently swelling sea" of humanity. The nearest faces were visible, but the others faded "into mere ghostly outlines" with a "weird, spectral beauty" enhanced by the "hum of voices that rose above the sea of forms."

Lincoln spoke from the center window, reading awkwardly with a candle in one hand and his speech in the other. Standing near his side, Brooks watched him make "a comical motion with his left foot and elbow, which I construed to mean that I should hold his candle up for him, which I did." Brooks stayed behind a curtain while Tad snatched up the pages that his father dropped one by one as he read them, all of them generous to the South. Less charitable people sent rope to the White House with which to hang Jeff Davis.

The festivities lasted yet another day. Mrs. Lincoln sent notes to Sumner and Lafayette's grandson the Marquis de Chambrun. General Grant would be at the White House that evening. They should come too. "Superb fireworks" exploded in Lafayette Square, says Fanny Seward's diary, some like bursting shells, others delicate and subtle. "The signal lights of red, yellow and green were very beautiful."

*   *   *

Good Friday was a raw, overcast, windy day, and the celebrations were over. Bob Lincoln arrived that morning. At breakfast with his father, he shared his experiences in the Appomattox campaign and described Lee's surrender, which he had witnessed. The president welcomed Grant to a cabinet meeting and took the rest of the day off to chat with a few friends, a nearly unheard-of indulgence. A messenger was sent to Ford's Theater. The president and the first lady would like a box for the evening's performance of *Our American Cousin*.

The coachman, Ned Burke, brought the carriage around with the footman, Charlie Forbes, at about 8:30 p.m. An important Massachusetts congressman approached the president under the portico, and Lincoln scribbled him a note that would get him admitted in the morning. The Union Light Guard stayed home, respecting Lincoln's wishes for no visible protection on his way to and from public places. He climbed into his carriage with his wife and rolled up the gravel drive onto Pennsylvania Avenue.

The White House policeman John Parker was assigned to protect him that night. Already disciplined for addressing "vile and insolent language" to a superior, Parker would later be charged with sleeping on duty in a streetcar and insulting a woman who asked for protection. He was not at his post when John Wilkes Booth talked his way past Charlie Forbes into the president's box.

*   *   *

White House servants were preparing an after-theater supper for the Lincolns and their guests when they heard the crazy rumor that the president had been

Robert Lincoln. Library of Congress.

shot. The doorman, Tom Pendel, watched a group of men and boys rush through the east gate with Senator Sumner at their head. Sumner asked Pendel what he knew, Pendel told him that the Lincolns had gone to Ford's Theater, and the senator hurried away with his friends.

Minutes later, an official came to the door and told Pendel that the president had been shot in the head. Pendel went up to Bob Lincoln's room and found him with a vial of medicine in one hand and a teaspoon in the other. He must have read Pendel's face. "As I stepped up to his side," Pendel recalled, "the teaspoon and the vial seemed to go involuntarily down on the table." Pendel lacked the heart to repeat what he had heard. "Captain," he said, "something happened to the President. You had better go down to the theater and see what it is."

"Go and call Major Hay."

Pendel went to Hay's room. "Major," he said, "Captain Lincoln wants to see you at once. The President has been shot."

The bloom on Hay's cheeks disappeared. "Don't allow anybody to enter the house," he said, and rushed to the theater with Bob.

Tad was taken home from a performance of *Aladdin's Wonderful Lamp* and ran upstairs shouting to Pendel: "Oh Tom Pen! Tom Pen! They have killed Pappa dead. They've killed Papa dead!" Pendel soothed him for an hour then took him to the bed that was kept for him in his father's room. Tad put on his nightclothes and got into bed. Pendel lay down beside him, put his arm around him, and quietly talked him to sleep.

At the Union Light Guard's barracks, someone shouted up to a sleeping sergeant that Lincoln and Seward had been killed. The cavalrymen saddled up, reached the White House in minutes, and found it quiet. A policeman let them know that the president had been shot at Ford's and the rest of their company had gone there. They galloped up to 10th Street and secured the house across the street from the theater, where Lincoln had been taken to die. "All night I rode up and down the street in front of that house," the sergeant said.

Lawrence Gobright of the Associated Press hurried to Seward's house on Lafayette Square and was told he had been savagely knifed but was still breathing. Then Gobright ran to the White House. Soldiers surrounded the mansion, keeping everyone away at bayonet point. "It was then, for the first time," Gobright said, "we learned that the President had not been brought home."

*   *   *

Soldiers and bareheaded officers escorted Lincoln's body to the White House on Saturday morning. Silent crowds watched the flag-draped coffin through the windows of the hearse. The body was brought upstairs to the Prince of Wales room where Willie died. Two army pathologists performed an autopsy observed by seven physicians. The embalming was done in the afternoon. The usher William Slade washed the body, snipped a lock of its hair, and dressed it in the suit that Lincoln had worn to the second inaugural. French planned the funeral under Stanton's loose direction.

Mrs. Lincoln refused to enter her bedroom or her husband's and collapsed in a spare room over the north portico, beyond the comfort of Mrs. Gideon Welles, who stayed with her all night, relieved by Mrs. Keckly in the morning. At midday, she dissolved in "unearthly shrieks" and "terrible convulsions" in Tad's presence. When he pleaded with her not to break his heart, "she would calm herself with a great effort, and clasp her child in her arms."

Gideon Welles made his way to the Executive Mansion that morning.

> There was a cheerless cold rain and everything seemed gloomy. On the Avenue in front of the White House were several hundred colored people, mostly women and children, weeping and wailing their loss. The crowd did not appear to diminish through the whole of that cold, wet day; they seemed not to know what was to be their fate since their great benefactor was dead, and their hopeless grief affected me more than almost anything else, though strong and brave men wept when I met them.

Lincoln's last mailbag came to Edward Neill on Saturday and "was opened amid an awful stillness." People filled the streets around the White House, "and everything seemed to weep."

Hay lay on his office sofa after an all-night deathbed vigil, on his way back from Cuba at sea, Nicolay knew nothing, and Neill took it on himself to sort through the papers that had accumulated in the president's office since 1861. "Few men's papers can be found in this world so free from anything objectionable," he said, "or sentiments which it would be desirable that the public should not know, as were these." He did not say what these few problematic papers were, or whether he destroyed them.

The north portico's white columns were swathed in black crepe, and heavy black cloth draped the door. After Hay suggested that President Johnson might give Mrs. Lincoln time to leave, two senators speaking on his behalf told Bob Lincoln in his father's office that she should not go in haste. Johnson moved from the Kirkwood House Hotel to a congressman's home and did business in a room at the Treasury Department, its door flanked by the flags that had decorated Lincoln's box at Ford's.

*   *   *

On Sunday, Nicolay heard at Hampton Roads that Lincoln was dead, and could not believe it. It might be one of a thousand wartime rumors. But when the ship reached Point Lookout at the mouth of the Potomac on Monday at dawn, "the mournful reports of the minute guns" and "the flags at half-mast left us no ground for further hope."

The body was brought down that night by men who removed their shoes to keep Mrs. Lincoln from hearing. The East Room's mirrors were covered with white fabric, an old superstition the chandeliers with black. John Alexander, who had managed the room's refurbishment, provided its funeral decorations. The coffin was set on a pillared cataflaque designed by French, its roof so high that the central chandelier had to be disconnected from the gas and taken down. Workmen hammered through the night. Mrs. Lincoln screamed that there were gunshots in the house.

While the body lay in state, members of "the African race" stood on Pennsylvania Avenue like sentinels, "weeping and moaning at the gateway." On Tuesday morning, thousands of mourners passed in two lines through the dimly lit Green Room into the East Room past the coffin, surrounded by spring flowers and a senior officers' guard. Nicolay wrote Therena: "I cannot describe to you the air of gloom which seems to hang over this city." Almost every house was draped in black, "and men stood idle and listless in groups on street corners." The White House was "dark and still as almost the grave itself," the silence as heavy "as if some greater calamity still hung in the air, and was about to crush and overwhelm everyone."

The funeral was held in the East Room on Wednesday. Grant and Farragut were there, with many other officers, most senior members of every branch of the federal government, many governors and state delegations. No one got in without a pass. Stands were set up, but someone underestimated the space, and the room was not quite full. Mrs. Lincoln was unfit to attend.

The service started at noon. Four clergymen of four denominations spoke for two hours. Dr. Phineas Gurley, the Lincolns' pastor at the New York Avenue Presbyterian Church, went first. The Marquis de Chambrun thought his hour-long eulogy was "a stock of dry commonplaces marshaled in good order," but in life Lincoln had found him a solace and a friend. On nights when he could not sleep, he had sent a servant for Gurley, and the two of them had walked the south portico until dawn.

Tad had been distraught until the sun came out on Sunday morning. He took it as a sign. "Do you think my father has gone to heaven?" he asked a caller. The gentleman said he was sure of it. "Then I am glad he has gone there," Tad said, "for he was never happy after he came here. This was not a good place for him."

A month after the funeral, the *New York World*'s correspondent sat in Lincoln's battered chair and wrote at his little desk as Hay gathered his effects.

The room "is so thickly hung with maps," the reporter wrote, "that the color of the wall cannot be discerned." When he stood up to examine them, he wondered if Lincoln had made the pencil marks tracing the movements of armies. The brilliant new carpet put down in 1862 had worn dull and thin, "and the emptiness of the place on this sunny Sunday" brought back the desolation that the country had scarcely begun to shed.

Tad ran in and out in a mourning suit with a gold fob chain. With the passage of a little time, his father's death had made "only the light impression which all things make upon childhood." Some books lay on a table—a thesaurus, a manual of parliamentary procedure, and two works of rustic humor published under the pseudonyms Artemus Ward and Orpheus C. Kerr, a play on "office seeker." Lincoln had told a friend that anyone who had not read Orpheus C. Kerr was a heathen.

EPILOGUE

THE WHITE HOUSE

Mrs. Lincoln haunted the White House for five weeks after her husband's murder, in what she later called "almost positive derangement," never leaving the room to which she had been taken. With no president in residence, the police were withdrawn, and relic hunters plundered the house like barbaric tribes. Dozens of unguarded mementos were sliced from carpets and upholstery. Bric-a-brac disappeared under the noses of the demoralized staff. Even some heavy furniture was carried away.

On May 23, Mrs. Lincoln was led from the White House for the last time, heavily veiled in black. Much of what was left went with her. According to various witnesses, ninety boxes and seventy crates were stuffed into fifteen carts and shipped to Illinois. In 1866, the *New York Daily News* called it no wonder that the house looked dismal and empty, and the *World* mourned the fortune spent on renovations, "shocked at the downright shabbiness" of the place. Whether due to public pilfering, Mrs. Lincoln's crates, or both, the steward said several years later there was "not silver enough in the White House to set a respectable free lunch table."

President Johnson repaired the "utterly dilapidated and ragged" public rooms, as the *Chicago Tribune* described them. His daughter rescued the state dining room and "redeemed it from wreck." Johnson also fixed the absurd constraint on the authorized professional staff, which grew from one private secretary to six, supported by half a dozen clerks. There was no more need to turn the president's secretaries into majors or call them Interior Department clerks.

Lincoln's office furnishings were still too rickety to venerate. During the Grant administration, a secondhand furniture company disposed of his desk, the cabinet table, Andrew Jackson's chair, and other treasures. Mrs. Calvin

Coolidge found Lincoln's rotting desk chair in what had been the attic. President Truman discovered his mice-gnawed cabinet chairs under the Treasury Department's eaves. Many presidential couples added and subtracted furnishings and fixtures and lived with sagging floors, groaning beams, and frightening receptions under quivering chandeliers until Truman moved his family across Pennsylvania Avenue to Blair House in 1948 while the house was gutted and rebuilt. Jacqueline Kennedy oversaw the most famous renovation of all.

MRS. LINCOLN

As Mrs. Lincoln had predicted, flocks of odious birds came home to roost when her husband left the White House. Among other indignities, Justice Davis was presented as administrator of his estate with a $2,000 invoice for her second inaugural gown, a staggering furrier's bill, and a notice that Lincoln had refused to pay for three hundred pairs of kid gloves. In 1866, Mrs. Cuthbert asked Orville Browning to help her find work. She had never seen a cent of her White House stewardess's salary, she said. Mrs. Lincoln had taken it all, "and she was left penniless."

The Lincoln estate's net value exceeded $110,000, not counting real estate, an impressive sum divided equally between his widow, Bob, and Tad. Championed by Senator Sumner, who overcame testimony that she "had been a curse to her husband," Mrs. Lincoln got over $22,000 from Congress—the unpaid balance of her husband's 1865 salary—and an annual $3,000 pension, $500 more than Nicolay's salary as private secretary.

Mrs. Lincoln said pride "made me endeavor, for the sake of our country and position, to keep up a genteel appearance." Convinced, despite Bob's constant reassurances, that she lived on the edge of poverty, she wrote self-pitying letters begging friends and former servants for help. In 1867, she ignited a new scandal by pressuring wealthy men to buy her old clothes.

Clara Rathbone, who had been in the box at Ford's Theater when Lincoln was shot, called on President Rutherford B. Hayes and left Tom Pendel touched when she told him that Mrs. Lincoln had asked her to inquire about the old employees.

Mrs. Lincoln died at sixty-three in 1882. Stoddard called her one of the best friends he ever had, long after it could do him any good: "She was a woman much misrepresented and scandalously abused."

TAD LINCOLN

Soon after the assassination, Tad looked up at the servant who was dressing him. "Pa is dead," he said, "and I am only Tad Lincoln now, little Tad, like other little boys." In the summer of 1865, after Crook wrote to Mrs. Lincoln, she passed along Tad's inquiries: "Tell us how Charlie is coming on and Dana Pendel—none of them ever write. Tell us about the new people in the house. All news will interest us."

Starting in October 1868, Mrs. Lincoln toured Europe with Tad and lived with him in Frankfurt and other places. When she brought him home in May 1871, just turned eighteen, Hay found Tad to be a tall, "modest and cordial young fellow" who showed his mother "a thoughtful devotion and tenderness beyond his years" and had outgrown "the mischievous thoughtlessness of his childhood." He was beautifully mannered and spoke quite clearly, with a trace of a German accent. Two months later, he died bolt upright in bed, fighting for breath in the presence of his mother and brother, probably from tuberculosis.

ROBERT LINCOLN

Bob Lincoln grew rich as a lawyer and a railroad man, served three presidents as Secretary of War and Minister to London, and rebuffed several attempts to persuade him to run for president. The White House, he said, was "a gilded prison." Early one morning, shortly before his death at the age of eighty-two in 1926, a clergyman watched his valet and his chauffeur help him up the steps at the Lincoln Memorial. "Moving forward, he knelt with bowed head in the attitude of prayer" and was gently lifted up and led back to his automobile.

SOLOMON JAMES JOHNSON

In 1867, Lincoln's barber became the federal government's first black clerk. In 1881, he wrote to President Garfield's Secretary of the Treasury, seeking advancement after seventeen years. "I am a colored man and a voter," he said, who had served since 1864, starting as a messenger "upon the request of the lamented Abraham Lincoln, whose trusted attendant I was at that time." He had acquired "a fair knowledge of the law which I have read at the Howard

University, and I have endeavored to improve myself in such liberal culture as becomes a good citizen." He hoped that his service would be recognized "and that my unfortunate race relations may not be a bar to such recognition." He died in 1885 as a first-class clerk.

ELIZABETH KECKLY

Mrs. Keckly "taught young colored girls" to make dresses, and employed up to twenty at a time. Mrs. Lincoln's recommendation may not have been jarring when written: "Elizabeth Keckley [*sic*], although colored, is very industrious, and will perform her duties faithfully." In later life she taught Domestic Arts at Wilberforce University in Ohio and gave her students bits and pieces of fabric and lace from which she had made Mrs. Lincoln's dresses, to be turned into pincushions. She died in Washington at the Home for Destitute Women and Children in a little dingy basement room "with one window facing the setting sun. Over the dresser was a picture of Mrs. Lincoln."

WILLIAM SLADE

William Slade continued on as the White House usher under Andrew Johnson, who later appointed him steward. When he died in 1868 at fifty-three, President Johnson and his daughters came to the funeral. Having speculated in real estate, he had left his family over $100,000, nearly as much as Lincoln had.

WILLIAM STODDARD

Stoddard began writing reminiscences of Lincoln's White House only weeks after he left it, and never stopped. In 1866 he left Arkansas for New York, where he made and lost fortunes and wrote over seventy books for boys, "not exactly what they call fame," he said, "but it will do." He returned to the White House often, once to help Grover Cleveland with his biography and gather material for a boy's historical novel. After losing his wife and three daughters to tuberculosis, he died at the age of ninety in 1925. A child's adulation speaks well of any man, and Stoddard's son worshipped him.

He had kept the tarnished key that had opened the White House door since

1800. Until the locks were changed, late in the Grant administration, he enjoyed stopping by the Executive Mansion at all hours and astonishing the doorkeepers by walking right in "without any help from them." The key passed to his descendants and was hammered down at Christie's in 2005 for $54,000.

JOHN GEORGE NICOLAY

Nicolay married Therena Bates and returned with her from Paris in 1869 to edit the *Chicago Republican*. Remarkably enough, he did not become a naturalized American citizen until 1870. With Bob Lincoln's influential help he was appointed marshall of the U.S. Supreme Court in 1872 and wrote a ten-volume Lincoln biography with Hay. After Nicolay died in 1901 at the age of sixty-nine after more than half a century of friendship with Hay, Hay sent a telegram to Nicolay's daughter and put himself at her disposal "precisely as if I were your father's brother."

JOHN HAY

Hay married Clara Stone, an heiress of the Gilded Age, and earned his own place in history as one of the leading men of his generation, distinguishing himself as a writer, a poet, William McKinley's ambassador to the Court of Saint James's, and the warlike Theodore Roosevelt's peace-loving Secretary of State, the post to which McKinley had elevated him after his service in London. On a hot night in 1901, his son was about to become McKinley's assistant private secretary at the age of twenty-four, following in his father's footsteps, when he fell sixty feet from a hotel window in New Haven in the midist of a Yale reunion. The coroner concluded that he had dozed off on the windowsill, escaping the heat. His father was never the same. "My boy is gone," he wrote, "and the whole face of the world is changed in a moment."

Hay died in office as Secretary of State in 1905. He was sixty-six years old. His diplomatic accomplishments were memorable, and so were his instinctive charm and his seemingly effortless talent with his pen. John Hay was "the most delightful man to talk to I ever met," Roosevelt said, though the Rough Rider thought the poet's preference for men of "refined and cultivated tastes" reflected a certain timidity and a missing "robustness of fiber." In 1891, Hay had written a grateful note to John Russell Young, an accomplished author and diplomat who had honored Hay's youthful service in Lincoln's White House:

> I have read what you said of me with the tender interest with which we hear a dead friend praised. The boy you describe in such charming language was once very dear to me, and although I cannot rate him as highly as you do, I am pleased and flattered, more than I can tell you, to know that he made an impression on a mind like yours.

AUTHOR'S NOTE AND ACKNOWLEDGMENTS

To avoid unnecessary distractions in material quoted in the book, some abbreviations were written out, ellipses and bracketed capital letters signaling partial quotations were omitted when the omissions were not misleading, and spelling and punctuation errors were corrected. Instructive abnormalities were preserved.

For their help and support I am grateful to my wife and children and my daughter-in-law; my literary agent, Alice Martell, the sine qua non of my writing career; Janice Goldklang, who edited my first book and patiently taught me how to write one; James M. Cornelius, Ph.D., Curator of the Lincoln Collection at the Abraham Lincoln Presidential Library and Museum, who read the manuscript, saved me from several errors and omissions, and contributed ideas for improvements; Clarence Lusane, Ph.D., Chairman of the Political Science Department at Howard University, who helped me understand Lincoln's interactions with African American leaders and White House staff; many helpful librarians, including Kristin Cook, Carolle Morini, and Mary Warnement at the spectacular Boston Athenaeum; Jonathan Sisk, my editor; his assistant editor, Christopher Utter; Elaine McGarraugh, the book's production editor; Josh Zeitz, who sent me copies of Hay's diaries and letters and Nicolay's correspondence with Therena Bates; Karen Needles and her Lincoln Archives Digital project; and Joan Brancale, whose watercolors brought the cover's engraving to life, advancing the proposition that a book can be judged by its cover.

NOTES

INTRODUCTION

1. *gates*: Noah Brooks. *Lincoln Observed: Civil War Dispatches of Noah Brooks.* Edited by Michael Burlingame. Baltimore: Johns Hopkins University Press, 1998 (*"Lincoln Observed"*), p. 80.

1. The Union Light Guard: George Ashmun. "Recollections of a Peculiar Service," *Magazine of History* 3 (April 1906): 277–92 ("Ashmun"), *passim*; Robert McBride. *Lincoln's Body Guard: The Union Light Guard of Ohio.* Indianapolis, IN: E. J. Hecker, 1911 ("McBride, *Body Guard*"), *passim*; Robert McBride. *Personal Recollections of Abraham Lincoln.* Indianapolis, IN: Bobbs-Merrill, 1926 ("McBride, *Recollections*"), p. 61; Smith Stimmel. "Experiences as a Member of President Lincoln's Bodyguard 1863–65," *North Dakota Historical Quarterly* 1 (January 1927): 7–33 ("Stimmel") *passim*.

1. Gaslight: William Seale. *The President's House: A History.* 2 vols. Washington: White House Historical Association, 1986 ("Seale"), p. 331.

1. Bucktails: Thomas Chamberlin. *History of the One Hundred and Fiftieth Regiment Pennsylvania Volunteers.* Philadelphia: F. McManus Jr., 1905, *passim*; H. S. Huidekoper, "On Guard at White House," *National Magazine* 29 (February 1909): 510–12, *passim*.

1. *ornamental*: McBride, *Recollections*, pp. 1, 24; Noah Brooks, *Mr. Lincoln's Washington: Selections from the Writings of Noah Brooks, Civil War Correspondent.* Edited by P. J. Staudenraus. South Brunswick, NJ: Thomas Yoseloff, 1967 (*"Lincoln's Washington"*), p. 250; George A. Sala. *My Diary in America in the Midst of War*, 2 vols. London: Tinsley Brothers, 1865 ("Sala"), vol. 2, pp. 142–44; Seale, p. 324.

1–2. Lincoln on the portico: McBride, *Body Guard*, pp. 13–15; McBride, *Recollections*, pp. 33–42.

2. English writer: George Borrett. "An Englishman in Washington in 1864," *Magazine of History with Notes and Queries* 38 (Extra no. 149, 1929): 2–15 ("Borrett"), pp. 5–6.

CHAPTER 1

5. *March 4*: *New York Times*, March 6, 1861.

5. Washington under threat: George Williamson Smith. "A Critical Moment for Washington," *Records of the Columbia Historical Society* 21 (1918): 87–113 ("A Critical Moment"), p. 87; Gideon Welles. *Diary of Gideon Welles, Secretary of the Navy Under Lincoln and Johnson*, 3 vols. New York: W. W. Norton & Company, 1960 ("Welles"), vol. 1, p. 10; L. A. Gobright. *Recollection of Men and Things*. Philadelphia: Claxton, Remsen & Haffelfinger, 1869 ("Gobright"), p. 286; Bryan, vol. 2, pp. 461–72; Charles P. Stone, "Washington in March and April, 1861," *Magazine of American History* 14 (July 1885): 1–24 ("Washington in March and April") and "Washington on the Eve of the War," *The Century Magazine* 26 (July 1883): 458–66 ("Washington on the Eve"); Isaac N. Arnold, *Life of Abraham Lincoln*. Chicago: Jansen, McClerg & Company, 1885 ("Arnold, *Life*"), p. 189; Carl Schurz. "Reminiscences of a Long Life," *McClure's Magazine* 28 (March 1907): 453–69 ("Schurz"), p. 461.

5–6. Parade: *Id.*; W. B. Bryan. *A History of the National Capital*, 2 vols. New York: The Macmillan Company, 1916 ("Bryan"), vol. 2, p. 469; Benjamin B. French. *Benjamin Brown French, Witness to the Young Republic: A Yankee's Journal, 1828–1870*. Edited by Donald B. Cole and John J. McDonough. Hanover, NH: University Press of New England, 1989 ("*Witness*"), p. 349; Harold Holzer. *Lincoln President-Elect*. New York: Simon & Schuster, 2008, pp. 447–50; Jay Monaghan. *Diplomat in Carpet Slippers: Abraham Lincoln Deals with Foreign Affairs*. Indianapolis, IN: Bobbs-Merrill Co., 1945) ("Monaghan"), pp. 35–36.

5–6. Pennsylvania Avenue: William A. Croffut. "Lincoln's Washington," *Atlantic Monthly* 145 (January 1930): 55–65, p. 55; Edward Dicey. *Six Months in the Federal States*. London: Macmillan, 1863, 2 vols. ("Dicey"), pp. 92–95.

6. Trollope: Anthony Trollope. *North America*. Philadelphia: J. B. Lippincott & Co., 1862 ("Trollope"), pp. 301–5.

6. *Bullfrogs*: J. G. Kohl, "The Federal City of Washington," *Bentley's Miscellany* 50 (July–December 1861): 381–93 ("Kohl"), p. 389.

6. *menagerie*: *William Howard Russell's Civil War: Private Diary and Letters, 1861–1862*. Edited by Martin Crawford. Athens, GA: University of Georgia Press, 1992 ("*Russell's Civil War*"), p. 22.

6. *dingy-looking*: McBride, *Recollections*, p. 31.

6. *President's Park*: Laura Wood Roper. *FLO: A Biography of Frederick Law Olmsted*. Baltimore: The Johns Hopkins University Press, 1973 ("Roper"), p. 163; Isometrical View of the Presidents [*sic*] House, the Surrounding Buildings, and Private Residences, Library of Congress ("LOC") Document No. LC-USZ62–40367 ("Isometrical View").

6. *sidewalk*: Lois Bryan Adams. "Meeting Father Abraham, Washington, D.C., February 1864," in *The Civil War: The Third Year Told by Those Who Lived It*, edited

by Brooks D. Simpson, pp. 693–700. New York: Library of America, 2012 ("Adams"), p. 694.

6–7. Lafayette Square: William O. Stoddard. *Lincoln's White House Secretary: The Adventurous Life of William O. Stoddard*. Edited by Harold Holzer. Carbondale, IL: Southern Illinois University Press, 2007 (*"White House Secretary"*), p. 267; Trollope, pp. 312–13; Seale, pp. 300, 310, 325.

7. *moonlight night*: Dicey, vol. 1, p. 98.

7. *innocence*: Kohl, p. 389.

7. *Fence and grounds*: Adams, p. 695; Seale, pp. 202–5; William O. Stoddard. *Lincoln at Work: Sketches from Life*. Boston: United Society of Christian Endeavor, 1900 (*"Lincoln at Work"*), p. 105; *Lincoln's Washington*, p. 250; Seale, p. 324; Isometrical View; William O. Stoddard. *Inside the White House in War Times: Memoirs and Reports of Lincoln's Secretary*. Edited by Michael Burlingame. Lincoln, NE: University of Nebraska Press, 2000 ("Stoddard-Burlingame"), p. 169.

8. *long breath*: Charles Francis Adams. *Charles Francis Adams, 1835–1915: An Autobiography*. Boston: Houghton Mifflin, 1916 ("Charles Francis Adams"), p. 99.

8. *the shadows . . . wrinkle*: William Hayes Ward, ed. *Abraham Lincoln: Tributes from His Associates, Reminiscences of Soldiers, Statesmen, and Citizens*. New York: T. Y. Crowell & Company, 1895 (*"Tributes"*); William O. Stoddard. *Inside the White House in War Times*. New York: Charles L. Webster & Co., 1890 ("Stoddard, *Inside*"), p. 11.

8. *Uncle Abe*: Horatio King. *Turning on the Light: A Dispassionate Survey of President Buchanan's Administration from 1860 until Its Close*. Philadelphia: J. B. Lippincott Company, 1895, p. 283.

8. *entirely ignorant*: David H. Donald. *Lincoln*. New York: Simon & Schuster, 1995 ("Donald"), p. 285.

8. *frontier community*: A Critical Moment, p. 90.

8–9. Buchanan and his parting: Elizabeth Todd Grimsley. "Six Months in the White House," *Journal of the Illinois State Historical Society* 19 (October 1926–January 1927): 43–73 ("Grimsley"), p. 46; Washington on the Eve, p. 466; Philip Auchampaugh. "Squire in the White House," *Pennsylvania Magazine of History and Biography* 58 (1934) ("Auchampaugh"): 270–85, p. 274; Papers of John George Nicolay ("Nicolay Papers"), LOC, file labeled "The White House from James Madison to Abraham Lincoln," p. 56; John Hay. *At Lincoln's Side: John Hay's Civil War Correspondence and Selected Writings*. Edited by Michael Burlingame. Carbondale, IL: Southern Illinois University Press, 2000 (*"At Lincoln's Side"*), p. 119.

9. *storm entrance*: Seale, p. 216; Stoddard, *Inside*, p. 11; Viator [Joseph Bradley Varnum]. *The Washington Sketch Book*. New York: Mohun, Ebbs & Hough, 1864 ("Viator"), p. 185.

9. *porter's lodge*: Seale, p. 195; Thomas Pendel. *Thirty-Six Years in the White House*. Washington: The Neale Publishing Company, 1902 ("Pendel"), p. 35.

9. *McManus . . . Burns*: At Lincoln's Side, 68; Stoddard, *Inside*, p. 10; Charles G.

Halpine. "Miles O'Reilly at the White House," in *The Life and Adventures, Songs, Services and Speeches of Private Miles O'Reilly*. New York: Carleton, 1864 ("Halpine"), p. 158; Stoddard, *Inside*, pp. 10, 46; Helen Nicolay. *Lincoln's Secretary: A Biography of John G. Nicolay*. New York: Longmans, Green, 1949 ("Helen Nicolay, *Biography*"), p. 121; "Data on White House Expenditures from Files of General Accounting Office, Nat. Archives" ("Expenditures"), Papers of J. G. Randall, LOC ("Randall Papers").

9–10. *vestibule*: "The City of Washington III," *United States Magazine* 3 (September 1856): 193–205, pp. 197–98; Seale, p. 216; Pendel, p. 169; Stoddard, *Inside*, p. 11; William H. Russell. *My Diary North and South*, 2 vols. Boston: T. O. H. P. Burnham, 1863 ("Russell"), vol. 1, p. 37.

10. Servants: Seale, p. 337; "The City of Washington III," *United States Magazine* 3 (September 1856): 193–205, pp. 203–4 (Doorkeepers, messengers, and watchmen were often described interchangeably.); John Washington. *They Knew Lincoln*. New York: E. P. Dutton, 1942 ("*They Knew Lincoln*"), pp. 106–7, 127, 129, and *passim*; Abraham Lincoln. *The Collected Works of Abraham Lincoln*, 9 vols. Edited by Roy P. Basler. New Brunswick, NJ: Rutgers University Press, 1953–55 ("CW"), vol. 5, p. 474, vol. 6, pp. 8–9.

10. Blue Room: Seale, p. 215; *Lincoln Observed*, pp. 81–82; *New York Herald*, March 10, 1861; *The White House: An Historic Guide* ("*Historic Guide*"). Washington: White House Historical Association, 2011, p. 48; "The White House and Its New Decorations," *Daily Alta California*, May 12, 1862 ("*Daily Alta*").

10. Benjamin French: *Witness*, pp. 1–11.

10. *kiss*: *Id.*, pp. 348–49.

11. *sovereigns*: e.g. *id.*, p. 386.

11. *excellent mood*: *National Intelligencer* (Washington), March 5, 1861.

11. *rudeness*: *New York Times*, March 5, 1861.

11. Gloves: *Tributes*, p. 109; Ward Hill Lamon. *Recollections of Abraham Lincoln, 1847–1865*. Edited by Dorothy Lamon. Chicago: A. C. McClurg and Company, 1895 ("Lamon"), p. 99.

11. *royalty apers*: *Boston Journal*, "Waifs from Washington," December 1, 1863.

11. *called the White House*: CW, vol. 4, p. 348; Seale, p. 163.

11. *tongs*: Elizabeth Keckley. *Behind the Scenes*. New York: G. W. Carleton, 1868; rept. Oxford University Press, 1988 ("Keckley"), p. 154.

11. Lamon: Lamon, p. 17; Leonard Swett. "The Conspiracies of the Rebellion," *North American Review* 144 (February 1887): 179–190 ("Swett"), p. 186; W. W. Orme to Judge David Davis, May 11, 1861, David Davis Papers ("Davis Papers"), Abraham Lincoln Library and Museum ("ALLM"), Box 2.

11–12. Nicolay's pay and title: See *Lincoln's Washington*, p. 402 for an admiral's comparable pay; Jesse W. Weik. *The Real Lincoln*. Boston: Houghton Mifflin Company, 1922 ("Weik"), p. 285.

11–13. Nicolay: John G. Nicolay, Scrapbook 1856–1870, typescript dictation by Nicolay to Helen Nicolay, October 14, 1897, Nicolay Papers, Box 1; Helen Nicolay,

Biography, pp. 3–6, 11–19, 24–27, 31–36, 44, 84, 114; John Nicolay. *With Lincoln in the White House: Letters, Memoranda and Other Writings of John G. Nicolay, 1860–1865*. Edited by Michael Burlingame. Carbondale, IL: Southern Illinois University Press, 2000 (*"With Lincoln"*), pp. xii–xvi; Harold Holzer. *Lincoln and the Power of the Press*. New York: Simon & Schuster, 2014 (*"Power of the Press"*), p. 244; Weik, p. 283.

13–16. Hay: John Taliaferro. *All the Great Prizes: The Life of John Hay from Lincoln to Roosevelt*. New York: Simon & Schuster, 2013 ("Taliaferro"), pp. 14–37; A. S. Chapman, "The Boyhood of John Hay," *Century Magazine* 46 (July 1904): 432, 444–54; Lorenzo Sears. *John Hay, Author and Statesman*. New York: Dodd, Mead and Company, 1914 ("Sears"), pp. 6, 16, 19, 24; William Roscoe Thayer. *The Life and Letters of John Hay*, 2 vols. Boston: Houghton, Mifflin Co., 1915 ("Thayer"), vol. 1, p. 87; *At Lincoln's Side*, pp. xii, xiii, xix; *Russell's Civil War*, p. 144; Alexander K. McClure: *Colonel Alexander K. McClure's Recollections of Half a Century*. Salem, MA: The Salem Press Company, 1902 ("McClure"), p. 210; John Hay. *Inside Lincoln's White House: The Complete Civil War Diary of John Hay*. Edited by Michael Burlingame. Carbondale, IL: Southern Illinois University Press, 1997 ("Hay, *Inside*") pp. xiii, xvi; Joseph B. Bishop. *Notes and Anecdotes of Many Years*. New York: Charles Scribner's Sons, 1925 ("Bishop"), p. 778; Michael Burlingame. *Abraham Lincoln: A Life*, 2 vols. Baltimore: Johns Hopkins University Press, 2008 ("Burlingame"), vol. 2, p. 74; *A College Friendship: A Series of Letters from John Hay to Hannah Angell*. Boston: Privately Printed, 1938, p. 62; John Hay. *Letters of John Hay and Extracts from Diary*, 3 vols. Edited by Clara Hay. Washington: Privately printed, 1908 ("Hay Letters"), p. 7.

16. Lincoln enters his office: Lincoln got Anderson's note in his office "when I came from the inauguration," according to a memorandum written by Nicolay, July 3, 1861, Nicolay Papers, Box 2.

16. *since Jackson*: Wendell Garrett, ed. *Our Changing White House*. Boston: Northeastern University Press, 1995 ("Garrett"), p. 118.

16. *the shop*: William O. Stoddard, *Lincoln's Third Secretary*. Edited by William O. Stoddard Jr. New York: Exposition Press, 1955 (*"Third Secretary"*), p. 208.

16. *business stairs*: Stoddard, *Inside*, p. 12.

16. *steps . . . lower*: Seale, p. 185.

16. *worn and soiled*: Albert G. Riddle. *Recollections of War Times: Reminiscences of Men and Events in Washington, 1860–1865*. New York: G. P. Putnam's Sons 1895 ("Riddle"), p. 17.

16. *waiting room*: Seale, pp. 339, 403; Harold Holzer, "Abraham Lincoln's White House," *White House History* 25 (Spring 2009): 5–17 ("Holzer, White House"), p. 8; *Frank Leslie's Illustrated Newspaper*, April 6, 1861, p. 309.

16–17. *anteroom*: Issac Arnold. *Sketch of the Life of Abraham Lincoln*. New York: John B. Bachelder, 1869 ("Arnold, *Sketch*"), p. 67; Auchampaugh, p. 273.

17. The President's office: *Id.*; Seale, pp. 183, 339–40, 364; Auguste Laugel. "A

Frenchman's Diary in Our Civil War Time – III." *The Nation* 75 (July 31, 1902): 88–89 ("Laugel"), p. 88; Stoddard-Burlingame, p. 145; George A. Townsend. *The Life, Crime, and Capture of John Wilkes Booth*. New York: Dick and Fitzgerald, 1865 ("George Townsend"), p. 58; *Lincoln at Work*, p. 60; Garrett, p. 118; Frederick W. Seward. *Seward at Washington, as Senator and Secretary of State*, 3 vols. New York: Derby and Miller, 1891 ("*Seward at Washington*"), vol. 1, p. 520; Seale, p. 340.

17. *too rickety*: *Daily Alta*.

17. *bastard Gothic*: Trollope, p. 19.

17. *first thing*: Memorandum by Nicolay, July 3, 1861, Nicolay Papers, Box 2; Orville H. Browning. *The Diary of Orville Hickman Browning*, 2 vols. Edited by Theodore Calvin Pease and James G. Randall. Springfield, IL: Illinois State Historical Library, 1925–1933 ("Browning Diary"), vol. 1, p. 476.

17–18. *dinner*: Grimsley, p. 48; Harry E. Pratt. *The Personal Finances of Abraham Lincoln*. Springfield, IL: The Abraham Lincoln Association, 1943 ("Pratt"), p. 72.

18. Serenades: CW vol. 4, p. 272; *At Lincoln's Side*, p. 40; Seale, p. 409; Frank B. Carpenter. *Six Months at the White House with Abraham Lincoln: The Story of a Picture*. New York: Hurd and Houghton, 1867 ("Carpenter"), p. 248.

18. *absent in part*: Henry Adams. *The Education of Henry Adams*. Boston: Houghton, Mifflin Company, 1918, p. 107.

18. Todds: Katherine Helm. *The True Story of Mary, Wife of Lincoln*. New York: Harper, 1928 ("Helm"), pp. 180–83; Grimsley, 48; Edna Colman. *Seventy-Five Years of White House Gossip*. New York: Doubleday, 1925 ("Colman"), p. 319.

18. *quick, lively, gay*: Douglas L. Wilson and Rodney O. Davis, eds. *Herndon's Informants: Letters, Interviews, and Statements about Abraham Lincoln*. Urbana: University of Illinois Press, 1998 ("*Herndon's Informants*"), p. 443.

18–19. Horse and carriage gifts: *New York Tribune*, February 25, 1861; *At Lincoln's Side*, pp. 190, 272–73 nn. 24–27; *New York Times*, March 7, 1861.

CHAPTER 2

21–23. Lincoln besieged: Stoddard-Burlingame, pp. 157, 161; Allen Thorndike Rice, ed. *Reminiscences of Abraham Lincoln by Distinguished Men of His Time*. New York: North American Publishing Co., 1886 ("Rice"), pp. 480–81; Gideon Welles, "Memoranda and Documents: Two Manuscripts of Gideon Welles," *New England Quarterly* 11 (January 1, 1938), pp. 576–605, p. 594; *National Intelligencer*, March 21, 1861; April 9, 1861; Carpenter, p. 129; William O. Stoddard. *Abraham Lincoln: The True Story of a Great Life*. New York: Fords, Howard, & Hulbert, 1885 ("*True Story*"), p. 215; Grimsley, p. 48; Stoddard, *Inside*, p. 12; *Frank Leslie's Illustrated Newspaper*, April 6, 1861, p. 310; *With Lincoln*, pp. 32, 33; John G. Nicolay. "Lincoln's Personal Appearance," *Century Magazine* 42 (October 1891): 932–38 ("Personal Appearance"), p. 937; *At Lincoln's Side*, p. 109.

21. *which end of a ship*: Julia Taft Bayne. *Tad Lincoln's Father*. Boston: Little, Brown, and Company, 1931 ("Bayne"), p. 157.

23–25. Stoddard: *White House Secretary*, pp. 1–5, 216, 234, 274, 317, 320, 384 n. 6.; Stoddard-Burlingame, pp. vii–xi; *Third Secretary*, p. 12.

25. McManus: Stoddard-Burlingame, p. 151 (misnaming McManus "Moran"); Life in the White House, p. 34; Stoddard, *Inside*, pp. 46–47.

25–26. Doorkeeping: *E.g.*, Camille Ferri-Pisani. *Prince Napoleon in America, 1861*. Translated by Georges J. Joyaux. Bloomington, IN: Indiana University Press, 1955 ("Pisani"), p. 94; Sala, vol. 2, p. 143; *Lincoln Observed*, p. 80; Riddle, p. 11; Sala, vol. 2, pp. 143–45.

26. Keys: Stoddard, *Inside*, p. 10.

26–27. Lincoln importuned: John Hay. "Life in the White House in the Time of Lincoln," *The Century Magazine* 41 (November 1890): 33–37 ("Life in the White House"), p. 34; Frederick W. Seward. *Reminiscences of a War-Time Statesman and Diplomat, 1830–1915*. New York: G. P. Putnam's Sons, 1916 ("Seward, *Reminiscences*"), pp. 147–48; Seale, p. 368; Rice, p. 50; *With Lincoln*, p. xix; Life in the White House, p. 33; *At Lincoln's Side*, p. 159; Russell, vol. 1, pp. 33, 51; Grimsley, *passim*; *Concerning Mr. Lincoln*, pp. 73–75; Harry J. Carman and Reinhard H. Luthin. *Lincoln and the Patronage*. New York: Columbia University Press, 1943 ("*Lincoln and the Patronage*"), p. 61; *Lincoln and the Patronage*, p. 54; Burlingame vol. 2, p. 95; Stoddard-Burlingame, p. 161.

27–28. Springfield job seekers: O. C. Dake to Leonard Swett, May 7, 1861, Davis Papers, Box 2; Hatch to Nicolay, March 11, 1862, Nicolay Papers, Box 2; Harold Holzer, ed. *Dear Mr. Lincoln: Letters to the President*. Reading, MA: Addison-Wesley, 1993 ("*Dear Mr. Lincoln*"), p. 80.

28. *bayonets*: Burlingame vol. 2, p. 72.

28. *waited days or weeks*: Life in the White House, p. 33.

28. *Thank God*: Rufus Rockwell Wilson, ed. *Intimate Memories of Lincoln*. Elmira, NY: The Primavera Press, 1945 ("Wilson"), p. 454.

28. *patience*: Life in the White House, p. 33; Stoddard-Burlingame, p. 161.

28. *pigeonholes*: Life in the White House, p. 33.

28. *a simple man*: *True Story*, pp. 344–45.

28. *locusts . . . never left*: *With Lincoln*, p. 175; Life in the White House, p. 33.

28–29. Whipple: William H. Crook, "Lincoln as I Knew Him," *Harper's Monthly Magazine* 114 (June 1907): 41–48 ("Lincoln as I Knew Him"), p. 41.

29–30. William Johnson: *They Knew Lincoln*, pp. 106–7, 127–32; Roy P. Basler, *President Lincoln Helps His Old Friends*. Springfield, IL: Abraham Lincoln Association, 1977 ("Basler, *President Lincoln*"), p. 14; CW vol. 4, pp. 277, 288, vol. 5, p. 33, vol. 6, p. 69 n.; Roy P. Basler, "Did President Lincoln Give the Smallpox to William H. Johnson?" *Huntington Library Quarterly* 35 (May 1972): 279–84 ("Basler"), p. 282.

30. *Marque and Reprisal*: CW vol. 6, p. 126.

30. *On March 7 . . . blank*: *Id.*, vol. 4, p. 277; *Seward at Washington* vol. 1, p. 520.

30. *Nicolay wrote*: Nicolay to Hatch, March 7, 1861, Nicolay Papers, LOC, Box 2.

31. Past presidents' guards: Seale, pp. 158, 204, 218, 240–41, 284, 296, 309.

31. Tuckerman: Charles K. Tuckerman, "Personal Recollections of Abraham Lincoln," *Magazine of American History* 19 (January–June, 1888): 411–15 ("Tuckerman"), pp. 411–12.

31. Cocky Nicolay and Hay: Nicolay to Bates, April 7, 1861, Nicolay Papers; Hay Letters, p. 7.

CHAPTER 3

33. Mrs. Lincoln shopping: Helm, p. 153; Wayne C. Temple, "Mrs. Lincoln's Clothing," *Lincoln Herald* 62 (Summer 1960): 54–65 ("Mrs. Lincoln's Clothing"), p. 57; Edwin G. Burrows and Mike Wallace. *Gotham: A History of New York City to 1898.* New York: Oxford University Press, 1999, pp. 666–68, 945–46; Leonard Wheeler to Lyman Trumbull, January 11, 1861, Lyman Trumbull papers, LOC, reel 8.

33. *dilapidated mansion*: Mary Todd Lincoln. "Unpublished Mary Todd Lincoln." Edited by Thomas F. Schwartz and Kim M. Bauer. *Journal of the Abraham Lincoln Association* 17 (Summer 1996): 45–52 ("Unpublished Mary Todd Lincoln"), p. 10; Riddle, p. 15.

33. White House tours: *Baltimore Sun*, March 2, 1861; Turner, p. 84.

33–34. The basement: John B. Ellis. *The Sights and Secrets of the National Capital.* Chicago: Jones, Junkin & Co., 1869, p. 229; Stoddard, *Inside*, p. 49; Stoddard-Burlingame, p. 145; Stoddard, *Inside*, p. 178; Seale, pp. 194–95, 258.

34. The kitchen and cook: Seale, pp. 194–96; *They Knew Lincoln*, p. 119; Bayne, pp. 100–10.

34. *state of the art*: Seale, *passim*.

34. furnace and heat: *Id.*, pp. 216–17, 268, 315–16; Nicolay to Bates, February 17, 1864, Nicolay Papers.

34. Pump: Emmanuel Hertz. *Abraham Lincoln: A New Portrait* (New York) 2 vols. Horace Liveright, Inc. (1931) vol. 1, pp. 320–22.

34–35. *lamps and candles*: Lincoln Home National Historic Site.

35. Gas: Seale, pp. 268–69, 331, 340, 413; *Witness*, p. 456; *With Lincoln*, p. 86; William H. Crook. *Memories of the White House.* Edited by Henry Rood. Boston: Little, Brown, 1911 ("Crook, *Memories*"), p. 7.

35. *on his couch*: *Washington Star*, February 11, 1920.

35. *only elegance*: Grimsley, p. 47.

35. *inaugural delegations*: Riddle, p. 17.

35. he East Room: Stoddard, *Inside*, p. 13, Seale, pp. 186, 268–69; *Lincoln Observed*, p. 82.

35–36. The Green Room: *Daily Alta*; Stoddard, *Inside*, p. 13.

35–36. The Red Room: *Id.*, pp. 13, 145, 173; *Lincoln Observed*, p. 81; *Lincoln at Work*, p. 99; Crook, *Memories*, p. 34; "Lincoln's Attendance at Spiritualist Séances," *Lincoln Lore*, Numbers 1499 and 1500 (January and February 1963) ("Seances"), pp. 2–4.

36. The walls: *Lincoln Observed*, p. 81; Stoddard-Burlingame, p. 155.

36. The State Dining Room: *Id.*, p. 145; Seale, pp. 156, 195, 350; William O. Stoddard. *Dispatches from Lincoln's White House: The Anonymous Civil War Journalism of Presidential Secretary William O. Stoddard*. Edited by Michael Burlingame. Lincoln, NE: University of Nebraska Press, 2002 ("*Dispatches*"), p. 207; Jean H. Baker. *Mary Todd Lincoln: A Biography*. New York: W. W. Norton & Company, 1987 ("Baker") p. 182; Carpenter, p. 83; Mary Clemmer Ames. *Ten Years in Washington: Life and Scenes in the National Capital, as a Woman Sees Them*. Hartford, CT: A. D. Worthington, 1873 ("Ames"), p. 171.

36. The Family Dining Room: *Lincoln Observed*, p. 80; Seale, p. 409.

36. The hall: *Lincoln at Work*, pp. 46–47; Stoddard, *Inside*, pp. 13, 15; Life in the White House, p. 34; Seale, p. 366.

36–37. The furniture: Mary Todd Lincoln. *Mary Todd Lincoln: Her Life and Letters*. Edited by Justin G. Turner and Linda Levitt Turner. New York: Knopf, 1972 ("Turner"), pp. 326, 330; Helen Nicolay. *Personal Traits of Abraham Lincoln*. New York: The Century Company, 1912 ("Helen Nicolay, *Traits*"), pp. 205–6; Grimsley, p. 59.

37. Connecting bedrooms: *Donald*, pp. 198, 309; *With Lincoln*, p. 208 n. 129; M. A. De Wolfe Howe, ed., *The Life and Letters of George Bancroft*, 2 vols. New York: Scribner's, 1908 ("Bancroft"), p. 145.

37. Willie and Tad's rooms: Donald, p. 309.

37. Bob's room: Pendel, p. 42.

37. Guestrooms: Burlingame, vol. 2, p. 250.

37. Servants' rooms: www.whitehousemuseum.org.

37. Plumbing and water: Seale, pp. 90, 199, 316–17, 379; Dana Family Papers ("Dana Papers"), Massachusetts Historical Society, Richard Henry Dana to his wife, May 4, 1864; "Appropriations for the White House Taken from Statutes at Large" ("Appropriations"), Randall Papers.

37–38. The Library and books: Stoddard-Burlingame, p. 145; Seale, pp. 272, 292, 380; George G. Evans. *Visitor's Companion at Our Nation's Capital*. Philadelphia: George G. Evans, 1892, pp. 82–83; Grimsley, p. 68. *Dear Mr. Lincoln*, pp. 82–83; National Archives, GAO Accounting Office Records, First Auditor's Record Group 217 ("RG 217"), document 347-277-141775; CW, vol. 5, p. 394; Louis A. Warren, "A. Lincoln's Executive Mansion Library," *The Antiquarian Bookman* 5 (February 11, 1950): 569–70; Welles, vol. 1, p. 383; Stoddard, *Inside*, 227.

38–41. Willie and Tad: Burlingame, vol. 2, p. 261; Life in the White House, p. 35; Grimsley, pp. 48–49; Turner, p. 399; Keckley, pp. 197–98; Lincoln as I Knew Him, pp. 113–14; Bayne, pp. 31, 69, 112, 134–38, 193–94; *At Lincoln's Side*, pp. 111–12; Life in the White House, p. 35; Helen Nicolay, *Biography*, p. 134; Stoddard-Burlingame, p. 187; Stoddard, *Inside*, pp. 50–51; *They Knew Lincoln*, p. 124; Elbert B. Smith. *Francis Preston Blair*. New York: Free Press/Macmillan, 1980, p. 313; Crook, *Memories*, p. 25.

40. Pianist: David R. Barbee. "The Musical Mr. Lincoln," *Abraham Lincoln Quarterly* 5 (December 1949): 435–54 ("Musical Mr. Lincoln"), p. 443.

40–42. Williamson: Seale, pp. 374, 378–79; CW, vol. 6, pp. 144–45; Bayne, p. 153; Burlingame, vol. 2, p. 271; Crook, *Memories*, p. 22.

42. The grounds: Turner, p. 82; Lincoln as I Knew Him, p. 112; Herbert R. Collins. "The White House Stables and Garages," *Records of the Columbia Historical Society* 45 (1963/1965): 366–85 ("Stables and Garages"), p. 378; Seale, pp. 344–45.

42. Wings: *Morrison's Stranger's Guide and Etiquette for Washington City*. Washington: W. H. & O. H. Morrison, 1862 ("Morrison's"), p. 26; Seale, p. 194, 198; Isometrical View.

43. *greenhouse*: Seale, pp. 272, 312.

43. Conservatory and flowers: *Id.*, pp. 206, 313, 345, 391–92; Stoddard, *Inside*, pp. 13 and 106; *French aristocrat*: Adolph de Pineton, Marquis de Chambrun. *Impressions of Lincoln and the Civil War*. New York: Random House, 1952 ("Chambrun"), p. 21; Bayne, pp. 6, 82; Turner, p. 82; Crook, *Memories*, p. 17; Grimsley, p. 62; Seale, p. 392; Turner, pp. 129, 172, 177, 188; Russell, p. 53; Bancroft, p. 144; *At Lincoln's Side*, 186; Bayne, p. 82; Stoddard-Burlingame, p. 182; Julia S. Wheelock. "Excerpts of Diary of Susan Wheelock," *Lincoln Herald* 46 (October 1944): pp. 42–46 ("Wheelock"), p. 45.

43–44. Watt: Bayne, pp. 4–5, 133; Appropriations; *At Lincoln's Side*, pp. 192–93, 274, and notes 41, 64; Seale, pp. 205, 299, 324, 351, 392.

CHAPTER 4

45. Receptions tradition: *Id.*, *passim*, *e.g.*, pp. 91, 127–29, 159, 220, 243, 263, 315.

45. *hard in the face*: Sala, p. 124.

45–49. First levee: Riddle, p. 17; *New York Herald*, March 10, 1861; *Lincoln's Washington*, pp. 63, 250; Seale, pp. 12, 282, 320, 332, 349–50, 363, 403, 405, 1101 n. 5; Grimsley, pp. 49–50 and 62; William Makepeace Thayer. *Character and Public Services of Abraham Lincoln*. Boston: Dinsmoor & Co., 1864, p. 22; *Witness*, pp. 386–87, 417–18; Stoddard, *Inside*, pp. 52–53; 88–90, 96–97, 153–55; *Morrison's*, p. 51; Agnes Macdonnell. "America Then and Now: Recollections of Lincoln." *Contemporary Review* 3 (1917): 567–68 ("Macdonnell"), p. 567; Crook, *Memories*, p.

37; *Lincoln at Work*, p. 61; Russell, vol. 1, p. 390; Musical Mr. Lincoln, p. 445; www.marineband.marines.mil; Nicolay to Bates, March 10, 1861, Nicolay Papers; Helen Nicolay, *Biography*, p. 75; *New York Herald*, March 10, 1861; Mrs. E. F. Ellet. *The Court Circles of the Republic.* Hartford, CT: Hartford Pub. Co., 1869 ("Ellet"), pp. 535–36; Gobright, p. 311; Wilson, p. 370; Colman, p. 288; Regis de Trobriand. *Four Years with the Army of the Potomac.* Boston: Ticknor and Company, 1889, pp. 146–47; *New York Herald*, March 10 and March 13, 1861; *Charles Francis Adams*, pp. 99–100; *Lincoln at Work*, p. 65; Life in the White House, p. 35; Stoddard-Burlingame, p. 179; Osborn Hamiline Oldroyd. *The Lincoln Memorial: Album Immortelles.* London: G. W. Carleton & Co., 1883, pp. 414–15; *With Lincoln*, p. 67; John B. Blake to Harriet Lane, Harriet Lane Johnston Papers ("Lane Papers"), LOC.

49. New servants: Seale, pp. 337, 391.

49–50. arriet Lane: Virginia Clay-Clopton. *A Belle of the Fifties.* New York, Doubleday, Page & Company, 1905, pp. 114–15; "USS *Harriet Lane*," www.americancivil war.com; Sara Agnes Rice Pryor. *Reminiscences of Peace and War.* New York: Macmillan, 1905, p. 50; Grimsley, p. 48; Harriet Lane to an unspecified friend, February 26, 1861, Lane Papers.

50–53. Impressions of the Lincolns: Grimsley, p. 59; Burlingame, vol. 1, pp. 63, 173–75. 168, 201–2, vol. 2, p. 263; *Old Abe's Jokes Fresh from Abraham's Bosom.* New York: Hurst & Co., Publishers, 1864 ("*Jokes*"), p. 29; W. H. Herndon, "Mrs. Lincoln's Denial, and What She Says," January 19, 1874, Ruth Painter Randall Papers, Box 71; *Charles Francis Adams*, p. 97; Roper, p. 176.

50–53. Washington society: Stoddard, *Inside*, pp. 51, 144, 155; Stoddard-Burlingame, pp. 144 and 155; Benjamin Perley Poore. *Perley's Reminiscences of Sixty Years in the National Metropolis*, 2 vols. Philadelphia: Hubbard Brothers Publishers, 1886 ("Poore"), vol. 2, p. 115; Russell, vol. 1, pp. 53–54; Grimsley, pp. 50–51.

52–53. Mrs. Lincoln's receptions: Stoddard-Burlingame, pp. xv and 154; Colman, p. 289; *Tributes*, p. 235; Sala, p. 149; *Lincoln's Washington*, pp. 283–84; *Lincoln Observed*, p. 93; Mrs. Lincoln's Clothing, p. 61; Russell, vol. 1, pp. 53–54; *The Sydney Morning Herald*, June 7, 1864, www.trove.nla.gov.au; Jane Gray Swisshelm. *Half a Century.* Chicago: Jansen, McClurg & Company, 1880, pp. 236–37; Bancroft, vol. 2, p. 145; Helm, *passim*.

52. Dana: Diary of Richard Henry Dana, January 7, 1862, Dana Papers.

52–53. Flattery and snickers: Russell, vol. 1, pp. 53–54; Burlingame, vol. 2, pp. 271–73.

53. *Clash of cultures*: Stoddard, *Inside*, pp. 175–76.

53. Diplomatic reception: Grimsley, p. 50; Geoffrey Madan, *Madan's Notebooks.* Oxford. Oxford University Press, 1981, p. 34.

53. *Holland and Bremen*: J. W. Schulte Nordholt. "The Civil War Letters of the Dutch Ambassador," *Journal of the Illinois State Historical Society* 44 (Winter 1961): 341–73, p. 361.

53. *a list*: Helen Nicolay, *Biography*, p. 78.

53. *memorandum*: Nicolay Papers, Box 9, folder on "Etiquette & Official Intercourse 1861–1865."

53. *Mr. Lyon*: CW, vol. 5, p. 225.

53. *Unlike everyone else*: E.g., Donald, pp. 412–13.

54. *French . . . concerns*: White House Secretary, p. 236; Randall Papers, Box 19, folder marked "Nicolay, John G.," notes of Helen Nicolay.

54. *Bertinatti*: Russell, vol. 1, p. 37.

54. *cold shock*: Adam Goodheart. *1861*. New York: Alfred A. Knopf, 2011 (*"1861"*), p. 153.

54. *possible to survive*: Abraham Lincoln. *Recollected Words of Abraham Lincoln*. Edited by Don E. and Virginia Fehrenbacher. Stanford, CA: Stanford University Press, 1996 ("Recollected Words"), p. 344.

54–55. *Mrs. Lincoln's letter*: Turner, p. 82; Grimsley, p. 57.

55. *into the conservatory*: William H. Herndon and Jesse W. Weik. *Herndon's Lincoln*. Edited by Douglas J. Wilson and Rodney O. Davis. Urbana: University of Illinois Press, 2006 ("Herndon's Lincoln"), pp. 304–5.

55–56. The state dinner: Seale, pp. 350–51, 367–68; Grimsley, p. 50; Russell, vol. 1, pp. 41–44; Helen Nicolay, *Biography*, p. 79; Noah Brooks, "Personal Reminiscences of Lincoln," *Scribner's Monthly* 15 (March 1878): 673–81 ("Brooks, Reminiscences"), p. 680; *1861*, pp. 153–54.

56–57. *Melville*: Laurie Robertson-Lorant. *Melville: A Biography*. Amherst: University of Massachusetts Press, 1996, pp. 428–29.

57. Smith's letter: National Archives. Office of Secretary of Interior, Patents & Miscellaneous Division, Outgoing Letters Concerning Finance, p. 95.

57. Mrs. Lincoln's correspondence with Lamon: Turner, p. 83.

CHAPTER 5

59. Buchanan and Stone: Washington in March and April, pp. 3, 7–8; Bryan, vol. 2, pp. 461–68, 472; Marcus Benjamin. *Washington during War Time*. Washington: National Tribune Co., 1902, pp. 19–22.

59. *sentry challenged*: With Lincoln, p. 33; Grimsley, p. 52.

59–60. Helm: Washington in March and April, pp. 7–8; R. Gerald McMurtry. *Ben Hardin Helm, "Rebel" Brother in Law of Abraham Lincoln*. Chicago: The Civil War Roundtable, 1943 ("McMurtry"), *passim*; Helm, pp. 181–88.

60. *on fire*: James R. Gilmore. *Personal Recollections of Abraham Lincoln and the Civil War*. Boston: L. C. Page & Co., 1898 ("Gilmore"), p. 22.

60–61. Siege atmosphere: White House Secretary, p. 221; A Critical Moment, pp. 94, 105; Stoddard, *Inside*, pp. 11, 18, 22; Helm, p. 179; Henry Villard. *Memoirs of*

Henry Villard, Journalist and Financier, 1835–1900, 2 vols. Boston: Houghton, Mifflin and Company, 1904 ("Villard"), vol. 1, pp. 166–68; Schurz, p. 465.

60–62. Clay Battalion and Frontier Guard: Frontier Guard File, LOC; Burlingame, vol. 2, p. 140; *White House Secretary*, pp. 217, 337; H. Edward Richardson. *Cassius Marcellus Clay: Firebrand of Freedom*. Lexington: University Press of Kentucky, 1976, pp. 69–70; Edgar Langsdorf. "Jim Lane and the Frontier Guard," *Kansas Historical Quarterly* 9 (No. 1, February 1940): 13–25 ("Jim Lane"); "The Soldiers of Kansas: The Frontier Guard at the White House, Washington, 1861," *Kansas Historical Collections* 10 (1908): 419–21; Monaghan, p. 77; "The Clay Battalion," *Lincoln Lore* 1450 (December 1958), pp. 2–3 ("Clay Battalion"); *Tributes*, p. 44; Bryan, vol. 2, p. 474; Hay, *Inside*, pp. 1–2; *With Lincoln*, pp. 35, 39; *Seward at Washington*, vol. 1. p. 551; Washington in March and April, pp. 7–8; John G. Nicolay and John Hay. *Abraham Lincoln: A History*, 10 vols. New York: Century Company, 1917 ("N&H"), vol. 4, p. 107; *Washington Evening Star*, April 19, 1861.

62. Ladies with a warning: Hay, *Inside*, pp. 1–2.

62. *anxious citizens*: *New York Tribune*, April 25, 1861.

62–63. 6th Massachusetts: *With Lincoln*, p. 35.

63. *The Baltimore secessionists*: *With Lincoln*, p. 39; *Seward at Washington*, vol. 1, pp. 550–51; L. E. Chittenden. *Recollections of President Lincoln and His Administration*. New York: Harper Bros., 1891, p. 120.

63. *autograph book*: CW, vol. 4, p. 339.

63–64. Frontier Guard and Clay Battalion again: *White House Secretary*, p. 216; Lamon, p. 269; Edward L. Pierce, ed., *Memoir and Letters of Charles Sumner*, 4 vols. Boston: Roberts Brothers, 1893 ("Pierce"), vol. 4, p. 128; Adam Gurowski. *Diary of Adam Gurowski*, 3 vols. Boston: Lee and Shephard, 1862 ("*Gurowski Diary*"), vol. 1, p. 24; Hay, *Inside*, pp. 3, 6, 8, 11, 13, 276 n. 39; Clifford Arrick's diary, Frontier Guard File, LOC; *Washington Evening Star*, April 24, 1861; CW, vol. 4, p. 342; Helen Nicolay, *Biography*, p. 95; *New York Times*, May 1, 1861; N&H, vol. 4, p. 153; *Third Secretary*, pp. 83, 226; *New York Times*, May 1, 1861; Grimsley, p. 52; Villard, pp. 170, 175; Jim Lane, p. 20; *Washington Evening Star*, April 27, 1861; CW vol. 4, pp. 345, 352–53; Clay Battalion, p. 3; Clay Battalion, p. 3; Soft-bound ledger book, Frontier Guard file, LOC.

64–65. Seventh New York: *Frank Leslie's Illustrated Newspaper*, April 30, 1861, p. 381; *Third Secretary*, p. 83; *New York Times*, May 1, 1861; Grimsley, p. 52; *White House Secretary*, p. 226; Villard, p. 170.

65. *quickly followed*: Villard, p. 175.

65. *Providence Marine Corps*: CW, vol. 4, p. 352; *Washington Evening Star*, May 2, 1861.

65. *Splendid bands*: Stoddard, *Inside*, p. 18.

65–66. Sentries: Grimsley, pp. 51, 58; Stoddard, *Inside*, p. 145; *White House Secretary*, p. 292; McBride, *Body Guard*, pp. 13–14; McBride, *Recollections*, pp. 1, 24; Adams, p. 695.

66. Helm: McMurtry, pp. 19–23.

CHAPTER 6

67. *dreamlike and unreal . . . martial music*: *True Story*, p. 246.

67. *charming weather . . . blankets*: Elizabeth Lindsay Lomax, *Leaves from an Old Washington Diary*. New York: E. P. Dutton, 1943, p. 151; Hay, *Inside*, p. 14.

67. *lancers*: *Dispatches*, p. 68.

67. *Mrs. Grimsley wrote*: *Concerning Mr. Lincoln*: pp. 76–77.

67. *telescope*: Hay, *Inside*, p. 13; W. W. Orme to Davis, May 11, 1861, Davis Papers, Box 2.

67. *The President has suspended*: *New York Times*, May 1, 1861.

67–68. Rush for commissions: *White House Secretary*, p. 236; Stoddard, *Inside*, pp. 26, 79; N&H, vol. 5, p. 141; *Lincoln's Washington*, p. 64; Helen Nicolay, *Biography*, pp. 27, 113; Stoddard-Burlingame, p. 178.

68. *Potawatomie Indian chiefs*: Hay, *Inside*, p. 14.

69. Lincoln's dress: Personal Appearance, pp. 936–37; Stoddard-Burlingame, p. 149; Wilson, p. 472; Elizabeth Peabody. "Elizabeth Peabody Visits Lincoln, February 1865." Edited by Arlin Turner. *New England Quarterly* 48 (March 1975): 119–24 ("Peabody"), p. 118; 47 *The Independent*, "Lincoln Number," New York, April 4, 1895, p. 1, letter from George William Curtis; *New York Tribune*, January 23, 1887; C. Van Santvoord. "A Reception by President Lincoln," *Century Magazine* 25 (February 1883): 612–14 ("Van Santvoord"), p. 612; Bayne, p. 33; Lincoln as I Knew Him, p. 111; Wilson, p. 465; Hay, *Inside*, p. 320 n. 223; L. C. Baker. *History of the United States Secret Service*. Philadelphia: L. C. Baker, 1867, p. 242; George Townsend, p. 60.

69–70. Lincoln's posture and demeanor: *E.g.*, Moncure D. Conway. *Autobiography of Moncure Conway*. 2 vols. Boston: Houghton, Mifflin and Company, 1904 ("Conway"), vol. 1, p. 381; "An October Visitor at the White House, 1864," *Lincoln Lore* 809 (October 9, 1944), p. 1; Russell, vol. 1, pp. 147–48; Charles G. Halpine. *The Life and Adventures of Private Miles O'Reilly*. New York: Carleton, 1864 ("Halpine"), p. 174; Carpenter, pp. 185, 235, 279; Gilmore, pp. 212, 218, 240; Gobright, p. 335; Wilson, pp. 472, 559–60; Stoddard, *Inside*, 220; *L's WH Secretary*, 317–19; J. M. Winchell. "Three Interviews with President Lincoln," *Galaxy* 16 (July 1873): 33–41 ("Three Interviews"), pp. 36, 38, 40; John G. Nicolay, *An Oral History of Abraham Lincoln: John G. Nicolay's Interviews and Essays*. Edited by Michael Burlingame. Carbondale: Southern Illinois University Press, 1996 ("*Oral History*"), p. 81; Tuckerman, p. 413; *Oral History*, p. 52; *Lincoln at Work*, p. 120.

70–71. Artlessly dignified humility: Brooks, Reminiscences, p. 675; Lamon, p. 98; Bayne, pp. 90–91; *Third Secretary*, p. 74; Stoddard-Burlingame, p. 150. Silas W. Burt. "Lincoln on His Own Story-Telling," *Century Magazine* 73 (February 1907): 499–502 ("Burt"), p. 502; Brooks, Recollections, p. 222; Life in the White House, p. 36; George Templeton Strong. *The Diary of George Templeton Strong*, 3 vols. New York: The Macmillan Company, 1952 ("Strong"), vol. 3, pp. 188, 204; Borrett, pp. 13–14.

71. The grounds: *Morrison's Stranger's Guide to the City of Washington.* Washington: W. M. Morrison & Co., 1855 (*"Morrison's"*); Seale, pp. 217, 270–71, 295, 324–25, 391; Stoddard, *Inside,* p. 153; Lincoln as I Knew Him, p. 112; Pendel, p. 31; Robert V. Bruce. *Lincoln and the Tools of War.* Indianapolis: Bobbs-Merrill Co., 1956 ("Bruce"), p. 102; Bryan, vol. 2, p. 495.

71–72. Concerts: Nicolay to Bates, June 2, 1861, Nicolay Papers; Viator, pp. 182–83; David R. Barbee. "Lincoln and the Music of the Civil War," *Lincoln Herald* 63 (Summer 1961): 67–76 and (Fall 1961): 121–27 ("Music of the Civil War"); p. 75 n. 11; Musical Mr. Lincoln, pp. 445–47; Russell, vol. 1, pp. 389–90; *Lincoln at Work,* p. 61; Monaghan, p. 94; Thayer, vol. 1, p. 103; *New York Tribune,* May 12, 1861, p. 1.

72. *12th New York:* Horatio Nelson Taft. *Washington During the Civil War: The Diary of Horatio Nelson Taft, 1861–1865, 3 vols.* Edited by John R. Sellers. www.memory.loc.gov/ammem/tafthtml/tafthome.html ("Taft Diary"), May 13, 1861; Stoddard, *Inside,* pp. 18–19.

72–73. Insecurity: *Dear Mr. Lincoln,* p. 336; Stoddard, *Inside,* p. 173; N&H, vol. 5, p. 141; Lincoln as I Knew Him, p. 110; Crook, *Memories,* pp. 37–38; Stoddard-Burlingame, p. 171; McBride, *Body Guard,* pp. 13–15; McBride, *Recollections,* 33–42; William H. Crook. *Through Five Administrations: Reminiscences of Colonel William H. Crook.* Edited by Margareta Spaulding Gerry. New York: Harper & Brothers, 1910 (*"Five Administrations"*), p. 9; Pendel, p. 24.

CHAPTER 7

75. The secretaries: Seale, p. 380; *White House Secretary,* pp. 6, 331, 234, 274; Stoddard, *Inside,* pp. 150, 156; "The Executive Mansion Secretariat," *Lincoln Lore* 1061 (August 8, 1949); Stoddard, *Inside,* pp. 10, 157; *Lincoln at Work,* pp. 65–66; *True Story,* p. 243.

75–76. Nicolay's office: Stoddard, *Inside,* pp. 14, 49, 104–5, 226; *Lincoln Observed,* pp. 83–84; *With Lincoln,* pp. 30, 115, 168; Ames, p. 75; Seale, pp. 183–84; Browning Diary, vol. 1, p. 479; CW, vol. 6, p. 308; letters from Horace Greeley to Nicolay, Nicolay Papers, Box 2.

76. The Northeast Room: Stoddard, *Inside,* pp. 14, 38, 45, 50, 100, 165–66, 184, 226; *Daily Alta;* Hay, *Inside,* p. 95; *White House Secretary,* p. 235; *Lincoln at Work,* p. 66; Stoddard-Burlingame, p. 145.

76. Nicolay and Hay's bedroom: *With Lincoln,* p. 30.

76–77. Stoddard's residences: *White House Secretary,* pp. 233, 286, and 317.

77. Meals: Hay, *Inside,* pp. 101, 106, 322 n. 229, 335 n. 1; Nicolay Papers, Box

17, scrapbook of invitations; Stoddard, *Inside*, p. 57; *At Lincoln's Side*, p. 12; Sala, vol. 1, pp. 71–72; Russell, p. 33; Hay Letters, vol. 1, p. 6.

77. Nicolay: Stoddard, *Inside*, p. 104; *True Story*, p. 243; Stoddard-Burlingame, pp. 151, 157; *With Lincoln*, pp. xvii, 115–16, 125, 131, 142, 146, 154–57, 163–65; Gilmore, p. 218; Helen Nicolay, *Traits*, pp. 182–83; Helen Nicolay, *Biography*, p. 85.

77–78. Nicolay and Hay: James T. DuBois and Gertruse S. Mathews. *Galusha A. Grew: Father of the Homestead Law.* Boston: Houghton Mifflin, 1917, p. 266; Stoddard, *Inside*, p. 165; Hay, *Inside*, pp. 1, 2, 4; Helen Nicolay, *Biography*, p. 88; Welles, vol. 1, p. 71; *At Lincoln's Side*, pp. 24, 222 n. 131; Nicolay to Hay, August 9 and September 8, 1862, Nicolay Papers, Box 2.

78. *Didn't talk about himself*: John Hay and Tyler Dennett, eds. *Lincoln and the Civil War in the Diaries and Letters of John Hay.* New York: Dodd, Mead & Company, 1939, p. 225.

78. Nicolay and Hay's missions: John G. Nicolay, "Hole-in-the-Day," *Harper's New Monthly Magazine* 26 (January 1863): 186–91; N&H, vol. 9, pp. 2–13, 189; Hay, *Inside*, p. 204; *At Lincoln's Side*, p. 110.

78–79. Hay's role: Hay, *Inside*, p. 98 and *passim*; Helen Nicolay, *Biography*, p. 85; *At Lincoln's Side*, pp. xvii, 85.

79–80. Stoddard's role: Stoddard, *Inside*, pp. 14, 35, 173; *Lincoln at Work*, pp. 66, 122; *White House Secretary*, pp. 128, 220, 235–36, 342–43, 286–88, 303, 317; *The Independent* 47 New York (April 4, 1895), p. 5; Helen Nicolay, *Biography*, p. 87; Stoddard-Burlingame, pp. xv–xvi; Grimsley, p. 57.

80. Stoddard and Hay: *Power of the Press*, p. 486; *White House Secretary*, p. 235; Stoddard-Burlingame, p. 143.

80. *speculating*: *Id.*, pp. xvi–xviii; *White House Secretary*, pp. 240–41, 274, 312.

80. Stoddard on Nicolay: *Id.*, p. 236; Stoddard-Burlingame, pp. xii, 151.

81. *typically started . . . into the night*: Hay, *Inside*, p. 194; *Browning Diary*, vol. 1, p. 475; Stoddard-Burlingame, p. 168.

81. *caravan . . . explanations*: *Id.*, pp. 158, 185.

81. access to Lincoln: *White House Secretary*, p. 264; Rice, p. 316; *Tributes*, p. 103.

81. *hours . . . to the press*: *The Independent* 47 New York, April 4, 1895, p. 5; Gobright, p. 338.

81–82. Unbalanced callers: Stoddard, *Inside*, pp. 78–79; *With Lincoln*, pp. 109–10, 231–32 n. 59.

82. Lincoln's messages: Hay, *Inside*, p. 119; *White House Secretary*, pp. 235, 240, 287; Stoddard, *Inside*, p. 139; Helen Nicolay, *Biography*, p. 88.

82. Nicolay and Hay as messengers: *Id.*, p. 238; Gideon Welles. *Lincoln and Seward.* New York: Sheldon & Company, 1874, p. 69.

82. Patronage: Nicolay papers, Nicolay to Hatch, March 31, 1861.

82–83. *sensitive issues*: Nicolay memorandum, "A Private Paper. Conversation with the President, October 2nd 1861," Nicolay Papers; Hay, *Inside*, pp. 30–31, 68, 191, 211, 208, 238.

83. Nicolay and Hay's miscellaneous duties: *With Lincoln*, pp. 48–49, 55, 61, 86, 115–16, 131, 138, 142–43, 154–57, 162, 170–71, 224 n. 183, 254 n. 237; CW, vol. 7, pp. 376–78, 442; *At Lincoln's Side*, pp. 31–45, 226 n. 15, 295–96 n. 1; Helen Nicolay, *Biography*, p. 142; Hay, *Inside*, pp. 115–16, 252–54; Benjamin B. French to Henry Flagg French, March 6, 1861, Papers of Benjamin B. French ("French Papers"), LOC; *Power of the Press*, p. 486.

83. Speeches: Stoddard-Burlingame, pp. 171–72; Wayne C. Temple. "Charles Henry Philbrick: Private Secretary to President Lincoln," *Lincoln Herald* 99 (Spring 1997): 6–11 ("Philbrick"), p. 10; Brooks, Recollections, p. 230; *They Knew Lincoln*, 111–12; Stoddard, *Inside*, pp. 227–28; *White House Secretary*, pp. 320–21.

83–84. The secretaries critiqued: Helen Nicolay, *Biography*, p. 84; *Lincoln Observed*, pp. 83–84; Wayne C. Temple and Justin G. Turner. "Lincoln's 'Castine': Noah Brooks," *Lincoln Herald* 72 (Fall 1970): 113–89; and *Lincoln Herald* 73 (Fall 1971): 163–80 ("Lincoln's Castine"), p. 169; "Lincoln and Hamlin," *Philadelphia Times*, July 9, 1891; *At Lincoln's Side*, pp. xxiv, 210 n. 85; Mary T. Higginson, ed. *Letters and Journals of Thomas Wentworth Higginson 1846–1906*. Boston: Houghton Mifflin Company, 1921 ("Higginson"), p. 202.

84. Lincoln's trust in his secretaries: N&H, vol. 9, pp. 375–76; Hay, *Inside*, *passim*.

84. *a workshop*: *Tributes*, pp. 44–45.

84. *her diary*: Frances Seward Diary ("Seward Diary"), August 31, 1861, available online in "Lincoln and His Circle," University of Rochester Rare Books & Special Collections.

84. *comicality*: *Lincoln at Work*, p. 90.

84–86. Workload: Nicolay to Bates, March 29, 1861, January 5, 1862, Nicolay Papers; *At Lincoln's Side*, pp. 24, 222 n. 13; *With Lincoln*, p. 127; *Tributes*, p. 45; Homer Bates. *Lincoln in the Telegraph Office*. New York: Century Co., 1907 ("Bates"), pp. 139–40, 144; Charles A. Dana. *Recollections of the Civil War*. New York: D. Appleton and Company, 1898 ("Dana"), p. 173; Wilson, pp. 131–32; *Recollected Words*, p. 192; Helen Nicolay. *Our Capital on the Potomac*. New York: The Century Co., 1924 ("Helen Nicolay, *Capital*") p. 380; Francis Fisher Browne. *The Every-Day Life of Abraham Lincoln*. Chicago: Browne & Howell Company, 1886 ("Browne"), 354; Bayne, pp. 164–65, 216; *Lincoln at Work*, p. 64; Carpenter, pp. 127–28.

85. *smallpox hospital*: *At Lincoln's Side*, p. 69.

86. Sundays: Stoddard-Burlingame, pp. 176–77; *With Lincoln*, p. 30; Stoddard, *Inside*, pp. 164 and 219; *White House Secretary*, p. 227; *They Knew Lincoln*, p. 78; Rice, p. 60; *Lincoln's Washington*, p. 58.

86–87. Hay's story: Stoddard, *Inside*, pp. 165–66; *Lincoln at Work*, pp. 66–69 (a slightly different telling).

87. Mornings: *Lincoln Observed*, p. 84; Lincoln as I Knew Him, p. 111; Randall

Papers, Box 12, folder marked "Bellows, Henry W.," Bellows to his wife, April 23, 1863 ("Bellows"); Grimsley, p. 55; *At Lincoln's Side*, p. 109.

87. Lunch: Life in the White House, p. 34

87–88. Afternoons: Bayne, p. 33; Grimsley, p. 55; Lincoln as I Knew Him, p. 111; Life in the White House, p. 34; *True Story*, p. 403.

88. Dinner: *At Lincoln's Side*, p. 110; *Inside*, Stoddard 58–59.

88. When Mrs. Lincoln was away: Burlingame, vol. 2, p. 254; Carpenter, p. 272.

88. Lincoln's tastes: *They Knew Lincoln*, pp. 118–19, 125; Crook, *Memories*, p. 19; Seale, p. 409; *Herndon's Lincoln*, p. 305; *Herndon's Informants*, p. 445; *Noah Brooks, Washington D.C. in Lincoln's Time*. Edited by Herbert Mitgang. Chicago: Quadrangle Books, 1971 ("*Washington D.C.*"), p. 246.

88–89. Evenings and nights: *At Lincoln's Side*, p. 110; Life in the White House, pp. 35–36; Musical Mr. Lincoln, pp. 435–36; Burlingame, vol. 2, p. 249; Lamon, pp. 147–49; *At Lincoln's Side*, p. 110; "Guarding Mr. Lincoln." *The Ohio Soldier* (April 28, 1888) ("Guarding"); *At Lincoln's Side*, p. 109; Lincoln as I Knew Him, p. 111; Edward D. Neil, "Reminiscences of the Last Year of President Lincoln's Life" in *Glimpses of the Nation's Struggle* (St. Paul, MN: St. Paul Book and Stationary Company, 1887): 29–53 ("*Glimpses*"), p. 33; Hay, *Inside*, pp. 345–46 n. 140.

CHAPTER 8

91. Gold spoons: Seale, p. 221.

91. *almost every first lady*: Id., *passim*.

91. *$22,000 worth*: Id., pp. 341–42.

91. *continued work*: Seale, p. 385.

91–92. *near the lady*: Turner, p. 86.

92. Mrs. Lincoln shopping: Wayne C. Temple, "Mary Todd Lincoln's ("Travels")," *Journal of the Illinois State Historical Society* 52 (Spring 1959): 180–94, p. 182; Turner, p. 87; Harry Pratt and Ernest East. "Mrs. Lincoln Refurbishes the White House," *Lincoln Herald* 47 (February 1945): 13–22, p. 17; Grimsley, p. 59; Travels, p. 183; Harry Pratt and Ernest East. "Mrs. Lincoln Refurbishes the White House," *Lincoln Herald* 47 (February 1945): 13–22; Seale, pp. 382–86; Baker, pp. 187–89; Gerald R. McMurtry, "Lincoln White House Glass and China," *Lincoln Herald* 49 (June 1947): 33–34, 43; p. 34; "What Mrs. Lincoln Bought for the White House," *Lincoln Lore* 1492 (June 1962) ("What Mrs. Lincoln Bought"), p. 4; Expenditures, Randall Papers; CW, vol. 4, p. 348; Carryl invoice, July 31, 1861, RG 217.

92–93. *newspapers all over the country*: Seale, pp. 383–84; *Chicago Tribune*, August 31, 1861.

92–93. The renovations: *Historic Guide*, pp. 71–72; Garrett, p. 149; *Daily Alta*; Seale, pp. 86, 383–86; Lincoln as I Knew Him, p. 107; invoices and receipts, RG 217, 1861–62; RG 217, Mrs. Lincoln's annotation, October 12, 1861.

93. Art: *Lincoln Observed*, p. 81; Stoddard-Burlingame, p. 155; *Dear Mr. Lincoln*, pp. 230–31.

93–94. *first diplomatic dinner*: *Washington Evening Star*, June 7, 1861; Grimsley, pp. 62–63.

94. Nicolay and Hay's offices: *Alta California*.

94–96. Lincoln's Office: *Id.*; *Bancroft*, p. 144; *Historic Guide*, pp. 73, 128; Stoddard, *Inside*, pp. 24–26, 50, 167–68; George Townsend, pp. 56–58; Seale, pp. 183, 339, 385; Turner, p. 228; Arnold, *Life*, p. 452; Robert Gould Shaw. *Blue-Eyed Child of Fortune: The Civil War Letters of Colonel Robert Gould Shaw*. Edited by Russell Duncan. Athens: University of Georgia Press, 1992, pp. 90–91; E. V. Smalley, "The White House," *The Century Magazine* 77 (April 1884): 803–15; *Glimpses*, p. 35; Three Interviews, p. 36; Nicolay Papers, Box 8, folder marked "A Lincoln during the Administration—Loaves and Fishes (folder marked "Not Used in 'Personal Traits' "), Typescript, Paul Selby, p. 229; Halpine, p. 169; *True Story*, p. 245; Browne, p. 354; Carpenter, pp. 100, 215–16; Browning Diary, vol. 1, p. 562; Diary of John A. Dahlgren, January 15, 1863, Nicolay Papers, Box 13; Hay, *Inside*, p. 15; *The Independent*, New York, April 4, 1895, p. 1; *Lincoln at Work*, p. 60; Sala, vol. 2, p. 152; *Seward at Washington*, vol. 1, p. 520, vol. 2, p. 265; *Washington D.C.*, pp. 110, 264–65; Gilmore, p. 78; Arnold, *Sketch*, p. 66; *Oral History*, p. 81; Wilson, p. 559; *Tributes*, p. 257; George Townsend, pp. 56–58; Arnold, *Life*, p. 452; Helen Nicolay, "Lincoln's Cabinet," *Abraham Lincoln Quarterly* 5 (March 1949): 255–92 ("Lincoln's Cabinet"), p. 279; " 'Abe' Lincoln's Comrade," *Hartford Herald*, November 12, 1890. Illustrations at Seale, vol. 1, illustration 42; N&H, vol. 8, p. 225; and W. O. Stoddard, *Abraham Lincoln: The Man and the War-President*. New York: Fords, Howard & Hulbert, p. 342.

96–97. The Cabinet: *Lincoln Observed*, p. 86; *True Story*, p. 265; Stoddard, *Inside*, pp. 24, 148; Life in the White House, p. 34; Stoddard-Burlingame, pp. 157, 182; N&H, vol. 6, p. 125; CW, vol. 4, p. 416, vol. 5, p. 144; Hay, *Inside*, p. 36; Welles, vol. 1, p. 136; Helen Nicolay, *Biography*, p. 161; Carpenter, p. 55; Helen Nicolay, *Traits*, p. 243; *Witness*, p. 395; Phineas Taylor Barnum. *Struggles and Triumphs*, Hartford: J. B. Burr & Company, 1869, pp. 22, 572–73.

97. Overspending and coverup: October 16, 1861, French to Smith, National Archives, Office of Secretary of Interior, Patents and Miscellaneous Division, Box 58; Appropriations; *At Lincoln's Side*, pp. 186, 193, 197, 217 n. 65; Turner, p. 84; Ames, p. 239; Stoddard, *Inside*, p. 63; Seale, pp. 392–93; Expenditures, Randall Papers; *With Lincoln*, p. 61; Burlingame, vol. 2, p. 700; Manton Marble to David Goodman Croly, October 7, 1862, Manton Marble Papers, LOC ("Marble Papers"), bound correspondence. For Burlingame's overwhelming evidence of Mrs. Lincoln's corruption see *At Lincoln's Side*, pp. 185–203.

97–98. Wood's appointment: Seale, p. 387; Stephen Berry. *House of Abraham: Lincoln and the Todds, a Family Divided by War*. Boston: Mariner Books, 2009, p.

102; *At Lincoln's Side*, pp. 191, 273 nn. 31–37; Burlingame, vol. 2, p. 267; National Archives, Commissioner of Pub. Bldgs. Outgoing Letters, vol. 12, p. 476.

98. Mrs. Lincoln's Loyalties: Keckley, p. 136; *They Knew Lincoln*, pp. 208, 213, 215–16; Helm, pp. 212–13; McMurtry, p. 33; Turner, p. 155.

98. Skirmishes: *With Lincoln*, p. 44; Strong, vol. 3, p. 153; *Dispatches*, p. 263 n. 52; A. M. Waterman, "Washington at the Time of the First Bull Run," in *Military Essays and Recollections*, vol. 2. Chicago: A. C. McClurg and Company, 1894, p. 28.

98–99. *political business*: Stoddard-Burlingame, p. 154.

99. Mrs. Lincoln's salon: Turner, pp. 96–106; Baker, p. 231; Seale, p. 159.

99–100. Wikoff: Villard, p. 157; Seale, pp. 396–97; *At Lincoln's Side*, pp. 198–200; Matthew Hale Smith. *Sunshine and Shadow in New York*. Hartford: J. Burr and Company, 1869 ("Smith"), pp. 284–89; *Russell's Civil War*, p. 182; *At Lincoln's Side*, pp. 198–99; Poore, vol. 2, pp. 52, 143; Burlingame, vol. 2, p. 274; Burlingame, vol. 2, p. 273–75.

100. Sickles: Baker, p. 232 and n. 55; Thomas Keneally. *American Scoundrel*. New York: Anchor Books, 2002, pp. 125–30; Burlingame, vol. 2, p. 275.

100. Newell, Halsted, and Willis: Turner, pp. 98, 105; Baker, p. 232, n. 55.

100. Sumner: Lincoln as I Knew Him, p. 45; Turner, p. 455; *With Lincoln*, p. 152; *Oral History*, p. 84; Monaghan, p. 39.

100–102. Mrs. Lincoln: Turner, pp. 106, 108, *passim*; Seale, p. 337; *Herndon's Informants*, p. 461; Dana, p. 3; Keckley, pp. 124–25; *Tributes*, p. 110; *At Lincoln's Side*, pp. xxv, 67; Burlingame, vol. 1, p. 211, vol. 2, p. 263; Villard, vol. 1, p. 175; Ames, p. 237; Lamon, p. 21; Carpenter, p. 41; Stoddard, *Inside*, p. 173.

102. Supervision of servants: *Id.*, p. 62; CW, vol. 5, p. 143; W. A. Evans, *Mrs. Abraham Lincoln: A Study of Her Personality and Her Influence on Lincoln*. New York: A. A. Knopf, 1932, pp. 182–83; *White House Secretary*, p. 242; Crook, *Memories*, pp. 16–17; *They Knew Lincoln*, pp. 78, 119; *Herndon's Informants*, p. 729; Brooks, Recollections, p. 225.

102–103. Honesty, loyalty, and dismissal of servants: *They Knew Lincoln*, pp. 77–78, 100, 133, 244; Stoddard, *Inside*, p. 174; Seale, pp. 395–96; *Lincoln Observed*, pp. 80–81; Nicolay to Bates, September 29, 1864, Nicolay Papers.

103. Mrs. Wells and Mrs. Brooks: *They Knew Lincoln*, pp. 77–78.

103. The Browns: *They Knew Lincoln*, pp. 121–26.

103–104. Irish servants: *Lincoln Observed*, p. 49; Lincoln as I Knew Him, p. 114; *Glimpses*, p. 32; Pendel, p. 32; Frederick Hatch. "Lincoln's Missing Guard," *Lincoln Herald* 106 (Fall 2005): 106–17 ("Missing Guard"), p. 109; Seale, p. 378; Crook, *Memories*, p. 29.

CHAPTER 9

105. Washington in summer: Trollope, p. 313; *With Lincoln*, p. 30; Russell, vol. 1, p. 483; Nicolay to Therena, July 20, 1861, Nicolay Papers; Stoddard, *Inside*, pp. 149, 189; Strong, vol. 3, p. 164; Seale, p. 374; *Lincoln at Work*, p. 74.

105–107. Smells and disease: *Lincoln's Washington*, pp. 55, 187; Taft Diary, June 28, 1864; Bryan, vol. 2, p. 509; Viator, pp. 114–15; Grimsley, pp. 43, 51, 54, 57–58; Stoddard, *Inside*, pp. 41, 190–91, 217–18, 226; Turner, p. 81; Stoddard-Burlington, p. 145; Trollope, p. 314; *Lincoln's Secretary*, p. 225; Seale, p. 278; *True Story*, p. 345; *Lincoln's Washington*, p. 277; Stoddard, *Inside*, p. 189; Helen Nicolay, *Biography*, p. 115; *Dispatches*, p. xxiii; *White House Secretary*, pp. 235, 240.

107. Balloon: Bruce, pp. 85–86.

107. Flag raising: *Glimpses*, p. 30; *Washington Evening Star*, June 28 and July 1, 1861; *New York Tribune*, June 30, 1861; Washington *National Intelligencer*, July 1, 1861; Music of the Civil War, pp. 72, 75 n. 18. *Witness*, p. 362.

107. Olmsted: Roper, p. 167.

107. Evening of music: Music of the Civil War, pp. 121–22; *New York Herald*, July 6 and 8, 1861; *New York Times*, July 6, 1861, *Home Journal*, July 20, 1861; *New York Tribune*, July 8, 1861; *Witness*, p. 363.

108. Parade: Russell, vol. 1, pp. 376–83 and 583; Taft Diary, July 4, 1861; Montgomery Meigs diary ("Meigs Diary"), July 4, 1861, Nicolay Papers, Box 13; *With Lincoln*, p. 47; *New York Tribune*, July 6, 1861; *New York Times*, July 6, 1861; Seale, p. 373; E. D. Townsend, ed. *Anecdotes of the Civil War in the United States*. New York: D. Appleton and Co., 1884 ("E. D. Townsend"), p. 17; Villard, pp. 171, 174.

108–109. Mrs. Lincoln's letter: Turner, p. 94.

109. *council of war . . . Manassas*: Nicolay Papers, Box 16, folder marked "The White House from James Madison to Abraham Lincoln," p. 57; E. D. Townsend, p. 57.

109. *Howard*: Oliver O. Howard, "Lincoln's Loving Kindness," *The Congregationalist and Christian World*, The Pilgrim Press, Boston, Chicago, January 30, 1913, p. 168; Oliver O. Howard, "Personal Recollections of Abraham Lincoln," *Century Magazine* 75 (1908): 873–77.

109. Spotting Lincoln: Russell, vol. 2, p. 194; *Witness*, p. 365.

109–110. Bull Run: *With Lincoln*, p. 52; Grimsley, pp. 65–66; *Dispatches*, p. 34; N&H, vol. 4, pp. 352–57; *Herndon's Lincoln*, p. 325; Burlingame, vol. 2, p. 183; Russell, vol. 1, pp. 467–71; Seward, *Reminiscences*, p. 181; French Papers, French to his brother, July 22, 1861.

110. Caryl's bill: RG 217, Caryl invoice, July 31, 1861.

110. *bouquet . . . scandal*: At Lincoln's Side, p. 186.

110–111. The levee: Russell, vol. 1, p. 480.

111. Whitney: *Herndon's Informants*, pp. 404–5.

111. *Prince and suite*: Turner, p. 96.

111. *hotter and more detestable*: Strong, vol. 3, p. 172.

111–112. Pennsylvania Avenue: *Lincoln's Washington*, p. 116; Russell, vol. 1, p. 487; Philip Van Doren Stern. *An End to Valor*. Boston: Houghton Mifflin Company, 1958, p. 2.

112–114. Napoleon at the White House: Pisani, pp. 94–113; Daniel B. Carroll. "Abraham Lincoln and the Minister of France," *Lincoln Herald* 70 (Fall 1968): 142–

53, pp. 146–47; *Witness*, p. 370; *Seward at Washington*, vol. 1, p. 607; Seward, *Reminiscences*, pp. 182–83; Browning Diary, vol. 1, p. 492; Music of the Civil War, pp. 124–26; Russell, 482–85; *Russell's Civil War*, p. 100; *McClellan's Own Story*. New York: C. L. Webster & Company, 1862, p. 84; Mrs. Lincoln's Clothing, p. 60; Pratt, p. 73; Grimsley, pp. 69–70; *With Lincoln*, p. 54.

   113. Lincoln at his window: *At Lincoln's Side*, 215 n. 50.

   114. Costs: *At Lincoln's Side*, pp. 193–94.

   114. Willie: Allan Clark. "Abraham Lincoln in the National Capital," *Records of Columbia Historical Society* 27 (1925): 1–175 ("Clark"), p. 25.

   114. *three miles*: Taft Diary, August 10, 1861.

CHAPTER 10

   115. heat: *Russell's Civil War*, p. 101.

   115. *Voila*: Nicolay to Hay, August 11, 1861, Nicolay Papers.

   115. *Hay took a break*: *Washington Star*, August 14, 1861.

   115. *damp oven*: *At Lincoln's Side*, p. 11.

   115–116. Lincoln's relaxations: *At Lincoln's Side*, p. 48; CW, vol. 7, p. 506; Dicey, pp. 221–22.

   116. Wood and Watt: Burlingame, vol. 2, pp. 267–68; Turner, pp. 102–4.

   116. French and Mrs. Lincoln: *Witness*, p. 375; French to Mrs. Lincoln, September 28, 1861, National Archives, Commissioner of Pub. Bldgs. Outgoing Letters, vol. 14, p. 18; *Historic Guide*, p. 128.

   116–117. Watt's commission: CW, vol. 5, p. 25; Burlingame, vol. 2, p. 192; Turner, p. 103.

   117. *quite unnoticed*: Russell, vol. 1, p. 536.

   117. Wood's accusations: *Witness*, pp. 375–76; CW vol. 5, p. 25; *At Lincoln's Side*, p. 193; Turner, pp. 103–4.

   117. Stackpole: Turner, pp. 129, 133, 167; *At Lincoln's Side*, p. 190.

   117. *idler . . . insanity*: William P. Wood in the *Sunday Gazette*, D.C., January 16, 1867; Burlingame, vol. 1, pp. 179–81.

   117–118. *bedrooms . . . astonished*: Turner, p. 106.

   118. Sofa and chairs: RG 217, document 142–060.

   118. *It begins to feel*: *With Lincoln*, p. 58.

   118. *rebel flag*: *Witness*, p. 376.

   118. Olmstead: Fredrick Law Olmsted, edited by Charles Capen McLaughlin, *The Papers of Frederick Law Olmsted*, 9 vols. Baltimore: The Johns Hopkins University Press, 1986 ("Olmsted"), vol. 4, pp. 207–8, 213.

   118. *leaned forward . . . Your folks*: Carpenter, p. 75.

   118–119. *service stairs*: Pendel, p. 179; Seale, pp. 374, 377.

   119. *uniformed aides*: Lincoln's Cabinet, p. 275.

119. *survivors*: *Washington, D.C.*, pp. 77–78.

119. *French*: French to his brother, October 13, 1861, French Papers; excerpt from French's address at the dedication of a statue of Lincoln, 1868, Randall Papers.

119. *East Room . . . untaxed*: *Dispatches*, p. 38; Seale, p. 385; CW, vol. 4, p. 557.

119. *insufficient funds*: October 16, 1861, French to Smith, National Archives, Office of Secretary of Interior, Patents and Miscellaneous Division, Box 58.

119–122. Upperman scandal: *At Lincoln's Side*, pp. 194–95, 275 n. 47; *Witness*, p. 385; Turner, pp. 111–12; Travels, p. 186; *Russell's Civil War*, p. 162; Russell, vol. 1, p. 567; Bancroft, pp. 144–45; *At Lincoln's Side*, p. 14.

122. *new carpets*: *Dispatches*, p. 45.

122. *fireworks*: *Russell's Civil War*, p. 171; Hay, *Inside*, p. 31.

122. *cold day . . . directly*: Russell, vol. 1, p. 573; *Russell's Civil War*, p. 77; CW, vol. 5, p. 25; Burlingame, vol. 2, p. 276; *At Lincoln's Side*, pp. 195–96.

122. Gayety: Life in the White House, p. 34; *With Lincoln*, p. 170; Nicolay to Bates, February 15, 1863, February 17, 1865, Nicolay Papers; scrapbook of invitations, Nicolay Papers, Box 17.

123. White House entertainment: Pendel, 39; Stoddard, *Inside*, pp. 13, 59, 173; Stoddard-Burlingame, p. 145; Hay, *Inside*, p. 196; *The National Republican*, January 19, 1863; Kenneth A. Bernard. *Lincoln and the Music of the Civil War*. Caldwell, ID: Caxton Printers, 1966 ("Bernard"), pp. 56–58, 121–22; CW, vol. 7, p. 34; *Washington Evening Star*, February 20, 1864; *National Republican*, February 20, 1864; Musical Mr. Lincoln, *passim*; Music of the Civil War, *passim*; Peabody, p. 123; *Dispatches*, p. 49.

123–124. Hermann: *Russell's Civil War*, pp. 182–85; *With Lincoln*, 63; Samuel Heintzelman's Journal, November 25, 1861, Heintzelman Papers, LOC; *Witness*, p. 381; Benjamin P. Thomas. *Abraham Lincoln: A Biography*. New York: Alfred A. Knopf, 1952, pp. 477–78; *Recollected Words*, p. 312.

124. *Thanksgiving*: Turner p. 117; *Russell's Civil War*, p. 189.

124. *change of base*: *With Lincoln*, p. 94.

124–125. The *Herald* leak: Smith, pp. 285–89; *Power of the Press*, pp. 369–71.

125–126. Flub dubs: *Witness*, pp. 382–83; French to his sister, December 24, 1861, French papers; Seale, pp. 389–90.

126. *storm . . . worked up*: *Russell's Civil War*, p. 212; *Witness*, p. 383.

126. *Congress took care of it*: Carryl to French, April 12, 1862, RG 217.

126. *Christmas*: Browning Diary, vol. 1, p. 518; *Russell's Civil War*, p. 213.

126–127. Wikoff's exposure: Smith, pp. 288–89; Seale, p. 397.

CHAPTER 11

129. *Every President*: *Id.*, pp. 129, 159, 220, 243, 263, 315; *McClure*, p. 79.

129. Lincoln's open door: Pendel, pp. 20–22; Helen Nicolay, *Biography*,

pp. 117–18; CW, vol. 6, p. 508, vol. 7, p. 361; Stoddard-Burlingame, p. 176; *Lincoln at Work*, pp. 46–47; Stoddard, *Inside*, p. 15; Grimsley, p. 48; Seale, p. 366.

129–130. Open door policy critiqued: Donald, p. 285; *Lincoln's Washington*, p. 256; *Herndon's Informants*, p. 562; Dicey, vol. 1, p. 217; *Recollected Words*, p. 31; Bellows, *At Lincoln's Side*, p. 109; Life in the White House, p. 33.

130. Running the gauntlet; callers high and low: Life in the White House, pp. 33–34; *Herndon's Lincoln*, p. 303; *Recollected Words*, pp. 31, 388; Carpenter, p. 352; *At Lincoln's Side*, p. 126; CW, vol. 5, p. 32, vol. 7, p. 10; Stoddard-Burlingame, p. 188; Edourd de Stoeckl, Frank A. Golder, ed. "The American Civil War Through the Eyes of a Russian Diplomat," *American Historical Review* 26 (April 1921): 454–63, pp. 457–58; Conway, p. 345.

131. Respites: Stoddard, *Inside*, pp. 169–70; *At Lincoln's Side*, p. 22.

131–132. *almost noone . . . on the fly*: Stoddard-Burlingame, p. 157; Stoddard, *Inside*, pp. 37–38.

132. Order of admission: Arnold, *Sketch*, p. 68; Stoddard-Burlingame, p. 171.

132. *While they waited*: Arnold, *Sketch*, p. 68.

132. Bergdorf: Stoddard-Burlingame, pp. 151–52; Seale, pp. 336–37; *At Lincoln's Side*, pp. 68, 242 n. 175; *Tributes*, p. 102; Halpine, pp. 196–97; Stoddard, *Inside*, pp. 27, 50, 102; CW, vol. 6, pp. 175, 436; Expenditures, Randall Papers.

132–133. In Lincoln's office: Wilson, p. 561; *Herndon's Informants*, pp. 404–5; Elizabeth Peabody, p. 122; Crook, *Memories*, p. 28; Poore, vol. 2, pp. 143–44; *Glimpses*, p. 34; E. D. Townsend, p. 106.

133. *broke down*: *Lincoln Observed*, pp. 211–12.

133. *partition*: Carpenter, p. 234, George Townsend, pp. 38–39; Seale, p. 377.

133. Bores: *With Lincoln*, p. xix.

133. People wanting nothing: "Life in the White House," p. 34; Van Santvoord, pp. 613–14; *Recollected Words*, pp. 266, 353.

134. Browning: Browning Diary, vol. 1, pp. 542, 559, 596, 599–600.

134. Trollope: *North America*, p. 313.

134–135. Impatience, incivility, concealed generosity: Stoddard-Burlingame, p. 190; Van Santvoord, p. 613; Bishop, p. 780; Tuckerman, p. 412; Browning Diary, vol. 1, p. 659; Wilson, p. 432; Pendel, pp. 17–18; Joshua Speed. *Reminiscences of Abraham Lincoln*. Louisville: J. P. Morton and Co., 1884, pp. 27–28; Carpenter, p. 40.

135. Beggars' Opera: *Glimpses*, p. 37.

135–137. Group sessions: Life in the White House, p. 34; Thomas B. Bancroft. "An Audience with Abraham Lincoln," *McClure's Magazine* 32 (February 1909): 447–50, p. 447; Ivan Doig, "The Genial White House Host and Raconteur," *Journal of the Illinois State Historical Society* 62 (1969): 307–11 ("Doig"), pp. 310–11.

137. Men and women: Mary Livermore. *My Story of the War*. Hartford, CT: A. D. Worthington and Company, 1888 ("Livermore"), p. 569; Stoddard-Burlingame,

pp. 185 and 187; Helen Nicolay, *Traits*, pp. 204, 286; Carpenter, pp. 132–33; Stoddard, *Inside*, p. 102.

137. *Manufactured cheer*: E.g., Helen Nicolay, *Biography*, p. 83; Doig, p. 310; *Lincoln Observed*, p. 85.

137. Vanderbilt: CW, vol. 6, p. 432.

137. Hackett: Life in the White House, pp. 127–28; Brooks, Reminiscences, p. 675.

137. Black-eyed lady: Stoddard, *Inside*, p. 136.

138. Talk with Halleck's aide: Carpenter, pp. 278–81.

138. *not sheer waste*: Life in the White House, p. 34.

138. *What are people talking about?*: Brooks, Reminiscences, p. 677.

138–139. Religious visitors: Lamon, p. 94; Stoddard, *Inside*, p. 56; Stoddard-Burlingame, pp. 176–77; *With Lincoln*, p. 90; CW, vol. 5, pp. 212–13, vol. 7, p. 365; Carpenter, p. 242.

139–140. Hawthorne and the whip: Wilson, pp. 464–66; CW, vol. 5, p. 158; *New York Times*, March 22, 1862.

140. Secular delegations: *Lincoln Observed*, pp. 64, 86; Conway, p. 378; *At Lincoln's Side*, pp. 57–64, 110, 238 n. 131; Hay, *Inside*, p. 89; CW, vol. 4, pp. 486–87; N&H, vol. 8, pp. 215–16.

CHAPTER 12

143–144. New Year's Day: Seale, pp. 103, 108, 149, 192, 319; *Lincoln's Washington*, p. 284; Stoddard-Burlingame, pp. 153–54; *Dispatches*, p. 198; *Seward at Washington*, vol. 2, p. 151; *New York Times*, January 3, 1862; Poore, vol. 2, pp. 105–6; Browning Diary, vol. 1. p. 521; *Witness*, p. 384; *With Lincoln*, pp. 65, 67.

144–145. Party plans and preparations: *Id.*, p. 67; Helen Nicolay, *Biography*, p. 80; *White House Secretary*, pp. 260–62; "The Grand Presidential Party," *Lincoln Lore* 1550 (April 1967): 2–4 ("Grand Party").

145–146. Emerson and Gordon: Taft Diary, February 2, 1862; Ralph Waldo Emerson. *The Journals and Miscellaneous Notebooks of Ralph Waldo Emerson*, 16 vols. Edited by Linda Allardt, David W. Hill, and Ruth E. Bennett. Cambridge, MA: The Belknap Press of Harvard University Press, 1982 ("Emerson"), vol. 15, pp. 186–87, 194; CW, vol. 5, p. 128.

146–148. The party: Taft Diary, February 3, 1862; Grand Party, *passim*; David McCulloch. *Mornings on Horseback*. New York: Simon & Schuster, 1981, pp. 59–60; Emerson, vol. 15, p. 191; *At Lincoln's Side*, p. 67; Randall Papers, James Nesmith to his wife, February 5, 1862; French Papers, French to his brother, February 7, 1861; Browning Diary, vol. 1, p. 529; *With Lincoln*, pp. 67–68; *White House Secretary*, pp. 260–62; *Poore*, vol. 2, pp. 106, 116–20; Stoddard-Burlingame, pp. xiv, 154;

Dispatches, p. 58; Keckley, p. 102; *Alta California*; Ames, p. 171; *Washington Sunday Morning Chronicle*, February 9, 1862.

148–153. Willie's death: Keckley, pp. 100–17; Seale, pp. 397–99; Milton Shultes. "Mortality of the Five Lincoln Boys," *Lincoln Herald* 57 (Spring–Summer, 1955): 3–13 ("Shultes"); *Third Secretary*, 147; *With Lincoln*, pp. 69–71, 217 n. 39; *True Story*, p. 345; Carpenter, p. 117; Burlingame, vol. 2, pp. 283, 300; *The Christian Register*, September 7, 1872, "A Kindly Word for Abraham Lincoln's Widow," *New York Sunday Mercury*, February 16, 1862; Bernard, p. 65; Turner, p. 127; Bellows; "Mrs. Lincoln's Clothing," pp. 61–62; Erika Holst. " 'One of the Best Women I Ever Knew': Abraham Lincoln and Rebecca Pomeroy," *Journal of the Abraham Lincoln Association* 31 (Summer 2010): 12–20; Ames, pp. 239–40; Alan Peskin, "Two White House Visits: Congressman James H. Campbell Prods President Lincoln and Shares 'A Dish of Gossip with the First Lady,' " *Lincoln Herald* 94 (Winter 1992): 157–58, p. 158.

151. Watt's confessions: *At Lincoln's Side*, p. 186; Manton Marple to David Goodman Croly, October 7, 1862, Marble Papers.

151. French's interview: French to his brother, March 23, 1862, French Papers.

152. Hay on Mrs. Lincoln: *At Lincoln's Side*, pp. xxv, 18, 20.

152–153. Tad: *At Lincoln's Side*, pp. 111–12; Life in the White House, p. 35; Stoddard-Burlingame, p. 187; *Washington, D.C.*, p. 248; Colman, p. 294; "Recollections of the Home Life of Abraham Lincoln," Randall Papers; Bayne, pp. 78–79; CW, vol. 8, pp. 319–20; Wilson, p. 433.

CHAPTER 13

155. Payne: Daniel A. Payne. *Recollections of Seventy Years*. Nashville: Publishing House of the A.M.E. Sunday School Union, 1888, pp. 146–49.

155. *Hay went riding*: Nicolay to Therena, May 4, 1862, Nicolay Papers.

155–156. Mrs. Lincoln on concerts: Unpublished Mary Todd Lincoln, pp. 4–5, nn. 13, 14; Gideon Welles. *Diary of Gideon Welles, Secretary of the Navy under Lincoln and Johnson*, 3 vols. New York: W. W. Norton & Company, 1960, vol. 1, p. 325.

156. *shopping . . . appointment*: Matthew Pinsker. *Lincoln's Sanctuary: Abraham Lincoln and the Soldiers' Home*. New York: Oxford University Press, 2005 ("Pinsker"), p. 199; Unpublished Mary Todd Lincoln, p. 5.

156. *absolutely necessary*: French annotation on June 21, 1862, invoice, RG 217.

156. *Independence Day*: *New York Tribune*, July 7, 1863; Helen Nicolay, *Biography*, p. 147.

156–158. Lincoln's vulnerability: James Freeman Clarke. *Autobiography, Diary and Correspondence*. Edited by Edward Everett Hale. Boston: Houghton, Mifflin and Company, 1892, p. 280; Bruce, p. 142; *Lincoln's Washington*, p. 64; Carpenter, pp. 65–67, Stoddard-Burlingame, p. 168; Wilson, pp. 429, 475; Stimmel, p. 33;

William McCarter. *My Life in the Irish Brigade: The Civil War Memoirs of Private William McCarter, 116th Infantry*, edited by Kevin E. O'Brien (Da Capo Press, 2003) p. 13; *Recollected Words*, pp. 274, 353, 440; Brooks, Reminiscences, p. 674; *Washington D.C.*, p. 44; Wilson, p. 475; *Tributes*, pp. 189–90.

158. *Soldiers' Home*: Pinsker, *passim*.

158. *intervention*: Swett, p. 188; *Recollected Words*, p. 73.

158–159. *11th New York and sentries*: Thomas West Smith. *The Story of a Cavalry Regiment: "Scott's" Eleventh New York Cavalry.* Chicago: Veteran's Association of the Regiment, 1897, pp. 25–28; Colman, p. 299; Rice, p. 469; Lamon, p. 266; Carpenter, p. 67; Stoddard-Burlingame, p. 82; Brooks, Recollections, p. 224; *Lincoln at Work*, p. 105, 111.

159. *bugdom*: With Lincoln, p. 86.

159–161. *Committee of colored men*: CW, vol. 5, pp. 370–75; Kate Masur. "The African American Delegation to Abraham Lincoln: A Reappraisal," *Civil War History* 56 (June 2010): 117–44 ("Masur"); *Power of the Press*, pp. 396–98.

161–163. Slade: *They Knew Lincoln*, pp. 100–14; Natalie Sweet. "A Representative 'of Our People': The agency of William Slade, Leader in the African American Community and Usher to Abraham Lincoln," *Journal of the Abraham Lincoln Association* 34 (Summer 2013): 21–41 ("Sweet"); Masur, pp. 125, 132–33; *Glimpses*, pp. 47, 50–51.

163–165. 150th Pennsylvania: Thomas Chamberlin, *History of the One Hundred and Fiftieth Pennsylvania Volunteers.* F. McManus Jr. & Co. Philadelphia, 1905 ("Chamberlin"); Pinsker; McBride, *Body Guard*; McBride, *Recollections*; Stimmel; On Guard; Pendel, p. 31; Bruce, p. 103; Emmanuel Hertz, *Abraham Lincoln, a New Portrait*, 2 vols. New York: H. Liveright, Inc., 1931 ("Hertz"), vol. 1, p. 256.

165–166. Pennsylvania Avenue: William Tindall. "Beginnings of Street Railways in the District of Columbia," *Records of the Columbia Historical Society* (1918): 24–86, p. 77; Helen Nicolay, *Capital*, pp. 375–76; Kohl, pp. 391–93; Adams, p. 694; Clark, pp. 53–56; Riddle, p. 7; Sala, p. 75; Bryan, vol. 2, p. 496; Chamberlin, p. 55.

166. Fredericksburg: Stoddard-Burlingame, p. 214 n. 2.

166–167. New weapons: Meigs Diary, December 22, 1862; Stoddard-Burlingame, pp. 162–63, 196–97; *White House Secretary*, pp. 247–50; Stoddard, *Inside*; pp. 20, 39–42; Monaghan, p. 263; *True Story*, p. 272. Brooks, Reminiscences, p. 679; Sala, p. 68; Hay, *Inside*, p. 75; Life in the White House, p. 34.

CHAPTER 14

169. Stoddard's correspondence desk: Stoddard, *Inside*, pp. 27, 30–31, 170; *White House Secretary*, pp. 243–44; *Lincoln at Work*, pp. 72, 75–76, 82; Stoddard-Burlingame, pp. 157–58.

169–170. death threats: Stoddard, *Inside*, p. 33; *Lincoln at Work*, p. 86; *Lincoln at Work*, pp. 75, 86; *Recollected Words*, p. 353; *White House Secretary*, p. 246.

170. vitriol, oddity, and insanity: *Id.*, pp. 245–46; Hay, *Inside*, p. 10; *Lincoln at Work*, pp. 79–80; Stoddard, *Inside*, p. 31; Stoddard-Burlingame, pp. 157–58.

170. *P. T. Barnum*: Helen Nicolay, *Biography*, p. 117.

170–171. delegated and manipulated mail: Stoddard, *Inside*, pp. 32–33; *White House Secretary*, p. 244; Stoddard-Burlingame, pp. xviii, 159.

171. *personal services*: *Lincoln at Work*, p. 76.

171. *autographs*: Stoddard-Burlingame, p. 159; Dickens to Lincoln May 27, 1864, Lincoln papers, LOC ("Lincoln Papers").

171. *bundles and bales*: Stoddard, *Inside*, p. 28; *Lincoln at Work*, p. 79.

171–172. vetting and ghostwriting: *At Lincoln's Side*, p. 110; Stoddard-Burlingame, p. 158; Michael Burlingame, "New Light on the Bixby Letter," 16 *Journal of the Abraham Lincoln Association* (Winter 1995): 59–71; CW, vol. 5, p. 333, vol. 6, pp. 17, 167.

172. *Crazygrams*: Bates, pp. 167–70.

172–173. outgoing letters: *At Lincoln's Side*, pp. 88, 110; Hay, *Inside*, p. 19; *Glimpses*, p. 36; Helen Nicolay, *Traits*, p. 189; *Recollected Words*, p. 452; Browning Diary, vol. 2, pp. 24–25; CW, vol. 5, pp. 436, 491, vol. 6, pp. 130, 356; *With Lincoln*, pp. 65–66; Helen Nicolay, *Biography*, p. 86; N&H, vol. 7, p. 279, vol. 8, p. 215, vol. 9, p. 221.

173–174. pens, paper, copies: Brooks, Recollections, p. 229; *Glimpses*, p. 36; Helen Nicolay, *Biography*, p. 189; Bates, p. 141; Eugenia Jones Holt, "My Personal Recollections of Abraham Lincoln and Mary Todd Lincoln," *Abraham Lincoln Quarterly* 3 (March 1945): 235–52, p. 251; Leslie J. Perry, "Appeals to Lincoln's Clemency," *Harper's Magazine* 51 (November 1895–April 1896): 251–56 ("Perry"), p. 254; *White House Secretary*, p. 235; Appropriations.

174. Rough draft, e.g., August 12, 1864, Nicolay Papers, Box 3; stationary, seals, and franks in Ozias M. Hatch Papers ("Hatch Papers"), Box 3, ALPLM.

174. diplomatic correspondence: E.g., CW, vol. 4, pp. 417, 468, vol. 5, pp. 106, 125–26, 137.

174–175. gifts: Joseph Singer to Lincoln, January 24, 1862, Lincoln Papers; *Dear Mr. Lincoln*, pp. 200–1, 205–6; CW, vol. 4, p. 319, vol. 5, pp. 177, 200, vol. 8, p. 257; *At Lincoln's Side*, p. 24; Pendel, pp. 19–20; *White House Secretary*, p. 260; *Lincoln at Work*, pp. 98–100; Grimsley, pp. 54–55, 59; Turner, p. 162; Higginson, p. 164; *Lincoln's Washington*, p. 166.

175–177. Newspapers and reporters: *Washington D.C.*, p. 261; *Power of the Press*, *passim*, especially pp. 390–91, 394–97, 401, 465, 477; *At Lincoln's Side*, p. 110; Stoddard, *Inside*, pp. 27, 54–55; Stoddard-Burlingame, pp. xviii, 149; *With Lincoln*, pp. 115–16, 175, 234 n. 90; *White House Secretary*, pp. 239, 243; Carpenter, pp. 151–54; Nicolay Papers, folder marked "First Meeting Between Lincoln & Grant etc. 1861–1865," typescript of Nicolay notes; *Lincoln at Work*, p. 72; CW, vol. 6,

p. 120; Gobright, pp. 334–35; Three Interviews, pp. 37–38; Hay, *Inside*, pp. 85, 188.

CHAPTER 15

179–180. New Year's Day 1863: Taft Diary, January 1–3, 1863; Turner, p. 144; *Lincoln Observed*, pp. 15–17; Seale, p. 331; *Washington D.C.*, pp. 48, 68–69; Frederick Hatch. *Protecting President Lincoln: The Security Effort, the Thwarted Plots and the Disaster at Ford's Theater*. Jefferson, NC: McFarland & Co., 2011 ("Hatch"), p. 39; N&H, p. 429; Helen Nicolay, *Biography*, pp. 163–64.

180–181. spiritualists: Browning Diary, vol. 1, pp. 608–9; "Lincoln's Attendance at Spiritualistic Seances," *Lincoln Lore* 1499 (January 1963); "Baker's Spirit Message to Lincoln," *Lincoln Lore* 1497 (November 1962); *Lincoln at Work*, p. 80; Bates, p. 210; Richard N. Current, *The Lincoln Nobody Knows*. New York: Hill and Wang, 1958, p. 67; Terry Alford, "The Spiritualist Who Warned Lincoln Was Also Booth's Drinking Buddy," *Smithsonian Magazine* (March 2015); *Washington D.C.*, pp. 66–67.

181. social mores: Turner, p. 188; diary of Virginia Woodbury Fox, January 8, 1863, Levi Woodbury Family Papers, LOC.

181–182. Tom Thumb: Keckley, p. 123; *Tributes*, pp. 108–12; "Tom Thumb Visits the White House," *Lincoln Lore* 1467 (May 1960); French to his sister, February 19, 1863, French Papers; *Witness*, p. 417.

182–184. Indians: CW, vol. 6, pp. 151–52; Herman J. Viola. *Diplomats in Buckskin: A History of Indian Delegations in Washington City*. Washington: Smithsonian Institution Press, 1981, pp. 99–102; *Witness*, p. 419; *With Lincoln*, p. 107; Stoddard, *Inside*, pp. 99–100; *Washington D.C.*, pp. 293–94.

184–185. Chancellorsville and its aftermath: Nicolay to Hatch, May 5, 1863, Hatch Papers; Brooks, Reminiscences, p. 674; *Washington D.C.*, pp. 60–61; *Lincoln Observed*, pp. 50–51; Stoddard, *Inside*, pp. 198, 201–3; *White House Secretary*, pp. 307–9; *Tributes*, pp. 46–49.

185–186. black troops: CW, vol. 6, p. 239; Stoddard-Burlingame, pp. 172–73.

186. Independence Day celebration 1863: Burt, p. 499; Stoddard, *Inside*, pp. 207–9; *White House Secretary*, pp. 310–13.

186. *eighty odd years*: CW vol. 6, pp. 319–20.

186. *orgy*: At Lincoln's Side, p. 45.

186. *awkward address*: CW, vol. 6, pp. 319–20.

186–187. clemency: *At Lincoln's Side*, pp. 45–46; CW, vol. 6, p. 335. Stoddard-Burlingame, pp. 170–71, 187, 218 n. 3; *Herndon's Lincoln*, p. 320; Hay, *Inside*, p. 64; Rice, pp. 342–43; *Recollected Words*, p. 148; Lamon, pp. 86–87; Carpenter, pp. 171–72.

187–188. Matile and Howe: *At Lincoln's Side*, pp. 49, 85, 249–50 n. 60; *With Lincoln*, pp. 125, 237 n. 12; Stoddard-Burlingame, p. 210 n. 1.

188. *obsolete almanac*: Thayer, vol. 1, p. 146.

188. Hay on Stoddard: *At Lincoln's Side*, pp. 53, 105.

188–189. Douglass: Fredrick Douglass. *The Life and Times of Frederick Douglass*. Hartford: Park, 1883 ("Douglass"), pp. 421–25; Rice, pp. 185, 193; Hay, *Inside*, p. 72.

189. *leaves . . . light work*: *Dispatches*, p. 182; *At Lincoln's Side*, p. 103; *Washington Chronicle*, November 15, 1863; *Lincoln Observed*, p. 92; Taft Diary, November 18, 1863; Pendel, p. 41.

189. *nineteen loads*: RG 217, document 148–947.

189. O'Reilly: Halpine, p. 158.

189–190. *varioloid*: Basler, Smallpox; *Recollected Words*, p. 13; Carpenter, p. 273; *They Knew Lincoln*, pp. 133–34; Hay, *Inside*, p. 327 n. 299; Stoddard, *Inside*, pp. 189–92; *At Lincoln's Side*, pp. 70, 118, 327 n. 299; Helen Nicolay, *Biography*, p. 83; CW, vol. 7, p. 34; *White House Secretary*, p. 305; Browne, p. 460.

190–191. Johnson: *They Knew Lincoln*, pp. 135–36.

191–195. Emilie Helm: Burlingame, vol. 2, pp. 556–56; McMurtry, pp. 50–62; Helm, pp. 220–33; Seale, p. 410; CW, vol. 6, p. 517, vol. 7, pp. 484–85, 647; *Recollected Words*, p. 234; Grimsley, p. 57; Paul D. Escott, *Lincoln's Dilemma*. Charlottesville: University of Virginia Press, 2014 ("Escott"), pp. 250–51; *With Lincoln*, pp. 136–37; Turner, pp. 154–56.

195. Russian fleet: Travels, 189–90; *Witness*, p. 442; *At Lincoln's Side*, pp. 128–29.

195. Hay's Christmas: *Id.*, p. 133.

195. New Year's Day: Anna Ridgely, "A Girl in the Sixties," *Journal of the Illinois State Historical Society* (October 1929): 401–46, p. 432; *Lincoln Observed*, pp. 99–100; *Dispatches*, p. 198.

195–197. Union Light Guard: McBride, Body Guard, *passim*; McBride, Recollections, *passim*; Stimmel, *passim*; Borrett, pp. 6–7; Stoddard-Burlingame, p. 182; Rice, p. 470 n; Sala, pp. 142–44; National Archives, Judge Advocate General's Official Records, Record Group 153, File no. LL2712–4, court martial of Arthur H. White.

197. Death threat: *Dear Mr. Lincoln*, p. 345.

197. *plump lady*: *Recollected Words*, p. 482.

197. *walk with him*: Brooks, Reminiscences, p. 674; *Washington D.C.*, p. 44.

198. Sprague imbroglio: *With Lincoln*, pp. 124–25.

198–199. French on Mrs. Lincoln: French to his relatives, December 24, 1861, February 19, 1863, January 31, 1864, July 9, 1865, French Papers; *Lincoln's White House Secretary*, p. 242.

199. Nicolay's tour: *With Lincoln*, p. 176.

199. *replacing it*: *Lincoln's Washington*, p. 312; *Boston Journal*, December 1, 1863, "Waifs from Washington," signed "Perley."
199–200. *English girl*: MacDonnell, pp. 566–68.
200. *Lafayette's grandson*: Chambrun, p. 22.
200. Blacks at levees: Stoddard-Burlingame, p. 172; William Makepeace Thayer. *Character and Public Services of Abraham Lincoln*. Boston: Dinsmoor & Co., 1864, p. 22; David E. Long. *The Jewel of Liberty: Abraham Lincoln's Re-Election and the End of Slavery*. Mechanicsburg, PA: Stackpole, 1994, p. 171: Livermore, pp. 581–82.

CHAPTER 16

201. Carpenter: Carpenter, pp. 18–20, 30, 79, 83, 149, 216, 255; "Carpenter's Painting: 'The First Reading of the Emancipation Proclamation Before the Cabinet,'" *Lincoln Lore* 1482–83 (August and September 1861); Charles Hamilton and Lloyd Ostendorf. *Lincoln in Photographs: An Album of Every Known Pose*. Dayton, OH: Morningside, 1985, pp. 186, 211.
201. February 6 reception: Adams, *passim*; Sala, vol. 2, p. 143.
201. *My subs*: *With Lincoln*, pp. 125, 237 n. 12.
202. *pull of weeks*: *Lincoln's White House Secretary*, p. 317.
202. Neill: Edward D. Neill: *Abraham Lincoln and His Mailbag*. Edited by Theodore C. Blegen. Saint Paul: Minnesota Historical Society, 1964 (*"Mailbag"*), *passim*; *Glimpses*, pp. 31, 37; Helen Nicolay, *Biography*, p. 87; *At Lincoln's Side*, p. 87.
203. The mail: *Mailbag*, pp. 47–50; *Lincoln at Work*, p. 82; *Glimpses*, pp. 45, 49.
203. Condemned soldier: *Id.*, p. 35.
203–205. Stable fire: Nicolay to Hay, February 10, 1864, Nicolay to Stevens, February 15, 1864, Nicolay Papers; "The White House Stable Fire of 1864" http://rogerjnor
ton.com/Lincoln100.html; McBride, *Body Guard*, pp. 16–17; McBride, *Recollections*, pp. 44–46; Stimmel, pp. 15–16; *Washington Star*, February 11, 1864; *Washington Chronicle*, February 11, 1864; *Stables and Garages*, pp. 378–81; Robert J. Havlik, "Lincoln's Washington Carriages Revisited," *The Lincoln Herald* 112 (Fall 2010): 155–80, p. 169; *With Lincoln*, pp. 126, 237 n. 16; Bates, p. 209; Elizabeth Blair Lee. *Wartime Washington: The Civil War Letters of Elizabeth Blair Lee*. Edited by Virginia J. Lass. Urbana: University of Illinois Press, 1991 ("Lee"), p. 346; Carpenter, p. 45; Seale, p. 411; French to Rice, February 12, 1864, National Archives, Commissioner of Public Buildings Outgoing Letters; Viator, p. 183.
205. *Oliver Twists*: *White House Secretary*, p. 235.
205. Bancroft: Bancroft, pp. 155–56.
205. Drums: Taft Diary, February 26, 1864.
205–207. Grant: N&H, vol. 8, p. 340; Welles, vol. 1, p. 539; Nicolay memorandum, Nicolay Papers, Box 3; Arnold, *Life*, pp. 370–71; The *National Republican*,

February 22, 1923; *With Lincoln*, pp. 129–31, 238–40; CW, vol. 7, pp. 234, 236; Helen Nicolay, *Biography*, pp. 194–97; Noah Brooks. "Lincoln, Chase, and Grant," *The Century Illustrated Magazine* 49 (February 1895): 617–19, p. 618; *Washington D.C.*, pp. 134–35; McBride, *Body Guard*, pp. 1, 52–53; Stimmel, pp. 18–19; *Glimpses*, pp. 41–42; Gobright, p. 339; *Recollected Words*, p. 348; *Washington Star*, March 9, 1864; *Jokes*, p. 111; Stoddard, *Inside*, p. 220.

207. Julia Grant: Julia Dent Grant. *The Personal Memoirs of Julia Dent Grant*. Edited by John Y. Simon. New York: Putnam, 1975, p. 130.

207. Father Abraham: *White House Secretary*, pp. 310, 394 n. 6.

207–208. French and Usher: French to his brother, April 10, 1864, French Papers; CW, vol. 7, pp. 266–67.

208. *stay patient*: Turner, pp. 174–75.

208. *wandered in*: Hay, *Inside*, p. 194.

208. *the Herald*: *New York Herald*, May 2, 1864.

208. Lincoln photographed: *Photographs*, pp. 13, 188–90; "Carpenter's Painting: " 'The First Reading of the Emancipation Proclamation Before the Cabinet,' " *Lincoln Lore* 1482 (August 1961), p. 3.

208–209. Tad outraged: Carpenter, pp. 91–92; Lamon, p. 164.

209. *Quinine*: Grimsley, p. 57; CW, vol. 7, pp. 484–85; Escott, pp. 250–51; *With Lincoln*, 136–37; Turner, 154–56; Emilie Todd Helm, "Open Letters," *The Century Magazine* 52 (June 1896): p. 318.

209. Martha: Welles, vol. 2, p. 21; *With Lincoln*, pp. 243–44 nn. 75, 81, 82, 84; Helm, pp. 181–83.

209. Lincoln's face: Carpenter, pp. 30–31; Rice, p. 337.

209. *suddenly in summer . . . not so good*: Lee, p. 377; CW, vol. 7, p. 332; Carpenter, p. 143; Hay, *Inside*, p. 197.

210. *children*: Carpenter, pp. 130–31.

210. tobacco juice and mud: *American Notes*, pp. 297–98; Riddle, p. 17.

210. vandals: *Lincoln Observed*, pp. 82–83, 148; Stoddard-Burlingame p. 183; *Historic Guide*, p. 128.

210–211. *Daily Telegraph*: Sala, vol. 2, pp. 142–44.

211. Howe: Hay, *Inside*, p. 196.

211. Arkansas: *Id.*, p. 197; *True Story*, p. 3.

211. Pipes: Carpenter, pp. 160–61; CW, vol. 7, p. 34.

211. *drowned cats*: At Lincoln's Side, p. 85.

211–212. Sunday School picnic: CW, vol. 7, p. 420; Hay, *Inside*, p. 220; William E. Doster. *Lincoln and Episodes of the Civil War*. New York: G. P. Putnam's Sons, 1915 ("Doster"), pp. 241–42, 244; Carpenter, p. 196.

CHAPTER 17

213. Lincoln on the path: Carpenter, p. 352.

213–214. Early's raid: *Experiences*, pp. 20–23; Hay, *Inside*, pp. 221–23, 357 n.

225; *At Lincoln's Side*, p. 128; Carpenter, 301; *Glimpses*, p. 43; Bates, pp. 253–54; Doster, p. 253; *Lincoln's Sanctuary*, 136–40.

215. *California congressman*: Henry B. Rankin. *Intimate Sketches of Abraham Lincoln*. Philadelphia, J. B. Lippincott Company, 1924, p. 289.

215. Conrad: Thomas N. Conrad. *A Confederate Spy*. New York: J. S. Ogilvie Publishing Company, 1892, pp. 70–71. (Conrad's chronology may be wrong. See Pinsker, p. 180)

215. *impossibility . . . heat*: N&H, vol. 9, p. 250; Nicolay to Bates, August 14, 1864.

215–216. Mrs. Lincoln's debts: Turner, pp. 164–66; Keckley, pp. 149–51.

216. Douglass: Douglass, pp. 434–37; CW, vol. 7, pp. 506–8; Carpenter, p. 204.

216. black leaders: CW, vol. 7, p. 295; vol. 8, pp. 272–73; Douglass, p. 439.

216. 166th Ohio: CW, vol. 7, p. 512.

216–219. Philbrick, Hay, and Stoddard: Philbrick, *passim*; *With Lincoln*, p. 151; *At Lincoln's Side*, pp. xxiii, 27, 93; Philbrick to Nicolay, March 1, April 18, August 8, 1861, October 28, 1864, Nicolay Papers; Hay Letters, vol. 1, p. 223; *White House Secretary*, pp. 272, 339–40; Stoddard, *Inside*, pp. 218–19, 243; *Third Secretary*, p. 216; *Dear Mr. Lincoln*, p. 29.

218. *shut up shop . . . dinner*: *White House Secretary*, pp. 331–32.

219. *class of men . . . disgrace him*: Keckley, pp. 145–46; *Oral History*, p. 3.

219. French: French Papers.

219. Davis: *At Lincoln's Side*, p. 187.

219–220. New Yorkers: *Id.*, pp. 187–88; Burlingame, vol. 2, pp. 264, 279; Turner, p. 181; www.mrlincolnandnewyork.org; Welles, vol. 2, p. 122.

220. *five times*: David H. Donald. *Lincoln at Home: Two Glimpses of Abraham Lincoln's Domestic Life*. Washington: White House Historical Association, 1999, p. 20.

220. Gould: Wilson, pp. 470–71.

220. Sojourner Truth: Carpenter, pp. 201–3; "An October Visitor at the White House, 1964," *Lincoln Lore* 809 (October 9, 1944).

220–221. Whitman: Grace Seiler. "Walt Whitman and Abraham Lincoln," *Lincoln Herald* 52 (December 1950): 42–47, 53 ("Seiler"), p. 42.

221. Gurowski: Lamon, p. 269; *Recollected Words*, p. 291; Pierce, vol. 4, p. 128; Emerson, vol. 15, p. 189; Poore, vol. 2, pp. 139–40; Welles, vol. 2, pp. 100–1; Monaghan, p. 120.

221. *Lamon slept*: Swett, p. 188.

221. *vagabonds*: Seale, p. 401.

221. *deserters*: *Lincoln's Washington*, p. 393.

221. *Joe Hall's*: Stoddard, *Inside*, pp. 66–67.

221. lunatics: Nicolay Papers, Box 9, folder marked "Lincoln Memoranda Mostly Clippings," undated clipping, *New York Leader*; *Washington Star*, March 28, 1864; "Mr. Lincoln and the Petitioners," *Putnam's Magazine* 6 (November, 1870): 527–36, p. 534.

222–223. Police guard: Missing Guard, pp. 106–7; Lincoln as I Knew Him, pp.

107, 110; Pendel, pp. 11–14, 23; Guarding; Hatch, pp. 111–12; Crook, *Memories*, pp. 15, 38.

224. White House staff and the war: *Id.*, p. 176; CW, vol. 8, pp. 53, 328; Lincoln as I Knew Him, p. 42; Turner, p. 212; *At Lincoln's Side*, p. 235 n. 97; *Washington Star*, October 1 and October 3, 1864; Stoddard, *Inside*, pp. 15–17; *With Lincoln*, p. 55; Taliaffero, pp. 78–79.

224–225. Election day: Brooks, *Reminiscences*, p. 675; CW, vol. 8, p. 96; Hay, *Inside*, pp. 243–46; N&H, vol. 9, p. 378.

225. November 9: *Oral History*, p. 83; CW, vol. 8, p. 98.

225. *cavalrymen patrolled*: Ashman, p. 285.

225. *Mecca . . . informally*: Turner, pp. 187, 200.

226. Mrs. Lincoln's shopping: Taft Diary, January 2, 1863, and December 14, 1864.

226. *November 12*: Philbrick to Nicolay, Nicolay Papers, letters to Nicolay.

227. *About three days*: *Id.*, Nicolay to Hay, November 10, 1864; *With Lincoln*, p. 167.

227. *December 10*: Risley to Nicolay, December 10, 1864, Nicolay Papers; Lamon, pp. 274–75; Hatch, p. 10.

227. *tried Nicolay*: Lamon to Nicolay, December 15, 1864, Lincoln Papers.

227. News of Nashville: Bates, p. 317.

227–228. Edward's dismissal and replacement: Stoddard-Burlingame, pp. 151, 209–10 n. 9; Pendel, p. 37; Turner, pp. 197, 200 n. 2, 202; Carpenter, p. 41; *At Lincoln's Side*, p. 202.

228. Philbrick's letter: Philbrick to Hatch, December 30, 1864, Hatch Papers.

CHAPTER 18

229. New Year's Day: Carpenter, pp. 205–6; *Washington Star*, January 2, 1864; Lamon to Nicolay, January 4, 1865, Nicolay Papers; Ashman, pp. 287–89; Richtmyer Hubble, Marc Newman, ed. *Potomac Diary: A Soldier's Account of the Capital in Crisis, 1864–1865.* Charleston, SC: Arcadia Publishing, 2000, pp. 48–49; John S. C. Abbott. *Lives of the Presidents of the Unites States.* Boston: B. B. Russell & Co., 1880, pp. 419–20; Stoddard-Burlingame, pp. 214–15 n. 6.

229–230. *B&O*: CW, vol. 8, p. 209.

230. *China*: Turner, pp. 129, 199.

230. *junior officer*: C. H. Howard, "Some Glimpses of Abraham Lincoln," *Northwestern Christian Advocate*, Chicago, February 7, 1894.

230–231. Crook's story: Crook, *Memories*, pp. 3–4, 8–9, 14; Lincoln as I Knew Him, pp. 108–10.

231. Swayne: "William Marshall Swayne, The Man Who Made a 'Mud Head' of Lincoln," *Lincoln Lore* 1493 (July 1962).

231–232. Everett and Agassiz: Brooks, Reminiscences, p. 678; Brooks, Recollections, p. 224.

232. *crush* me: Carpenter, p. 276.

232–234. Inauguration Day: *With Lincoln*, p. 175; Welles, vol. 2, p. 252; Stimmel, pp. 27–28; Colman, p. 307; Pendel, pp. 35–36; Ashman, pp. 287–89; Allan Clark. "Abraham Lincoln in the National Capital," *Records of Columbia Historical Society* 27 (1925): 1–175, p. 63; *Witness*, p. 466; Seiler, p. 42; Rice, p. 192; Lincoln As I Knew Him, p. 42.

234. Brooks, Nicolay, and Hay: *At Lincoln's Side*, p. 103; *With Lincoln*, p. 175; Lincoln's Castine, pp. 113–14, 169–70.

234. *death threat*: *Glimpses*, p. 49.

234. *exhausted . . . directions*: *Id.*, pp. 170–71; *Lincoln Observed*, p. 176; Clark, p. 87.

234–235. *burned down*: Turner, pp. 205 n. 7, 210.

234–235. Cuthbert: Seale, pp. 395, 409; CW, vol. 5, p. 492.

235. *thoroughly sick*: *At Lincoln's Side*, p. 103.

235. *Anxious*: Philbrick to Hatch, April 4, 1865, Hatch Papers.

235. Wikoff: *With Lincoln*, p. 176.

235. April 3: *Washington D.C.*, p. 219; *Witness*, pp. 468–69.

235. *That evening*: Turner, pp. 212–13; Monaghan, pp. 35, 137.

235–236. April 4: Turner, p. 213; *Washington D.C.*, p. 222; Philbrick to Hatch, April 4, 1865, Hatch Papers; *Lincoln's Washington*, p. 440; E. D. Townsend, pp. 122–23.

236. Hay's note to Philbrick: *At Lincoln's Side*, p. 104.

236–237. April 9–11: Turner, p. 216; Charles Henry Philbrick, p. 8; *Lincoln Observed*, pp. 181–82; Welles, vol. 2, p. 278; *Glimpses*, pp. 44–46, N&H, vol. 9, p. 456; Stimmel, pp. 28–30; CW, vol. 8, pp. 395, 399–405; Gobright, p. 345; *Washington D.C.*, pp. 224–25; *Lincoln's Washington*, pp. 440–41; Keckly, pp. 175–78; Brooks, Reminiscences, p. 567.

237. *another day*: Turner, p. 219; Seward Diary, April 13, 1865.

237. Good Friday: Lincoln's Castine, p. 174; Helm, p. 259; Browne, pp. 701–2. CW, vol. 8, p. 413; *Washington, D.C.*, p. 229; *Five Administrations*, pp. 72–74; Pendel, pp. 39–40.

237–239. Assassination news: *They Knew Lincoln*, p. 126; Pendel, pp. 41–44; Keckley, pp. 185–86; Stimmel, p. 31; Gobright, p. 350.

239–240. Saturday: *Witness*, p. 470; Wheelock, p. 46; *Washington D.C.*, pp. 232–33; Pendel, p. 45; *Mailbag*, p. 50; *Glimpses*, pp. 49–51; Welles, vol. 2, pp. 289–90; Sweet, p. 8; Keckley, pp. 189–91; Seale, p. 419.

240–241. *Hampton Roads . . . overwhelm*: *With Lincoln*, pp. 176–77; Seale, pp. 419–24; Garrett, p. 149; Carpenter, p. 197; *Washington D.C.*, p. 232.

241. The funeral: *Id.*, pp. 232–35; Wheelock, p. 46; Chambrun, pp. 113–15; Pendel, p. 45; Seale, p. 422; *They Knew Lincoln*, p. 111.

241. Tad: Carpenter, p. 293.

241–242. *A month . . . heathen*: George Townsend, pp. 56–58; Browne, p. 334.

EPILOGUE

243–244. The White House: Seale, pp. 423–25; Ames, pp. 171–72, 240; Stoddard-Burlingame, p. 183; *At Lincoln's Side*, pp. 200–1; *White House Secretary*, p. 349; Turner, pp. 225, 326–27; Keckley; pp. 201–5; Robert Klara, *The Hidden White House*. New York: Thomas Dunne Books, 2013, p. 238.

244. Mrs. Lincoln: *At Lincoln's Side*, p. 187; Pratt, pp. 139, 184–85; Burlingame, vol. 1, p. 208; Turner, p. 220 *et seq.*; Pendel, p. 50; Stoddard-Burlingame, p. xv.

245. Tad: Keckley, p. 197; *At Lincoln's Side*, pp. 111, 113; Turner, pp. 584–85; Shultes, pp. 6–7.

245. Robert: *Id.*, pp. 10–11; Holzer, White House, p. 14.

245–246. *They Knew Lincoln*, pp. 137–40.

246. Keckly: *Id.*, pp. 208, 213–16, 221–22, 227.

246. Slade: *Id.*, pp. 114–15; *Glimpses*, p. 51; Sweet, n. 72.

246–247. Stoddard: Stoddard-Burlingame, pp. vii, xx–xxi; *White House Secretary*, p. 305; William O. Stoddard Jr. to J. G. Randall, July 17, 1951, Randall Papers; *White House Secretary*, pp. 220, 347–49, 361–65; www.christies.com/lotfinder/Lot DetailsPrintable.aspx?intObjectID=4606565.

247. Nicolay: *With Lincoln*, pp. 78, 181 n. 2, 182–83 n. 17; *Oral History*, pp. 124–25 n. 24; Some Correspondence Between John Hay and Helen Nicolay, *Lincoln Lore* 1547 (January 1967), p. 2.

247–248. Hay: Taliaferro, pp. 107–552; *At Lincoln's Side*, p. 12; Heather Neilson, *Political Animal: Gore Vidal on Power*. Clayton, Australia, 2014, p. 158.

BIBLIOGRAPHY

PRIMARY SOURCES

Manuscript Collections Consulted

American Antiquarian Society, Worcester, Massachusetts
    Original newspapers and magazines
Boston Athenaeum, Boston, Massachusetts
    Original newspapers, magazines, pamphlets, and tracts
Library of Congress
    Papers of James Buchanan and Harriet Lane Johnston; Papers of Benjamin
    B. French; Gist-Blair Family Papers; Papers of John Hay; Papers of Robert
    R. Hitt; Robert Todd Lincoln collection, Papers of Abraham Lincoln;
    Papers of Manton Marble; Papers of John Nicolay; Papers of J. G. Randall;
    The Frontier Guard File; Williams, Margaret, "A Brief Reminiscence of
    the First Inauguration of Abraham Lincoln as President," Miscellaneous
    Papers.
Abraham Lincoln Library, Springfield, Illinois
    Ozias M. Hatch Papers; Anson Henry Papers; Stuart-Hay Papers
The National Archives, files of the Lincoln Administration's General Accounting
    Office, Secretary of the Interior, Judge Advocate General, and Commissioner of
    Public Buildings, assembled and made available electronically by The Lincoln
    Archives Digital Project.

Books and Pamphlets

Ames, Mary Clemmer. *Ten Years in Washington: Life and Scenes in the National Capital, as a Woman Sees Them.* Hartford, CT: A. D. Worthington, 1873.
Arnold, Isaac N. *Life of Abraham Lincoln.* Chicago: Jansen, McClerg & Company, 1885.
———. *Sketch of the Life of Abraham Lincoln.* New York: John B. Bachelder, 1869.
Bates, David Homer. *Lincoln in the Telegraph Office.* New York: Century Co., 1907.
Bayne, Julia Taft. *Tad Lincoln's Father.* Boston: Little, Brown, and Company, 1931.

Brooks, Noah. *Lincoln Observed: Civil War Dispatches of Noah Brooks.* Edited by Michael Burlingame. Baltimore: Johns Hopkins University Press, 1998.

———. *Mr. Lincoln's Washington: Selections from the Writings of Noah Brooks, Civil War Correspondent.* Edited by P. J. Staudenraus. South Brunswick, NJ: Thomas Yoseloff, 1967.

———. *Washington D.C. in Lincoln's Time.* Edited by Herbert Mitgang. Chicago: Quadrangle Books, 1971.

Browne, Francis Fisher. *The Every-Day Life of Abraham Lincoln.* Chicago: Browne & Howell Company, 1886.

Browning, Orville H. *The Diary of Orville Hickman Browning,* 2 vols. Edited by Theodore Calvin Pease and James G. Randall. Springfield: Illinois State Historical Library, 1925–1933.

Carpenter, Frank B. *Six Months at the White House with Abraham Lincoln: The Story of a Picture.* New York: Hurd and Houghton, 1867.

Chamberlin, Thomas. *History of the One Hundred and Fiftieth Regiment Pennsylvania Volunteers.* Philadelphia: F. McManus Jr., 1905.

Crook, William H. *Memories of the White House.* Edited by Henry Rood. Boston: Little, Brown, 1911.

———. *Through Five Administrations: Reminiscences of Colonel William H. Crook.* Edited by Margareta Spaulding Gerry. New York: Harper & Brothers, 1910.

Douglass, Frederick. *The Life and Times of Frederick Douglass.* Hartford, CT: Park, 1883.

Editors of *The Independent. Abraham Lincoln: Tributes from His Associates, Reminiscences of Soldiers, Statesmen and Citizens.* New York: Thomas Y. Crowell & Company, 1895.

Ferri-Pisani, Camille. *Prince Napoleon in America, 1861.* Translated by Georges J. Joyaux. Bloomington: Indiana University Press, 1955.

French, Benjamin B. *Benjamin Brown French, Witness to the Young Republic: A Yankee's Journal, 1828–1870.* Edited by Donald B. Cole and John J. McDonough. Hanover, NH: University Press of New England, 1989.

Halpine, Charles G. "Miles O'Reilly at the White House." In *Life and Adventures, Songs, Services and Speeches of Private Miles O'Reilly.* New York: Carleton, 1864.

Hamilton, Charles, and Lloyd Ostendorf. *Lincoln in Photographs: An Album of Every Known Pose,* rev. ed. Dayton, OH: Morningside, 1985.

Hay, John. *At Lincoln's Side: John Hay's Civil War Correspondence and Selected Writings.* Edited by Michael Burlingame. Carbondale: Southern Illinois University Press, 2000.

———. *Inside Lincoln's White House: The Complete Civil War Diary of John Hay.* Edited by Michael Burlingame. Carbondale: Southern Illinois University Press, 1997.

Helm, Katherine. *The True Story of Mary, Wife of Lincoln.* New York: Harper, 1928.

Herndon, William H., and Jesse W. Weik. *Herndon's Lincoln.* Edited by Douglas J. Wilson and Rodney O. Davis. Urbana: University of Illinois Press, 2006.

Holzer, Harold, ed. *Dear Mr. Lincoln: Letters to the President.* Reading, MA: Addison-Wesley, 1993.

Keckly, Elizabeth. *Behind the Scenes.* New York: G. W. Carleton, 1868; rept. Oxford University Press, 1988.

Lamon, Ward Hill. *Recollections of Abraham Lincoln, 1847–1865.* Edited by Dorothy Lamon. Chicago: A. C. McClurg and Company, 1895.

Lincoln, Abraham. *The Collected Works of Abraham Lincoln*, 9 vols. Edited by Roy P. Basler. New Brunswick, NJ: Rutgers University Press, 1953–1955.

———. *Recollected Words of Abraham Lincoln.* Edited by Don E. and Virginia Fehrenbacher. Stanford, CA: Stanford University Press, 1996.

Lincoln, Mary Todd. *Mary Todd Lincoln: Her Life and Letters.* Edited by Justin G. Turner and Linda Levitt Turner. New York: Knopf, 1972.

Maynard, Nettie Colburn. *Was Abraham Lincoln a Spiritualist?* Philadelphia: n. p., 1891.

McBride, Robert. *Lincoln's Body Guard: The Union Light Guard of Ohio.* Indianapolis, IN: E. J. Hecker, 1911.

———. *Personal Recollections of Abraham Lincoln.* Indianapolis, IN: Bobbs-Merrill, 1926.

Morrison's Stranger's Guide to the City of Washington. Washington, D.C.: W. M. Morrison & Co., 1855.

Morrison's Stranger's Guide and Etiquette for Washington City. Washington, D.C.: W. H. & O. H. Morrison, 1862.

Neill, Edward D. *Abraham Lincoln and His Mailbag.* Edited by Theodore C. Blegen. Saint Paul: Minnesota Historical Society, 1964.

Nicolay, John G. *An Oral History of Abraham Lincoln: John G. Nicolay's Interviews and Essays.* Edited by Michael Burlingame. Carbondale: Southern Illinois University Press, 1996.

———. *With Lincoln in the White House: Letters, Memoranda and Other Writings of John G. Nicolay, 1860–1865.* Edited by Michael Burlingame. Carbondale: Southern Illinois University Press, 2000.

Nicolay, John G., and John Hay. *Abraham Lincoln: A History*, 10 vols. New York: Century Company, 1917.

Pendel, Thomas. *Thirty-six Years in the White House.* Washington, D.C.: Neale Publishing Company, 1902.

Pratt, Harry E., ed. *Concerning Mr. Lincoln, in which Abraham Lincoln is pictured as he appeared to letter writers of his time.* Springfield, IL: The Abraham Lincoln Association, 1944.

Rice, Allen Thorndike, ed. *Reminiscences of Abraham Lincoln by Distinguished Men of His Time.* New York: North American Publishing Co., 1886.

Russell, William H. *My Diary North and South.* Boston: T. O. H. P. Burnham, 1863.

———. *William Howard Russell's Civil War: Private Diary and Letters, 1861–1862.* Edited by Martin Crawford. Athens: University of Georgia Press, 1992.

Sala, George A. *My Diary in America in the Midst of War*, 2 vols. London: Tinsley Brothers, 1865.

Smith, Thomas West. *The Story of a Cavalry Regiment: "Scott's" Eleventh New York Cavalry.* Chicago: Veteran's Association of the Regiment, 1897.

Stoddard, William O. *Abraham Lincoln: The True Story of a Great Life.* New York: Fords, Howard, & Hulbert, 1885.

———. *Dispatches from Lincoln's White House: The Anonymous Civil War Journalism of Presidential Secretary William O. Stoddard.* Edited by Michael Burlingame. Lincoln: University of Nebraska Press, 2002.

———. *Inside the White House in War Times: Memoirs and Reports of Lincoln's Secretary.* Edited by Michael Burlingame. Lincoln: University of Nebraska Press, 2000.

———. *Lincoln at Work: Sketches from Life.* Boston: United Society of Christian Endeavor, 1900.

———. *Lincoln's Third Secretary.* Edited by William O. Stoddard Jr. New York: Exposition Press, 1955.

———. *Lincoln's White House Secretary: The Adventurous Life of William O. Stoddard.* Edited by Harold Holzer. Carbondale: Southern Illinois University Press, 2007.

Taft, Horatio Nelson, edited by John R. Sellers. *Washington during the Civil War: The Diary of Horatio Nelson Taft, 1861–1865*, 3 vols. Online at www.memory.loc.gov/ammem/tafthtml/tafthome.html.

Townsend, George A. *The Life, Crime, and Capture of John Wilkes Booth.* New York: Dick and Fitzgerald, 1865.

Viator [Joseph Bradley Varnum]. *The Washington Sketch Book.* New York: Mohun, Ebbs & Hough, 1864.

Ward, William Hayes. *Abraham Lincoln: Tributes from His Associates, Reminiscences of Soldiers, Statesmen, and Citizens.* New York: T. Y. Crowell & Company, 1895.

Washington, John. *They Knew Lincoln.* New York: E. P. Dutton, 1942.

Welles, Gideon. *Diary of Gideon Welles, Secretary of the Navy under Lincoln and Johnson*, 3 vols. New York: W. W. Norton & Company, 1960.

Wilson, Douglas L., and Rodney O. Davis, eds. *Herndon's Informants: Letters, Interviews, and Statements about Abraham Lincoln.* Urbana: University of Illinois Press, 1998.

Wilson, Rufus Rockwell, ed. *Intimate Memories of Lincoln.* Elmira, NY: Primavera Press, 1945.

———. *Lincoln Among His Friends.* Caldwell, ID: Caxton Printers, Ltd., 1942.

Articles and Chapters of Books

Adams, Lois Bryan. "Meeting Father Abraham, Washington, D.C., February 1864." In *The Civil War: The Third Year Told by Those Who Lived It*, edited by Brooks D. Simpson, 693–700. New York: Library of America, 2012.

Anonymous. "Guarding Mr. Lincoln." *The Ohio Soldier* (April 28, 1888).

Anonymous. "Lincoln's First Levee." *Journal of the Illinois State Historical Society* 11 (October 1918): 386–90.

Anonymous, "Mr. Lincoln and the Petitioners." *Putnam's Magazine* 6 (November 1870): 527–36.

Anonymous. "The White House and Its New Decorations." *Daily Alta California* (May 12, 1862): 1, col. 7.

Ashmun, George. "Recollections of a Peculiar Service." *Magazine of History* 3 (April 1906): 277–92.

Bancroft, Thomas B. "An Audience with Abraham Lincoln." *McClure's Magazine* 32 (February 1909).

Bishop, Joseph Bucklin. "A Friendship with John Hay." *Century Magazine* 71 (March 1906): 777–80.

Borrett, George. "An Englishman in Washington in 1864." *Magazine of History with Notes and Queries* 38 (Extra no. 149, 1929): 2–15.

Brooks, Noah. "Lincoln, Chase, and Grant." *Century Illustrated Magazine* 49 (February 1895): 617–19.

———. "Personal Recollections of Abraham Lincoln." *Harper's New Monthly Magazine* 31 (July 1865): 222–30.

———. "Personal Reminiscences of Lincoln," *Scribner's Monthly* 15 (March 1878): 673–81.

Chambrun, Adolph de Pineton, Marquis de. "Personal Recollection of Mr. Lincoln." *Scribner's Magazine* 13 (January 1893): 26–38.

Crook, William H. "Lincoln as I Knew Him," *Harper's Monthly Magazine* 114 (December 1906): 107–14 and (June 1907): 41–48.

Dicey, Edward. "Washington during the War." *MacMillan's Magazine* 6 (May 1862): 16–29.

Doig, Ivan. "The Genial White House Host and Raconteur." *Journal of the Illinois State Historical Society* 62 (1969): 307–11.

Grimsley, Elizabeth Todd. "Six Months in the White House." *Journal of the Illinois State Historical Society* 19 (October 1926–January 1927): 43–73.

Hay, John. "Life in the White House in the Time of Lincoln." *The Century Magazine* 41 (November 1890): 33–37.

Helm, Emilie Todd. "President Lincoln and the Widow of General Helm." *Century Magazine* (June 1895): 318.

Huidekoper, H. S. "On Guard at White House." *National Magazine* 29 (February 1909): 510–12.

Laugel, Auguste. "A Frenchman's Diary in Our Civil War Time–III." *The Nation* 75 (July 31, 1902): 88–89.

Lincoln, Mary Todd. "Unpublished Mary Todd Lincoln." Edited by Thomas F. Schwartz and Kim M. Bauer. *Journal of the Abraham Lincoln Association* 17 (Summer 1996): 45–52.

Macdonnell, Agnes. "America Then and Now: Recollections of Lincoln." *Contemporary Review* 3 (1917): 567–68.

Neil, Edward D. "Reminiscences of the Last Year of President Lincoln's Life." In *Glimpses of the Nation's Struggle*. St. Paul, MN: St. Paul Book and Stationary Company, 1887, 29–53.

Nicolay, John G. "Lincoln's Personal Appearance." *The Century Magazine* 42 (October 1891): 932–38.

Paton, William Agnew. "A Schoolboy's Interview with Abraham Lincoln." *Scribner's Magazine* 54 (December 1913): 709–10.

Peabody, Elizabeth. "Elizabeth Peabody Visits Lincoln, February 1865." Edited by Arlin Turner. *New England Quarterly* 48 (March 1975): 119–24.

Perry, Leslie J. "Appeals to Lincoln's Clemency." *Harper's Magazine* 52 (December 1865): 251–56.

Peskin, Alan. "Two White House Visits: Congressman James H. Campbell Prods President Lincoln and Shares 'A Dish of Gossip with the First Lady.'" *Lincoln Herald* 94 (Winter 1992): 157–58.

Sala, George A. "Mr. George Augustus Sala's Interview with Mr. and Mrs. Lincoln, the London *Daily Telegraph*, reprinted in *The Sydney Morning Herald*," June 7, 1864. http://trove.nla.gov.au.

Smalley, E. V. "The White House." *Century* 27 (April 1884): 803–15.

Smith, George Williamson. "A Critical Moment for Washington." *Records of the Columbia Historical Society* 21 (1918): 87–113.

Stimmel, Smith. "Experiences as a Member of President Lincoln's Bodyguard 1863–65." *North Dakota Historical Quarterly* 1 (January 1927): 7–33.

Stone, Charles P. "Washington in March and April, 1861." *Magazine of American History* 14 (July 1885): 1–24.

———. "Washington on the Eve of the War." *Century Magazine* 26 (July 1883): 458–66.

Swett, Leonard. "The Conspiracies of the Rebellion." *North American Review* 144 (February 1887): 179–90.

Tuckerman, Charles K. "Personal Recollections of Abraham Lincoln." *Magazine of American History* 19 (January–June 1888): 411–15.

Van Santvoord, C. "A Reception by President Lincoln." *Century Magazine* 25 (February 1883): 612–14.

Wentworth, M. "Mr. Lincoln and the Petitioners: A Record from the Executive Chamber." *Putnam's Magazine* 16 (November 1870): 527–36.

Wheelock, Julia S. "Excerpts of Diary of Susan Wheelock." *Lincoln Herald* 46 (October 1944): 42–46.

Wilson, James G. "Recollections of Abraham Lincoln." *Putnam's Magazine* 5 (March 1909): 672.

Winchell, J. M. "Three Interviews with President Lincoln." *Galaxy* 16 (July 1873): 33–41.

SECONDARY SOURCES

Books and Pamphlets

Alfers, Kenneth G. *Law and Order in the Capital City: A History of the Washington Police.* Washington, D.C.: George Washington University, 1976.

Baker, Jean H. *Mary Todd Lincoln: A Biography.* New York: W. W. Norton & Company, 1987.

Benjamin, Marcus. *Washington during Wartime.* Washington, D.C.: National Tribune Co., 1902.

Bernard, Kenneth A. *Lincoln and the Music of the Civil War.* Caldwell, ID: Caxton Printers, 1966.

Bruce, Robert V. *Lincoln and the Tools of War.* Indianapolis, IN: Bobbs-Merrill Co., 1956.

Bryan, W. B. *A History of the National Capital*, 2 vols. New York: Macmillan Company, 1916.

Burlingame, Michael. *Abraham Lincoln: A Life*, 2 vols. Baltimore: Johns Hopkins University Press, 2008.

Carman, Harry J., and Reinhard H. Luthin. *Lincoln and the Patronage.* New York: Columbia University Press, 1943.

Donald, David H. *Lincoln at Home: Two Glimpses of Abraham Lincoln's Domestic Life.* Washington, D.C.: White House Historical Association, 1999.

Escott, Paul. *Lincoln's Dilemma.* Charlottesville: University of Virginia Press, 2014.

Garrett, Wendell, ed. *Our Changing White House.* Boston: Northeastern University Press, 1995.

Goodwin, Doris Kearns. *Team of Rivals: The Political Genius of Abraham Lincoln.* New York: Simon & Schuster, 2005.

Hatch, Frederick. *Protecting President Lincoln: The Security Effort, the Thwarted Plots and the Disaster at Ford's Theater.* Jefferson, NC: McFarland & Co., 2011.

Hertz, Emanuel. *Abraham Lincoln, a New Portrait*, 2 vols. New York: H. Liveright, 1931.

Holzer, Harold. *Lincoln and the Power of the Press.* New York: Simon & Schuster, 2014.

Kimmel, Stanley. *Mr. Lincoln's Washington.* New York: Coward-McCann, 1957.

Leech, Margaret. *Reveille in Washington.* New York: Harpers, 1941.

Lusane, Clarence. *The Black History of the White House.* San Francisco: City Light Books, 2011.

McMurtry, Robert G. *Ben Hardin Helm, "Rebel" Brother in Law of Abraham Lincoln.* Chicago: The Civil War Roundtable Chicago, 1943.

Monaghan, Jay. *Diplomat in Carpet Slippers: Abraham Lincoln Deals with Foreign Affairs.* Indianapolis, IN: Bobbs-Merrill Co., 1945.

Nicolay, Helen. *Lincoln's Secretary: A Biography of John G. Nicolay.* New York: Longmans, Green, 1949.

———. *Personal Traits of Abraham Lincoln*. New York: The Century Company, 1912.

Pinsker, Matthew. *Lincoln's Sanctuary: Abraham Lincoln and the Soldiers' Home*. New York: Oxford University Press, 2005.

Powell, C. Percy. *Lincoln Day by Day: A Chronology 1809–1865*. Washington, D.C.: Lincoln Sesquicentennial Commission, 1960.

Pratt, Harry E. *The Personal Finances of Abraham Lincoln*. Springfield, IL: The Abraham Lincoln Association, 1943.

Seale, William. *The President's House: A History*, 2 vols. Washington, D.C.: White House Historical Association, 1986.

Taliaferro, John. *All the Great Prizes: The Life of John Hay from Lincoln to Roosevelt*. New York: Simon & Schuster, 2013.

Temple, Wayne C. *Alexander Williamson: Friend of the Lincolns*. Racine, WI: The Lincoln Fellowship of Wisconsin. Serial Publication No. 1, 1997.

Viola, Herman J. *Diplomats in Buckskin: A History of Indian Delegations in Washington City*. Washington, D.C.: Smithsonian Institution Press, 1981.

The White House: A Historic Guide. Washington, D.C.: White House Historical Association, 2011.

Zeitz, Joshua. *Lincoln's Boys: John Nicolay, John Hay, and the War for Lincoln's Image*. New York: Viking, 2014.

Articles and Chapters of Books

Allman, William G. "The Lincoln Bedroom: Refurbishing a Famous White House Room." *White House History* 25 (Spring 2009): 56–63.

Anonymous. "The President's Carriages." *Lincoln Lore* 685 (May 25, 1942).

Anonymous. "What Mrs. Lincoln Bought for the White House." *Lincoln Lore* 1492 (June 1962).

Barbee, David R. "Lincoln and the Music of the Civil War." *Lincoln Herald* 63 (Summer 1961): 67–76 and (Fall 1961): 121–27.

———. "The Musical Mr. Lincoln." *Abraham Lincoln Quarterly* 5 (December 1949): 435–54 (corrected by F. Lauriston Bullard, "A Correction of 'The Musical Mr. Lincoln.'" *The Abraham Lincoln Quarterly* 6 (March 1950): 37–39.)

Basler, Roy P. "Did President Lincoln Give the Smallpox to William H. Johnson?" *Huntington Library Quarterly* 35 (May 1972): 279–84.

Bernard, Kenneth A. "Glimpses of Lincoln in the White House." *Abraham Lincoln Quarterly* 7 (December 1952): 161–87.

Burlingame, Michael. "New Light on the Bixby Letter." *Journal of the Abraham Lincoln Association* 16 (1995): 59–71.

———. "Nicolay and Hay: Court Historians." *Journal of the Abraham Lincoln Association* 19 (Winter 1998): 1–20.

Carroll, Daniel B. "Abraham Lincoln and the Minister of France." *Lincoln Herald* 70 (Fall 1968): 142–53.

Chapman, A. S. "The Boyhood of John Hay." *Century Magazine* 46 (July 1904): 444–54.

Collins, Herbert R. "The White House Stables and Garages." *Records of the Columbia Historical Society* 45 (1963–1965): 366–85.

Cowden, Gerald S., ed. " 'My Dear Mr. W': Mary Lincoln Writes to Alexander Williamson." *Journal of the Illinois State Historical Society* 76 (Spring 1983): 71–74.

Croffut, William A. "Lincoln's Washington." *Atlantic Monthly* 145 (January 1930): 55–65.

Hatch, Frederick. "Lincoln's Missing Guard." *Lincoln Herald* 106 (Fall 2005): 106–17.

Havlik, Robert J. "Lincoln's Washington Carriages Revisited." *Lincoln Herald* 112 (Fall 2010): 155–80.

Holst, Erika. " 'One of the Best Women I Ever Knew': Abraham Lincoln and Rebecca Pomeroy." *Journal of the Abraham Lincoln Association* 31 (Summer 2010): 12–20.

Holzer, Harold. "Abraham Lincoln's White House." *White House History* 25 (Spring 2009): 4–17.

———. " 'Too Rickety to Venerate' (The Truth about the Lincoln Bedroom)." *American Heritage* 48 (July–August 1997).

Johnson, Martin P. "Did Abraham Lincoln Sleep with His Bodyguard? Another Look at the Evidence." *Journal of the Abraham Lincoln Association* 27 (Summer 2006): 42–55.

Langsdorf, Edgar. "Jim Lane and the Frontier Guard." *Kansas Historical Quarterly* 9, no. 1 (February 1940): 13–25.

"Lincoln's Attendance at Spiritualist Séances." *Lincoln Lore* 499 and 1500 (January and February 1963).

Masur, Kate. "The African American Delegation to Abraham Lincoln: A Reappraisal." *Civil War History* 56 (June 2010): 117–44.

McMurtry, R. Gerald. "Lincoln White House Glass and China." *Lincoln Herald* 49 (June 1947): 33–34, 43.

Pratt, Harry, and Ernest East. "Mrs. Lincoln Refurbishes the White House." *Lincoln Herald* 47 (February 1945): 13–22.

Rietveld, Ronald D. "The Lincoln White House Community." *Journal of the Abraham Lincoln Association* 20 (Summer 1999): 17–48.

Seiler, Grace. "Walt Whitman and Abraham Lincoln." *Lincoln Herald* 52 (December 1950): 42–47, 53.

Shultes, Milton. "Mortality of the Five Lincoln Boys." *Lincoln Herald* 57 (Spring–Summer 1955): 3–13.

Sprague, Ver Lynn. "Mary Lincoln, Accessory to Murder." *Lincoln Herald* 81 (Winter 1979): 238–42.

Sweet, Natalie. "A Representative 'of Our People': The Agency of William Slade,

Leader in the African American Community and Usher to Abraham Lincoln." *Journal of the Abraham Lincoln Association* 34 (Summer 2013): 21–41.

Temple, Wayne C. "Charles Henry Philbrick: Private Secretary to President Lincoln." *Lincoln Herald* 99 (Spring 1997): 6–11.

———. "Mary Todd Lincoln's Travels." *Journal of the Illinois State Historical Society* 52 (Spring 1959): 180–94.

———. "Mrs. Lincoln's Clothing." *Lincoln Herald* 62 (Summer 1960): 54–65.

Temple, Wayne C., and Justin G. Turner. "Lincoln's 'Castine': Noah Brooks." *Lincoln Herald* 72 (Fall 1970): 113–89; and *Lincoln Herald* 73 (Fall 1971): 163–80.

Websites

www.mrlincolnswhitehouse.org is an excellent compilation of information and sources on Lincoln's White House. It gave this book a jump start.

www.whitehousemuseum.org assembles photographs, floor plans, and other sources on the White House, many of which concern Lincoln's time.

INDEX

ABOUT THE AUTHOR

James B. Conroy, a trial lawyer in Boston for more than thirty years, is the author of *Our One Common Country: Abraham Lincoln and the Hampton Roads Peace Conference of 1865* (Lyons Press, 2014), a finalist for the Gilder Lehrman Lincoln Prize for 2014. Conroy served on Capitol Hill in Washington, D.C., as a House and Senate aide in the 1970s and early 1980s, and earned his JD degree from the Georgetown University Law Center in 1982. He and his wife, Lynn, are the parents of two grown children and the grandparents of two young boys.

Conroy is an elected fellow of the Massachusetts Historical Society and a member of the Boston Bar Association. He lives in Hingham, Massachusetts, on Boston's South Shore, where he serves as a member of the Hingham Historical Commission, and the Community Preservation Committee, has coached youth baseball and basketball teams, and has chaired the Town's Advisory Committee, which advises the Hingham Town Meeting, an exercise in direct democracy through which the Town has governed itself since 1635.

Learn more about the author at his website, www.jamesbconroy.com.